Ceramic Technology for Potters and Sculptors

Les Manning

Ceramic Technology for Potters and Sculptors

Yvonne Hutchinson Cuff

Line Drawings by Peter Bramhald

University of Pennsylvania Press

Philadelphia

Printed in the United States of America
First published in the United States 1995 by the University of Pennsylvania Press
First published in the United Kingdom 1995 by A & C Black (Publishers) Limited

Library of Congress Cataloging-in-Publication Data

Cuff, Yvonne Hutchinson.
   Ceramic technology for potters and sculptors / Yvonne Hutchinson Cuff ; line drawings
by Peter Bramhald.
      p.   cm.
   Includes bibliographical references (p.   –   ) and index.
   ISBN: 0-8122-3071-X (cloth : alk. paper). — ISBN 0-8122-1377-7 (pbk. : alk. paper)
      1. Ceramics.   I. Title.
   TP807.C84   1996
   666 — dc20   95-43944
                                                                                     CIP

Frontispiece: Les Manning, Canada. *Rundle View.* 28 cm. high. The work is created from a porcelain body and three stoneware bodies each with different qualities and colors. These are wedged separately and then paddled together. During throwing Les pushes the porcelain into the bottom of the piece producing a "lining" that seems to counteract the different shrinkage rates of the clays. (Thus we have a classic example of clays with very different rates of shrinkage being joined together.) Once thrown, the form is trimmed from top to bottom exposing the patterns achieved from the clays; it is then altered to accentuate these patterns. The work is biscuit fired, then sprayed with a Celadon glaze in varying degrees: thick, firing green, for a feeling of more depth; thin, giving transparency, to enhance the colored clay pattern. Finally the work is fired to 1263°C/2305°F or only a little above so as not to put extra pressure on the different shrinkage rates of the clay. Photo: Les Manning.

Contents

Part I. Background Sciences, Workshop Practice, and Raw Materials

Part II. Clay Bodies, Slips, and Casting Slips

Part III. Glaze and Color

Preface and Acknowledgments

This book had its origins a long time ago, when, on sunny winter Sundays, my parents used to take my sister and me for bush picnics in the Western Australian hills. There my mother and I made miniature rock gardens using the loose brown and white pebbles which littered the ground. Much later I discovered that they came from a large deposit of bauxite, the source rock of aluminum. These little gardens were decorated with marvellously crooked crystals of quartz, bits of chalcedony, and chunks of pink feldspar collected from a disused quarry farther north. From making these rock gardens and trekking through the bush sprang an overwhelming interest in rocks of all kinds, including the clay deposits derived from these same rocks, which bordered the ancient river valley, where on hotter days, I made "mud pies" (my mother's definition) and baked them in the hot Australian sun.

This was a milestone in my life that led eventually to studies in science, especially geology, and art. The last two, however, did not come together until, after research in England, I returned home to Australia for a visit to find that my mother, having won acclaim for an Ikebana flower arrangement, had put her prize piece on a Georgian piecrust table. Next morning there was a white circle on the table where the vase had stood and my analysis began, to find the reason for the porosity of the pot. It was then that I started to take a deeper interest in the materials and the part played by the firing cycle in ceramics. I discovered that my much loved minerals were involved: the clays, feldspar, quartz, limestone, and flint pebbles such as those found on English beaches, and many others from which clay bodies were compounded and glazes made.

My thanks go to Chris Topley, for his inspired teaching of mineralogy and the hours spent discussing phase diagrams with reference to ceramics, and to David Stoodley, for whom I worked as technician in a very busy pottery at the College of Further Education, Oxford. David gave unstintingly of his considerable knowledge by word and demonstration. I must also thank David Garbitt and Ken Bright, who gave me the opportunity to undertake advanced studies at Goldsmith's College, University of London, and later an appointment as lecturer in Theory of Ceramics; Jonathan Switzman and Steve Arlow, our wonderful technicians; and the late James Tower, my examiner, who suggested that I should turn my thesis into a book.

Thanks must also go to Colin Pearson, my tutor in glaze formulation, and to Johnson's Tile Factory, Stoke-on-Trent. For a short time I was able to study there with their chief chemist, Ron Leek, who led me into a world of molecular theory and made it as fascinating as a crossword puzzle is for others. Further thanks go to Harry Fraser of Potclays; to Christopher Hogg of English China Clay; and to Mrs. Gould and her late husband, Brian, through whom a direct link was forged between artist-potters and English China Clay. Finally my gratitude to Paul Rado, chief chemist at the Worcester Royal Porcelain Factory for many years and author of a textbook for the Institute of Ceramics, Stoke-on-Trent (see Bibliography), who took on the awesome task of reading the first manuscript for this book; to Fran and Geoff Kenwood for much encouragement and support; to Janet Kovesi-Watt who read the second and final versions with many helpful suggestions; to the ceramists who generously allowed me to include photographs of their work with notes on the technology involved; to the Perth Potters' Club, Western Australia; and to all my colleagues and students past and present, whose ideas and energy are deeply ingrained in this book. Most of all, thanks must go to my family, especially Lesley who suffered the paperwork, and Corinne who translated the manuscript from one computer system to another.

Yvonne Hutchinson Cuff

Abbreviations and Equivalent Measures

Abbreviations

C.	cones (see Orton)
°C/°F	degrees Celsius/degrees Fahrenheit
°TW	degrees Twaddell
e/w	earthenware
FW	formula weight
g	gram
HT	high temperature (range over 1200°C/2192°F)
l.o.i.	loss on ignition
LT	low temperature (range 600–1150°C/1112–2102°F)
mol	The standard abbreviation for mole.
MT	middle temperature (range 1168–1222°C/2134–2232°F)
MP	melting point of a substance
MW	molecular weight
"O"	oxidation
"R"	reduction
SG	specific gravity
SI	système international (international system of metric weights and measures)
s/w	stoneware
u	atomic weight units
+%add.	addition in excess of 100 percent recipe. This indicates an addition to the percentage recipe, i.e., a material added "in addition to" the percentage recipe, e.g., +2%add. color = 100 g recipe plus 2 g color.
* * *	end of Exercise
■ ■ ■	end of Advanced Section

Equivalent Measures

U.S./UK	Metric
1 gal (U.S.)	3780 ml = 3.78 l

1 gal (UK)	4520 ml = 4.52 l
1 pt (U.S.)	473 ml = 0.473 l
1 pt (UK)	568 ml = 0.568 l
1 fl oz (U.S.)	29.57 ml
1 fl oz (UK)	28.4 ml
1 lb	454 g = 0.454 kg
1 oz	28.35 g
1 in	2.54 cm
1 ft	30.48 cm = 0.305 m

Figures

Introduction

This book is intended for college students, potters, and sculptors working alone, and as an auxiliary text for student archaeologists and those hoping to enter the ceramic industry. It opens with a discussion of the chemistry necessary for an understanding of ceramic processes, followed by a similar section on geology (special consideration is given to those readers who have not previously studied these subjects). All information given in these sections is directly pertinent to ceramics and enables students to follow with ease the chapters on making and firing bodies and glazes.

Next comes a more detailed study of minerals and rocks and a comparison with their pre-fused counterparts, the frits. The principle is established here that it is impossible to succeed in this subject without a thorough knowledge of the raw materials of ceramics.

The introduction to clay, Chapter 4, is accompanied by fieldwork which includes practical experiments that may be carried out on site. These are continued when students return to the studio/pottery. The Exercises pass from the study of natural clays and the effects of combining them with other materials, to the making of clay bodies for special purposes from dry powdered raw materials. The works of leading potters/sculptors are illustrated to support these Exercises.

The section on the Clay-Glaze Relationship is designed so that through practical work the student discovers the differences between clay, vitreous slip, and glaze. The section on glazes takes up this theme by simple blends of raw materials followed by an intensive assessment of the results. The melting history of a glaze has been updated in the light of new knowledge and personal research, and is written in such a way that the student is presented with a reasoned table of proportions of oxides for the various glazes, firing temperatures, and firing cycles. This is followed by a carefully organized series of Exercises which introduce the formulation of glazes in such a way that the theory behind them is automatically revealed. The method follows the thinking required for using computer programs for glaze formulation (though the student without such facilities is not disadvantaged).

Color is presented by directly linking it, through practical work, with the correct glaze needed to give the hue desired. This is accompanied by a theoretical discussion of the origin of coloring oxides, the making of colored stains, and the compatibility of oxides and stains with one another.

The division of the book into sections allows alternative approaches. The first four chapters, for example, could be studied separately, either as private reading or as home study before joining a course; they could also run parallel with the Exercises in Part 1. Ideally, the texts in Parts 2 and 3 should be read in the order given, whether or not all the Exercises are undertaken; in that way knowledge will be gradually built up. Reference to the periodic table (Appendix Figure A.2) should be made frequently until the reader is thoroughly familiar with the way the elements are grouped together. The list of abbreviations at the front of the book should be read before commencing study.

In each Exercise a standard layout is used which begins with a clearly defined aim and concludes with a guide to an assessment of the fired result. These assessments are supported by line drawings, tables, and colored illustrations.

Throughout the book there are short "Advanced Sections," organized in such a way that the text reads consecutively whether they are included or omitted.

Part I
Background Sciences, Workshop Practice, and Raw Materials

Chapter 1
Essential Chemistry

Introduction

It is remarkable that, so far as we know at present, everything in the world is made from around 90 *elements*. Some artificial ones have been created in the laboratory but these are few in number.

The *periodic table*, in which the elements are arranged in a definite order, can be found in most introductory chemistry books. This table was compiled as the result of some brilliant scientific detective work, mainly conducted during the nineteenth century, when it was realized that elements with similar properties could be grouped together. This modern list of elements replaces many earlier theories, in particular, the ancient philosophical idea that there are but four elements: earth, air, fire, and water.

A shortened version of this table is given in Appendix Figure A.2. It is suggested that you make a copy of this table, preferably using color to identify the various groups, and keep it beside you as you study. In this table the elements of particular interest to ceramists have been given with an abbreviation, or *symbol*, derived from one or two letters taken from its name. For example, Mg stands for magnesium and O for oxygen. Where the name has been taken from a Greek or Latin source, the abbreviation may not be immediately obvious; four of the elements that get their symbols in this way are

Potassium = K (from Kalium)
Sodium = Na (from Natrium)
Lead = Pb (from Plumbum)
Tin = Sn (from Stannum).

When two or more elements combine chemically (in ways to be described below), the abbreviation for the resulting compound is called a *chemical formula*. For example, MgO is the formula for magnesium oxide, a compound of magnesium (Mg) and oxygen (O). Many artist-potters shy away from using these abbreviations as being too academic. However they can be extremely useful, for they tell you, very simply, what each ceramic material contains and, most important, as we shall see, the proportions of one element to another in a particular substance. Water is an example where hydrogen and oxygen combine in the proportion of two to one, H_2O (two units of hydrogen to one unit of oxygen).

Some elements combine with themselves in nature. For example, individual units, *atoms*, of the element gold (Au) can link together in all directions to form a nugget of gold. Some, like oxygen (O), combine with themselves in definite proportions (the formula for the air we breathe is O_2). Most elements combine, or *bond*, together with other elements in definite proportions by weight to make stable compounds, the individual units of which are called *molecular units* (some compounds are unstable, as we will see when we study carbonates). In the example of water, given above, hydrogen and oxygen combine to give the compound H_2O, a single unit of which is sometimes referred to as a *molecule*.

Atoms, Molecules, and Moles

Atoms and molecules are so tiny that they cannot be seen through an optical microscope; it is therefore exceedingly difficult to count them. We shall have to use these terms in the next few pages, but after that we shall use a much larger unit of quantity, called the *mole*. In Figure 1.1 the first illustration represents an atom and the second a molecule in which two atoms have combined together. The third illustration represents a mole of lead and a mole of lead oxide. Although the individual atoms and molecules cannot be seen by the naked eye, a mole of pure lead and a mole of lead oxide can be seen, and indeed weighed (see Plate 1).

A mole is a unit of quantity containing a particular number of particles of the same chemical matter. In more formal terms a mole is the quantity of a chemical substance which consists of a specific (though vast) number of units. (For an explanation of the number, see p. 21.)

Thus, if we call this number n we would say that we have a mole of atoms

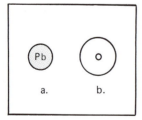 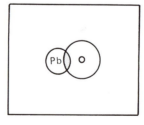 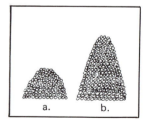

Figure 1.1. Diagrammatic representation of an atom, molecule, and mole: (left) atoms of lead (Pb, wt = 207 u) and oxygen (wt = 16 u); (middle) molecule of lead oxide (PbO, wt = 223 u); (right) moles of lead (molar wt = 207 g) and lead oxide (molar wt = 223 g). See also Plate 1.

(n units of pure lead, Pb) or a mole of molecules (n units of lead oxide, PbO), or a mole of more complex materials (n units of potassium feldspar, $K_2O \cdot Al_2O_3 \cdot 6SiO_2$). The value of the mole as a unit is that it is large enough for us to see and weigh in the ordinary way.

Chemical Reactions and Ions

Atoms are made up of a central nucleus containing particles of matter called *protons* and *neutrons*. This nucleus is surrounded by smaller units of matter called *electrons*. An atom with exactly the same number of protons as electrons is electrically neutral. If, however, an atom loses or gains one or more electrons such that it has fewer or more electrons than protons, it is electrically charged and is then called an *ion* (see Appendix 1). The process of interaction between ions so as to achieve overall electrical neutrality is called a *chemical reaction*. For example,

Sodium ions (Na^+) and chlorine ions (Cl^-) bear opposite charges. It is well known that opposite charges attract each other. This electrical attraction is responsible for the formation of the compound sodium chloride, (NaCl). Nentwig, Kreuder and Morgenstern (1992).

Valence is the combining power of an atom expressed in terms of the valence of hydrogen as 1. For example, the valence of oxygen in water, H_2O, is 2. That is, one oxygen unit can combine with two hydrogen units.

Oxygen and Oxides

Oxygen is present in the air in two stable gaseous forms. The most common form consists of two atoms of oxygen bonded together (O_2).

Most geologists consider that oxygen was produced in large quantities when the world was first formed and reacted with the metals originally present as uncombined elements. This is the reason compounds of an element with oxygen, called oxides, are numerous. For example, calcium combines with oxygen to form calcium oxide. A simple way to express this is $2Ca + O_2 \rightarrow 2CaO$. Here the arrow indicates that a chemical reaction has taken place.

How to Read the Formulas of Compounds

It is important to note that when a number appears in front of two or more elements it refers to all the elements that follow it, thus:

2CaO = 2 calcium and 2 oxygen.

A number that follows an element as a subscript refers only to the element to which it is attached. For example, Na_2O represents two atoms of sodium for each oxygen atom. Other important examples are

K_2O = 2 potassium atoms and 1 oxygen atom
H_2O = 2 hydrogen atoms and 1 oxygen atom
SiO_2 = 1 silicon atom and 2 oxygen atoms

In more complicated formulas a dot separates the names of various oxides, but they are all still a part of the same compound. For example, the formula for talc is $3MgO \cdot 4SiO_2 \cdot H_2O$. Thus this mineral consists of a ratio of

$3MgO$ (magnesium oxide) : $4SiO_2$ (silicon dioxide) : H_2O (water).

To determine the numbers of each element in this compound, you must also consider the subscripts where they appear after an element:

$3MgO$ = 3 magnesium + 3 oxygen
$4SiO_2$ = 4 silicon + $(4 \times 2 = 8)$ oxygen
$1H_2O$ = 2 hydrogen + 1 oxygen

So this compound contains $3Mg : 4Si : 2H : 12O$.

This is the most complicated kind of material that we deal with in ceramics. Study the above pages, learn the definitions, and test yourself (preferably with a second person).

Oxides and Carbonates of Importance in Ceramics

The following oxides are described in the order in which the elements they contain appear in the short version of the periodic table given in Appendix Figure A.2.

Group 1: Alkali Metal Oxides

The elements in Group 1, which are called *alkali metals*, typically link with oxygen in the ratio of 2 : 1, that is, two atoms of the alkali metal to one atom of oxygen. These are stated here together with their common names, now used by ceramists (see Hamer and Hamer, 1991).

Li_2O, lithium oxide, lithia
Na_2O, sodium oxide, soda
K_2O, potassium oxide, potassa

Group 2: Alkaline Earth Metal Oxides

Group 2 elements are called *alkaline earth metals*. They generally bond with oxygen in a 1 : 1 ratio:

MgO, magnesium oxide, magnesia
CaO, calcium oxide, calcia

SrO, strontium oxide, strontia
BaO, barium oxide, baria

All these oxides are made up of three-dimensional arrays of alternating positively and negatively charged *ions*. The metal atoms form positive ions (*cations*) by transferring (losing) one or more electrons to the oxygen atoms. Each of the latter gains two electrons to form a negative ion (*anion*) with a 2⁻ charge (O^{2-}). The chemical formula of the oxide that a given metal forms depends on its position in the periodic table. Group 1 metals (Li, Na, K) lose one electron to form cations with a 1⁺ charge (e.g., Na^+). To form the electrically neutral oxide, two Na^+ ions combine with one O^{2-} ion to give the compound sodium oxide (soda), whose formula unit is Na_2O. Similarly, Group 2 metals (Mg, Ca, Sr, Ba) lose two electrons to give cations with a 2⁺ charge (e.g., Mg^{2+}). The latter can combine in a 1 : 1 ratio with oxide ions to form magnesium oxide (MgO).

In this text we shall study the effect two or more oxides have on one another to lower the temperature at which they begin to melt. We shall also see that materials containing the oxides of Groups 1 and 2 can have a dramatic effect on lowering the melting temperature and for this reason are called *fluxes*, and the materials containing them may be called flux-containing materials. This topic is further discussed in Chapter 6 under "The Functions of Oxides in Ceramics."

Group 3: Oxides of Aluminum and Boron

Al_2O_3, aluminum oxide, alumina
B_2O_3, boric oxide, no common name

In these two oxides the ratio is 2 : 3, as shown by their formulas. This would seem to indicate that they have something in common. Looking at the periodic table shows, however, that a zigzag line is drawn across the table to separate the metals from the nonmetals. This places aluminum among the metals and boron, together with silicon, among the nonmetals. We may infer from this that while aluminum and boron have some characteristics in common, they are dissimilar in other ways. It is as a nonmetal glass-former that boric oxide, along with silica (discussed below), plays an important role in ceramics. For this reason boric oxide and silica will be grouped together in many places in this text. In doing this the author follows the ceramic classification originally used by Hermann Seger in contrast with that of Felix Singer.

Group 4: Oxides of Carbon, Silicon, Tin, and Lead

These elements have some properties that place them in the same group, but as with boron and aluminum in Group 3, they are divided by the zigzag line on the periodic table. This division shows that carbon and silicon are classed as nonmetals, and tin and lead as metals.

The Nonmetals

Carbon (C)

Carbon may be found in its elemental state in such diverse forms as graphite, charcoal, and diamond. The differences among these three are due simply to the different ways in which carbon atoms can link together. In graphite each carbon atom bonds to three others in a planar triangular way to form two-dimensional sheets. Interactions between the sheets are rather weak, so they can slide across each other, hence the lubrication qualities of graphite. Charcoal consists of carbon atoms linked in irregular geometries. In diamond the crystal structure consists of a regular three-dimensional array of carbon atoms, each bonded to four others in a tetrahedral geometry, hence diamond is very hard.

In chemical combinations, carbon normally loses or shares four electrons. It has the ability to link with one, two, or three atoms of oxygen to make oxides.

Carbon Monoxide (CO)

Carbon monoxide is a poisonous gas. It forms during incomplete combustion of fuels containing carbon. It is present in exhaust fumes from automobiles and when kilns are fired with insufficient oxygen for complete combustion. As the formula indicates, carbon links with oxygen in a $1:1$ ratio.

Carbon Dioxide (CO_2)

Carbon dioxide (1 carbon : 2 oxygen) is a more common combination of carbon and oxygen, and small amounts are present in the atmosphere. This gas is given off when plant or animal matter (whether live or decayed) is burned in a normal atmosphere, that is, one containing plenty of oxygen. Such carbon-containing matter is called carbonaceous (or organic) matter. The first term is the best one for potters to use because it is a reminder that carbon is contained in pottery materials. Carbon dioxide is not poisonous, but if a person is exposed to a relatively high concentration in the air the concentration in the blood may increase to a point where the body responds by hyperventilation.

Carbonates (CO_3^{2-})

The combination of carbon and oxygen in a $1:3$ ratio gives a negatively charged ion (anion), and it is associated in this form with other elements, generally metals. Several carbonates are extremely important in ceramics: these are the carbonates of the alkali metals and alkaline earth metals.

Carbonates of Group 1 metals	Carbonates of Group 2 metals
lithium carbonate, Li_2CO_3	magnesium carbonate, $MgCO_3$

sodium carbonate, Na_2CO_3 calcium carbonate, $CaCO_3$

potassium carbonate, K_2CO_3 barium carbonate, $BaCO_3$

Carbonates of the Group 2 Metals

The carbonates of Group 2 metals are far less soluble than those of Group 1. Thus in nature considerable quantities of calcium carbonate accumulate to give great beds of calcium carbonate rock (e.g., limestone, marble, chalk).

Remember that carbonate compounds have one or more elements besides carbon and oxygen. For example, lithium carbonate has lithium, carbon, and oxygen, and calcium carbonate has calcium, carbon, and oxygen. This fact is important when you need to calculate the weight of a carbonate: many students ignore the C (carbon) and so get the wrong total weight. Also, on burning in a kiln the carbonate breaks down and CO_2 goes up the chimney, leaving behind an oxide. For example: $CaCO_3$ on burning gives $CaO + CO_2\uparrow$ (the arrow indicates that the CO_2 escapes up the chimney). This leaves an oxide, CaO, which the potter wants to keep. If you look at the periodic table, Appendix Figure A.2 you will see that the total weight of $CaCO_3$ is:

$Ca = 40$ u; $C = 12$ u; and $(O \times 3u) = 48$; giving a total of $CaCO_3 = 100$ g.

Silicon, Silica, and the Silicates

The element silicon (Si), is now well known for its use in microelectronic circuits, for example, the silicon chips in computers.

Silica (silicon dioxide, SiO_2) is a compound of silicon with oxygen; silicates are combinations of silicon with oxygen and one or more metals. Together they give the most important group of rock-forming minerals found in the earth's crust. SiO_2 gives the silica mineral quartz (also flint, chalcedony, and opal, which is a hydrated form), while potassium feldspar, $K_2O \cdot Al_2O_3 \cdot 6SiO_2$, is the most important and well-known silicate.

The fundamental building unit of these minerals is the tetrahedron. Using the model suggested by Arthur Holmes (1978), if you imagine the oxygen units as three tennis balls set up as a triangular base with a fourth ball balanced on top to form a pyramid and a much smaller marble (representing the silicon) inserted in the middle you will have some idea of the arrangement of a single silica tetrahedron (see Figure 1.2). Such a model is magnified about 65 million times! These tetrahedral units combine to form stable and extremely strong minerals.

Quartz

Quartz has this type of structure, with tetrahedral units linked together in three dimensions through the oxygen atoms. Thus, although the basic structural unit (the silica tetrahedron) has an overall ratio of (1 silicon : 4

oxygen), the compound quartz has a ratio of (1 silicon : 2 oxygen), which is expressed as SiO_2. Figure 1.3 (left) shows a simple two-dimensional representation. Note that, although the silicon atom is surrounded by four oxygen units, the circle demonstrates that the oxygen is shared, such that the proportion is one silicon atom to the equivalent of two oxygen atoms, SiO_2.

Feldspars and Feldspathoids

The feldspar family is the most important of the many other silicate minerals. In these minerals the tetrahedra are again linked together by oxygen, as in quartz, but some silicon atoms are replaced by aluminum. Aluminum has one valence electron fewer than silicon, so the structure would be electrically unbalanced. However, metals such as potassium, sodium, and calcium, which readily form positive ions, enter the network and balance the structure again (see Figure 1.3, right). These are further discussed in Chapter 2.

Group 4 Metals

Tin Oxide

Tin (Sn) forms compounds with oxygen in the ratio of $1 : 2$, to give SnO_2. The rock from which it is mined is called cassiterite (or tinstone), which, apart from possible impurities, has the formula SnO_2.

Do not confuse Sn (tin) with Si (silicon). Because of the similarity in their atomic symbols, you are advised to refer to tin and tin oxide by their full names.

Lead Oxide

Lead (Pb) is able to combine with oxygen in several ratios (e.g., lead monoxide, PbO). In general, lead compounds are poisonous and thus rarely used in ceramics today. However, there are now available certain compounds of lead with silica, called *lead frits*, which are prefused mixtures of minerals that lock the lead into the glassy structure and render them safe provided they are properly used. Frits can be made in the studio, but, particularly with lead frits, it is easier to buy them from a pottery supplier who has extremely accurate equipment to weigh and make them to the exact (safe) formula. The two most well-known lead frits are lead sesquisilicate and lead bisilicate.

Group 5: Phosphorus

The only oxide in Group 5 of importance to the potter is an oxide of phosphorus in which phosphorus and oxygen are combined in a $2 : 5$ ratio. This is commonly called phosphorus pentoxide, P_2O_5, although the actual molecular formula is P_4O_{10}. It is a constituent of many wood ashes, especially fruit woods.

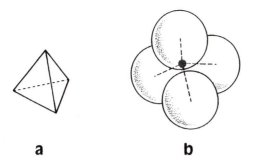

a   **b**

Figure 1.2. (a) Model illustrating a tetrahedron, the fundamental structural array of all silicate minerals. In a unit of silica, solid lines drawn joining the centers of four oxygen ions surrounding a central silicon ion would make a tetrahedral form. (b) An artist's impression showing the large cloudlike areas occupied by four oxygen ions with a tiny silicon ion at the center. In silica this unit extends in three dimensions; similarly for the silicates with some silicon ions replaced by other elements.

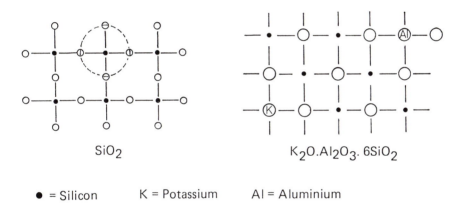

SiO_2 $K_2O.Al_2O_3. 6SiO_2$

● = Silicon   K = Potassium   Al = Aluminium

Figure 1.3. Silicate structures. Left: each silicon ion (·) is surrounded by four oxygen ions (o). Because the tetrahedra are linked in three dimensions so that each oxygen ion is shared by two silicon ions, the overall ratio of silicon to oxygen is one to two, expressed in the formula SiO_2. Right: In potassium feldspar some of the silicon ions are replaced by aluminum and potassium ions to give a theoretical formula of $K_2O \cdot Al_2O_3 \cdot 6SiO_2$.

In the compound calcium phosphate (bone ash), calcium is combined with phosphorus and oxygen to give $Ca_3(PO_4)_2$. The chemical formula is sometimes also represented as if it were the mixed oxide, $3CaO . P_2O_5$. This compound is obtained by burning animal bones, a typical analysis being 55% CaO, 40% P_2O_5 by weight (mass) with 5 percent impurities (organic and mineral matter). Bone ash is an important constituent of bone china ware. Both bone ash and selected wood ashes are used in glaze making, for which P_2O_5 can have an important effect on the quality and color of the glaze.

Groups 6 and 7: Volatiles

Volatiles are materials that convert readily to vapor and escape into the atmosphere. Only the volatiles that involve metals are discussed here.

In many cases metals combine with elements of Groups 6 and 7 to give compounds that are stable at room temperature but volatilize at higher temperatures. An important example of volatilization in ceramics occurs during salt glazing. For example, when ordinary table salt (sodium chloride, NaCl) is thrown into a hot kiln containing clay or biscuit-fired objects, the salt decomposes and volatilizes according to the chemical reaction

$$4NaCl \text{ (table salt)} + O_2 \overset{heat}{\rightarrow} 2Na_2O \text{ (soda)} + 2Cl_2\uparrow \text{ (chlorine gas)}.$$

The metal oxide settles on the surface of the objects and reacts with silica and a little alumina from the clay to give a "salt glaze" consisting of sodium (or potassium) aluminum silicates, while the chlorine escapes up the chimney as chlorine gas.

Warning: Because chlorine gas is toxic, the chimney of the kiln should pull a good draft and the working area near the kiln should be well ventilated. Preferably the kiln should be situated out-of-doors under a fireproof and weatherproof shelter (roof) with the chimney built through the roof and well away from buildings where people are living and working.

Other reactions involving the formation of volatiles that may occur during firing are

$$4FeS + 7O_2 \overset{heat}{\rightarrow} 2Fe_2O_3 + 4SO_2\uparrow$$
$$\text{(iron sulfide)} \quad \text{(oxygen)} \quad \text{(iron oxide)} \quad \text{(sulfur dioxide)}$$

$$CaF_2 \text{ (calcium fluoride)} + O_2 \overset{heat}{\rightarrow} CaO \text{ (calcium oxide)} + F_2O\uparrow$$

Because these gases do not participate in the final products (they go up the chimney) they need only be considered insofar as it is essential to fire carefully in the range 700–900°C/1292–1652°F. Between these temperatures released sulfur and chlorine gases combine with oxygen in the air.

These compounds are poisonous, so plenty of ventilation must be arranged so that they may escape not only from the kiln but from the kiln room or kiln area.

The potter does not need to study sulfides, sulfates, and so on in depth, but it is worth noting that galena, the source mineral for lead oxide, is PbS (lead sulfide) and that iron pyrite is FeS_2 (iron sulfide). There is also some sulfur dioxide in most clay bodies, and this burns away as sulfur dioxide gas during the early stages of firing. Because gases are released during firing, precautions as stated above are particularly important in the early stages of firing clay. *Observe this warning: do not have your kiln in a living or sleeping area.*

Hydrogen (H)

Hydrogen is dealt with separately, for it plays a very important part in ceramics (as well in the world around us). Such compounds as water and clay depend on hydrogen for their existence. Because it is the lightest element, having the simplest atomic structure, scientists originally assigned to it the relative atomic weight of 1 and expressed the atomic weights of all other elements in terms of this unit weight. For example, an atom of sodium is 23 times heavier than an atom of hydrogen, so its atomic weight is 23.

More recently, carbon-12 has been selected as the atom (isotope) on which to base the relative weights of all other atoms. This decision fixed the weight for hydrogen as 1.00797, but the nearest whole number (1) is still used for most purposes.

Hydrogen can combine with oxygen in the ratio of $2:1$, giving H_2O, which we know in its various physical forms, or phases, as ice, water, and steam. Hydrogen and oxygen also combine in a $1:1$ ratio to form OH^- (the hydroxide ion). It is found in compounds with other elements called hydroxides, for example, sodium hydroxide ($NaOH$, or caustic soda), potassium hydroxide (KOH), and aluminum hydroxide ($Al(OH)_3$).

Transition Metals

Lying between Group 2 and Group 3 in the periodic table are the transition metals. These are of great importance to the potter, for among their oxides are the coloring oxides, which will be explored in Chapter 13. Chemically, they are significant for the variety of ways in which they combine with oxygen to give oxides (e.g., Cu_2O and CuO) and in some cases with other elements, (e.g., $CuCO_3$) so that there is more color in some than in others. The table in Figure 1.4 sets out the oxides, carbonates, and hydroxides with their formulas; the purpose of this table is not for you to learn them, but to demonstrate the differences among them. When you order a coloring oxide from a supplier, you are not necessarily told which oxide or carbonate is being supplied, whether it is a mixture of different oxides, or even whether it includes some of the hydroxide forms. Without this information, you cannot be sure of the molar weight of the oxide supplied. For this reason studio ceramists should not include color in percentage recipes but rather treat the small amount of color as an addition to the recipe (see Chapter 13). The exception to this rule is iron oxide when it is used in amounts over 5 percent.

Besides the transition metals listed in the periodic table in the Appendix, the following elements are also used for preparing colored stains and precious liquid metals (usually bought mixed as named colors or lusters ready to use): praseodymium (Pr), antimony (stibium, Sb), molybdenum (Mo), gold (Au), silver (Ag), bismuth (Bi), cadmium (Cd), and selenium (Se).

Metal	Oxide(s)	Name(s)*	Carbonate	Hydroxide
Fe Iron	FeO	IRON (II) OXIDE ferrous oxide *black iron oxide*	$FeCO_3$ *iron carbonate* Siderite	$FeOH \cdot nH_2O$ iron hydroxide; limonite and other hydrated forms includ- ing *ochre*
	Fe_2O_3	IRON (III) OXIDE ferric oxide *red iron oxide* Hematite		
	Fe_3O_4	IRON (II, III) OXIDE Magnetite		
Cu Copper	Cu_2O	COPPER (I) OXIDE cuprous oxide (red) *red copper oxide*	$CuCO_3$ *copper carbonate* Malachite	$CuCO_3 \cdot Cu(OH)_2$
	CuO	COPPER (II) OXIDE cupric oxide (black) *black copper oxide*		
Co Cobalt	CoO	COBALT (II) OXIDE cobaltous oxide	$CoCO_3$ *cobalt carbonate*	$Co_2CO_3(OH)_2$ basic cobalt carbonate
	Co_2O_3	COBALT (III) OXIDE *cobaltic oxide*		
	Co_3O_4	COBALT (II, III) OXIDE *cobalt oxide*		
Mn Manganese	MnO_2	MANGANESE (IV) OXIDE *manganese dioxide* PYROLUSITE MANGANITE $MnO_2 \cdot nH_2O$	$MnCO_3$ *manganese carbonate* RHODOCHROSITE	
Cr Chromium	Cr_2O_3	*chromia* CHROMIUM (III) OXIDE		
V Vanadium	V_2O_5	*vanadium pentoxide* VANADIUM (V) OXIDE		
Ni Nickel	NiO	NICKEL (II) OXIDE *nickel oxide,* nickelic oxide		
	Ni_2O_3	NICKEL (III) OXIDE		

Figure 1.4. Transition metals that supply coloring oxides, carbonates, and hydroxides. Common mineral names are given in italics.

Oxides of Titanium, Zirconium, and Zinc

These elements are also transition metals. Although their oxides are not coloring oxides in the normal sense, they have a considerable influence on color. The oxides of interest are

TiO_2, titanium dioxide, at high temperature during firing dissociates to give TiO (titanium oxide, titania)

ZrO_2, zirconium dioxide (zirconia), sometimes referred to as zirconium oxide

ZnO, zinc oxide, an auxiliary flux, particularly useful in the middle temperature range, heightens the color of copper and cobalt in alkaline glazes, but with other coloring oxides may produce a mottled or muddy effect.

Study the periodic table in Appendix Figure A.2 and refer back to it often. Gradually, you will become so familiar with it that a glance will solve many problems. It will be a relief to those who have not studied chemistry to know that only those elements listed in the shortened version of the periodic table are commonly used in ceramics. The symbols for copper (Cu), and cobalt (Co) are given, but they look so much alike that it is better to write copper and cobalt out in full when you are working. Similarly with zinc (Zn) and zircon (Zr). Think of the periodic table as a convenient list, not as a complicated chart. Teachers have tended to shy away from using it as being too academic, but it can provide a clear and simple understanding of our raw materials and what happens to them when we mix and fire them.

Crystal Structure and Crystal Form

Elements combine with each other in an orderly fashion. That is to say, not only do they combine in definite ratios to give particular chemical compounds, but they also usually arrange themselves into definite three-dimensional structures. Furthermore, if the structures are able to grow freely, characteristic crystal forms often develop. Where the space to grow is constricted, the external form may not be recognizable, but the internal order, though distorted, will remain the same. Where crystals develop in solutions (e.g., in a cooling molten magma), very often a number of tiny crystallites develop and aggregate to form large crystals or clusters of crystals. If these are worn down, for instance when exposed to the weather, so that they are not immediately recognizable (though crystalline inside), they are more often referred to as particles of a particular mineral.

Growth Around a Nucleus

In some instances, crystal growth may be stimulated by the presence of a nucleus. A tiny particle of matter can act as a seed around which other constituents accumulate and arrange themselves into a crystal structure, just as a pearl develops around a point of irritation inside the shell of an oyster. This phenomenon is relevant to macro-crystalline glazes where the crystals are visible, and to other glazes where minute crystal growth causes the glazes to be opaque and sometimes matte.

Impurities

An occasional site in a crystal may be replaced by an element that is foreign to the pure form, but in most cases this occurs at so few sites that the proportion is negligible in the overall composition. For most purposes the impurities are ignored in chemical analyses, or simply noted by adding up all the impurities and stating them as, for example, "2% impurities," and the mineral is assigned the pure formula. Note that this is the case in most minerals: few things in nature are absolutely pure.

Broken edges of crystals may also offer sites where elements alien to the particular mineral can attach themselves. These are usually the ions of elements and are referred to as _adsorbed ions_. (The prefix "ad-" means "added on" and is used here because the ion is added onto the surface and not absorbed.) Whether the added ions are noted in the chemical analyses and formulas depends on the amount involved. We shall deal with these as we come to them.

Ion Exchange

Impurities adsorbed onto the surfaces of crystals are not bonded to the crystal as tightly as those involved in the crystal structure. They may therefore be knocked off and replaced by other species where certain conditions prevail or when conditions change. The most important of these occurs where the particles are immersed in water. With simple ions, for example, some attach themselves more strongly than others, and there is an order of bonding strength (the symbol > means "greater than"):

> hydrogen > aluminum > barium > calcium > magnesium > potassium > sodium > lithium

Here the hydrogen ion has a greater bonding strength than the aluminum ion, aluminum greater than barium, and so on. Of particular interest to ceramists are the metal ions. An example of metal ion exchange occurs where a calcium ion enters a solution containing mineral particles to which potassium or sodium ions are adsorbed. Calcium ions, capable of making a stronger attachment than potassium or sodium ions, knock them off and exchange places with them. The ions knocked off enter the water as dissolved potassium or sodium ions. (The term "cation exchange" is often used when metal ions are involved. Some textbooks use the expression "base exchange.")

The Chemical Composition of Glass and Glaze

The composition of glass, like that of crystals, may be expressed by its oxide content, but unlike crystals, glass does not have a regular internal structure. The reason for this is that, when a mixture of materials used to produce a glass is heated to a temperature sufficient to melt it completely and the heat source is then withdrawn, the molten material cools too quickly to a rigid state for crystallization to take place: the glass remains noncrystalline (amorphous).

Glaze is a glass made from a mixture of materials that will produce a viscous melt that remains on vertical surfaces during the molten state. Special techniques can be employed to produce some crystals in a glass or glaze, but the matrix (i.e., the bulk of the glaze or glass) consists of a noncrystalline material. Glazes are discussed in depth in Chapter 11.

Stating the Formula of a Glaze

The introduction of molar weights (where one mole of a substance may be seen, weighed, and divided into, say 0.5 moles, by weight, in grams) introduces a rationale into formulas and formulation of glazes, which formerly were quoted as molecular formulas. The traditional method of stating a glaze formula is, for example:

$$0.3 \, K_2O \quad 0.5 \, Al_2O_3 \quad 4 \, SiO_2$$
$$0.7 \, CaO$$

In this example, it is realistic to take 0.5 of a mole of alumina when one mole of alumina weighs 102 grams. We have the same proportions but the bulk amount is larger. Our formula unit is now the mole, and the moles of materials required in a glaze can be weighed out in grams (see Plate 1).

Remember simply that the values assigned to molecules and mole are the same and therefore an amount stated in molecules will have the same value in moles (e.g., a substance with the molecular weight of 50 MW will have a molar weight of 50 g).

Weights and Numbers

In practice, the weight of a ceramic material is simply looked up in a reference book or calculated quickly from the periodic table. Here we give the theoretical background; atomic weights are considered first, then formula weights. After this discussion we shall be able to use molar weights without concerning ourselves with atoms and molecules. There will be occasional references to active chemical substances such as ions in accordance with the definition already given, but these will be kept to a minimum.

The following should be read by all students before tackling the glaze chapters, but this may be done in easy stages while studying further chapters. For this reason it has been placed in an advanced section.

ADVANCED SECTION

Atomic Weights

Scientists are able to measure the precise atomic weights of elements with the mass spectrograph, an instrument developed just after World War I. In 1961, carbon-12 was designated by the International Bureau of Standards as the standard unit of atomic weight. The weight of one ultimate particle of carbon-12 was defined as exactly 12 atomic weight units (u):

1 atom of carbon-12 weighs 12u

Using the same technique, hydrogen was found to be 11.905116 times lighter than carbon-12; therefore:

$$1 \text{ atom of hydrogen} = \frac{12,000000}{11.905116}, \quad \text{which is } 1.00797\,u$$

However, because hydrogen is 12 times lighter than carbon-12 *to the nearest whole number*, for most purposes it is considered that 1 atom of hydrogen weighs 1 u.

All other weights are stated relative to this figure. For instance, potassium is 39 time heavier than hydrogen, and therefore weighs 39 u. Calcium weighs 40 times more than hydrogen, and weighs 40 u. The atomic weights of elements used in ceramics are given in the periodic table in the Appendix.

Formula Weights (FW)

Formula weights (called "molecular weights" in some earlier works) are calculated by adding together the atomic weights of the elements involved in the compound. For example,

$$CaO = 40u\ (Ca) + 16u\ (O) = 56\ FW.$$

To calculate the formula weight of potassium feldspar, $K_2O \cdot Al_2O_3 \cdot 6SiO_2$, first find the weight of each oxide by adding up the weights of the constituent elements (remember there are $6SiO_2$):

$$
\begin{aligned}
K_2O &= (\text{potassium} \times 2) + (\text{oxygen} \times 1) \\
&= (39 \times 2) + (16 \times 1) &&= 94.00\ FW \\[4pt]
Al_2O_3 &= (\text{aluminum} \times 2) + (\text{oxygen} \times 3) \\
&= (27.00 \times 2) + (16.00 \times 3) &&= 102.00\ FW \\[4pt]
6SiO_2 &= 6(\text{silicon} \times 1) + 6(\text{oxygen} \times 2) \\
&= 6(28.00 \times 1) + 6(16 \times 2) = 6 \times 60.00 &&= \underline{360.00\ FW} \\[4pt]
\text{Total} &&& 556.00\ FW
\end{aligned}
$$

The formula weight of potassium feldspar is 556, that is, it is 556 times heavier than hydrogen.

(In the above discussion, the theoretical formula for potassium feldspar has been used, and whole numbers have been taken for the constituent oxides. If more precise figures had been used, the result would be nearer 557. In your general reading, you will find that some authors give 556, others 557 for the theoretical formula weight for potassium feldspar. The calculation for a regionally available feldspar is given on p. 397.)

The Mole and Molar Weight (molar mass)

The mole was discussed above. The scientific definition, relating the mole to carbon-12, is as follows:

A mole contains the same number of fundamental particles (atoms, molecules, or ions) as are contained in precisely 12 g of carbon-12.

Using modern methods scientists calculated the number of fundamental units in 12 grams of carbon-12 as 602,200,000,000,000,000,000,000 units. As there are 23 digits after the 6, this number may be written: 6.022×10^{23}. Using this expression in the following examples gives

6.022×10^{23} atoms in 1 mole of lead
6.022×10^{23} formula units in 1 mole of silica
6.022×10^{23} formula units in 1 mole of feldspar

This huge number is called the Avogadro number in honor of the brilliant Italian scientist, Amadeo Avogadro. We do not have to remember this number, any more than we need to know the number of grains in a pound (or kilogram) packet of sugar. It is sufficient to know that there are nearly a trillion billion units in one mole of a substance.

The important thing to remember is that there is always the same number of units in one mole, and that a mole may be used to describe a quantity of any chemical substance that contains 6.022×10^{23} fundamental units (e.g., a mole of atoms contains 6.022×10^{23} atoms; a mole of molecules contains 6.022×10^{23} molecules; and a mole of K_2O contains 6.022×10^{23} molecular units).

Fixing the Mass (Weight) of a Mole of a Chemical Substance

The molar mass of a substance is the weight in grams of 1 mole of the substance. Hydrogen is 12 times lighter than carbon-12 (to the nearest whole number), so, if

1 mole of carbon weighs 12 g,

then

1 mole of hydrogen must weigh 1g.

Since potassium, K, is 39 times heavier than hydrogen it follows that

1 mole of potassium weighs 39 g.

From here it is easy to calculate the weight mass of all other substances against the weight of hydrogen, as we did above for atomic and formula weights.

■   ■   ■

A Useful Point

It will be seen that, because formula weights and molar weights are both based on the "number of times heavier than hydrogen," it follows that the values assigned to molar weights will be the same as the values assigned to formula weights of chemical substances. This means that, if only formula weights are given in a textbook (or molecular weights, MW, in older texts) you may take the values given and use them as molar weights in grams. For example, since the formula weight of $CaO = 56$ FW, its molar weight is 56 g. In this text we shall refer to *molar weights*.

Chapter 2
The Natural Process: The Crystallization of Minerals and Formation of Rocks

Introduction

In early history, study of the earth was inseparable from religion. In the fifteenth century Leonardo da Vinci (1452–1519) recognized the origin of many features in the world about him. He realized that landscapes had been sculpted by the action of wind, rain, and frost and that shells found in rocks high in the Apennine Mountains were the fossil remains of sea organisms that must have once settled in great beds of sediments under the sea that later were raised up into mountains by some remarkable action. Only in the last hundred years, however, has geology developed into an indispensable science in an age of technology. Modern geology studies all aspects of the evolution of the earth. As ceramists, we are concerned mainly with the formation and transformation of minerals and rocks.

Magma

The planet Earth is believed to consist of several concentric layers (see Figure 2.1). The lighter, less dense rock collects like scum on boiling soup, and floats on the denser mantle in the way that an iceberg floats on denser water. It is this lighter rock, together with a cover of looser sediments and organic deposits, that forms the continental land masses. It consists of several types of rock, each with a different composition, though overall they are rich in silica and possess an abundance of alumina. Among them are some denser rocks that increase in proportion with depth, until both pass into the core that has metallic properties (probably largely iron) of very high density. The mantle rocks are believed to have just sufficient mobility to be in constant, very slow, circular motion (convection), and it is this motion that carries the hot rock upward where it is able to expand as the pressure drops and to become more fluid. This is one of the causes of the existence of volcanos and fissure eruptions along a crack.

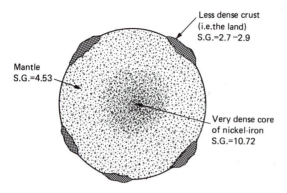

Figure 2.1. Concentric layers of the earth, from the outer crust to the inner core (S.G. = specific gravity).

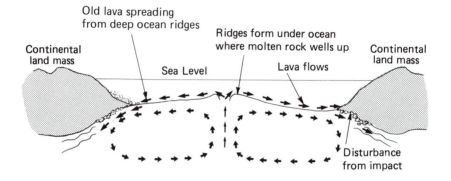

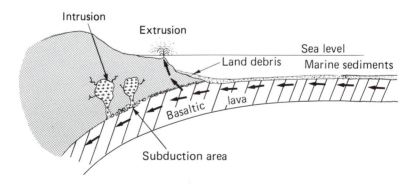

Figure 2.2. Sea floor spreading and the impact of magma on the crust.

One of the most exciting discoveries of recent times is that there are vast mountain ridges running down the mid-Atlantic Ocean, across the Indian Ocean, and down the eastern side of the Pacific Ocean deep below the surface of the sea. Here fluid molten magma, called lava, wells up and spreads out on either side across the ocean floor at the slow but steady rate of 1 to 6 cm/year. This is called "sea floor spreading." Disturbances occur as the lava, together with sediments that have settled on it, impinges on and slides down under the lighter, less dense continental land mass (see Figure 2.2). It is believed that earthquakes result from this activity. Heat from friction and pressure causes the mixture of broken lava and local rock material to melt and water vapor to form. Thus we get a new mixture of oxides and the formation of a magma with a new composition. Where it can, the newly formed magma pushes upward. If it reaches the surface, eruptions through the continental crust may occur, or large masses called batholiths may be trapped below the surface, where they cool very slowly. The types of new rock that form depend on the composition of the new magma as well as the rate of cooling.

Fluidity of Magma

The fluidity of a magma depends on the pressure, the composition and nature of the molten rock, as well as its temperature. A magma that flows with ease is said to be fluid; if it moves sluggishly, it is said to be viscous. (The term rheidity is used by geologists for the study of the ability to flow.)

Composition and Nature of Magma

The constituents of a magma are

1. Simple elements, oxides, and/or silicates (or substances capable of forming them when the temperature and pressure drop).
2. Small amounts of volatiles, such as water, sulfur, chlorine, and fluorine (including boron fluoride).

The volatiles escape when they can, and as they do, they push the magma up toward the surface of the earth.

Hatch, Wells and Wells (1972) explain, "It so happens that in the silicates, the ratio of the other elements to oxygen is always such that their formulae may be written down in terms of oxides; for example, orthoclase (potassium feldspar) $KAlSi_3O_8$ may be written as $K_2O \cdot Al_2O_3 \cdot 6SiO_2$ (i.e., as oxides)." Given this fact, chemists and geologists have adopted the convention of stating the composition of rocks (including molten rock, i.e., magma) in terms of oxides. Potters follow this convention, and it is used in this text.

Silica is the most important component of a magma, but there may be as little as 35 percent (in which case it combines with other oxides as the magma cools) or as much as 75 percent (in which case most of the resulting rock could be composed of silica alone). Alumina is the next most important component; thus it is not surprising that many aluminum silicates form in the cooling magma. Considerable quantities of calcia, magnesia, iron oxide, potassa, and soda are also present, and only a very small proportion of the magma contains the many other rarer oxides and trace elements, such as gold, copper, zinc, and so on. The potter is extremely fortunate, for these seven widely occurring oxides provide the bulk of the raw materials used in ceramics.

Types of Magma

Siliceous magma. Molten silica is extremely viscous; thus, even when potassa and soda are present, a siliceous magma never forms a "river of fire" but congeals quickly around the vent, forming thick tongues and conical piles of solidified rock. It is also less likely to reach the surface. Thus there are many batholiths containing rocks derived from silica-rich magmas.

Basaltic magma. This is a molten magma low in silica and high in calcia, magnesia, and iron. It is therefore fluid and erupts vigorously to flow out in great sheets or lava flows and is responsible for the distinctive landform known as columnar basalt. Basaltic lava flows are also the origin of *aa* (block lava) and *pahoehoe* (ropy lava), their names being of Hawaiian origin.

Temperature and Crystallization of Magma

When a magma is under pressure at great depths, its temperature may be well over 2000°C/3632°F; as it nears the surface of the earth and the pressure eases off, the temperature begins to fall. When a magma is able to cool slowly (in geologic time) more and more compounds come out of solution to form minerals, and the magma is said to be crystallizing. Where crystallization is able to take place slowly and where there is room to grow, very large crystals may form. Diamonds are believed to form at very high temperatures and pressure, but it is not until the temperature cools to under 2000°C/3632°F that common minerals are able to form. A magma that erupts and flows at the earth's surface usually registers temperatures of about 1200°C/2192°F down to 900°C/1652°F. When it falls below 900°C/1652°F it begins to consolidate and form rocks, though minerals still crystallize at temperatures as low as 400°C/752°F.

Among the first to crystallize is calcium feldspar, $CaO \cdot Al_2O_3 \cdot 2SiO_2$, and other silicates containing calcium, magnesium, and iron (e.g., olivine, a magnesium/iron silicate, and diopside, a calcium/magnesium silicate). Once the magma is depleted of many of the common elements, it becomes proportionately richer in the rarer elements and richer in volatiles, such as chlorine, sulfur, and fluorine (including boron fluorides). The temperature of the magma at this stage is about 400–600°C/752–1112°F. Very large crystals may form in this gaseous environment, notably tourmaline, topaz, and fluorite. (Geologists call this the *pneumatolytic* stage.) After these have formed, the residual liquid falls to lower temperatures where aqueous (watery) conditions prevail. In this *hydrothermal* (hot water) stage the magma is relatively enriched with water, which is necessary for the formation of minerals containing the hydroxyl (OH$^-$) group. Alkali-rich feldspars also form because of the concentration of potassium and sodium. Any silica left over will crystallize out as the mineral quartz.

This is a simplified account of crystallization from a cooling magma. There are many complexities. In nature, particularly at great depths, the pressure affects the exact temperature at which crystallization takes place. Some minerals that form at high temperatures can react with the residual liquid at low temperatures and begin to decompose again. Calcium feldspar is one that is thus affected. Other minerals retain their chemical composition but change their crystalline form as the temperature drops. The changes in the crystalline forms of silica are an example of this, and a knowledge of these changes is important in ceramics.

On cooling to 1713°C/3115°F, silica will begin to form crystals of cristobalite, SiO_2. These are stable down to 1470°C/2678°F. At this temperature the silicon and oxygen atoms in the crystals change their position in relation to one another, and a new crystal form, called tridymite, develops. Tridymite is stable down to 870°C/1598°F, when a further rearrangement takes place in response to the changing environment giving rise to quartz. This is the stable form from then on in the cooling magma and subsequently in rocks. It is for this reason that we are more familiar with silica in the form of quartz than with the high-temperature varieties. There are further modifications within each phase; we shall deal with them when we study the heating of silica.

Of all these complications, the most important is the way in which the oxides and/or minerals react with one another and mutually lower the temperature at which crystals may form. Of further importance to the ceramist is the fact that, where the pressure and the rate of cooling and heating remains the same, the crystallization point on cooling is the same as the melting point on heating. Thus, although it is rather confusing, the initials MP are used for both "melting point" and "crystallization point."

ADVANCED SECTION

The best way to understand how minerals react with one another in a cooling magma is to study a definite example in which the cooling history is traced on a diagram, called a *phase diagram*. This shows the various phases or states that a material may assume (those with which we are most familiar are ice, water, and steam).

Before you proceed to study an example, however, certain points should be drawn together. We are discussing here a magma buried deep in the earth. As already mentioned, in nature most magmas have many constituents, including volatiles, which are held under pressure and cannot escape. Thus the temperature decreases slowly: the magma cools over geologic time, and crystallization proceeds in an orderly fashion. It is therefore not always possible to correlate the cooling of a magma with the results of pottery firings, most of which are completed within a few days and many in under 24 hours. A final point that should be noted is that a phase diagram shows compositions and temperatures: there is no indication of the time taken for reactions to happen. These diagrams are therefore given as a quick, but academic, method of understanding the history of heating and cooling mixes of mineral materials. Other, more practical methods will be discussed later in this text. Let us consider a magma of the following composition which is able to cool slowly so that all the liquid is able to crystallize out in correct order.

calcium feldspar, $CaO \cdot Al_2O_3 \cdot 2SiO_2$
diopside, $CaO \cdot MgO \cdot 2SiO_2$

Experiment shows that the crystallization point of calcium feldspar is 1550°C/2822°F and that of diopside is 1390°C/2534°F. Addition of diopside to calcium feldspar lowers the crystallization point of the feldspar, and, surprisingly, addition of calcium feldspar to diopside lowers the crystallization point of diopside (see Figure 2.3). Point A represents a magma with the composition of pure calcium feldspar. Crystallization of composition A therefore begins at 1550°C/2822°F to give pure calcium feldspar. Similarly, pure diopside, at point B, would start to crystallize at 1390°C/2534°F. One might expect the crystallization points of mixtures of these two materials to be somewhere along a straight line drawn from A to B but not lower than this, but experimental results show otherwise. With a composition containing a small amount of diopside, giving a composition of, say, 90 percent calcium feldspar and 10 percent diopside, the feldspar does not begin to crystallize until temperature A^1 is reached. With an increase in the proportion of diopside (giving, for example, 80 percent calcium feldspar and 20 percent diopside) the temperature of crystallization of feldspar is lowered further to A^2, then A^3, and so on. Eventually, point E is reached, where the composition of the magma is 42 percent calcium feldspar and 58 percent diopside, the temperature at this point being 1270°C/2318°F. With further additions of diopside the crystallization point does not continue to fall but, in fact, starts to rise again.

Similarly, if we start wth pure diopside and add calcium feldspar, the lowest crystallization point is achieved with a composition of 58 percent diopside and 42 percent calcium feldspar, and the addition of further calcium feldspar starts to raise the temperature of crystallization of the mixture. The mixture of 58 percent diopside and 42 percent calcium feldspar is said to be the *eutectic mixture* for these two materials. Point E therefore represents the composition of calcium feldspar and diopside with the lowest crystallization point. It is called the eutectic point, and 1270°C/2318°F the eutectic temperature of this particular combination of materials. At the

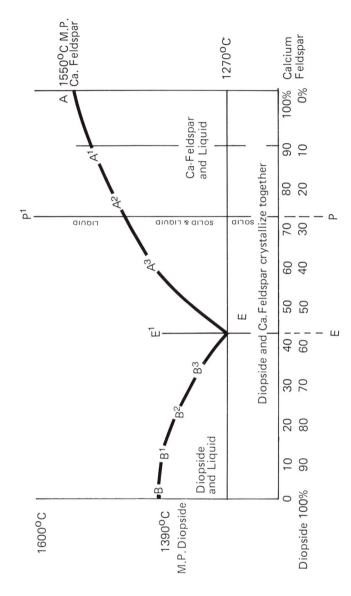

Figure 2.3. Phase diagram for the crystallization of mixtures of diopside and calcium feldspar (anorthite). The solid black line joins the temperatures at which the various mixtures melt. Points A_1–A_3 and B_1–B_3 mark the temperatures at which various mixtures of calcium feldspar and diopside (horizontal axis) begin to crystallize. After E. F. Osborne, "Equilibrium Diagram of the System Diopside-Anorthite," *American Journal of Science* 240 (1942), fig. 4; reprinted courtesy of Kline Geology Laboratory, A. J. Science.

eutectic temperature both minerals crystallize simultaneously until all the magma has disappeared. This means that, if a magma with a composition of 58 percent diopside plus 42 percent calcium feldspar is cooled, it will remain liquid until the temperature falls to 1270°C/2318°F and then crystallize at that point. But if a mixture richer in one or the other is used, there will be an excess of that mineral, which will cause the excess mineral to crystallize out until the *eutectic composition* is reached, and then both will crystallize together.

■　■　■

Texture of Rocks Formed from Cooling Magma

If magma is able to cool at a slow and regular rate, crystallization occurs as described above, and visible crystalline development will occur, giving the resulting rock a coarse texture. If, on the other hand, the magma is chilled fairly quickly, only small crystals will form, and the cooled rock will be fine-grained. In the extreme case, where the magma is suddenly chilled, a situation may occur where virtually no crystals have time to form, and the rock has a noncrystalline (amorphous) or glassy texture.

There are several interesting exceptions. For instance, if a magma cools to a temperature at which calcium feldspar forms and is held at this temperature for some time, large, well-developed calcium feldspar crystals may form. If the magma is then chilled rapidly, these large crystals will be enclosed in a fine-grained or glassy background called a matrix. Again, as the result of extremely slow cooling from a magma rich in volatiles, a very coarse-grained crystalline rock may form. This is called a *pegmatite*.

If one particular mineral predominates in the composition of a magma, for example potassium feldspar, $K_2O \cdot Al_2O_3 \cdot 6SiO_2$, that mineral is referred to as being found in the *massive* form (e.g., massive feldspar). Such occurrences are the sources of minerals that are mined commercially. The amount of the mineral available for mining in a particular area is referred to as the reserve (e.g., the economic reserve of potassium feldspar).

Types of Igneous Rocks and Their Mineral Content

Igneous rocks are literally fire rocks (cf. "ignite" and "ignition"). Rocks that form from cooling magma may be classified as either *extrusive*, or *volcanic* rocks, or as *intrusive*, or *trapped*, rocks.

Extrusive or Volcanic Rocks

If a siliceous magma cools rapidly in air, it forms either a fine-grained rock called rhyolite or a noncrystalline glassy rock called obsidian. When a volcanic eruption flings ash high into the air, it cools immediately, forming glassy splinters that settle and consolidate as *tuff* (see Figure 2.4).

On subsequent alteration in the presence of water, the clay minerals

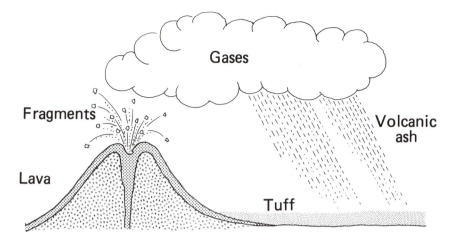

Figure 2.4. Volcanic eruption and the formation of tuff.

montmorillonite and beidellite may form to give deposits of bentonite (see p. 68).

If a basaltic magma cools in contact with the atmosphere, as in the case of a lava flow, an extremely fine-grained rock called *basalt*, consisting of calcium-magnesium-iron minerals, will form inside the lava flow, while on the surface, in immediate contact with air, basaltic glass will form.

Intrusive or Trapped Rocks

These solidify below the surface, where slow cooling permits large crystals to grow and therefore coarse-grained rocks to form. The most important of these are derived from magmas which are siliceous and therefore too viscous to reach the surface, hence they form silica-rich rock intrusions, or *batholiths* of granite (see "intrusion" in Figure 2.2). In these rocks the crystalline minerals quartz, mica, and feldspar, of which the granite is composed, are large enough to be seen and identified with the naked eye.

Even after the formation of the granite, volatiles and high-pressure steam continue to force their way up, carrying with them concentrates of the rare and often valuable elements such as gold, silver, and lead. Being under pressure, the volatiles often penetrate the rock (called country rock), surrounding the intrusion and change its physical and/or chemical properties. Cracks form in the country rock and in these the magma cools to form sheets often several meters thick, called dykes or intrusions. When they contain minerals of economic importance they are called veins or lodes.

Of these, tourmaline is a veritable cocktail among minerals, containing boron, silicon, aluminum, and varying amounts of alkali metals (lithium, sodium, and potassium), alkaline earth metals (magnesium, calcium, and barium), iron, and manganese. With the injection of the right concentrations of boron together with the volatiles into rocks of granite composition, the above elements (particularly iron) can be drawn from other minerals to form tourmaline, which is extremely tough and resistant to weathering. This leaves a rapidly decomposing granite where the formation of tourmaline has removed the iron and left some potassium feldspar, mica, and quartz in a virtually iron-free granite.

Important changes occur in the feldspars. We have seen how calcium feldspar, which crystallizes from a cooling magma at high temperature, disintegrates early in the cooling process. In the alkali feldspars, any alteration that occurs is thought to be due to liquid inclusions occurring during the hydrothermal stage: water enters the crystal structure, and gradually it is converted into the ultrafine flaky mica mineral sericite and the all-important white clay mineral *kaolinite*. However, it must be remembered that not all of the feldspars will be transformed and that alkali feldspars resist change more than the calcium feldspars.

In a few areas where iron-free light-colored feldspathic granite has been altered in this way, the bulk of the rock becomes a thoroughly rotted granite known by such names as China stone, Cornish stone, Carolina stone, D.F. stone, Graven, or Amakusa. Where the rotting is taken to its conclusion, the potassium feldspar in the granite disintegrates, loses its potassium (which is taken up in the formation of mica or washed away), and the remaining alumina and silica combine with water to form the clay mineral kaolinite. This, together with the remaining quartz (which is reduced to grains of quartz sand) and the mica/sericite (both residual from the rock and newly formed), gives the massive beds of white clay called *kaolin* (also called china clay).

The famous batholiths of southwest England, such as Dartmoor and Bodmin Moor, were formed 200 million years ago at the end of the carboniferous period but were not exposed until the overlying rock had been worn away, 160 million years later in the cretaceous period (see Figure 2.5). Since then, further erosion has carried away the surrounding softer rocks, and no doubt some of the exposed kaolin, to leave the higher points of the domes as "tors," with pockets of kaolin at various points on the perimeters. Fortunately for ceramists, the occurrences of the deposits are funnel-shaped, widening as they go downward, and are thus protected from erosion, providing very large reserves of clay.

Important Magmatic Minerals for Potters

If possible you should study the following notes in conjunction with hand specimens of the minerals and rocks described below. Your school, college, local museum, or library should be able to advise you where these may be seen. If you are not able to see specimens, ask for an illustrated book in color.

The two most important minerals used in ceramics, which are formed from magma, are those of the feldspar family and quartz.

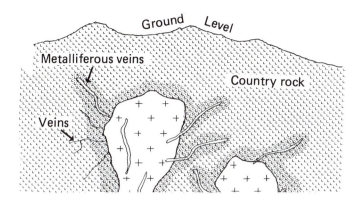

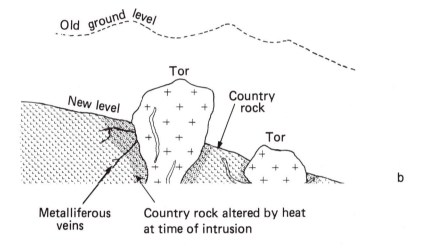

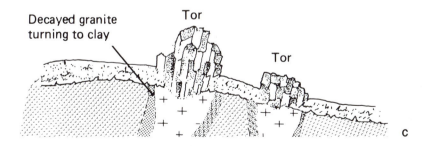

Figure 2.5. (a) Intrusion of granite batholiths into country rock; (b) erosion removes overlying rock, exposing the intrusion; (c) weathering sculpts the outcrop.

The Feldspar Family

Feldspar is the most abundant constituent of igneous rocks and may be found as small and large crystals, as well as in massive form. From the potter's point of view, feldspars may be classified by the dominant alkali or alkaline earth metal present and assigned the following theoretical formulas:

Potassium feldspar $K_2O \cdot Al_2O_3 \cdot 6SiO_2$
Sodium feldspar $Na_2O \cdot Al_2O_3 \cdot 6SiO_2$
Calcium feldspar $CaO \cdot Al_2O_3 \cdot 2SiO_2$

Calcium feldspar contains less silica than the other two because it crystallizes out of the magma at a higher temperature than potassium feldspar when co-crystallization of silica is not so favorable.

Feldspars are never found in nature in this degree of purity. Potassium feldspar, for example, will usually contain a little sodium and a small amount of other impurities. An example, in which a full formula for potassium feldspar is set beside a theoretical formula, will demonstrate this point:

Theoretical formula	*Full formula*
$K_2O \cdot Al_2O_3 \cdot 6SiO_2$	$0.70\ K_2O \cdot Al_2O_3 \cdot 6SiO_2$
	$0.20\ Na_2O$
	$0.05\ CaO$
	$\underline{0.05\ MgO}$
	1.00 mole total

The full formula reveals that a little of the K_2O has been replaced by Na_2O and even smaller amounts of CaO and MgO. The $Al_2O_3 : 6SiO_2$ ratio remains the same.

Where it is necessary to emphasize the presence of a significant amount of soda in potassium feldspar, the formula may be written $(K,Na)_2O \cdot Al_2O_3 \cdot 6SiO_2$. Placing the K first shows that potassa is the major oxide component but that a significant amount of soda is also present. If soda is predominant, the feldspar is called sodium feldspar and the formula may be written $(Na,K)_2O \cdot Al_2O_3 \cdot 6SiO_2$.

In the early stages of study, students may find that the simplified theoretical formulas of feldspars are perfectly adequate and are indeed preferable if confusion is to be avoided. In advanced work, you may find it necessary to take into consideration the detailed analysis of a particular feldspar given by the supplier.

Feldspathoids

These minerals are closely related to the feldspars. They contain the same oxides but the proportion of silica is lower. The important feldspathoid for ceramists is nepheline, which is contained in the rock *nepheline syenite*. In the rock spectrum, nepheline syenite is intermediate in composition between basalt and granite (see p. 38). It consists of the mineral nepheline with some alkali feldspar and, as is usual in rocks, a small amount of other minerals. It is important to remember that this is a rock and therefore variable in composition. However, because nepheline forms a major part of the rock, and the other chief component, alkali feldspar, consists of the same oxides (though introducing a little more silica), it is accorded the same generalized formula as the mineral. It should be noted that other types of syenites also occur containing various iron and calcium minerals. Hatch, Wells, and Wells (1972) also report a "nearly" pure nepheline rock, nephelinite or nemafite.

It is believed that, during the cooling of a magma, the feldspathoid leucite, a potassium aluminum silicate, forms at high temperature, but becomes unstable and goes back into solution as the cooling magma changes composition, with the formation of other minerals (particularly alkali feldspar) that leaves a sodium rich magma. From this, nepheline, a sodium aluminum silicate, forms leaving only a few large crystals (phenocryst) of leucite in the cooled magma. Though not used in ceramics, leucite is important in the heating history of potassium feldspar and is studied in Chapter 11.

Nepheline syenite (a rock consisting of a mixture of the minerals potassium feldspar, sodium feldspar, and nepheline) is a useful material in ceramics because it has a high soda content coupled with a low proportion of silica. It therefore reacts at a lower temperature than potassium feldspar. The generally accepted theoretical formula for nepheline syenite is $(3Na_2O \cdot K_2O) \cdot 4Al_2O_3 \cdot 8SiO_2$. Dividing through by 4 gives $(0.75Na_2O \cdot 0.25K_2O) \cdot Al_2O_3 \cdot 2SiO_2$. In this form it is possible to see that there is less silica in nepheline syenite than in sodium feldspar, $Na_2O \cdot Al_2O_3 \cdot 6SiO_2$ or potassium feldspar, $K_2O \cdot Al_2O_3 \cdot 6SiO_2$.

Given that it is a rock, however, the composition from different localities varies. You are advised therefore, to use the generalized formula in your initial studies but at a later stage, obtain and use the formula of the type available to you or at least recognize the difference.

Petalite and Spodumene

These have a feldspathic crystal structure and a similar composition, but the potassa and soda are replaced by lithia (Li_2O):

Petalite $Li_2O \cdot Al_2O_3 \cdot 8SiO_2$
Spodumene $Li_2O \cdot Al_2O_3 \cdot 4SiO_2$

These minerals are of considerable value in ceramics, supplying lithium.

Quartz

This very hard mineral, composed of the oxide silica (SiO_2), gives the extremely strong crystal structure discussed in Chapter 1. It crystallizes from silica-rich magmas and often forms the matrix in which precious metals are found. It sometimes grows into beautiful individual crystals or clusters of crystals. The clear, transparent variety, "rock crystal," is used in jewelry. It is the most important ingredient in glazes. Occasionally, because of the presence of iron or manganese, quartz is found with a very attractive violet color and is called amethyst. There are also a rose quartz, a smoky quartz, and a common milky quartz (in which minute bubbles in the crystals disperse the light and make the quartz appear cloudy).

Mica

There are many types of mica. They are like feldspars in their chemical makeup, being silicates of aluminum and potassium. There is magnesium and iron in the darker varieties; there may also be small amounts of other elements such as fluorine and barium. In addition, micas contain water. They differ from feldspars in their crystal structure. The platelike crystals of the micas form layers that split into sheets as thin as paper; this feature distinguishes them from other minerals, and they are, in fact, referred to as *sheet silicates*. Micas are common constituents of granitic rock (seen as sparkling flecks). They weather to give shiny particles among sediments. The two most important micas are white mica (containing potassa, soda, and no iron), called muscovite, and black mica (containing iron, magnesia, and titania), called biotite. Among other varieties is lepidolite, in which the potassa and soda is replaced by lithia.

Iron and Ferro-Magnesium Minerals

Metallic iron (Fe) is found on the earth's surface, but its major occurrence is as oxides in igneous rocks. A little pure iron is found in some basalts, usually as an alloy with nickel and similar metals. As the iron minerals are exposed to conditions near the surface of the earth, FeO tends to oxidize to Fe_2O_3, which weakens the crystal structure, thus assisting the process of disintegration of the minerals and rocks containing it. It is important to note that the ability of iron to be oxidized and reduced depends on the availability of oxygen. Iron oxidizes in an environment where there is plenty of air, that is, it rusts. Iron is responsible for the color in many minerals. An important source of iron is *hematite* (Fe_2O_3), found chiefly in sediments and metamorphic rocks formed from these sediments. It is also called *kidney ore* because of the curious shape in which it is found.

Ferro-magnesium minerals are also silicates, but contain less silica than the feldspar or mica minerals, and not all of them contain alumina. Moreover, they are high in calcia, magnesia, and iron rather than in potassa and soda. A number of these colored minerals are present in basaltic-type rocks, giving these rocks their dark color. In weathered sediments they contribute magnesia, calcia, and particularly iron. Geologists refer to them as the *mafic* minerals, but their popular nickname *ferro-mags* might appeal more to potters. The formulas of some of these minerals are given below as a quick, visual way of displaying their oxide content, but you do not need to remember them. Olivine, augite, hornblende, and diopside are not used in the pottery as such, but they are constituents of the rock basalt, which is used as a raw material to produce rich brown glazes.

Common Ferro-Magnesium Minerals

Formulas are given below only where they are of value to the ceramist.

Olivine is a magnesium-iron silicate. This mineral is found in shades of red, brown, or yellow depending on the Mg : Fe ratio. A pale green olivine is the gemstone called peridot.

Augite is a magnesium-iron silicate with calcium. Its brown/black crystals are common in basaltic-type rocks, which are often distinctive and well-formed. It belongs to the same family as the gemstone jade.

Diopside is a calcium magnesium silicate. It is the mineral used in the discussion of phase diagrams above.

Hornblende is a common dark green to black mineral, of similar composition to those mentioned above, but hydrated. This mineral is found in rocks intermediate in composition between granite and basalt.

Magnetite (Fe_3O_4) is one of the most important and abundant minerals in igneous rocks, particularly in the basaltic types, where it may accumulate in massive form to provide deposits of considerable commercial value. Other commercial occurrences are found as deposits in loose sediments and sedimentary rocks.

Chromite, iron chromate, is a mineral that forms in basaltic rocks, usually in small grains but sometimes segregated into bands, thus forming important economic deposits for the extraction of chromium. It is also obtained from sediments.

Rutile (TiO_2) is a titanium mineral that contains a little iron. It occurs in a number of forms in igneous rocks, though it is usually obtained commercially from the sediments of weathered rocks, such as the beach sands of Australia. Geology books list another titania mineral, anatase, also with the formula TiO_2, but this mineral, like rutile, is seldom iron-free in nature. Pure titania (TiO_2) is prepared commercially.

Ilmenite ($FeO \cdot TiO_2$). This is an idealized formula for ilmenite, a complex oxide of iron and titanium, originating in basaltic rocks such as gabbro. Sometimes it occurs in veins where it may aggregate, giving valuable commercial deposits. There may be small replacements of iron by magnesium or manganese. This ilmenite may vary slightly from batch to batch. It is also collected as sediments such as beach sands, along with rutile and zircon. An alteration product of ilmenite is leucoxene, which is sometimes found between the structural layers of kaolinite, as a black gelatinous material. Lawrence and West (1982) report that it can be the cause of darkening of the fired color in some U.S. clays. However, it is possible that it can now be removed or treated during the refining process.

Other Magmatic Minerals

Cassiterite: tin dioxide
Galena: lead sulfide
Witherite: barium carbonate
Sphalerite: zinc sulfide
Pyrite: iron sulfide
Chalcopyrite: copper iron sulfide
Vanadium: traces in sulfides
Cryolite: sodium aluminum fluoride
Celestine: strontium sulfate (used in industry, but still little used by studio
    potters)
Tourmaline: hydrated silicate of sodium, potassium, magnesium, iron, man-
    ganese, and lithium, with boron and fluorine.

Classification of Consolidated Igneous Rocks

Rocks are variegated assemblages of minerals and do not fall into clearly
defined classes by virtue of their mineral content or percentage oxide composition. For example, the chief minerals in basalt are calcium feldspar and
the colored ferro-magnesium minerals, but one basalt may have an abundance of olivine and another none at all. Some contain a little alkaline
feldspar; in others some of the calcium feldspar is replaced by nepheline.
However, there are sufficient similar characteristics to group them together
into the rock family basalt. The same thing applies to other named groups of
rock. There are also some minerals found in the massive form (such that
they offer deposits which can be mined). It is interesting to see the way one
rock type passes into another by virtue of a slightly different composition:

High CaO, MgO, FeO, Low SiO_2 High Na_2O, K_2O, SiO_2

basalt — gabbro — nepheline syenite — quartzite — granite
    — dolerite — syenodiorite — pitchblende —

Chapter 3
The Changing Landscape and the Evolution of Clay

Introduction

Land masses are constantly changing. We are only aware of this on occasions when coastal erosion is so great that homes can be seen toppling over the edge of cliffs, or when an earthquake or volcanic explosion has a visible effect. Most of the time changes happen at an unnoticeable rate so that it takes thousands of years for a marked change in the landscape to occur (see Figure 3.1).

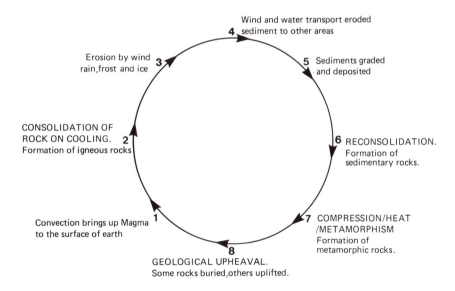

Figure 3.1. Rock cycle showing the formation of sedimentary, metamorphic, and igneous rocks.

Wind, rain, and frost destroy the rocks at the surface of the earth. Water gets into cracks in the rock; when the weather gets cold, it freezes, swells, and breaks up the rocks. Gradually the minerals are separated and disintegrate further. This process is known as mechanical weathering. Chemical weathering may also take place by the action of water or bacteria causing a change in the composition of minerals and the formation of new ones. The most important result of mechanical and chemical weathering from the potter's point of view is the formation of clay, which is discussed later in this chapter.

Occasionally, the resulting sediments stay in situ, but more often they slip and creep downhill or are carried away by wind and water and deposited elsewhere. The wind has been known to carry dust thousands of miles from desert areas before it is washed down from the air by rain and anchored by grass. These deposits are often known by local names, such as loess, the thick deposit of yellowish-brown dust made up of angular grains of quartz together with feldspar, calcite, and clay minerals, which covers parts of central and eastern Europe and China. In the Americas it is called adobe, and in Britain and Europe brickearth. Glaciers also erode the earth, grinding the rocks over which they pass, plucking off large chunks, and dumping them in a most erratic fashion.

An interesting situation occurs when small amounts of heavy minerals weather from rocks and slip downhill under the influence of gravity. As the movement slows down, their weight causes them to settle; this provides *selective deposition* in order of weight, giving separated valuable mineral deposits containing small amounts of heavy minerals, such as gold, diamond, tin, and witherite (barium carbonate), called placer deposits. However, erosion and transportation by water is the most universal and impressive. Fast-flowing rivers carve out deep valleys and transport sediments and pebbles; sometimes boulders are rolled along the river bed by fast-flowing water, gradually reducing them in size and making them smooth, rounded, and polished. As the gradient of the riverbed levels out and the river slows down, rock fragments are dropped, first the larger and then progressively the finer particles. In this way, sorting the transported materials takes place. With spring floods the banks of the river may be breached, leading to deposition on river flats. The final important deposition occurs when the river enters a lake or meets the sea (see Figure 3.2).

Only the finest grains are carried out to sea, the rest being deposited at the mouths of rivers where deltas and sand spits may form. Here the work of the river water is joined by that of the sea. Waves help to break up the rocks along the coast and sediments, mostly in the form of sand, are flung up to form beaches. Although beach sands are formed as described above, they are not necessarily only found along the sea coast. Geological upheavals may leave them far from the sea, where, given time, they are washed clean of salt by rain, rivers, and percolating water. The bulk of any sand consists of grains of quartz. Sand that also contains an important mineral in economically significant reserves is named by that particular mineral. For example, feldspathic sand is quartz sand containing an appreciable amount of feldspar;

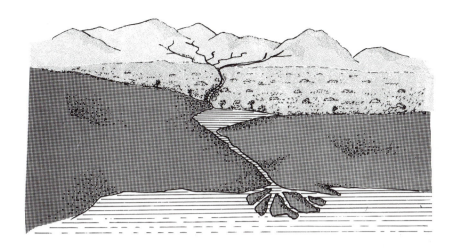

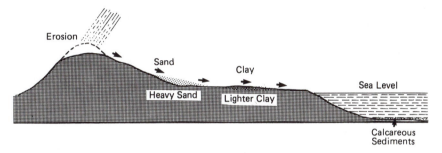

Figure 3.2. Transportation and deposition of sediments.

black sands ("ilmenitic sands") consist of quartz sand with ilmenite; mineralized sand contains quartz with one or more minerals of economic value. The pure white fine-grained silica sand called silver sand is used in glass-making and ceramics.

Weathering

Weathering is carried out by physical and chemical action and may be considered under the following headings:

1. resistant sediments
2. suspensions and colloids
3. solutions and saturated solutions, and
4. decomposition and further alteration by chemical action.

The first two result from physical weathering only; the third and fourth are the result of physical and chemical change.

Resistant Sediments

Quartz has such a strong crystal structure that a great deal of physical weathering is needed to break it into fragments. Even the smallest grains remain crystalline. It is because of this and its abundance in rocks that we find such quantities of quartz sand on the earth's surface. Other common minerals such as white mica break into tiny fragments but resist chemical weathering. Black (or brown) mica passes through a stage of decomposition in which it gives up its iron and is converted to white mica. It is then resistant to further chemical attack. Less common resistant minerals include zircon, tourmaline, olivine, tin, chromite, ilmenite, and rutile. These minerals are often found as components of mineral sands, and, where there are economic reserves of these minerals, they may be extracted by mechanical separation.

Suspensions and Colloids

Suspensions are rock fragments carried in suspension by the transporting water when the particles are light enough to be held up by the turbulence of the water and not simply rolled along the bottom.

Colloids are such ultrafine particles that they cannot be seen individually and do not settle even when the water is still. They may be carried very great distances, and sometimes are deposited only when the water evaporates.

Solutions and Saturated Solutions

Solutions in water. Natural water is never pure H_2O. It normally contains carbon dioxide (CO_2) from the air and from contact with organic (carbonaceous) matter in the soil and so is weakly acidic and chemically active. It helps to decompose minerals in the soil and in rocks to such an extent that, given geologic time, they eventually exist as molecules of various constituent oxides or elements attached to the water molecules. In this form they are dispersed evenly through the liquid.

Saturated solutions. As more and more solid material is dissolved into a particular volume of water, the concentration increases until a point is reached when no more can be taken into solution. A slight increase in the temperature normally enables more of the material to be dissolved, but on cooling the solution becomes supersaturated. This state is not stable. The slightest change, even a sudden movement, causes the excess material to combine again to form solids. If a lump of the same material or even a particle of foreign matter falls into or is placed in the supersaturated solution it will act as a "seed," and the dissolved constituents will start to precipitate and crystallize around this seed, or *nucleus* (a concept important in the making of crystalline glazes).

The classic experiment to illustrate this is to suspend a tiny piece of crystalline copper sulfate in a weak solution of copper sulfate and watch, over a short period of time, a large crystal grow around the nucleus crystal.

Solubility of Minerals

No mineral is completely insoluble in water, though some dissolve more readily than others. Crystals of borax dissolve easily, while it takes years to dissolve an appreciable amount of alumina or silica. Both silica and alumina can nevertheless dissolve and collect over geologic time, and eventually supersaturation is reached and silica *precipitates* and participates in the formation of new minerals. Laboratory experiments have shown that a solution of up to 144 parts per million (0.014%) silicon in water can exist. As the amount of silica is increased, chains of silica begin to link together until eventually the excess silica is precipitated.

There is an order of solubility among minerals, as follows (> stands for greater than): sodium > potassium > magnesium > calcium > iron > silicon > aluminum. The temperature of the water, and whether or not it is slightly acidic, affect the ability of the water to dissolve alumina and silica.

Decomposition and Alteration by Chemical Action

Iron has an interesting history. In Chapter 2, the oxidation of iron in minerals and rocks lying below but near the earth's surface was discussed. When exposed to the earth's atmosphere iron oxidizes rapidly; hematite, red iron oxide (Fe_2O_3), forms. Surfaces change to a fine yellow-red powdery form; that is, they rust.

Other minerals, such as calcium feldspar and the ferro-magnesium minerals, which begin to decompose in a cooling magma, are susceptible to further attack by chemical action when they are exposed to an oxidation atmosphere. Even potassium feldspar, which crystallizes at lower temperatures than calcium feldspar, may be attacked. However, there is such an abundance of it that much survives to provide feldspathic sediments, and it is largely from these sediments that clay minerals form (given geologic time).

The Evolution of Clay Minerals

The classic example of chemical decomposition and alteration is that of feldspar and the subsequent formation of the clay mineral *kaolinite*. This may occur as a response to a change in the environment, for example, the injection into feldspathic rock (e.g., granite) of magmatic water, a fluid of direct magma origin containing volatiles such as fluorine, a powerful promoter of change. The change may also come about by exposure of feldspathic rock to the atmosphere, causing disintegration of rocks and mineral decomposition (even rainwater containing a little carbonic acid is effective).

On the breakdown of feldspar, the potassa, soda, and a little of the silica are taken into solution and removed by percolating surface water. Water enters the relics of the feldspar crystals and, together with the alumina and

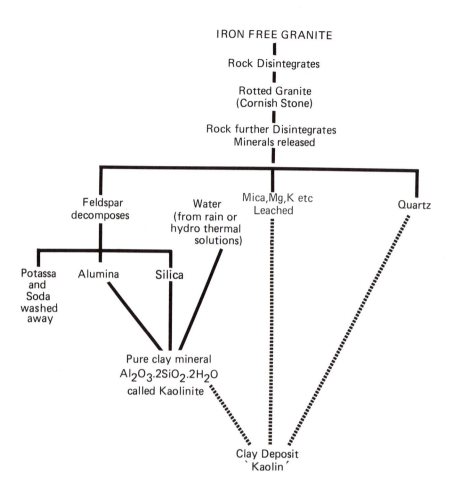

IRON FREE GRANITE

Rock Disintegrates

Rotted Granite
(Cornish Stone)

Rock further Disintegrates
Minerals released

Feldspar
decomposes

Water
(from rain or
hydro thermal
solutions)

Mica,Mg,K etc
Leached

Quartz

Potassa
and
Soda
washed
away

Alumina

Silica

Pure clay mineral
$Al_2O_3.2SiO_2.2H_2O$
called Kaolinite

Clay Deposit
`Kaolin´

Figure 3.3. Disintegration of granite and the formation of the mineral kaolinite.

remaining silica, forms a new crystal with the composition of $Al_2O_3 \cdot 2SiO_2 \cdot 2H_2O$. This is the pure clay mineral, kaolinite (see Figure 3.3).

Where rock debris from several rock types is transported and the finest sediments redeposited, less pure clay minerals will form, and the deposits will most likely be colored by iron. They form common clay, which is a widespread feature of the earth's surface. These clay minerals may subsequently change from one type to another. In one case, two exploratory drill holes were put down into the same stratum of rock many miles apart. On examining the core geologists found clay in both at the same level and clearly from the same stratum. In one core the clay mineral was pure kaolinite; in the other it was a sodium-bearing clay mineral. Furthermore, in the latter drill hole the presence of salt water was established. The conclusion was that, because of desert conditions in the latter area, salt water had become concentrated in the clay layer altering the clay, while in the first drill hole the clay remained unchanged.

ADVANCED SECTION

Chemistry of the Breakdown of Feldspar

When a feldspar crystal is exposed to water, oxygen ions at the surface of the crystal attract hydrogen ions from the water and link together forming strong bonds. This, in turn, weakens the crystal structure of the feldspar, and from this loosened structure, large potassium ions, sodium ions, and calcium ions migrate into the surrounding water. The crystal structure is distorted; it begins to break, gaps or holes appear, and water enters the broken structure. A greater surface area is then exposed to further disintegration. If the water is on the move (e.g., if it is river water washing over the feldspar, or water percolating through the rock), the metal ions of potassium, sodium, and calcium will be carried away in solution, and fresh supplies of water will continue to attack.

■ ■ ■

Deposits of Sediments

Primary or Residual Deposits

These sediments have formed above or adjacent to the parent rock. Their composition is dependent on, but not a replica of, that of the rock. Particularly important from the potter's point of view are deposits of rotted white feldspathic rock. In some cases the formation of tourmaline takes up the iron and other impurities from the disintegrating rock, leaving a partially decomposed deposit of Cornish (or Carolina) stone (see p. 32 for other regional names). With further change a deposit forms consisting of the iron-free clay mineral kaolinite, together with quartz and mica (the tourmaline can be removed during refining by mechanical separation). This clay, before refining, is called *raw kaolin*. An important feature of primary sediments is that they are coarse and angular because they have not suffered the abrasive action of transportation.

Secondary or Transported Sediments

In contrast to primary deposits, transported sediments are unrelated to the underlying rock, and usually result from the accumulation of sediments from several sources. As Figures 3.1 and 3.2 show, igneous rocks may be fragmented, transported, and consolidated, and these consolidated rocks eroded in turn to give fresh deposits of sediments. As these sediments are recycled, they are reduced to a smaller and smaller particle size, producing extremely fine sediments.

Lake Deposits

Where the sediments settle and remain for a very long time in a wet (and therefore chemically active) environment, new minerals may form. For example, clay minerals may develop where suitable oxides are dissolved in the water and large deposits can form. Again, clay minerals already formed are particularly vulnerable to chemical alteration. If the water is salty or becomes salty, metal ions (particularly potassium and sodium) not only attach themselves to the surface of clay crystals but also may enter the internal structure of the crystals and change them from one species of clay crystal to another. For instance, the pure clay mineral kaolinite, if in contact with potassium in solution, can be transformed to a new type of potassium-bearing clay mineral.

There is still a great deal of discussion as to whether clay minerals in this type of deposit are formed in the environment in which they have been found or whether they have been carried into it already formed. However, as such large areas contain deposits of the same type of clay mineral, they have probably been newly formed or transformed in situ.

A special type of lake deposit, called montmorillonite, can form as a result of a fall out of ash (called tuff) from a volcanic eruption. This is discussed in Chapter 2 (see Figure 2.4).

Salt Deposits

Where water has drained into depressions with no outlets, salts carried by the water gradually increase in concentration as the water evaporates (more rapidly in a hot climate), and gradually thick beds of salt accumulate. Where a part of the sea has been cut off, for instance, by the formation of a sand bank, vast beds of rock salt, $NaCl$ (table salt), may occur. In a few areas of the world such as volcanic regions, alkaline lakes may dry out to yield deposits of natron, a hydrated sodium carbonate ($NaCO_3 \cdot 10H_2O$) or deposits of borax, sodium borate ($Na_2O \cdot 2B_2O_3 \cdot 10H_2O$) and colemanite, calcium borate ($2CaO \cdot 3B_2O \cdot 5H_3O$).

Many natural salts contain water in their structure; hence when reheated (e.g., in a kiln) they give off steam causing problems (discussed later).

Hard Crust and the Formation of Bauxite (aluminum hydrate)

In climates where there are marked wet and dry seasons, mineral constituents may be *leached*. They are dissolved from the rock during the rainy season. During the dry season, the water is drawn to the surface and evaporates, leaving behind distinctive layers of the material previously held in solution. The least soluble minerals are dropped first at a lower level, while the more soluble ones are carried nearer the surface. Thus eventually the most soluble ones may be carried away, while those containing aluminum and iron remain and harden to give a crust, or hard-pan. Where the iron content is low and the aluminum high the deposit is called bauxite, the most important ore used in the production of the metal aluminum and the source of *alumina* and *aluminum hydrate* for ceramics. As the geological rock cycle continues these deposits can eventually contribute to the formation of high alumina clays.

The Effects of Environment on Sediments

In cold, dry climates, or in desert areas, the ground cover is thin or absent, and sediments are quickly blown away. By contrast, in hot, wet climates, rapid chemical action occurs. Deep weathering takes place in water-saturated rock material, while tropical vegetation prevents erosion. Under these conditions vast beds of clay may form. Then with a change in environment, clay may be transformed from one type to another by the process known as *ion exchange* (see below).

The Changing Character of Clay Crystals

We have already discussed the destruction of rocks and minerals and the formation of various types of sediments. We now come to an important change that takes place in the superficial character of clay minerals: not a change in the essential structure of the crystal but in the "clothes" it wears which it can change from time to time. When a clay is mixed with water some of the OH⁻ (hydroxyl) ions and metal ions (particularly calcium or sodium) held in solution in the water migrate to sites where they are *adsorbed* onto the broken edges of the clay crystals (see Chapter 1, "Crystal Structure"). The clay is then named by the dominant metal ion which has been adsorbed: Ca-clay (calcium-clay), or Na-clay (sodium-clay). As explained in Chapter 1, the calcium ion is capable of making a stronger bond than the sodium ion; thus most of the common clay found in nature is Ca-clay (Figure 3.4).

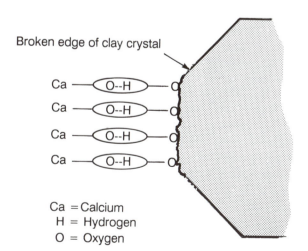

Figure 3.4. Calcium ions *ad*sorbed to clay crystal.

The Force of Numbers over Individual Strength and Ion Exchange

There are special circumstances in nature where Ca-clays may be transformed to Na-clays. If, for example, seawater inundates an area containing Ca-clay, then the sheer mass of sodium ions available in the new environment may knock off the calcium ions that had been previously attached to the broken edges of the clay crystals, and replace them by sodium ions. This process is called ion exchange. If subsequently the environmental conditions are reversed (e.g., if the salt water recedes and fresh water comes into the area, supplying calcium ions), the sodium ions may be knocked off and exchanged for calcium ions.

ADVANCED SECTION

The Chemical Explanation

Forces of attraction. There is a natural attraction between crystals of the same mineral. The nearer the crystals are to one another, the greater the mutual attraction. If for any reason there is a barrier between the crystals, the forces of attraction between them are affected.

Let us consider the case of Ca-clays and Na-clays suspended in water. Given the attachment of a layer of hydroxyl and metal ions, a double layer of ions surrounds each clay particle. The type of metal ion attached has an important bearing on the performance of a clay for ceramics, particularly in reducing a clay mass to a slip and in slip casting.

Characteristics of Ca-clay. Calcium ions are smaller than the sodium ions, and calcium ions form stronger bonds than sodium ions. For these two reasons, calcium ions pack in neatly among the adsorbed water and have little incentive to leave. This produces a neat, thin layer surrounding the clay crystal, which does not interfere with the forces of attraction between the crystals. They therefore attract one another and coagulate together to form larger particles, or flocs. They are said to *flocculate.*

Characteristics of Na-clay. Sodium ions form weak bonds and are constantly wandering back into the water, then reattaching themselves. Because they are larger than calcium ions they disrupt the hydroxyl layer around the crystal. These factors reduce the forces of attraction between the crystals. Furthermore, the hydrogen ions at the broken bonds on one clay particle, left free for most of the time by the wandering sodium ions, are not attracted by the hydrogen ions also left at the free ends on other clay particles, but are in fact repelled by them. There is therefore a considerable "stand-off" distance between adjacent particles. They do not coagulate, or floc together, but rather the opposite: they deflocculate, and a suspension of fine clay particles results.

■ ■ ■

Sedimentary Rocks

During the course of geologic time, sediments of whatever origin may accumulate to give layers hundreds of meters thick. With the growing pile of sediments, the pressure of the overburden squeezes out the water from deeper layers and heat is generated. As a result, consolidation of the sediments to sedimentary rocks takes place. Sediments have usually been neatly sorted by nature and deposited layer upon layer; thus we find that sedimentary rocks are fairly simple in composition (unlike the complexity of igneous rocks) and that they usually exhibit a banded appearance, or *stratification*. It is by this feature that many sedimentary rocks are recognized.

There are three main groups of sedimentary rocks:

1. Sandstone (mostly quartz)
2. Mudstone and shales (mostly clay minerals)
3. Limestone and chalk (mostly calcite); calcium magnesium carbonate rock, dolomite, may be included here.

Sandstone consists of compacted quartz sediments. These may be self-cementing (pressure and the heat generated softens the grains so that they stick together), or, they may be cemented together by silica carried into the deposit by percolating water, where it precipitates and fills the pore spaces. Other cementing materials may be ferruginous (iron oxides) or calcareous (calcium carbonate). The different cements give different characters to the resulting rocks.

Mudstone and *shales* consist of compacted clay in which much of the water has been squeezed out. As the compaction continues, the tiny clay crystals begin to align themselves, and shales develop. Many mudstones are laid down together with carbonaceous matter from decayed plants, which colors the shales dark gray. Sulfur is also released from plant matter, and if iron is present, iron sulfide (FeS_2), known as fool's gold or iron pyrite, forms and gives a lustrous effect.

Limestone, chalk, and *dolomite* are formed by all sorts of sea organisms extracting calcium from the water and using it to make shells and skeletons of calcite (calcium carbonate, $CaCO_3$). As these disintegrate they settle to form thick beds of calcite on the seafloor over eons of time and eventually consolidate to form limestone. Sometimes shells (or their forms) remain as fossils in the rock. When shells and calcite fragments settle slowly through great depths of water, they dissolve and eventually precipitate on the ocean floor as a very fine powdery calcium carbonate to form a pure white type of limestone called chalk. Coral polyps that live in warm and clear water also contribute; as one generation dies another builds its calcite homes on top, eventually forming coral reefs.

Where more than 15 percent of the mineral *dolomite*, $CaCO_3 \cdot MgCO_3$, is present in limestone, the rock is called dolomite; if there is under 15 percent the rock is called dolomitic limestone. It should be remembered that dolomite is a rock and therefore the composition is variable. The Dolomite Mountains in Italy are a famous source of dolomite.

Other Deposits

Flint (microcrystalline quartz) is an opaline form of silica ooze, probably deposited at the same time as calcitic sediments, the future chalk, and trapped in the sediments, where it creeps through them until it can accumulate and precipitate. Once revealed at the surface of the earth (by geological action) it is often seen as knobbly nodules or layers in the chalk. It is so fine-grained that it breaks in the same way as glass and was for a long time thought to be noncrystalline. The massive form is called chert. This is also found in limestones, sandstones, and shales; when it is colored with iron, the beautiful banded gemstone jasper forms. Flint usually contains about 1 percent water and some carbonaceous matter, which gives natural flint a dark gray color, but these burn away during the preparation of flint for use in ceramics.

Diatomaceous earth and *diatomite rock* are formed by tiny organisms that inhabit lakes and the sea and use silica instead of calcite to make their skeletons. On dying, they settle and accumulate to form thick beds of ooze. Having a cellular structure, the pure (100% silica) variety makes excellent high-temperature bricks. The impure variety also provides useful insulation materials up to 900°C/1652°F.

Boric Oxides and the Borates

Here we consider the oxide of boron and the boron salts. The nomenclature is confusing, so it is important to learn it correctly from the beginning, as all the terms are important in ceramics:

Boron, B, the element
Boric oxide, B_2O_3, the oxide
Borates, the general term given to oxides of boron combined with sodium, calcium, or magnesium in different varieties of borates, plus water

We have already seen that boron is one of the trace elements that accumulate in the final phase of a cooling magma and that tourmaline is one of the boron minerals that form (see p. 31). This is a complex mineral and is not a direct source of boron to the potter. Far more useful are the borates that are deposited, along with sulfur and other rare compounds, around hot springs and gas vents in volcanic areas.

Borax ($Na_2O \cdot 2B_2O_3 \cdot 10H_2O$). This hydrous sodium borate compound is highly soluble. Calcium may replace the sodium, forming a hydrous calcium borate, colemanite, variable between $CaO \cdot 2B_2O_3 \cdot 6H_2O$ and $2CaO \cdot 3B_2O_3 \cdot 5H_2O$. This, together with pandermite, also $2CaO \cdot 3B_2O_3 \cdot 5H_2O$, is relatively insoluble.

Colemanite is often found as nodules in clays, or as thick beds between layers of tuff (see Figure 2.4). Similar compounds supply boric oxide in a virtually insoluble form. However, because of the high water content of the natural minerals, commercially prepared dehydrated forms are often preferred.

Metamorphic Rocks

These rocks have been changed from one type to another. As the land is worn down in one place and built up in another, the balance of the lighter continental rock floating on the mantle is upset. Some parts subside while others are raised above sea level. Thus rocks like limestone, formed under the sea, may eventually become high mountains, and the cycle of erosion, transportation, deposition, and formation of new rocks begins all over again. Very often in this process rocks are changed by heat, pressure, and chemically active fluids. We can imagine the gigantic crushing that must take place as rocks are pushed against one another and become folded or thrust one over the other. Also it must be remembered that, where igneous matter is pushing its way up, direct contact with the magma or simply its heat can cause a change in the rocks. The changes most likely to occur are:

1. *Formation of new textures.* Minerals may be squeezed out into elongated shapes giving the rock a banded appearance. Shales become slates, and the terms schist and gneiss are used to describe rocks with a lamellar, or banded, appearance.

2. *Reforming of crystals.* With the softening of the rock by heat, crystals may reform. Of particular interest is a metamorphic rock consisting almost exclusively of microcrystalline quartz, which on recrystallization develops a hard, massive, interlocking fabric of quartz crystals, forming the rock known as quartzite. Similarly, a pure limestone may recrystallize into a harder, more compact rock in the presence of heat to form marble. This may also be used as a source of calcium carbonate ($CaCO_3$).

3. *Formation of new minerals.* As the rock is heated, carbon dioxide or water may react with the other constituents, or, in some cases, constituents may migrate. Thus, with a change in chemical composition of the rock, a new assemblage of minerals may form. Alternatively, where two different minerals exist in the same rock, they may, in the presence of high temperatures, react together to form a new mineral. Such is the case with impure limestone containing appreciable quantities of silica sand (SiO_2) giving

$$CaCO_3 + SiO_2 \xrightarrow{\text{heat}} CaSiO_3 + CO_2\uparrow$$

$$\underset{\substack{\text{calcium} \\ \text{carbonate}}}{} \quad \underset{\text{silica}}{} \quad \underset{\substack{\text{calcium silicate} \\ \text{(wollastonite)}}}{} \quad \underset{\substack{\text{carbon} \\ \text{dioxide}}}{}$$

The mineral wollastonite ($CaSiO_3$) is a very useful raw material in ceramics, supplying both calcia and silica. Another similar alteration caused by a reaction of dolomite with silica gives the mineral talc, $3MgO \cdot 4SiO_2 \cdot H_2O$:

$$3(CaCO_3 \cdot MgCO_3) + 4SiO_2 + H_2O \xrightarrow{\text{heat}} 3MgO \cdot 4SiO_2 \cdot H_2O + 3CaCO_3 + CO_2\uparrow$$

$$\underset{\text{dolomite}}{} \quad \underset{\text{silica}}{} \quad \underset{\text{water}}{} \quad \underset{\text{talc}}{} \quad \underset{\text{calcite}}{} \quad \underset{\substack{\text{carbon} \\ \text{dioxide}}}{}$$

A more useful source of talc is the rock steatite (soapstone) formed from the metamorphosis of basic or ultrabasic rocks. Steatite is largely composed of the mineral talc and is thus assigned the same formula. Talc and steatite are very soft and feel greasy when touched.

Changes in Clay and Shales

Clays and shales are even more sensitive to heat than sandstones or limestones. With pressure from great thicknesses of overburden or earth movements, clay is squeezed into thin, hard parallel platelets of shale, and this, in turn, becomes slate. With an increase in pressure and temperature, complete recrystallization may take place giving a hard granular rock called hornfels. The major changes with heat and pressure are shown in Figure 3.5.

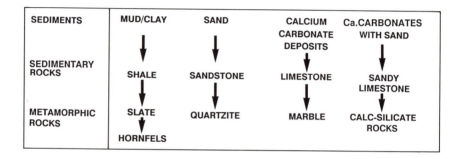

Figure 3.5. Changes in sediments due to heat and pressure.

Chapter 4
Clay Deposits and the Mineralogy of Clay

Introduction

In this chapter we study the mineral constituents of clay deposits and then make use of this knowledge in the practical fieldwork and workshop tests that follow. Everyone from a very early age is familiar with the terms sand, clay and soil, but when pressed for an explicit description or definition, most begin to falter. Clay gets sticky when wet and becomes rock hard as it dries out. Sand is gritty and blows everywhere when it is dry (it only becomes rock hard when consolidated into sandstone). The ceramist should be able to recognize the differences between a clay deposit and sand or soil, and to recognize in the field a deposit that shows promise of being a usable clay in ceramics.

Use of the Word Clay

In this text clay is used in four specific ways.

1. *Clay minerals* are those minerals in which the crystals have "a platy layered structure, and which chemically are hydrous aluminum silicates" (Pettijohn, 1974).

2. *Clay deposits* consist of mixtures of clay minerals, other minerals, and sometimes carbonaceous matter. There must be sufficient clay minerals to enable a handful of damp earth to hold its shape after being squeezed in the hand. For our purposes, deposits of clay found in nature are referred to as *natural clay* (or *local clay* when referring to natural clay found near a potter's workshop).

3. *Clay body* is a term used to describe the clay used to make objects that after firing form a permanent ceramic material. This includes the natural clays that can be used "as dug" or with only minimal cleaning and the clay bodies compounded by or for potters to meet specific requirements. They are made by mixing together definite proportions of natural and/or refined clays and other minerals, such as feldspar and quartz, to serve special purposes, either because natural clays are not available in precisely the

required composition, or because they are found in small deposits and are therefore expensive. After firing, the body is no longer a clay body; it should then be called pottery or a ceramic body (or simply ceramic). Note that archaeologists refer to the body as *fabric*.

4. *Clay slip* is the name for clay mixed with water to the consistency of thin cream. A clay slip is used as a cover coat or to decorate the surface of a clay object. When clays are being cleaned or recycled they are reduced to a slip; when clays are being mixed together it is best to do it while both are of slip consistency.

Detailed Description of Natural Clay Deposits

In order to study deposits of natural clay in greater detail, the constituents may be divided into three categories:

1. Essential clay minerals
2. Accessory minerals
3. Carbonaceous matter

The presence of soluble salts in some clays is also discussed.

Essential Clay Minerals

These provide the essential quality of plasticity. The two most important groups are the *kandites* (including kaolinite) and the *smectites* (including montmorillonite). Some authors also include the illites with the clay minerals. However, although they are an important group (they may be responsible for the smooth, silky sheen on Roman red gloss ware), they do not have the plasticity of true clay minerals. They are therefore placed with mica in the classification in Figure 4.5 below. The present classification is based on the list of "principal clay mineral groups" given by Deer, Howie, and Zussman (1986).

Chemically, all the clay minerals are hydrous aluminum silicates, the pure form being $Al_2O_3 \cdot 2SiO_2 \cdot 2H_2O$. The degree of plasticity that a deposit of wetted clay (as opposed to hard dry clay) can exhibit depends on which of the clay minerals are present and the proportion of these clay minerals to the other accessory minerals in the deposit, as well as the degree to which they have been abraded.

Crystals of the clay minerals are too small to see with the naked eye. However, because they have a structure similar to that of mica, the latter can be used as a model. Mica crystals have a flat plate-like structure and build up into layers or laminates tightly bonded together by potassium ions. It is possible to split the layers apart, but a little effort is required. In a similar but finer mineral, sericite, there are fewer potassium ions, and splitting occurs more readily. Thus very tiny particles exist. Although sericite does not have the plasticity of the clay minerals, if present in clay it fits into the physical

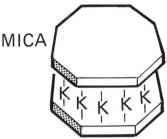

MICA

Mica layers are strongly bonded
together by Potassium,K.

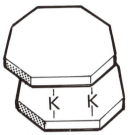

As the bonding by Potassium
decreases splitting occurs
more readily.

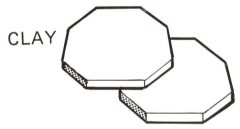

CLAY

In clay the layers are not bonded
and therefore separate with ease.

Figure 4.1. Layer structures of mica and the clay
minerals.

structure of clay so well that it does not detract from the plasticity of a wet
clay mass. Finally, in the clay minerals the layers are not bonded together by
potassium ions but are loosely linked together through oxygen and hydroxyl
ions at the surface of the clay layers and therefore separate with ease (see
Figure 4.1).

There are several different types of clay minerals. Each has a slightly
different crystal makeup, but all have a flat, plate-like form that is an expres-

sion of the internal structure. In simple language, this structure may be likened to a sandwich. One type of sandwich consists of two pieces of buttered bread with a filling. Another type, the open sandwich, consists of one piece of buttered bread on which is spread the filling, or topping; and these in turn are piled one on top of the other. Clay crystals are akin to these. The most important of the clay minerals, kaolinite, is of the open-sandwich type and is also chemically the purest type, with the formula of $Al_2O_3 \cdot 2SiO_2 \cdot 2H_2O$. The rest are of the closed sandwich type, of which montmorillonite has the smallest particle size.

In the "sandwich" shown in Figure 4.2, the bread represents layers (called sheets by some authors) of silica tetrahedra, while the butter and filling represent a layer of aluminum ions surround by OH^- ions, which in turn join with the silica layer. This is an ideal construct. In reality, the water content may vary, and other ions enter the structure to give us the several types of clay minerals that exist in nature.

The Clay-Water Relationship

Water is associated with clay in three different forms.

1. *Structural water* refers to the water that forms part of the crystal structure and is therefore the water recorded in the formula. The terms water of crystallization or combined water are used by some authors.

2. *Free water* or *water of plasticity* is rain (or tap) water, which, when added to clay lubricates it so that the particles can slide over one another. Some of this water is trapped in the pores (spaces between tiny particles of clay) and remains even when the clay appears to be dry. This is the water that is driven off in the early stages of firing.

3. *Interstructural,* or *interlayer, water* is the water that separates the crystal layers in the smectites. The interstructural water lying nearest a crystal is oriented with respect to the crystal with some of the OH^- ions adsorbed (attached) to the surface; further away it becomes increasingly disoriented and less tightly held, hence the ions tend to wander in and out, and the amount is variable. Thus the smectites are sometimes referred to as swelling clay crystals.

ADVANCED SECTION

Crystal Structure of Clay Minerals

In more scientific language, clay minerals may be described as hydrous aluminum silicates in which the fundamental structural units of clay crystals are composed of two clearly defined layers:

1. *A tetrahedral layer* composed of silica (see Figure 4.3). In this layer silicon may be replaced occasionally by aluminum, but not more than one aluminum ion to every three of silicon.

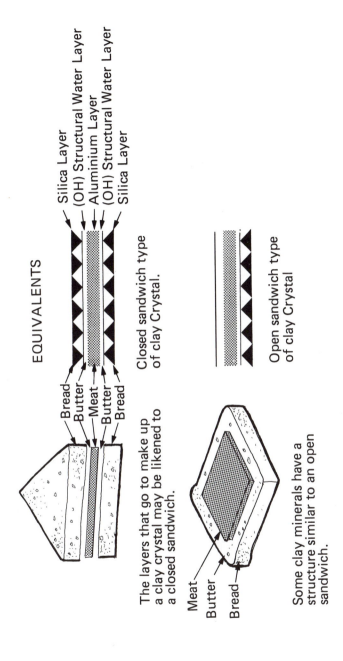

EQUIVALENTS

Silica Layer
(OH) Structural Water Layer
Aluminium Layer
(OH) Structural Water Layer
Silica Layer

Bread
Butter
Meat
Butter
Bread

Closed sandwich type
of clay Crystal.

The layers that go to make up
a clay crystal may be likened to
a closed sandwich.

Open sandwich type
of clay Crystal

Meat
Butter
Bread

Some clay minerals have a
structure similar to an open
sandwich.

Figure 4.2. General structure of the two types of clay crystals likened to a sandwich.

2. *An octahedral layer* or sheet in which aluminum ions are linked in six-fold coordination with hydroxyl ions, called a *gibbsite* layer. Sometimes the aluminum is replaced by magnesium, and the layer is then called a *brucite* layer, but more often there is a partial replacement of aluminum ions by iron and/or magnesium ions, in which case it is referred to as a modified gibbsite layer (see Figure 4.3). These layers combine in the ways described above to give the complex fundamental unit structures of the clay crystals.

The unit crystals are stacked one above the other. If they are stacked in a regular order, one unit crystal lying directly over another, the units tend to build up into (relatively) larger crystals with the same form. Primary kaolinite has this tendency. When the crystals have been weathered or transported or otherwise disturbed, the stacks may become disorganized and more prone to break into smaller particles. This structure is referred to as irregular stacking (see Figure 4.4).

The way in which the fundamental structural units are stacked and the extent to which silicon is replaced in the tetrahedral sheet and the aluminum replaced in the octahedral sheet, together with the presence or absence of extra metal ions and water between the fundamental structural layers, determines the type of clay crystal.

Classification of Clay Minerals According to Structure

Clay minerals have been classified by Deer, Howie, and Zussman (1986) into kandites and smectites. This classification, along with the nonclay, nonplastic minerals, the micas, sericite, and illites, is illustrated in Figure 4.5 so that a comparison of their structure may be made.

Gibbsite type layer

Silica tetrahedral layer

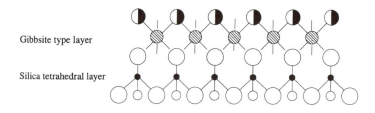

◑ Hydroxyl layer

◍ Aluminum

○ Oxygen

• Silicon

Figure 4.3. Structure of kaolinite, showing the tetrahedral layer composed of silicon and oxygen ions and the gibbsite-type layer composed of hydroxyl and aluminum ions with some replacement of aluminum by magnesium or iron. The layers, linked through oxygen ions in the overall crystal structure, are represented separately in the diagram for clarity.

Regular Stacking

Irregular Stacking

Figure 4.4. Regular and irregular stacking of clay crystals.

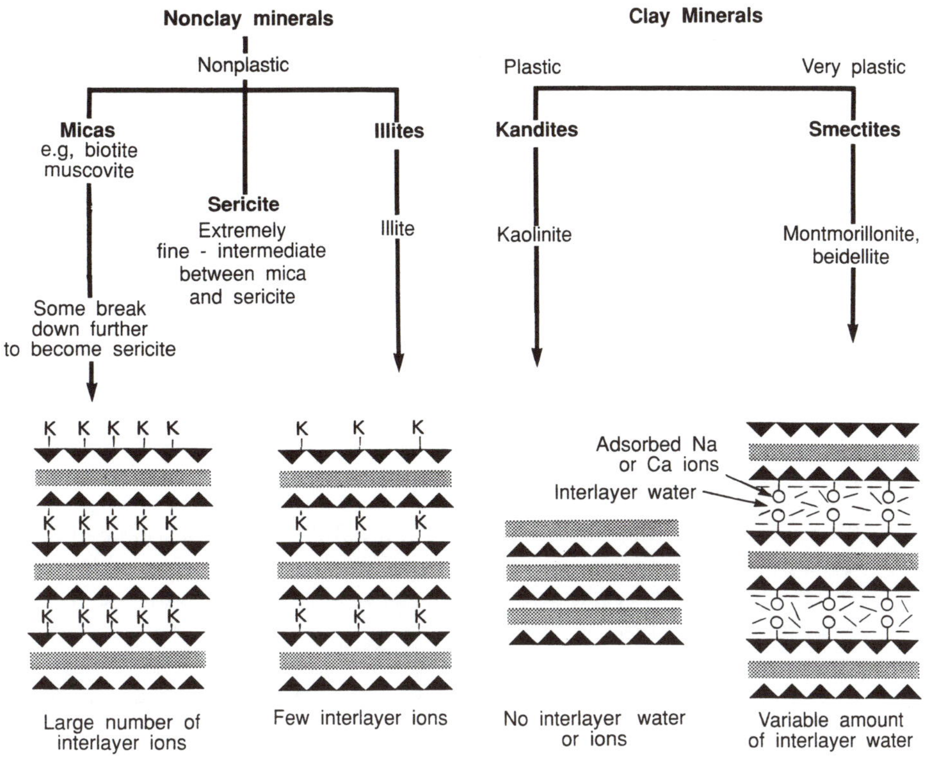

Nonclay minerals
Nonplastic
Micas
e.g, biotite
muscovite
Sericite
Extremely
fine - intermediate
between mica
and sericite
Illites
Illite
Some break
down further
to become sericite
Clay Minerals
Plastic
Very plastic
Kandites
Kaolinite
Smectites
Montmorillonite,
beidellite
K K K K K
K K K
Adsorbed Na
or Ca ions
Interlayer water
Large number of
interlayer ions
Few interlayer ions
No interlayer water
or ions
Variable amount
of interlayer water

Figure 4.5. Classification of clay crystals and allied minerals according to number of inter-layer ions. Based on the list of "principal clay mineral groups" given by Deer, Howie, and Zussman (1986).

Kandites consist of alternating silica tetrahedral and gibbsite octahedral layers. Kaolinite is the chief mineral of this type. In kandites that have not been disordered, the stacking is regular and they make slightly bigger stacks (though without potassium ions bonding them together, they do not grow as large as those of illite or mica). In addition, kandites with regular stacking have less surface area exposed to a lubricating film of water resulting in a less plastic clay. (This can be demonstrated by measuring the surface area of the six faces of a small block of clay, slicing it into four smaller blocks, and measuring the total surface area of the faces of all four blocks.) Kaolinite that has been mechanically abraded, so that the original orderly stacking is distorted, is called *disordered kaolinite.* Although easily recognized in white kaolin deposits, vast amounts in other clay sediments are not immediately recognized because of the presence of color from other minerals. Kaolinite lying adjacent to the rock from which it originated is coarse-grained and has little plasticity. By contrast, if transported and deposited elsewhere, it is usually disordered, broken, and reduced to a finer particle size. In this state the kaolinite may contribute to the plasticity of a deposit.

Smectites, montmorillonite for example, have a few of the silicon ions in the tetrahedral layer replaced by aluminum ions, and a few aluminum ions in the octahedral layer replaced by magnesium or iron ions. The resulting electrical imbalance is redressed by a small number of sodium ions or calcium ions between the layers, which are adsorbed onto the surface of the crystal. Interstructural water also occurs between the layers, and because the amount of water can vary from time to time, these minerals are described as swelling minerals. The metal ions of sodium or calcium are loosely held between the layers and tend to wander in and out. The calcium and sodium ion may therefore frequently replace each other. This is called *cation exchange* or *base exchange*. Because of this and because of the weak linkages between the layers, these clay minerals tend to break down into very small particles and are extremely slippery. Bentonite and fuller's earth are examples of deposits containing minerals of this type.

Detailed Classification of Clay Minerals

Within each clay mineral type there are a number of species. You need not learn them by name, but you should be aware that there are a great many, ranging from the very plastic montmorillonites to the less plastic, perfectly formed kaolinite crystals.

1. *Kandite* group: kaolinite, disordered kaolinite, dickite, nacrite, and halloysite.
2. *Illite* group: illite, hydromicas, phengite, brammalite, glauconite and celadonite.
3. *Smectite* group: montmorillonite, beidellite, nontronite, hectorite, saponite, and sauconite.
4. *Vermiculite.*
5. *Palygorskite*: palygorskite, attapulgite, and sepiolite.

■ ■ ■

Accessory Minerals

The chief accessory minerals are quartz and the mica minerals (including sericite). Others are the feldspars, calcium or iron-bearing minerals and trace minerals, depending on the parent rock(s) and on whether the deposit is primary or secondary (transported). Their grains may be sharp, angular fragments or rounded, particularly those of quartz, or they may be present as extremely fine-grained mineral flour (quartz flour, also called silica flour) and possibly a little amorphous (noncrystalline) material. In primary deposits the accessory minerals are usually coarse-grained, while transported minerals are well weathered and therefore fine-grained (see Chapter 3). The size of the fragments is important in ceramics. Any clay containing a considerable proportion of fragments larger than 2 or 3 mm in diameter (i.e., more than could be picked out by hand) should be viewed with extreme caution or discarded. For most clay work, grains that do not pass through 40s mesh (an approximate particle size of 0.2 to 0.3 mm) are too large and, in most cases, are considered to be undesirable. Grains of nonplastic minerals, 60s to dust, have been found to be the most useful. Accessory minerals do not have the slippery platelike structure of clay minerals. For this reason they do not contribute to the plasticity of clay. They do, however, balance the plasticity by helping to lock together the slippery clay particles, so that once a shape has been formed the clay will retain it. They also help to open the clay thus permitting water to enter the clay mass and then evaporate away, allowing the finished work to dry.

During firing, most (though not all, particularly large grains) of these materials contribute to the reactions in the kiln. This depends on the type of minerals and their oxide content (see pp. 32–33). Thus the accessory minerals make a significant contribution to the properties of clay: its workability, building strength, texture, color, and firing qualities. The chief minerals in clay are given below.

Quartz and *mica* are present in all clay deposits both primary and secondary.

Feldspar crystals are often found in raw kaolin and occasionally in other clay deposits in various stages of decomposition but are removed during refining.

Calcium and *calcite* are not found in kaolin but are often present in secondary clay. Calcium may be useful if adsorbed onto the clay crystal, but if present as lumps of limestone or chalk (calcium carbonate), plaster (calcium sulfate), or other calcium bearing materials, it is a contaminant. This, according to Fraser (1986), "is converted to lime by the firing but then absorbs moisture from the atmosphere causing it to hydrate and as it does so it swells." This swelling causes the clay lying over the lump to flake or "pop" off, or the piece to explode. This is called "lime popping." These clays are therefore useless in the pottery. A warning should therefore be given not to use sand from a building site as an addition to a clay body, since it may be contaminated with lime.

Iron oxide is abundant in the earth's crust, and is present in all clays, from traces in kaolin to appreciable amounts in common clays. It gives color to the red clays seen in nature and is also present in significant amounts in most other ochre or gray colored clays (though this can also be due to carbonaceous matter). Examples of iron coloration are the red clays of Albany, New York, USA, and the terracotta clays of Stoke-on-Trent, England. It is also present as particles of iron pyrite in the black clay of La Borne, France. However, the black color of this clay is mainly due to carbonaceous matter, which burns away, while the iron pyrite gives dark splotches in the fired ceramic.

Other minerals. Small quantities of sediments of a host of other minerals affect the color or other qualities of the clay. Many are present in such small amounts as to appear insignificant in the analysis. However, some have an adverse influence on the fired characteristics of the ceramic: among these could be some of the many ferro-magnesium minerals, such as rutile or ilmenite or those containing titanium. Sometimes a black noncrystalline gel, leucoxene, containing iron and titanium, is layered between the stacked kaolinite crystals. This can usually be washed away during refining.

Carbonaceous Matter

Most common surface clays will contain some decayed plant matter. The presence of moderate amounts is advantageous. It assists in the final stages of weathering and ageing of the clay, and assists plasticity by lubrication. It should fire away completely during the early stages of firing, leaving no trace of its original structure or color. If too much carbonaceous matter is present in the original clay, however, it can cause considerable difficulties during the making and firing stages of ceramics.

Soluble Salts

These are compounds such as potassium carbonate (K_2CO_3), sodium carbonate (Na_2CO_3), and sodium chloride ($NaCl$), which dissolve in water. Where clay has been contaminated by sea water it is usually of little value to the potter as the soluble salts migrate to the surface during drying, leaving an unpleasant scum on the clay surface. (The exceptions to this are bricks made with splotches of dried scum to imitate antique bricks.)

Terminology to Describe and Classify Natural Clays and Clay Bodies

The classification of natural clays depends on the clay minerals and accessory minerals present, their grain size, and the chemical and mechanical weathering to which the clay has been subjected. These factors, together with their firing characteristics, play an underlying role in the formulation, adjustment, and description of prepared bodies. To describe the firing characteristics of both natural and prepared clay bodies, the following terms *fusible, vitrifiable,* and *refractory* are used.

Fusible clays do not withstand high temperatures. They deform and even melt at temperatures regularly used by modern potters. Temperatures in the region of 1060–1120°C/1940–2048°F may be taken as the average top temperatures. Some deform before this point; some fire a little higher. Testing at several temperatures in this area is therefore advised (see Plate 3). Such clays contain calcium oxide, often appreciable amounts of iron oxide, and possibly other fluxes that cause melting to occur suddenly when the temperature at which they react is reached. For this reason, fusible clays are not fired too near the top end of their firing range.

Vitrifiable clays may be defined as clays in which sufficient glass can be formed during firing to render them nonporous without deformation. These clays have a longer firing range and a higher top temperature, extending from 1200°C/2192°F up to 1300°C/2372°F and over with some clays. At the bottom end of the range, reactions occur to change the clay into a ceramic fabric. As the temperature rises, more and more molten material forms which, on cooling, tightens the ceramic into a dense, non-porous body.

Refractory clays resist high temperatures without deforming. The studio potter considers clays that withstand 1300°C/2372°F as refractory. In the industry, clays that withstand even higher temperatures are needed for making kiln furniture and kiln building bricks. Kaolin and fireclay fall into this category, as do some prepared bodies made by mixing natural clays with other mineral materials, for example, clay for industrial porcelain and high-temperature refractories.

Classification of Natural Clays

Natural clays are classified into seven types:

1. Common clay and red brick clay
2. Natural stoneware clay
3. Kaolin (including English china clay)
4. Ball clay
5. Fire clay
6. Terracotta clay
7. Bentonite and fuller's earth

Common Clay and Red Brick Clay

With its origin in secondary (transported) accumulations of sediments lying at the surface of the earth in great abundance, common clay usually contains a considerable mixture of minerals making it highly fusible, though always with sufficient clay minerals to warrant being defined as clay (see Chapter 3). In the unfired body these tiny particles of other minerals act as a filler, giving nonplastic bulk to the body, and as part of the fine gritty material giving strength during the making stage. Very often the clay is contaminated with iron so that it fires red or brown. In some places (e.g., the Middle East) there are low-iron deposits that fire a dirty white. The calcium content in most common clays is high (true marls, i.e., calcareous clays, contain up to 20%). It is present either as ions adsorbed onto the clay crystal surface or as a constituent element in fragments of complex minerals, such as dolomite. Tiny particles of calcium carbonate may also be present and react quickly with other minerals during firing, once the carbonate has been broken down, to give quick melting, thus contributing to the fusibility of these clays. However, if present as larger fragments or lumps in the clay (more than, say, 3 mm) they can blow out during or after firing (see p. 61).

This type of low-temperature fusible clay has a short firing range, often in the region of only 50°C/90°F between the temperature at which a reasonably satisfactory ceramic body is formed and that at which it suddenly deforms and begins to melt. For many of them the optimum firing temperature is 1000–1060°C/1832–1940°F. We shall be undertaking a number of tests involving common clay.

Uses of common clay and red brick clay in ceramics
1. As a clay body for making low-temperature ware, particularly unglazed objects such as flower pots and butter coolers (the porous nature of low-fired unglazed pottery permits evaporation which keeps the contents cool).
2. As a constituent of manufactured clay bodies to which it brings plasticity, texture, and color in the case of common clays which are iron-bearing.
3. As a constituent of slips and glazes.

Natural Stoneware Clay

This clay type is similar in origin to common clay but accumulates in areas where most of the fluxes, in particular potassa and soda, have been washed away or absorbed by plant life, and the calcia content is low or absent. It is therefore vitrifiable and able to withstand temperatures over 1200°C/2192°F. Although fairly widespread, natural stoneware clay is not as abundant as common clay. The nature of this type of clay points to transported deposits: the kaolinite content is usually disordered, giving plasticity (which is further helped if the deposit contains carbonaceous matter). Also quartz and mica are usually present in small-particle size. However, the kaolinitic nature of the clay is not immediately recognized, as it is often discolored by a small amount of iron, carbon, or other impurities. It therefore fires to a dirty white, buff, gray, or red-brown to dark brown. The La Borne clay from France, mentioned earlier, is a stoneware clay. Stoneware clays are often found in association with fireclays, flint clays, or coal, having been buried at some point in geologic time. They are therefore not so often found lying at the surface of the earth and often must be won by mining. Natural stoneware clays vary considerably in their plastic qualities and in the amount they shrink on drying and firing.

If you can find a natural stoneware clay in sufficient quantities to use without adjustment, you will be extremely fortunate. More usually a natural stoneware clay is used as part of a mixture of clays, thus spreading its advantageous contribution over a larger quantity of clay body.

Uses of natural stoneware clay and prepared stoneware bodies.
The following applies to firings over 1200°C/2192°F when the fired product may be classified as stoneware.

1. It is a major constituent of stoneware bodies, where a dense, hard, impervious fired body is required.
2. Because it does not chip as easily as earthenware, it is valuable for domestic ware.

3. Having a wide firing range, the density increases gradually. Thus, by testing, a top temperature may be found that gives an optimum density without the risk of overfiring.
4. Many types give special effects when fired in a reduced atmosphere.

Kaolin (including English China Clay)

Kaolin is a white-firing, virtually iron-free refractory clay in which the clay mineral is kaolinite. Primary deposits are coarse-grained and have poor plasticity, whereas secondary kaolins may be fine-grained and more plastic, but are usually less pure. The generalized formula is $Al_2O_3 \cdot 2SiO_2 \cdot 2H_2O$, though fractional amounts of other oxides may be present. These are usually collected together and stated as a percent total of impurities or other minerals. The composition of two well-known varieties of English china clays are given below.

Grolleg	*Standard Porcelain*
81% kaolinite	84% kaolinite
15% micaceous material	13% micaceous material
1% feldspar	1% feldspar
3% other minerals	2% other minerals

The use of the word "porcelain" in "Standard Porcelain" merely implies that it is an ideal kaolin to use in the composition of porcelain bodies. It is not a porcelain body ready for use.

In general, American kaolin contains less K_2O and more TiO_2 than English china clays. The lower K_2O (average about 0.2%) means that they are more refractory than the English china clays (containing an average of 2% K_2O). It is therefore necessary to add more feldspar (or other fluxing material) to an American recipe when formulating a white clay body. Again, with higher TiO_2 (around 1–2%, which is very much higher than that contained in the English varieties), the American kaolins show a significant difference in fired color. In oxidation a slight cream to yellow color is produced, and in reduction a gray-white. It is also interesting to note that Celadon glazes containing American kaolin give a green tone in reduction, whereas the English variety favors a blue Celadon. Of the American clays, No. 6 Tile, produced by Dry Branch Kaolin, Georgia, or Edgar Plastic Kaolin (EPK), from Florida, is recommended for strong plastic kaolins. Of the English china clays, Grolleg and Standard Porcelain are recommended for white porcelain, as well as Super Standard Porcelain and Sovereign, which have a lower iron content than the Grolleg or Standard Porcelain and therefore fire whiter.

The processes of refining and blending kaolin to produce reliable specifications are generally adopted by large producers in most parts of the world. For example, during the digging and preparation, much of the sand and mica is removed and the clay is adjusted so that the overall composition of the refined kaolin is the same as that of the clay mineral, kaolinite, giving the formula $Al_2O_3 \cdot 2SiO_2 \cdot 2H_2O$. However, if you are planning to produce your own white body, particularly if it is to be a porcelain body, it is advisable to obtain a percentage analysis or the mineralogical composition (and sample for testing) from your supplier. If there is any iron present, or if the composition deviates considerably from that of a kaolin you have previously used, you may expect different results, and these should be taken into account.

Uses of kaolin in ceramics
1. Kaolin is an essential constituent of all white-firing clay bodies for all temperatures.
2. It is a common ingredient of slips and glazes.
3. It is used to increase the firing temperature of colored bodies and to lighten color, if required.

Ball Clays

The name ball clay does not refer to any characteristic of the clay itself, but simply to the way in which it was dug and rolled for transport in the early days of mining it in southwest England. Ball clay is an extremely fine-grained plastic clay containing highly disordered kaolinite, fine-grained quartz, varying amounts of micaceous material, and possibly carbonaceous matter. It is valued for its plasticity and low iron content. Up to 2 percent iron content will not affect the color significantly. If there is over 5 percent iron oxide, the clay should not be called a ball clay.

There are good reasons for suggesting that at least some ball clays may not be primary or secondary but rather tertiary deposits. They probably originated from the sediments of disintegrated secondary rocks, for instance fine-grained shales and slates, giving sediments of extremely fine particle size. These fine sediments, whether transported by water or air, would be carried further than coarse, heavy sediments and selectively deposited as thick beds of ultrafine clay, which, where the iron content is low, may be considered ball clays. In other words, nature has lent a hand in the refining process: the only additional processing is the blending of clays from different parts of the pit in order to be able to offer catalogued varieties with standard mineralogical and chemical compositions to the ceramic industry and craft market.

Refined ball clays have variable firing ranges. Some form sufficient glass and tighten at lower temperatures, becoming quite hard and dense in the region of 1300°C/2372°F. The chief deficiency of ball clay, from the potter's point of view, is that it has an extremely high shrinkage rate (15% in some cases) during drying and firing; see Chapters 7 and 8.

Uses of ball clay in ceramics
1. Small additions of ball clay to clay bodies increase plasticity.
2. It contributes good dry strength to green ware.
3. It increases the density of fired ware.

4. Some ball clays are included in clay bodies for their refractory nature or light color, despite their high shrinkage.
5. It helps prevent a burnt-orange color in reduced stoneware when this is not required.

Deficiencies
1. Ball clay has a high rate of shrinkage (averaging 15% as compared with 10% to 12% of other clays) during drying and firing, which must be allowed for.
2. It is too slippery and flabby to use by itself.

Fire Clays

Most fire clays are secondary (transported) clays, but a few are primary (residual) clays. Usually refractory, they withstand temperatures up to 1400°C/2552°F. A few fire clays fire white or near-white, but the majority fire buff or light brown, often with specks or splotches of iron pyrites (FeS). They are often found in association with coal deposits, and it is believed that they were once the earth in which the vegetation grew that subsequently rotted down to become coal. The plant life may have absorbed minerals from the clay, removing those elements that would otherwise have provided fluxing oxides in the clay.

Uses of fire clay in ceramics
1. The refractory fire clays are used for fire bricks and in the manufacture of kilns, furnaces, and boilers. They are also used for making crucibles, kiln shelves, and kiln furniture (see Figure 5.2).
2. Fire clay is used for making saggars, the ceramic boxes in which the ware is placed to protect it from direct contact with the flames, if necessary, or to isolate objects from other pieces in the kiln. Clay for saggar-making must be sufficiently plastic to model the shape required, and when fired to give a dense, tough body resistant to thermal shock and fatigue from repeated firings.
3. Fire clays are added to stoneware bodies to give tooth (grittiness) to the body. A fire clay that contains iron specks may be used to add character.
4. Fire clay is extremely useful in clay bodies for large terracotta sculptures; the open, coarse grain of some fire clays makes them an excellent addition for building and firing strength.
5. A few fine-grained, white or near-white firing plastic fire clays are available, and these, if cheaper, may replace part of the ball clay in clay bodies.
6. Fire clay is also used for "mudding in" kiln doors (filling cracks before firing, particularly kilns built on site that have kiln entrances that must be bricked up just before firing).
7. Fire clay is important for making grog (see Chapter 6).
8. Other uses include sanitary ware, drain pipes, and bricks.

Terracotta Clay

The name terracotta simply means "cooked earth," and this is a good description of its fired quality, as it fires to a rich red brown. It is classified as a type of fire clay, though it fires to a lower temperature than many fire clays. The exact temperature it will withstand depends on its mineral composition, especially the calcia content. If the calcia content is low, the clay may be used as a major component in bodies for all temperatures; if high, it may still be used as a major component in an earthenware body but only up to approximately 25 percent in a stoneware body.

Uses of terracotta clay in ceramics
1. It is traditionally used as a modeling clay, particularly for small figurines, like those of Eastern Mediterranean origin, called "terracottas."
2. It introduces color into clay.
3. It is used in slips and glazes.

Bentonite and Fuller's Earth

These are two special types of iron-free deposits composed of the clay minerals montmorillonite and beidellite. They have an exceptionally fine particle size and therefore an enormous surface area exposed to lubrication by water, which makes them extremely plastic.

Bentonite consists mainly of sodium montmorillonite and beidellite formed from volcanic ash or tuffs deposited in water, which seeps between the crystal structural layers and is also adsorbed onto the surface. Thus with tiny particles and a good clay-water relationship, it is extremely slippery or plastic.

Uses of bentonite in ceramics
Small amounts are added to clay, when required, to increase plasticity: about two to three percent is usually sufficient.

Fuller's earth consists chiefly of the clay mineral calcium montmorillonite and is iron-free.

Uses of fuller's earth in ceramics
In areas where bentonite is not obtainable fuller's earth may be used in small amounts as a plasticizer for clays (about 3%, as in the case of bentonite), but it must be remembered that it will introduce a small amount of calcia and not soda.

Fieldwork

If a field trip is being organized for your ceramics class, it is a good idea to arrange for a geologist to accompany the group or to arrange a combined geology/pottery trip to a clay pit. (If you are working alone you may be able to join a class excursion of a local college or university.) The main aim for ceramists would be to learn how to identify clay and to collect samples to test in the workshop. Large quantities should not be dug until fully tested. While in the field, look for other rock types. If you do not have a geologist with you, get advice regarding a suitable location to search and take home small specimens; a member of a geology department of a museum or school should then be able to assist in identifying them. Take one specimen of each type per group. When selecting samples you should remember that, in order to identify rocks, it is necessary to split the sample with a hammer so that you can examine a "fresh face." You should also check that the sample is in situ and not foreign to the locality; hence if you pick up a piece, check that it is the same as the local rock.

Equipment

If you intend to look for clay on a small scale, then all you need is a trowel or spade, some plastic bags, and a waterproof marker. If you wish to prospect on a larger scale, you should take, in addition to the above, a geological survey map (showing surface deposits) of the district you intend to search, a geological hammer, a strong cloth bag, a small (15 cm) bowl, a bottle of drinking water, a pocket magnifying lens (for looking at minerals in rocks), and materials for making a quick sketch map of the exact locality with the position of the deposits found (also mark on your map the area that you intend to search).

Possible Locations

Ideally, try to find a cutting or pit (or even a road construction site) where you can get permission to collect samples of clay, if possible, a meter down from the surface. It is also possible to find river "mud/clay" along banks of rivers and make a pinched pot as you walk along. For these initial exercises it does not matter how small the deposit is. For larger deposits the geological map can help locate potential sites, open cuts, and old workings. If possible, look for deposits in the close vicinity of your home or workshop because clay is very heavy and expensive to transport. Remember to obtain permission if necessary, close gates, and do not spoil the environment.

Methods of Identification

You should be able to recognize clay by its fine-grained but still scratchable surface when rock hard. If a wet deposit is found it will be sticky when very wet. If it is a pliable mass, try forming a shape by squeezing a little of the clay in the hand. If it holds this shape well, it is probably a useful clay. Carry out the finger test for plasticity (see Figure 5.6). If a rock hard deposit is found, break off a lump with your hammer, crush it to a fine powder, then mix it with just sufficient water to return it to a plastic state. This done, carry out the tests as above. If the rock mass is too hard to break with your hammer, or if it does not revert to a plastic state on the addition of water, it is probably not clay. If it crumbles too easily, it may be clay but with such a high content of silica sand that it will not be useful in the pottery. If possible, choose the wet season of the year to look for and identify clay. You may have to wait until it is a little less muddy to dig in large quantities.

Observations and Experiments

Scum. Clay found near the sea may be contaminated with salt and may leave white scum marks on your claywork and spoil glazes.

Calcium impurities. If the clay contains whitish lumps (and you are working in, or prospecting in, an area containing limestone), test them for calcium by pouring a few drops of a 50 percent hydrochloric acid (HCl) solution on a sample, or by dropping pieces into the HCl. If transported with care, a very small amount—about 10 ml—of the acid may be taken on the field trip *clearly* labeled "HCL ACID, POISON." Otherwise, the test is best done in a chemistry laboratory where a technician is available to help. If the lumps consist of $CaCO_3$, they will bubble furiously. Such clays should not be used.

Color. Make a note of the color of each clay you collect. Ideally this should be done when the clay is damp (splash some water on it if necessary). These recorded natural colors can be compared with their fired colors after completing the tests in the Exercises. Do not take for granted that the fired color will be the same as the natural color (this is studied in Chapter 7).

Texture. Feel the texture of each clay sample by rubbing a little clay between a finger and thumb. Does it feel gritty? If so, how gritty? Compare it with a standard workshop clay sample. You should be able to draw some conclusions about whether the clay is very fine grained and smooth, or gritty, and whether it might be useful.

Collecting Samples of Clay for Testing in the Workshop

Small samples are best collected by shaving thin slithers with a trowel or spade when the clay is in a damp state: it will probably roll up if you use a spade (see Figure 4.6). Dry clay lumps may be taken home for crushing (but test them first as described above).

The most difficult clay to collect is clay that is nearly dry. It can be neither dug with a spade nor split and crushed with a hammer. The best thing to do is to collect a number of small lumps, take them back to the workshop, and let them dry out thoroughly. They may then be split and crushed fairly easily. Do not attempt to wet the lumps, as this will result in a lot of very hard work. If the clay is wet (like mud), tie it up in cheesecloth or similar close-woven cloth, squeeze out the excess water, and hang it up, preferably in a warm, windy position, to dry back to the plastic state. Keep a careful eye on it as it can sometimes dry extremely quickly. Then put it

Figure 4.6. Digging slithers of clay. For production purposes the topsoil and about two meters below it are removed, and the less contaminated clay mined. River bank clay can, however, be used for pinched pots (provided there are no lumps of white calcium carbonate in it), and the pots can be fired.

through the field tests suggested above. If you are satisfied that you have found a clay worth further testing, collect a bucket or sackful of it and label it with the location where it was found, together with a grid reference from a geological survey map. Samples will be used in the Exercises in the following chapters.

Chapter 5
Workshop Practice and the Theory of Kiln Firing

Layout of the Workshop

The workshop should be designed to accommodate the flow of activities. Areas should be defined for recycling clay and for clay and glaze slip preparation and application. The kiln should be in a separate kiln room or an alcove lined with fireproof material (particularly the ceiling), with good ventilation or an extractor fan strong enough to cope with exhaust fumes. A spray booth with integral extractor fan for spraying glazes is important; otherwise spraying should be done outdoors. A porch or garden alcove gives wind protection and can be hosed down after use. The workshop floors should also be hosed down after vacuuming (do not use a broom on dusty floors unless they are sprinkled with oiled sawdust). Damp storage for work in progress away from drafts and extreme temperature changes is important, for example, rust-proof cupboards or an alcove lined with heavy-duty plastic, with humidifiers if necessary. This is particularly important for sculptural pieces that take time to complete. Further dust-free storage should be prepared for biscuit ware waiting to be glazed.

Health and Safety

You should be able to obtain a guide to health and safety issues, if possible one relevant to the country in which you are working (or if exporting, the area to which the work is destined) containing the local legal requirements (see "Health and Safety" in Bibliography for list of addresses).

Personal Health

Wherever possible, try to arrange the delivery and storage of clay and glaze materials at a point where a vehicle can park. If the workshop is not on the ground floor, some method of hauling the clay mechanically to an access bay should be considered, such as a simple outside pulley system to a window. Some of the most frequent visitors to physical therapists are potters; don't be one of them. Learn to lift correctly (bend your knees, not your back), carry correctly, and use a cart for heavy loads (or a small two-wheeled luggage trolley or wheeled bins for bags of materials). Do not sit in the same position for too long a period, and always compensate for physical activities at regular intervals. If you are huddled over a wheel for long periods, stretch every now and then in the opposite direction and bend your fingers back as far as they will go. If you work on the floor, do not spend too long on your knees (even on a cushion); it can cause permanent damage that can shorten your working life. Finally, when learning to wedge, make sure that the bench height is correct for your height (see Figure 5.1), and develop a rhythmic body movement, so that the whole body, not just the neck and shoulders, participates in the energy exerted on the clay.

Clothing and Hygiene

Wear overalls and wash them regularly to remove clay and glaze materials that have dried to dust. Use protective clothing for special activities, for example, dust goggles and kiln goggles, which do not melt and are fitted with special glass for looking into a red-hot kiln during firing; heat-proof (but not asbestos) gloves; and a leather (not a plastic) apron to wear when taking objects from a raku kiln (one can be made from imperfect or second-hand leather). If you have sensitive skin, try to obtain veterinary elbow-

Figure 5.1. Wedging bench. Make sure that you are wedging at a comfortable height.

length waterproof gloves or use a paddle for hand-stirring slip glazes, particularly ash glazes, that are caustic. Do not eat or smoke while preparing or applying glazes, and keep all working surfaces clean and free of dust.

Kilns and Machinery

Ensure that hot kilns cannot be opened by unauthorized persons, and do not open a hot kiln yourself unless you know exactly what you are doing. Never open an electric kiln until it has been switched off and isolated from the main electricity supply. Observe manufacturers' instructions and local ordinances or regulations on the use and safety precautions of all equipment and machinery, and have necessary guards fitted on equipment (e.g., to prevent hands and long hair being drawn into a machine).

Toxic and Other Dangerous Materials

Keep all toxic materials clearly labeled and stored in a locked cupboard. When weighing out dry ceramic materials, always wear a mask and turn on the extractor fan if there is one. Mineral dust is abrasive and damages the lung linings if inhaled. The fine-grained variety of quartz called flint is very hard and razor-sharp, and should always be handled with a 5 percent moisture content to prevent dust rising from it. Do not use articles or materials made from asbestos because its needle-like crystals are particularly dangerous when inhaled.

Lead release. If lead glazes are incorrectly compounded or underfired and used on vessels for containing acidic material (e.g., orange juice or vinegar), the lead may be released from the glaze and consumed by unsuspecting victims. Over a period of time, a person may develop lead-poisoning, which can be fatal. Color stains containing cadmium are ten times worse than lead. Although suppliers in most regions ensure that their prepared glazes are well below the toxic limits established by international legislation, if incorrectly used (e.g., a lead glaze with a copper or cadmium color added to the glaze or as a painted decoration), the fired object could cause illness or even be fatal. It is the responsibility of ceramists to see that items they make are safe.

Clay dust. Do not leave dried clay lying around the studio; it can quickly turn to dust. Clay scraps should be put into a soak bin half full of water for recycling (keep a separate bin for each type of clay).

Equipment

Kilns and Kiln Furniture

The subject of kiln type and design is a big one, and there are some good books and catalogues on the subject. Hence kiln types and kiln-building are not dealt with in this text.

Figure 5.2. Kiln furniture.

Key:
1. Castellated props.
2. Refractory kiln shelves.
3. Castellated prop collars.
4. Tubular props.
5. Prop collars for top and bottom.
6. Cones.
7. Cone holder.
8. Solid props.
9. Spurs.
10. Refractory bits.

Kiln furniture consists of shelves; bats (small shelves); props for supporting the shelves; cranks for holding tiles and plates; and stilts, saddles,
and bits for various supporting uses (see Figure 5.2). Kiln shelves and furniture are made from refractory fireclay plus grog for low temperature firings.
For temperatures up to 1305°C/2381°F they consist of cordierite and mullite. To achieve this, talc is mixed with mullite and the kiln furniture made
from this mix. On firing, this converts to cordierite and mullite. For temperatures 1305–1400°C/2381–2552°F, silicon carbide is used, as this allows
the heat to pass through efficiently.

Water and the kiln lining. The brickwork or fiber with which the kiln is
lined absorbs and retains moisture, particularly if the kiln has not been used
for some time or is kept in a damp place. Although only a little water may be
present in the kiln lining and in the kiln load of air dried clay objects ready
for firing, once this has been converted to steam it occupies a very large
space. It has been estimated that the water contained in an average kiln load
of clay pots, plus the moisture from the kiln lining, can generate steam
equivalent to several times the volume of the kiln space at atmospheric
pressure.

If preventive measures are not taken, this steam creates enormous pressure on the fabric of the kiln as the steam searches for every crack to escape,

gradually widening the cracks and causing the kiln fabric to crumble. It may even cause an explosion. It is therefore essential to dry off all moisture before closing the kiln vents during firing. Slow firing with all the vents open in the early stages accomplishes this. Alternatively, particularly where the kiln is suspected of being very damp, it may be preheated by leaving a gentle heat on for several hours the previous day with all vents open. If the kiln is in a locked safety cage, the door of a gas kiln or the brickwork of oil or wood kilns may be left slightly open. Whichever method is used, the kiln must be checked to see that all the moisture has been driven off. This is done by holding a cool, clean piece of clear glass or mirror over the top vent (or spy-hole of a test kiln if there is no top vent) for a few seconds, and then withdrawing it and running the finger across it to test for moisture on the glass. *The kiln vents must not be completely closed while moisture is still evident.* If moisture is still present at 900°C/1652°F, then it is best to hold the kiln at this temperature until all the water has gone and the mirror test shows no steam.

Methods Used to Monitor Kiln Firings

Three types of aids are discussed. For good firing practice you should use both pyrometric cones and a pyrometer or oxygen probe. This enables you to record the rate of temperature rise per hour, the amount of reduction in a reduction firing, and ensures that the kiln load of ceramics receives the required amount of heat treatment (or heat work).

A *pyrometer* is an instrument for measuring temperature. There are many types on the market, ranging from very simple devices to elaborate electronic ones. These should be checked regularly for accuracy.

An *oxygen probe* may be used to measure the amount of oxygen in the kiln atmosphere and therefore the degree of reduced (oxygen) atmosphere in which the work is being fired during a reduction firing. It also gives a digital reading of the kiln temperature, which is useful for monitoring the rate of temperature rise. A pyrometer or probe also tells you when the kiln is near top temperature: a warning that the cones should be watched.

Pyrometric cones are used to measure heat-work, that is to say, the joint effect of the temperature and the time that the work is subjected to heat. Cones are slender pyramids made from mixtures of minerals and mineral materials, the same as those used in ceramics. For example, high-temperature cones are composed principally of kaolin, quartz, feldspar, and calcite. Some low-temperature cones contain iron (identified by their brown color), others contain lead: these will not give reliable results if there is a reduced atmosphere in the kiln. However Orton makes some cones in which the lead is introduced in a low-solubility glass (frit) that "resists reduction much more than the old formula." The approximate range of temperature covered by this group is 576°C/1069°F to 625°C/1157°F and is used for firing gold, platinum, and lusters on artware. The actual temperature depends on heating rates and kiln atmosphere. There is also a series of *iron-free cones* covering the range C.010 to C.3 (approximately 894°C to 1168°C).

In the manufacture of cones, mixtures of minerals are used that interact gradually as the temperature rises, thus giving gradual melting. Setting the cones at the slight angle of 8 degrees from the vertical (see Figure 6.6 below) lets the cones *squat* gradually as melting proceeds. Using a series of compositions that are consecutively numbered, lets the cones complete their deformation at reasonably regular intervals that reflect the changes occurring in the work being fired.

In this text reference is made throughout to *Orton Standard cones*, which are 6.3 cm high. These must be supported in clay pats (see Figure 6.5). In the table in Appendix Figure A.5 each cone number is assigned an equivalent temperature, but remember that these temperatures are only relevant if the kiln is fired at the rate stated in the table. In Appendix Figure A.5 and the surrounding text, standard rates of 150°C per hour and 270°F per hour are given; if you fire at a different rate, the top temperature will be higher if the kiln is fired faster and lower if the kiln is fired more slowly (see Figure 6.10).

Small cones (also called *midget* cones) are 2.75 cm high. They are made of the same materials as the large cones and are useful for small kilns or kilns that have small spy-holes. The Orton Foundation quotes temperature equivalents for small cones when fired at a rate of 300°C per hour or 540°F per hour. These rates are intended for fast firing. Examples of squatting temperatures at this rate of firing are given here.

C.07 (1008°C/1846°F)   C.7 (1264°C/2307°F)
C.05 (1062°C/1944°F)   C.8 (1300°C/2372°F)
C.04 (1098°C/2008°F)   C.10 (1330°C/2426°F)
C.4 (1209°C/2208°F)

The author does not recommend such fast rates for normal pottery practice. Clays and glazes need to pass through certain temperatures at a moderate rate, the reasons are discussed later in this chapter.

Both standard large and small cones must be supported in clay pats or cone plaques or "holders" (see Figure 5.2). Self-supporting cones require no additional means of support and the correct angle is a built-in feature. The method of setting cones in the kiln and reading them during firing is discussed in Exercise 3 below.

Potters' Wheels

The type of drive and expertness of the operator dictate the smoothness of the running of an electric wheel and whether very slow revolutions are possible, an important feature for many techniques. If you intend to set the wheel up permanently out-of-doors then a simple kick wheel would be an ideal choice. If you intend to move around to give demonstrations, the weight and size may be important. A wheel with easily changeable trays is a great help if you work, say, in porcelain as well as a colored clay (see Appendix Figure A.11).

Weighing Equipment

Consider your needs carefully before making a purchase. Weighing instruments are not cheap but will last you forever if you buy the correct ones. Types of weighing instruments include

Apothecary (or laboratory) balance
Beam scale
Triple-beam balance
Electronic balance (with or without computer link-up)
Heavy-duty platform scales with weights (15 kg capacity)

A useful purchase would be a set of gram weights (see Figure 5.3). These can be used to check the accuracy of a second-hand balance before purchasing or used with a balance where the weights are missing or not in the metric system. They are also useful for periodic checks of a balance or scales (with weights of the same value on each pan, the scales should balance equally). Even an electronic balance may be checked using gram weights. The minimum number of weights required are 5 of 1 g; 2 of 5 g; 2 of 10 g; 1 of 20 g; 2 of 50 g. Also a selection of bits (small flat pieces of metal of exact weight) are needed ranging from 0.1 g to 0.9 g (including 0.25 g and 0.75 g).

A combination of heavy-duty platform scales and an apothecary balance would enable you to weigh large amounts and accurate amounts under 1 g. If you decide to buy only one balance, consider a balance that also has a micrometer setting, which allows accurate weighing under 1 g. However, give close consideration to the electronic balance, as they are now produced in a wide range of sizes and types. Furthermore, they are quick and easy to use as well as being extremely accurate.

Figure 5.3. Gram weights and bits. These are useful for checking the accuracy of your scales and to replace old or missing weights. Photo: Geoff Kenward.

Jar Ball Mill

A jar ball mill is used for grinding ceramic raw materials in slip form (see Appendix Figure A.11). It consists of a rotating cylindrical drum filled to 60 percent of its volume with grinding media, usually flint pebbles, and water.

Pug Mill

There are horizontal and vertical types (the latter usually fixed to a wall), also a de-airing type. A pug mill performs two functions. The blades in the upper (or wider) part of the shaft cut and mix slightly stiff clay with softer clay to give a homogeneous mass. (Do not expect it to cope with hard clay, and do not allow clay to dry out in the shaft. Cover the nozzle tightly with plastic sheeting when not in use.)

The lower part (or end) of the shaft narrows, forcing the clay to compact, giving a denser body, which is stronger and more workable. Many potters like to knead their clay after pugging and just before use because there is a slight drag at the contact surface between the clay and the shaft of the pug mill and a little kneading overcomes this unevenness.

Other Machinery

Other equipment worth considering if you are inclined toward mechanical aids may be an electric mixer, an electric vibratory sieve (or a manual sieve with a rotary action), and a blunger for mixing casting slips. A rock crusher should be considered if you plan to collect your own mineral material. These are not essential pieces of equipment but they do reduce much of the heavy work and save time (see Appendix Figure A.11).

Maturing Plastic Clays and Glazes

Clays in the plastic state or glazes in slip form should be left to stand before use so that the moisture can percolate right through the mass and wet the clay, or glaze, thoroughly and evenly. A few hours suffice for glaze slips, and occasional stirring helps. Plastic clays take longer. The process starts in its natural environment and may be divided into three stages: weathering, aging, and souring.

Weathering is the physical breaking down of rocks, and the chemical changes that produce fine-grained clays, many of which are plastic, have already been discussed in Chapters 1 and 2. This process is assisted by digging the clay and leaving it exposed to the weather throughout the winter.

Aging occurs when the clay is left to stand, in a soft wet state, in a place where it will not dry out. The water is then able to percolate through the entire mass, separating the particles and enveloping them in a film of water, and producing an even clay-water relationship. A moist, slightly warm environment is helpful.

Souring bacteria, naturally present in clay, or an added souring agent such as vinegar helps to break down any organic matter present. This forms a fine gel which spreads through the clay with the water. The presence of this mushy material increases the slipperiness, and therefore the plasticity of the clay but if taken to excess it is a nuisance. Note that this does *not* affect the fired color or other fired qualities of the clay.

Aging and souring, working together, improve clay newly arrived from a supplier, or waste clay from work in the pottery (left as a mass in a soft wet state). The clay also gradually compacts under its own weight, encouraging the alignment of the particles that improves its workability.

Working with Clay

Buying Clay

Clay may be bought in three forms: as plastic clay ready for use, in slip form, or as a powder that can be rendered down to the plastic state or slip by the addition of water. You should not purchase clay in large quantities until you have read the chapter on clay and carried out the practical work. You will then know what to look for in a clay and the type of clays and firing temperatures that you like to work with. The practical work in Chapters 7 and 8 will also enable you to assess bags of clay without labels or mixed clays. Before ordering large quantities of clay, ask your craft supplier for samples the catalog suggests would be suitable for the type of work you wish to undertake and the firing cycle you plan to use. Some suppliers will put up a selection of several different types of clay for a small charge. Test these thoroughly, making use of the Exercises in Chapter 7.

Grain Size or Coarseness of Clay

Clay contains some grit, either natural or added in the pottery. Generally speaking, a fine-grained clay is needed for fine work (e.g., porcelain), a fine- to medium-grained one for most thrown work, and a coarser one for hand-building, although individual choice is important. The fineness or coarseness is classified by the mesh size of sieves through which clay (in slip form) will pass (see Figure 5.4).

Figure 5.4. Mesh sizes, shown actual sizes.

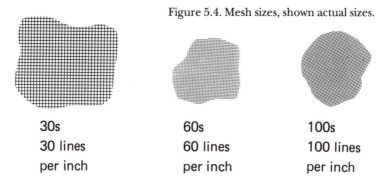

30s
30 lines
per inch

60s
60 lines
per inch

100s
100 lines
per inch

Mesh Sizes for Sieves

Mesh sizes were originally determined by the number of threads per linear inch which dictated the size of the holes. The illustrations in Figure 5.4 are true sizes and should help you to identify a sieve that is not numbered. Equivalent mesh numbers for the sizes shown in Figure 5.4, plus the mesh size commonly used in sieving glazes, that is, 120s, are given below along with the modern International Standard measurement in microns. For a full list of mesh size equivalents see Hamer and Hamer (1991).

UK	North America	International Standard
30s	35	500microns
60s	60	250microns
100s	100	150microns
120s	120	125microns

Care of Clay in the Workshop

Before accepting a consignment of ready mixed clay body, make sure that it is in good physical condition. It should be soft enough to poke a finger into it without undue pressure and to hold the shape of your finger. Clay that you dig and prepare yourself should also meet these requirements before use. Clay with these characteristics is said to have a good *yield point*: it yields to pressure but does not lose shape on release of the pressure (see Figure 5.5).

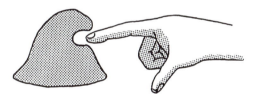

Finger pushes clay into shape
Shape remains after release
of finger.

Figure 5.5. Finger test for clay workability and yield point.

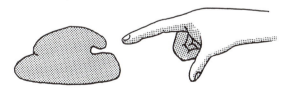

If a clay yields to pressure too easily it will exibit the unfavorable characteristic of slumping.

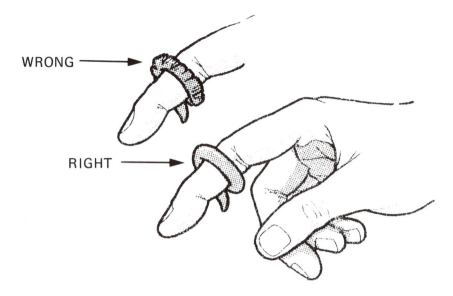

WRONG

RIGHT

Figure 5.6. Finger test for clay plasticity.

If the clay resists the pressure of your finger too much, it will not have good *workability*.

The plasticity of a clay may be checked by making a coil and wrapping it around a finger. It should make a smooth, firm ring (see Figure 5.6). If it cracks or breaks, it is said to be "short."

Keep your clay moist and closely wrapped in plastic sheeting, or in a bin with heavy-duty plastic completely covering and touching the clay. When clay is removed from the container, what remains should be resealed and made air-tight immediately. A special plea on behalf of technicians is not out of place here. It is hard work and time-consuming to prepare and recycle clay. If you are studying in a college or school, do help the technician by seeing that the clay is protected from drying out by keeping it properly covered. Never use clay that is too hard. It is exhausting and not conducive to good work. Recycle it, as explained below.

Clay should be made sufficiently wet so that it is soft enough to model into a shape with ease, yet not so soft that it does not hold the shape but tends to slump. There is usually a small leeway between these two conditions, so that an individual potter or sculptor may choose the degree of softness to work with say, a soft clay for molding into a curved shape or a stiffer clay for slab work. Again, some potters like to throw with a soft clay, others like it stiffer. Remember that you and your clay must work together, not against each other. Therefore the most important aspect of workshop practice is to ensure that your clay is kept in good condition and ready for use. A lot of enthusiasm is lost by students who, with great ideas, plan a creative session, only to spend their first, best energy in finding and preparing clay. There are two golden rules:

1. Always prepare clay well ahead so that it is in prime condition when you wish to use it.
2. Never glaze just before you fire. If you do, your pots will be wet, and you, and your kiln, will be all steamed up.

Beyond this, as old potters will tell you, "If it works, it's right!"

Wedging and Kneading

In both these hand processes, the clay is mixed and the air expelled. In addition, wedging helps to compact the clay, while kneading involves a circular motion in which the clay is slid over on itself in such a way that air is not trapped in it but is, in fact, expelled.

Wedging by Cutting and Dropping

Block up the lump of clay and cut it through with a cutting wire. Turn over the bottom half, then lift the top half. Turn it over, raise it above your head, and allow it to fall onto the first piece (do not throw it). Dropping the rounded side onto rounded side pushes air out sideways (flat side to flat side would arch in the middle and trap air). Do this several times until the texture is even. Turn the clay onto its side and repeat the above. Check the clay for air bubble cavities when you cut through with the wire. Do this several times (see Figure 5.7).

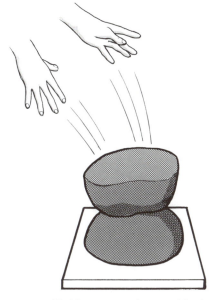

Wedging removes air trapped in clay

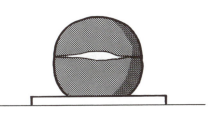

Air trapped-WRONG

Conical Kneading

Support a rounded lump of clay of comfortable hand size by cupping one hand behind the clay. As the clay is turned slightly, press down the heel of the other hand, sliding the clay over from the back and down the front of the lump. Then cup the lump in one hand again and turn it slightly, repeating the same motion. Eventually the lump takes on a conical appearance. This action pushes air out from the lump at the nose of the sliding clay, and should be repeated until all air bubbles have been removed and the texture is even and smooth. If the clay is drying too quickly, do this on a nonporous wedging surface. Take care, at this stage, that the clay is not "folded over" but is slid down the front of the lump; otherwise, air may be trapped and not removed (see Figure 5.8).

Spiral Kneading

This is the same as the above except that the clay is pushed away from the potter. Many potters who have the strength handle very large amounts of clay by these methods. Beginners and those with lesser strength are advised to use amounts that are comfortable to work with.

Ram's Head Kneading

Grasp the clay on either side using both hands, and let the heels of both hands slide the clay down the front of the lump toward you. Then lift the clay slightly, turn it toward you a little, and repeat the process. Gradually a shape builds up that looks like a ram's head. These processes must be carried out on a strong, stable bench or table. Two surfaces are needed: one porous (e.g., very smooth stone, plaster, wood, or porous low-temperature unglazed ceramic tiles, such as terracotta floor tiles), the other nonporous (e.g., a surface covered with stoneware tiles). You can then work on the porous surface if your clay is too moist and move it to the nonporous surface when you are beginning to feel that the water content is right but that the clay still needs a little more work to remove bubbles and to ensure that the texture is even. You should try to set up a rhythm of movement in which your whole body is completely involved.

The purposes of wedging and kneading are

1. *To remove air.* If air pockets in the clay are not removed they can cause bubbles and blisters to form as the temperature increases during firing. They can even cause explosions in the kiln. Air pockets in the clay body can also make it more difficult to center a lump of clay on the wheel. This is very important for beginners.
2. *To check correct water content.* If the clay is too sticky, knead it on a porous surface to a workable state; if it is too dry, recycle it, as described below.
3. *To find and remove any foreign bodies.* Hard lumps of clay, sticks, and

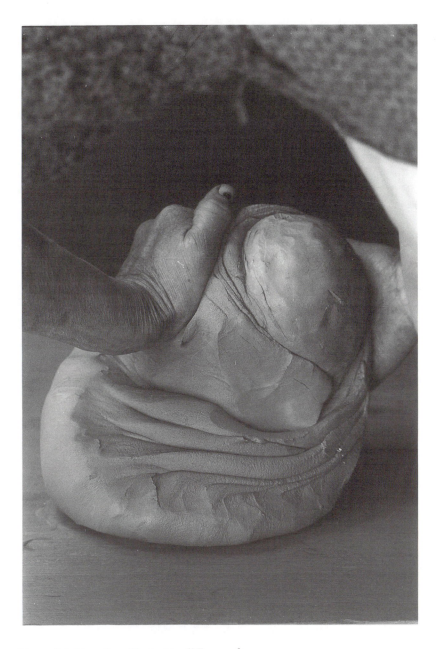

Figure 5.8. Kneading. Photo: Geoff Kenward.

stones should be removed to achieve a workable clay. If the contamination is considerable, the clay must be recycled.

4. *To check and improve plasticity.* Wedging and kneading help to align the particles of clay so that they slip over one another easily, thus increasing workability. You should also check the yield point (see above).

During all these preparatory stages, take the opportunity to become intimately acquainted with the clay. Rub a little of it between thumb and first finger, and feel the texture, its fineness or coarseness. If you are attentive when kneading, you will gradually develop the ability to tell when the clay feels right.

Recycling Waste Clay

Although clay is an extremely common commodity, it is quite expensive by the time it reaches the workshop. Therefore, reclaiming waste clay should be considered carefully. A soak bin should be kept ready for each clay type in which it can be completely immersed in water. Rock hard clay and hardened but still damp clay should be dried out completely, then broken into small pieces with a mallet and soaked. Cuttings from slab-making should be put in the soak bin together with clay left from coiling. Slurry from the throwing wheel, if it is fresh and has not been overworked on the wheel, may go straight to the plaster-dying slabs or into the soak bin. Remember to put each clay type into the correct bin.

Leave the clay to soak in plenty of water, stirring it occasionally, until it has the consistency of thin cream. Then sieve it through 40s, 60s, or 80s mesh (finer for porcelain) depending on the coarseness required. After sieving allow the clay to settle to the bottom of the container and pour away the clear water, then place the clay on plaster slabs to dry back to a workable state. Finally, pug-mill or wedge the clay by hand and put back into storage, close-covered with plastic, and left to rest (see "Aging" above). Ideally, the clay should be hand-wedged again just before use.

Reducing the Water Content of Clay

Large quantities of clay may be placed on slabs of plaster, preferably covered with close-woven canvas to prevent chips of plaster being mixed with the clay and to help remove the clay after it is dried back to the plastic state. A convection heater beneath the slabs of plaster helps to drive off the excess water. Separate slabs for white clays prevent contamination by colored clay. Provided the clay has reached a good plastic condition, it will come away from the cloth smoothly.

Look at the clay frequently; don't let it dry back too far. This is of particular importance for porcelain. If small pieces of dry porcelain drop back into the softer clay, they remain as hard lumps and do not reabsorb moisture. Even tiny particles cause serious problems in fine work. In extremely dry weather, it may pay to cover porcelain with another (slightly damp) cloth or turn the clay occasionally so that the outside does not dry too quickly, or use one of the methods described below.

Small quantities of clay slip may be poured into a biscuit-fired bowl or a flower pot lined with two thicknesses of cloth. When the excess water has drained away (this should only take a few minutes), the clay may be wrapped in cheese cloth like a cottage cheese and hung up to dry back to the plastic

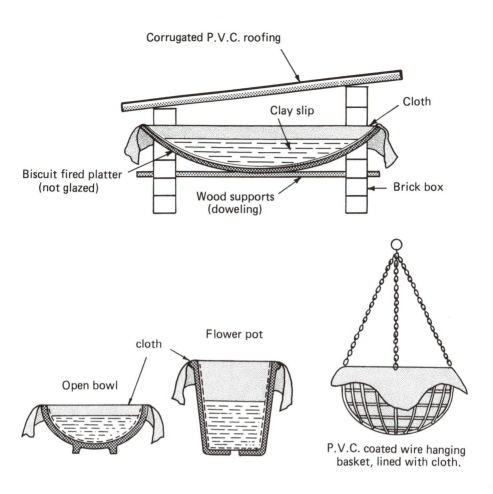

Figure 5.9. Quick methods of drying test quantities of clay slip back to the plastic state.

state. Make sure that the clay does not dry too much and become an unusable mass again.

A *brickbox* erected out-of-doors where the water can drain away naturally is useful in warm weather for larger quantities (see Figure 5.9).

The Making Stage

Because clay particles are flat and plate-like they tend to align themselves at right angles to the pressure exerted on them during the making stage (the plastic stage when the clay particles are surrounded by a film of water that allows movement). This occurs no matter what technique has been used, whether throwing, slabbing, coiling, pinching, or casting. In the last case,

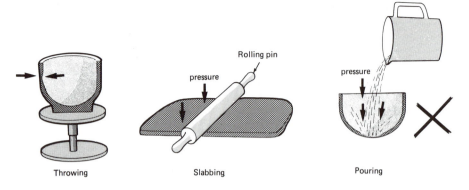

Rolling pin

pressure

pressure

Throwing

Slabbing

Pouring

Figure 5.10. Examples of faults in the making stage. Consistent, even pressure is essential.

the weight of the casting slip acts as the pressure. It is therefore necessary to ensure that even pressure is used; otherwise, the clay density is uneven. The clay wall may become thinner and stretched in areas subjected to extra pressure, and this affects the strength of the work before and after firing, which may cause cracking and breaking (see Figure 5.10).

The Drying Process

As the water is removed, the clay particles move closer together until they are touching; the clay particles stick together, and the clay mass shrinks. A useful exercise is to put some used postage stamps or tiny pieces of flat paper in a glass bowl of water and watch them "swim." Let this stand for a minute, and then gently pour off all the water. As you do so, the pieces of paper will align themselves and stick together in a small flat mass. The smaller the pieces of paper the tighter will be the pack. Similarly, the finer the particle size of a clay body, the greater the amount of shrinkage. When only a very small amount of water is left, the drying process may be hastened as there will be little further movement.

Throughout the drying process care must be taken so that water is not dried from the surface of the clay more quickly than it can be drawn from the center. If this happens, an air-lock develops and the water in the center of the ware has difficulty migrating to the surface and escaping. Fine-grained clays are prone to this. A remedy is to dry the clay in a warm, slightly humid atmosphere. In these conditions water moves readily toward the warmer air, while the humidity prevents the surface water evaporating too quickly.

A further important factor is the orientation of clay particles. Where a clay object has corners, the oriented plates of clay particles abruptly change direction, with a corresponding change in shrinkage patterns. At these points stresses build up. Careful joining is therefore necessary, particularly in slab work.

A similar situation may occur if a slab or wall of clay is compressed more in one place than another or is of uneven thickness. Stresses may develop between these areas and cause cracking or deformation of the piece. It is therefore important that walls are potted, or formed, as evenly as possible. Do not allow one part to become wetter than another, and dry evenly.

Ways in which even drying may be achieved:

1. Do not leave water lying at the bottom of a pot or object.
2. Do not leave a thrown pot on a wheel head so that the bottom remains damp while the top and rim become dry. Turn thrown pots over as soon as the rim is firm enough, or support objects so that the air can circulate underneath.
3. Place or suspend plastic sheeting over work while it is drying, particularly porcelain, so that the rims and edges do not dry before the rest of the work (though take great care that drops of water do not fall onto the work). Porcelain has a high shrinkage rate and tends to dry quickly, and can develop fine hairline cracks perpendicular to the rim, often not seen until after firing.

Sculptures that will take a long time to complete may be very lightly sprayed with water (do not soak them). After the glistening water has gone off, any areas likely to dry quickly should be close-wrapped with thin plastic, and then the whole loosely covered or wrapped with plastic. Where it is not possible to wrap, lightly spray the thinner or drier areas without soaking them, and place in a reasonably airtight container, with a humidifier if necessary.

After the making process has been completely finished, the clay objects should be allowed to dry thoroughly, often for a week or longer, before firing. At this stage the clay should feel warm against the cheek, and a spot of water on it should dry away immediately. Clay objects at this stage are usually called *greenware*. At this stage, all greenware requires careful handling. Always support the weight and never pick up greenware by a thinner part (e.g., a handle); it may look strong enough, but it is not.

Allowing for Shrinkage

One of the difficult things in ceramics is to calculate the size an object will be after firing and, what is more difficult, to calculate the size an object should be made to achieve a required fired size. Below are given the calculations for achieving this, where:

Sb = size *before* drying and firing (i.e., the original size).
Sa = size *after* firing.

Example 1. To find fired size where Sb = 11 cm and the rate of shrinkage is 12%:

$$Sa = \frac{(100 - \% \text{ shrinkage}) \times Sb}{100} = \frac{(100 - 12) \times 11}{100} = 9.68 \text{ cm}$$

Sa (finished size) will be 9.68 cm.

Example 2. To find the size an object should be made to give a finished size of 9.68 cm:

$$Sb = \frac{100 \times Sa}{(100 - \% \text{ shrinkage})} = \frac{100 \times 9.68}{(100 - 12)} = 11 \text{ cm}$$

The object should be made 11 cm to give a finished size of 9.68 cm.

The calculation above is essential if you have an architectural commission to make tiles or a wall sculpture to fit a particular space (see Plate 34). Also, if you use two different clays in a piece of work, the shrinkage rates must be compatible or special techniques developed to offset this problem (see frontispiece).

Firing Clay and the Ceramic Change

Although kiln building is not discussed in this book, it is essential for every potter to understand the theory of the firing process involved in turning clay into ceramic and mixtures of raw materials into glaze. To do this we shall study the firing of a kiln load of evenly potted work, which has been correctly dried and fired at a rate of temperature rise of not more than 150°C per hour, or 270°F per hour. The stages will be considered as follows:

1. The escape of water
2. The ceramic change
3. The escape of volatiles
4. Changes that occur in crystalline silica

The Escape of Water

In Chapter 4 we saw that there are three forms of water involved with clay crystals. Of these, much of the free water should dry off when the greenware is set to dry in the studio and the rest in the early stages of firing. When a temperature of 100°C/212°F is reached, the remaining free water becomes more active and starts vaporize. At 450°C/842°F the interlayer water begins to escape, but it is not until 600°C/1112°F that the structural water (which is bound more tightly in the crystal structure) is released. To ensure that all the water escapes, all ports, vents, and the spy-hole must be fully open and the kiln fired slowly. In the case of a solid fuel fired kiln, the back plate/damper (that is, the vent in the chimney, see Exercise 3: "Firing the Kiln") should be fully open: this causes a draft through the kiln and helps to carry the moisture out. If the kiln load is not as dry as it should be or if the kiln is fired too quickly, temperatures much in excess of those given above may be registered before all the water is expelled. The mirror test should be used to check that all the moisture has been driven off. To do this a clean, cold mirror should be held at an angle over the top vent (or spy-hole, if there is no top vent in a small kiln). If the mirror steams up, moisture is still present in the kiln. Do not use a warm mirror as steam will not settle on it. Do not close the kiln completely until all the steam has gone. The kiln fabric can be seriously damaged from steam pressure and explosions can occur if the above procedure is not observed.

The Ceramic Change

As the structural water in the clay crystal is driven off ($450°C–600°C/842°F–1112°F$), the crystals change their state to a new crystal form that does not contain water: the clay becomes a ceramic fabric. This new material, under normal circumstances, cannot revert to clay. Even if it is ground down to a powder and mixed with water, it will behave as a grit and display no plastic qualities. (Geologic time would be required to metamorphose it.)

Further changes occur as the temperature rises. For example, at about $600°C/1112°F$ the structural water in kaolinite is driven off, and a new form, called metakaolinite (changed kaolinite) takes its place. At $980°C/1796°F$, some amorphous (non-crystalline) silica is released and the metakaolinite enters an aluminum silicate transitional stage. Finally, at $1050°C/1922°F$ and higher, more amorphous silica is released and crystals of *mullite* begin to form.

There are two forms of mullite: primary mullite, consisting of small scaly crystals giving good mechanical and thermal shock resistance, and secondary mullite, longer needle-like crystals. These are important in a high-temperature glaze-body interface, binding them together giving greater strength.

The Escape of Volatiles (see Glossary for definition)

Many of the gases and volatiles escaping from a kiln, such as sulfur dioxide (SO_2), and chlorine gas (Cl_2), are harmful if inhaled. (They may be detected by smell, but do not rely on this.) Therefore, the kiln room must be well ventilated and should not be used for living purposes.

Between $700°C/1292°F$ and $900°C/1652°F$, when a kiln is fired at a rate of approximately $150°C$ per hour (or $270°F$ per hour), heat-labile substances decompose, and all or part of the decomposed materials volatilize. For this combustion to take place, there must be a normal atmosphere (i.e., plenty of oxygen) in the kiln and open vents to allow the gases to escape. It is essential that this process take place at this stage while the ceramic body is still porous, so that the gases can escape easily; otherwise, they become trapped. If the volatiles do not escape at this stage, they accumulate in the body and expand as the temperature rises, eventually forming unsightly blisters or bloating. This fault, formed at low temperature, is often not seen until after the high temperature firing. It is therefore a common mistake to think that something has gone wrong at top temperature instead of looking for bad practices during making or the early stages of firing. If you make and fire your work carefully and the fault persists, it is then reasonable to question the clay and to consult your clay manufacturer or supplier, but always send a sample of the fault and a statement of your firing cycle with your query.

Changes That Occur in Crystalline Silica

The crystallization of silica in a cooling magma has already been discussed in Chapter 2, and should be reviewed before continuing (see "Temperature and Crystallization of Magma").

During the quartz and cristobalite phases there are changes in the structural arrangement of the crystals giving rise to changes in size, setting up stress in the body that can result in cracking or breaking of the ceramic (sometimes with a noisy explosion). The temperatures of change are 225°C/437°F and 573°C/1063°F. When significant changes are expected, slow firing through these temperatures is necessary so that the changes can take place slowly. To be on the safe side, you should, until you thoroughly understand the theory given in the following Advanced Section, make a regular practice of firing slowly through a short range on either side of these temperatures and, if cracking occurs, reduce the firing time over 1100°C/2012°F or reduce the top temperature (or a little of both) in order to reduce the amount of cristobalite that rapidly forms over this temperature. You might also consider trying another clay body containing less crystalline silica, or one in which the quartz content has a much finer grain size (200s mesh or finer), so that it may more easily enter the melt and react with other constituents in the clay to form compounds that do not react in this way.

ADVANCED SECTION

The Conversion of Quartz to Cristobalite

In the following discussion tridymite (defined in Chapter 2) is considered with cristobalite; the changes are the same for both from the potter's point of view. Because quartz is the stable form of crystalline silica at normal temperature and pressure (N.T.P.), it will be the form found in clay. During firing some of the quartz in the clay can convert to the cristobalite form, but given the quick cooling of a studio firing (relative to the slow cooling of a magma under higher pressure), the cristobalite does not have time to change back into the quartz form during cooling or in any subsequent firing. Therefore, once formed, cristobalite remains as cristobalite unless drawn into the (noncrystalline) melt. Although a little cristobalite may form earlier, significant amounts do not occur until after 1100°C/2012°F in a studio firing; hence 1100°C/2012°F is taken as the working temperature at which the conversion of quartz to cristobalite starts when firing ceramics. The conversion takes place slowly and is dependent on the length of time the temperature remains above 1100°C/2012°F and on the top temperature of the firing (the higher the temperature the more rapidly it forms). In normal practice, only a portion of the quartz is converted to cristobalite. Thus, in bodies fired over 1100°C/2012°F, both quartz and cristobalite can be present and remain in the cooled ceramic. Indeed, in subsequent firings over 1100°C/2012°F more cristobalite can form; this can be a problem in high-fired ceramics, those fired a second time over 1100°C/2012°F, and in overfired work. The important factor to remember, discussed below, is that while a little cristobalite may be useful, too much is disastrous. Given this, we must now consider the further changes, called *inversions*, which take place in both of these crystalline forms or phases, that is, a change within the quartz phase and a change within the cristobalite phase.

The Quartz Inversion

During heating the quartz crystal structure begins to loosen (at about 550°C/1022°F). As the temperature reaches 573°C/1063°F, the low-temperature compressed form of quartz, known as the alpha-quartz crystal structure, is extended and straightened. This is accompanied by an increase in size as the new form, called beta-quartz, develops. This is called an inversion, and there is a quartz inversion from alpha-quartz to beta-quartz on heating and from beta-quartz back to alpha-quartz on cooling. Both these inversions occur suddenly, resulting in a shock to the body. (If you find this difficult to visualize, think of a Chinese paper lantern, which is sold twisted and compressed but, when pulled out to hang up, untwists and occupies a much larger space.)

The Cristobalite Inversion

This, also a change in the internal structure of the crystal phase, is accompanied by a sudden change in size. At 225°C/437°F, alpha-cristobalite changes to beta-cristobalite on heating, and the reverse happens on cooling.

If raw clay is being fired, no cristobalite will be present in it. This means that there is no danger of a sudden shock at 225°C/437°F on firing up for the first time or in firing objects that are never fired over 1100°C/2012°F. But once cristobalite has been formed, inversion in the crystal structure occurs at 225°C/437°F and thereafter when heating and cooling.

Problems of Too Much Cristobalite

Precautions must be taken against shock and possible cracking of the pottery. This is done either by controlling the amount of cristobalite that forms, which in turn, is controlled by the length of time the ware is fired above 1100°C/2012°F and the top temperature used (see Figure 6.10), or by taking steps to ensure that at least some of the cristobalite is drawn into the (noncrystalline) glassy melt.

Finally, it should be standard practice to fire slowly through the critical quartz inversion temperature of 573°C/1063°F. This also applies when firing through the inversion temperature for cristobalite of 225°C/437°F, on firing down for the first time, and both firing up and down in any further firings (plus a short range on either side of these temperatures is recommended for safety).

If a crack occurs during firing, it is called a *firing dunt*; if it occurs during cooling it is referred to as a *cooling dunt*. This is readily recognized in glazed ware: the cooling dunt is sharp-edged, while in a firing dunt the glaze melts after the dunt has occurred and flows over the edge covering it smoothly with glaze.

Formation of Glass During Firing

This process involves the reaction of microcrystalline silica, particularly flint, and amorphous (noncrystalline) silica released from decomposing minerals, with other mineral constituents present in the clay mix. Large grains of crystalline quartz are more resistant and usually react at the surface only (the center remaining crystalline) unless the temperature is very high. The temperature at which melting takes places depends on the composition of the body and the firing cycle. By 1000°C/1832°F a melt is normally well under way, and the molten material (glass on cooling) helps to bind the body together. If too much glass is formed, the ceramic may deform and the surface may have a tight appearance. It may also be brittle and prone to breakage. If too little glass is formed, the fabric is weak and, at worst, crumbly and, again, prone to breakage. This can be controlled by the top temperature used and the length of firing at and near the top temperature.

■ ■ ■

Glaze Fit and the Firing Cycle

A ceramic body and a glaze have a different chemical makeup and therefore different rates of expansion and contraction during firing and cooling. They also respond differently to changes in temperature during normal use. Fortunately, glaze fit can be controlled by the firing cycle and by adjusting the composition of the glaze or the clay body so that their rates of expansion and contraction are compatible and work together without setting up stresses that may cause the glaze, or the glaze as well as the fired body, to crack. When the kiln is switched off at top temperature, the ceramic body and the glaze begin to cool together, and the molten glaze covers the ceramic body in a smooth layer. Even if the ceramic body contracts at this stage, the glaze can adjust because it is still sufficiently mobile. However, by 1000°C/1832°F, it begins to lose its fluidity and become viscous. By about 550°C/1022°F for earthenware and 650°C/1202°F for stoneware, it is very nearly rigid. Thus, when the body passes through the changes in crystalline silica, the glaze cannot adjust by flowing and finding a new level, but still having a little mobility, it "wrinkles."

If the amount of wrinkling is correct, then in all subsequent expansions and contractions of the body the glaze has a slight elasticity and can stretch or contract to fit the body. If you open and close your hand and watch the skin on the back of your hand stretch and contract, you will see what this means in terms of body-glaze fit. The art of firing in this respect is to encourage the formation of just enough cristobalite in the body to produce the required amount of "squeeze" or wrinkle; but not too much or too little. If the amount of wrinkling is insufficient, the glaze is put into tension (it is stretched too much) and it will crack, or craze. If it is under too much compression, too much wrinkling occurs. The glaze may break at the peaks of the wrinkles or shoots over the edges of the body (sharp edges can sometimes be felt). This is called *shivering* or *peeling*. Peeling is less common than crazing, as a glaze can withstand much more compression than tension (see Fraser, 1986).

To eliminate cracking and crazing:

1. Alter the firing cycle or the body composition.
   a. Fire longer or higher over 1100°C/2012°F. More cristobalite forms in the body, the body shrinks more, putting the glaze under compression, and the glaze fits the body.
   b. Increase the crystalline silica content of the body and fire longer or higher over 1100°C/2012°F. More cristobalite forms, the body shrinks more and the glaze fits the body. In both cases several tests may be needed to achieve a good glaze fit.
2. Alter the glaze composition so that it does not shrink as much. Reduce the proportions of materials that have a high expansion and contraction rate. This can be done by reducing the alkali content or increasing the silica content. Either way, the proportion of alkalis (which have a high expansion/contraction rate) is reduced. This is the easiest method and the most sensible if you have bought a clay body and do not know its composition. To eliminate shivering reverse the above procedures.

Body compositions are discussed in Chapter 9, glazes in Chapters 11 and 12, where alkali (high expansion and contraction) glazes and lead borosilicate (low expansion and contraction) glazes for earthenware are discussed.

Firing Cycles

Ceramics may be once-fired or twice-fired.

Once-firing. The clay objects are set in the kiln, and the firing cycle is completed in one firing. If the work is to be glazed, this is applied to the raw pot, hence it is called *raw-glazing.*

Twice-firing. The unglazed work is first fired to a temperature that hardens the ware and converts the clay to a ceramic material. This is called the *biscuit firing.* The work is then removed from the kiln, the glaze applied, and it is fired a second time, usually called the *glaze firing.*

The expression "glaze firing" implies that the firing concerns only the glaze, but this is not the case. In the biscuit firing the clay body is fired high enough to convert it to a *ceramic body,* or *pottery,* so it is no longer clay. During the second firing, once the temperature rises above that obtained in the first firing, changes take place in both the body and the glaze, and they complete the higher firing together. This is of great value because the body and glaze are thus bound more tightly together. Each method has several advantages.

The advantages of twice-firing include:

1. The ware is hardened in a biscuit firing and will stand up to more wear and tear during glazing and setting in the kiln for the second firing.
2. If a biscuit-fired pot is dropped into a bucket of glaze during glazing, it does not contaminate the glaze as a raw pot will do.
3. Work may be close-packed in the first-firing of a twice-fired load, then examined, so that defective pieces may be rejected and not sent on to the glaze firing. This is a saving in time and firing costs as faulty work is not glazed before the second firing. The glaze on each piece must be checked, and at least the thickness of a piece of cardboard must separate them when they are set in the kiln.

The advantages of once-firing include:

1. The pots may be placed in the kiln and not handled again until they come out completely fired. This is a saving in terms of labor and firing costs, but it should be noted that, as in twice-firing, the thickness of a piece of cardboard must separate glazed pots.
2. The clay body and the glaze mature together throughout firing, giving a greater degree of integration between them.
3. The ware is less likely to chip, and the quality of the glaze is often better.

It is worth pointing out that once-firing is the traditional method of firing a kiln. Twice-firing is useful and convenient, particularly in the school situation. But after a ceramist has set up an independent studio, the pros and cons of both methods should be considered carefully.

Glaze Application

On *biscuit ware*. A slight porosity in the biscuit-fired body helps to suck the glaze onto the surface. If the biscuit ware is near the vitrification point, it is advisable to warm it before glazing so that the glaze dries quickly and does not run off the less porous surface.

On *raw ware*. An object may be raw-glazed at any stage from leatherhard to completely dry, but remember that if one side of a clay wall is glazed first, it will dry out through the clay wall as well as directly to the atmosphere. Some ceramists find that it is best to allow the application on one side to dry completely before glazing the other side. You must practice to discover the stage or method that suits you best. The various methods of application (spraying, dipping, etc., described below) may be used for both raw glazing and glazing after biscuit firing. However, if dipped, the object must never be held too long in a bucket of glaze slip, or it may disintegrate, particularly where parts of the object have been *luted* (stuck) onto the object, for example, a handle on a cup. This ruins not only the object but the bucket of glaze as well. There is also the difficulty of handling raw-glazed ware when wet inside and outside with glaze. Nevertheless, with practice this method may be perfected, and it gives excellent fired results. For large objects and hollow sculptural pieces, many potters glaze the inside first by pouring, then thoroughly dry the object and glaze the outside. (The glaze water thus can dry through the clay body to the outside and evaporate before the outside glaze is applied, which might otherwise lift off the surface.) Another important point is that if a thin-walled pot is glazed on one side only, the glaze may pull on the clay body as the piece dries, or during firing, and deform it (especially fine porcelain).

Glaze application should be practiced over and over again. Biscuit-fired rejects and a bucket of waste glaze could be kept for this purpose. When washing cups, plates, and large bowls, you might practice the way you would hold them and pass them through the water to "glaze" them evenly and quickly without dropping them or leaving too many finger marks on them.

All glaze must be cleaned from the parts of the objects (e.g., foot-rings) that will touch the kiln shelf before they are placed in a kiln. If this kiln packing routine is not done, objects will stick together and/or to the shelf.

Bisque and Glost

One industrial practice is to take the first firing to top temperature, usually 1200°C/2192°F (called bisque firing). This completes the firing of the body.

A low-temperature glaze (say, one for 1060°C/1940°F) is then applied and the ceramic(s) fired at the lower temperature (called the *glost firing*).

This method eliminates a great deal of breakage that would otherwise occur when unfired ware is handled during glazing. There are also great savings in production costs because the bisque ware can be thoroughly checked and all faulty pieces destroyed at an early stage. This method, however, does not have the advantage of completing the firing of the body and glaze together, whereby the body and glaze are fused together more strongly so that chipping is less likely to occur.

The above firing practice does not apply to hard-fired porcelain, which, in the industry, is biscuit-fired at 900–1000°C/1652–1832°F, that is, without the glaze, in order to harden the body before the second firing, during which the glaze and body are fired together to the high temperature of 1400°C/2552°F.

The following list sets out the average firing temperatures for the various firing cycles.

Biscuit Firing	980–1000°C/1796–1832°F
Glaze Firing Raku	800–1000°C/1472–1832°F
Earthenware and low-temperature bodies fired over 1100°C/2014°F	1000–1100°C/1832–2014°F (no appreciable cristobalite formed) 1100–1168°C/2014–2134°F (cristobalite formed)
Middle temperatures	1170–1240°C/2138–2264°F
Stoneware	1260–1305°C/2305–2381°F
Soft porcelain and studio porcelain	1260–1305°C/2300–2381°F (1305°C/2381°F and higher where the kiln is built to take such temperatures)
Hard porcelain (HT Industrial) and Industrial whiteware	1380–1400°C/2516–2552°F
Bisque firing	1100–1200°C/2012–2192°F
Glost	950–1100°C/1742–2012°F

This industrial firing cycle is now used by many studio potters and sculptors, particularly those using the slip-cast technique.

EXERCISE 1: Making a Set of Test Tiles

Introduction

If only one or two tiles are required, a single slab may be rolled out, and the tiles cut from this. If a number of identical tiles are to be made, the most efficient way is shown in Figure 5.11. This method may also be used to make tiles of different shapes and sizes. You should carry out this Exercise following the steps shown in Figure 5.11 in conjunction with the notes given below. These tiles will be used for glaze tests in Exercise 28 (see Plate 8 for finished tiles). By making them at this stage you not only practice the method of making a bulk amount of tiles but allow time for drying and biscuit firing.

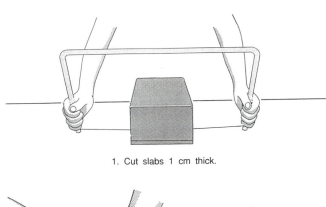

1. Cut slabs 1 cm thick.

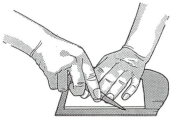

2. Cut out tiles using a cardboard template.

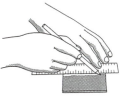

3. Mark the front of each tile by scoring with ballpoint pen.

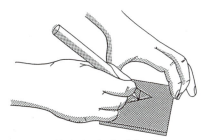

4. Mark the back of the tiles.

Figure 5.11. Four steps in making and marking tiles.

Method

Wedge a lump of buff-firing stoneware clay, and shape it into a block about 12 cm square and 10 to 12 cm high. Hold the wire horizontal and very taut as it cuts through the clay; otherwise, it will rise in the middle of the slab. Each slab should then be placed between two pieces of cloth (a finely woven cloth for the front of the tile, and a coarsely woven one for the back, which provides a good key for gluing the tile onto a board after firing). Using the rolling pin and guides (wooden sticks that ensure that the slab is finished to the required even thickness), roll each slab lightly through the cloth (see Figure 7.2). Loosen both cloths between each roll and finally smooth the front of the tile gently through the fine cloth with your hand. These small tiles could be as thin as 0.5 cm (larger tiles need to be proportionately thicker). When turning the slabs over, loosen the cloths but leave them in position, being careful not to bend the slabs, as this could throw the clay particles out of alignment and cause the tiles to warp on drying (hence the saying, "clay has a memory").

The edges of the tiles may be finished by polishing with a dry finger, gently pushing the rough grains back into the body. Never try to smooth the edge of claywork by wetting it. If you do, you will remove the very fine clay, leaving the coarser particles standing out and producing a rough edge (this also applies to the rims of thrown work, where a slightly moist chamois leather may be used, not a wet one). Brush on white slip where required (see Plate 8) when the tiles are leatherhard. If the tiles are red- or buff-firing, brush a stroke of white slip across the back. Prop up the tiles until the glistening water has gone off, then, using an old ball point pen, incise the reference letters (A to J) on the back of the tiles as shown in Figure 5.11 while the clay is still leatherhard. Also mark the divisions on the front of the tiles (see Figure 5.11 and Plate 8), using the same method. The recipes on the front of the tiles will be entered later.

Drying the Tiles

Two methods are given to prevent warping during drying.

1. Make stacks of not more than four or five tiles interleaved with several thicknesses of newspaper. The paper allows some movement so that the tiles may shrink without cracking and can be replaced from time to time to aid drying. A book placed on top of each stack helps to keep them flat, but do not put a very heavy weight on them. Ideally, the tiles should be allowed to dry slowly. This is especially important for large tiles, which should be dried separately, resting on several sheets of newspaper, and turned often.
2. Tiles may be dried a little more quickly by placing them singly between wire grids, or between two smooth, dry, flat, porous surfaces again between layers of newspaper.

Firing and Storing the Test Tiles

Biscuit fire the tiles to the standard biscuit temperature. Do not stack too many tiles on top of one another for the biscuit firing or they may crack. After firing, the tiles should be wrapped so that they do not get dusty and stored in a dry place until required.

Layout for Standard Test Tiles

Throughout the book, references are made to standard layouts for particular tests. To save repetition, those used regularly have been placed together in Appendix Figure A.7.

* * *

EXERCISE 2: Making a Glaze and Developing a Glaze Application Technique

Introduction

Efficient methods of making a glaze are illustrated in Figure 5.12. In these step-by-step instructions, a test glaze is illustrated although the same method applies to large-scale glaze making as well. Figure 5.13 illustrates the method of glazing a test pot. Other methods are described below.

These methods may also be used for applying clay slips, with the exception of spraying because coarser nozzles are necessary for spraying clay slips, slip glazes, and ash glazes.

Much good work is ruined by poor glaze technique. This exercise has therefore been devised as a guide to this important part of workshop practice. Always keep the glaze well stirred throughout the glazing session and make sure no glaze is stuck to the bottom of the container. After glazing, clean the glaze off any area that will touch the kiln shelf; otherwise the piece will stick to it. (This does not refer to white marking slip made from kaolin and a little ball of clay.) When making test pots you are advised to make them with foot-rings.

Method

Materials Required for Regular Glaze Practice

At least 12 or 15 biscuit-fired pots or sculptures of various shapes and sizes, a 9 liter (2 gallon) bucketful (or more) of waste glaze, a wide bowl, sponges, hand towels, and a small glaze mop, i.e., a full-bodied brush (see Figure 11.5). Some potters like to cover the foot-ring (or the base) of their work with latex or wax to prevent glaze adhering to the area in contact with

1. Weighing the materials on an electronic balance.

2. Powders placed in mortar separately for checking.

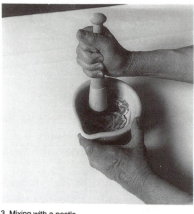

3. Mixing with a pestle.

4. Adding water.

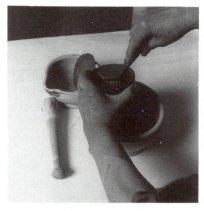

5. Seiving 120 mesh.

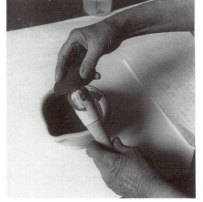

6. Wiping off ALL glaze with a rubber kidney.

Figure 5.12. Steps in making a test glaze. Photo: Ken Bright.

1. Testing for thickness: the finger should be covered smoothly without obscuring outline of finger nail. Hairs on back of the finger should break through.

2. Stir the glaze well and fill the pot to the brim.

3. Lower pot gently into glaze with rim exactly parallel with surface of the glaze, preventing glaze splashing inside.

4. The dip may be timed while learning by saying aloud 1-2-3-4 (seconds) from top of dip and back again; give the pot a little wriggle to loosen the last drip.

5. Place pot on bench still holding the foot rim only, this shows the value of foot rim, at least while learning.

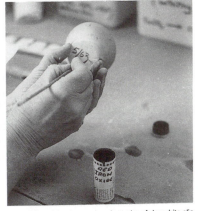

6. Mark base clearly over brush-stroke of dry white slip.

Figure 5.13. Steps in glazing a test pot by dipping. Photo: Ken Bright and Geoff Kenward.

the kiln shelf. A good method is to keep a layer of wax in an old electric fry pan and warm this gently when glazing to dip the base into it.

Glazing Methods

Again, a number of practice sessions should be carried out before attempting the glazing of final work. There are four well-known methods of applying glaze: dipping, pouring, brushing, and spraying.

Dipping and pouring. Dipping and pouring may be used separately or in combination as, for example, pouring the inside and dipping the outside as shown in Figure 5.13.

However, one of the simplest methods involves dipping alone. The work is held on its side and lowered into the glaze so that one half (both inside and outside in the case of a hollow vessel) is glazed. The work is allowed to dry sufficiently to touch and the other half is dipped in the same way. This technique may be used also for closed forms (where the inside is not to be glazed). There will be a slight overlap of glaze in the middle, but this will not matter if you are using a fluid (e.g., transparent) glaze, as it should merge and smooth out in the melt. If you are using a viscous glaze, the overlap may be gently rubbed down with a finger when the glaze is white dry before firing. This might be important in some sculptural work and any dribbles may be dealt with in the same way. Do this over a sink or the waste glaze bucket while wearing a mask. You should practice glazing until you can avoid leaving dribbles; a little twist of the wrist to make the last drop fall off helps. Some sculptural forms can be deep-dipped, but make sure that the container holding the glaze is deep enough to submerge the whole piece without flooding the glaze over the rim of the container and without the work touching the sides as it is removed. The work may be hand-held or held with tongs.

A useful but more difficult way to glaze the outside of a vessel that cannot be conveniently gripped by its foot is to hold it with the fingers splayed out and pressed against the inside and dip the pot up to the rim. The rim may then be glazed by brushing while the pot rotates on a whirler or potter's wheel (see below).

Sluicing is another useful method of dipping flatware and some sculptural forms. The work is held with tongs (or other manufactured aid), or by using the middle finger and thumb of both hands (one on each side or end of the work) and drawing it into a bowl of glaze at one side, through the glaze and out the other side. This technique might be practiced with household pieces and a large bowl or basin filled with water (e.g., a baby's bath).

Pouring is a very useful method for large or heavy work. For a hollow form the inside may be glazed by pouring as described above. The outside can be glazed by holding the foot or other suitable part of an object with one hand. Alternatively, the hand can be inside the pot or object supporting it. The hand and pot are then twisted round as far as possible, keeping the pot vertical, and the glaze poured on from a jug continuously as the hand and arm are "untwisted." A large bowl should be placed underneath to catch the excess glaze. Again, this process may be practiced using water (but not on the pot about to be glazed). A similar method is to place the work on a clean whirler (turntable) standing in a large bowl to catch the excess glaze as it is poured onto the turning piece (or as you walk around it). To prevent damage to the glaze on the inside a lump of clay can be centered on the wheel and covered with a soft dry cloth with the work suspended over it.

Brushing a glaze onto the inside of a round vessel can be carried out by using a potter's wheel. Start the wheel turning slowly and center the object on it. Secure the object with soft clay if necessary, then take a full-bodied, well-loaded glaze mop, and touch it down at the center of the piece. Draw it straight from the center to the rim while the object rotates. Practice until you can lay on a continuous stroke without gaps (the secret is to time the rate at which you move the brush outward to match the speed of rotation). To glaze the outside the brush may be drawn up the outside as the vessel is turned. Brushing may be used to glaze the rim of a vessel if a smooth surface has not been achieved with the other methods. For cups and mugs, a slightly more viscous glaze brushed on may keep the rim smooth and therefore pleasant for drinking.

Using a *chuck* is a method that may suit some work. A thick collar of clay thrown on the wheel is used to support the object while glazing it. This is called a chuck (manufactured chucks may be purchased from craft suppliers). If it is necessary to place the object so that the newly applied glaze has to touch the chuck, wait until the glaze is dry and put a fine cloth and/or padding over the chuck. Until you perfect this method take out the amount of glaze you need for the work in hand and put a little binder in it (see p. 123). This gives the glaze better adhesion and stops it from rubbing off. (Do not put the binder in the bulk glaze.) A chuck may also be used to balance a sculpture, or to hold a piece of work in a novel position in order to achieve decorative glaze effects.

When raw glazing (especially fine porcelain), you may need to glaze the inside first, then allow the pot to dry thoroughly before glazing the outside.

Spraying with a Spray Gun

Personal safety and care of equipment is important. Always wear a mask, and turn on the extractor fan. If you do not have a spray booth with an extractor fan, or a separate alcove, spray out-of-doors. Otherwise, do not spray in the studio since you will inevitably inhale the glaze dust and also leave a layer of glaze dust everywhere. You should equip your spray booth or area with a shower hose, and wash down the waste glaze into a clean bucket. It is possible to reclaim glaze in this way: let the glaze settle and pour off the excess water. If you do this remember to label the waste glaze.

Procedure After Spraying

A spray gun is a delicate piece of equipment, so always see that it is left clean. Spray two lots of clean water through the sprayer after tipping any unused glaze back into its correct container, and clean the nozzle thoroughly according to the manufacturer's instructions. Switch off the compressor, and follow the instructions for releasing the air in the compressor tank. Carry out these functions under proper supervision until you are thoroughly acquainted with the method, or get expert advice from the supplier.

Spraying Technique

Most glaze spray guns have very fine nozzles. They spray a glaze that has been properly sieved through a 120s mesh sieve without difficulty, but a much coarser spray nozzle is needed for ash glazes (preferably, these should be applied by dipping). Hold the gun far enough from the object for it to receive a wide spray of the glaze, and adjust the discharge so that you get a fine spray without splatter. Keep the gun and the object moving all the time. The usual method is to have the object on a whirler moving round laterally and the gun moving up and down. Practice frequently for glaze thickness: spray a trial area with four sweeps. Stop and let the glaze dry a little, then proceed as below.

Testing for Thickness

Thickness should be tested when the glistening water has gone off and the glaze has set but is not completely dry. A standard thickness is considered to be about 1 mm. There are several ways of checking this; a fine needle painted bright red up to a 1 mm mark is ideal. Another method is to run a clean potter's knife at right angles along the edge of the (unfired) glaze on a test tile and to observe the profile (or the edge of a broken glazed tile). In the case of sprayed glaze, several tests with different thicknesses of sprayed glaze should be fired (after recording the unfired thickness of each test in your notebook). These tests must be placed on large test areas at least 15 cm square. If you want a crackle glaze, it should be extra thick; try several thicknesses between 1 mm and 3 mm thick.

*   *   *

EXERCISE 3: Firing the Kiln

If you are firing a new kiln, monitor the rate of temperature rise throughout the first few firings until you know your kiln thoroughly. Also see "Pyrometric Cones" (in this chapter).

Aim

The aim here is to guide you through the general principles and practice of kiln firing. The instructions therefore apply regardless of the type of fuel used or whether you are firing in oxidation ("O") or reduction ("R").

For the purposes of this exercise a simple device for measuring and displaying temperature and pyrometric cones will suffice, although these principles also apply to more sophisticated equipment. Emphasis is placed on the changes that take place in the clay during firing and the procedure to ensure a successful firing. Your first few firings should be carried out under the supervision of a trained person; if this is not possible, carefully follow the steps given below and the manufacturer's instructions. These are important. If you have a new kiln or if it has not been fired for some time, it must be pre-fired empty with all the vents open to at least 600°C/1112°F to ensure that it is thoroughly dry. You will need a kiln load of well dried work ready for biscuit firing or glaze firing, a notebook (graph paper if you wish to construct a graph of the firing); a small flashlight (a tiny one that will fit into the kiln to light the cones while you view them and place them in position so that they can be seen through the spy-hole with the door closed); alternatively, matches stuck in a pad of clay; and heat-proof goggles for viewing the cones. Remember to remove the flashlight before firing.

Pyrometric Cones

You will need at least one set of three cones for the firing temperature to be used: a *guide cone* (warning you that the end of the firing is near), a *firing cone* (marking the "top of the firing cycle"), and a *guard cone* (warning you that you are in danger of overfiring!). The guard cone should be still erect when you finish the firing (do not use this cone again as it has already undergone a major part of its changes). To choose your cones, first select the firing cone that marks your selected firing temperature, then select the cone numbers immediately below and above it. For example, you might choose cones 7 (guide cone); 8 (firing cone); and 9 (guard cone, the overfiring warning cone). Set these up as shown in Figure 6.5, or in an Orton cone plaque with the lowest cone (no. 7 in the above example) on the right so that it does not fall on the others when it squats; the firing cone in the middle; and the guard cone on the left, all leaning 8 degrees from the vertical to the right (see Figure 6.6).

For the first few firings place several sets of cones in different places, particularly the top and bottom of the kiln, so that you may check after firing whether there are any cool spots in your kiln. If there are, you could make a practice of putting work with a slightly more fusible glaze (or unglazed pieces) in those areas.

Method

Packing the Kiln

For a biscuit firing, the pieces may be stacked touching one another when setting them in the kiln, but remember that they will shrink, and that different clays have different shrinkage rates. Hence, if you put one object inside another, make sure that you will be able to get it out after firing. If there are any sculptural pieces that are completely enclosed, make sure that there is a small air hole (several for complicated pieces) to let the air out as it heats up. Otherwise the object will explode. For complicated sculptures, particularly if there are several separate closed areas, ensure that expanding air can escape from all of them. This should be checked at the kiln packing stage (as well as at the making stage) and any piece without an air hole rejected for firing. If the firing contains glazed ware and is to be once-fired, or is a glaze firing (after biscuit firing), set the pieces in the kiln so that they do not touch. It should be just possible to get a piece of cardboard between them. Nevertheless, still try to get as tight a pack as possible since the hot ware will help to distribute the heat evenly. Make sure that nothing is resting against the elements in an electric kiln. In a gas or solid-fuel kiln, see that nothing obstructs the flow of fire up the channel behind the bag wall (the wall that deflects the flame so it does not strike the ware directly and gives a more even heat among the work being fired).

Positioning the Cones

Place the cones in position in line with the spy-hole. Place the flash-light, (or a match supported by a lump of clay), in the kiln shining on the cones, close the door and check that you can see the cones through the spy-hole with the door completely closed.

Remove the flashlight.

Close and fasten the door. In a school situation the door should be locked.

Biscuit Firing or Early Stage of Once-Firing

Turn on and set the controls (according to the instruction for your particular kiln). A biscuit firing or the early stages of once-firing may be fired slowly overnight with the air vents (air inlets) open. Slow firing (at about 10% to 25% heat input) at these low temperatures will not affect the cones. The aim at this stage is to drive off the moisture from the ware and the kiln fabric. Next morning, the rate of heat input may be gradually increased; at 600°C/1112°F check the moisture by holding a mirror over the top vent (taking proper safety precautions) or check at the spy-hole if the kiln is small and has no top vent. When all the steam has completely disappeared, remember that the volatiles still have to escape. If using gas or solid fuel you should leave sufficient openings to permit a flow of air through the kiln, thus maintaining an oxidation atmosphere during this stage. The more heavily contaminated your clay (as in some common clays), the slower you should fire. Once this is completed, continue at an average rate of 150°C per hour or 270°F per hour (the standard rate used in this book). If you use a different rate of temperature rise, record this for future reference.

Glaze Firing

Oxidation Firing When Twice-Firing

If you think the kiln or work has accumulated moisture from the atmosphere or from the application of glaze, start a glaze firing with 25 percent heat input and vents open as in the biscuit firing. Otherwise, you may start at 50 percent heat input for the first one half to one hour and double-check for steam before closing the vents. As for the biscuit firing, sufficient flow of air must be retained in a gas or solid fuel kiln if you are trying to maintain an oxidation atmosphere.

Some potters set the kiln to full on from the beginning or use a fast firing technique. However, most people need to gain some experience before trying this. If the pieces have been glazed just before being set in the kiln (though this practice is not recommended), or if the kiln is suspected of being damp, preheat the kiln load with all your vents open the night before firing. Ideally, glazing should be carried out at least 24 hours before firing (a week in damp cold weather) and the pieces thoroughly dried again before setting in the kiln.

Monitoring and recording your firing is important. Ideally, firing should be recorded in graph form. For this you need a pyrometer (or similar instrument). Put the time, in hours, along the bottom (horizontal) axis of the graph and the temperature on the vertical axis (see Figure 6.10). When you start firing, put a cross on the vertical axis representing the room temperature and time when you begin the firing. When all the moisture has been driven from the kiln, note the time and the temperature registered by your pyrometer and place a cross on the graph where they meet. So far, the graph tells you how long you have taken to rid the kiln of steam (this will help you adjust the rate of heat input, if necessary). Make a note on the graph when you (partially) close the vents.

Every hour from then on, read and mark the temperature. Although the temperature increase need not be exactly 150°C/270°F per hour, the firing should average this rate. During the last 100°C (180°F) you should look at the temperature and the cones every quarter of an hour, then every ten minutes, and finally every five minutes. Once the guide cone deforms, you should be extra alert and switch off when the firing cone squats (see Figure 6.6). If you use a different rate of temperature rise you will need to carry out several test firings to ascertain the exact top temperature at that rate of firing that gives the fired qualities you require (by noting the temperature and the time when your firing cone squats). The graphs should be dated and stored clipped in a folder for future reference and comparative analysis. These records become one of your most valuable firing aids.

The kiln should be set to soak when the firing cone stands at 3 o'clock and switched off when it reaches the 6 o'clock position. Alternatively, some potters continue the firing until the firing cone reaches the 6 o'clock position and either switch off without soaking or soak for 20 to 30 minutes. If you are using simple heat input controls this is done by turning back the setting to about 60 to 70 percent heat input. The exact setting differs for every kiln, so you must kiln-sit until you know the exact setting(s) at which your kiln soaks (holds top temperature). Some electronically controlled kilns can be set to soak for the required time at top temperature.

It is vital that you do not allow the kiln to climb over the top firing temperature during soaking. If you do, further chemical reactions may take place, causing glaze constituents to volatilize and leaving the glaze "thin." Gases may also be released, forming tiny bubbles in the glaze that do not have time to escape.

As a general rule the vents should be kept closed during cooling. It is essential that the kiln is allowed to cool very slowly through 573°C/1063°F and 225°C/437°F because of the quartz and cristobalite inversions. Some potters who want clear shiny glazes and have very efficiently constructed kilns find that they have to open the top vent slightly during the first 100°C/180°F drop in temperature; otherwise, the glazes cool so slowly that they start to recrystallize, and matte (nonshiny) glazes result. This is relevant to stoneware firings rather than earthenware firings. If you do need to do this, make sure that the kiln is completely closed well before the critical quartz and cristobalite inversion temperatures are reached. Do not open the kiln until it has cooled to under 200°C/392°F and make sure that there is not a draft of cold air being drawn through the kiln. This should be considered before opening the top vent and the door or other vents (particularly in cold or draughty weather). As a general rule, it is best to wait until the kiln is near room temperature before opening it.

Reduction Firing

The general instructions given above in "Oxidation Firing" apply to both oxidation and reduction firings. The following discussion is relevant to reduction firings only.

The aim of reduction firing is to fire in such a way that oxygen is drawn from the kiln load of work thereby reducing the oxidation state of some of the constituents in the body and the glaze. The principal reason for this is to change the texture and color of the body or the glaze. A classic example is the reduction of Fe_2O_3 to FeO, producing a toasted or earth-colored body. In glazes with very small amounts of Fe_2O_3 reduced to FeO, a celadon green or green-blue is produced.

To achieve reduction, carbon is introduced into the kiln atmosphere by burning gas, wood, or other carbon- or carbohydrate-containing material and then reducing the flow of air (containing oxygen) into the kiln. Given this reduced oxygen atmosphere, carbon dioxide (CO_2) can no longer be maintained, and the reduced oxide carbon monoxide (CO) forms. Carbon monoxide is unstable, and in the presence of a high temperature, combines with oxygen to form CO_2. This oxygen is drawn from any available source, in this case, from the kiln load of work, thus bringing about the reduced oxidation state of the body and glaze constituents.

It must be added that the flow of air into the kiln is controlled by closing the vents, but not completely or too much back pressure may build up in the kiln and cause an explosion. Careful adjustment of the air intake by adjusting the backplate in the chimney (also called the damper) and/or the top vent and the fuel supply produces the desired amount of reduction. This is an individual matter, and the desired effect is achieved by trial and error.

Generally speaking, reduction firings are normally carried out in wood, oil, or gas kilns. Electric kilns fired to 1300°C/2372°F and over may produce some reduction but not of the order of fuel-burning kilns unless moth balls or some other reducing agent are introduced. To use this method special kanthal electric elements should be installed.

1. All vents should be open at the commencement of the firing (even for biscuit-fired work). Some gas and solid fuel burning kilns will just not light up and keep lit unless there is plenty of air in the kiln to feed the flame at this stage. For once-fired work, the vents should be left open until the kiln reaches at least 800°C/1472°F, that is, through the biscuit firing stage.

2. A personal decision must then be made whether to reduce the body lightly, thus keeping warmer tones, or to reduce more heavily to obtain the earth tones commonly associated with a reduced body. In a red-firing body, this would mean earthy reds and browns; in porcelain, bluish tints (with some, depending on the kaolin used, a gray tint). Some potters prefer to reduce for 30 minutes to one hour at about 800–1000°C/1472–1832°F and at 1100°C/2012°F for a similar period and again near top temperature. Others prefer to keep a light reduction from 800°C/1472°F for the rest of the firing. Experiment, do not look for any rule of thumb, and keep detailed records, or the experiments will be useless. With more experience you may try to get special glaze effects that require holding the kiln in a reduced state during the initial cooling period. This may be done by "firing down," that is, keeping the kiln on and under reduction but, at the same time, allowing the kiln temperature to drop, usually 100°C/180°F by gradually reducing the heat input until the glaze has become sufficiently viscous to prevent too much reoxidizing. In all this, the kiln construction, age, and idiosyncracies must be taken into account. Every kiln has its individuality.

3. At the temperature at which you wish to reduce the body, the kiln may be partly "closed up." Closing the vents and the spy-hole prevents fresh supplies of oxygen entering the kiln. The damper or backplate, and/or the top vent should be partly closed (usually by pushing it in about halfway). Do not close it completely; these are your controls for adjusting the degree of reduction. Wait for a few seconds, then take out the bung at the spy-hole keeping yourself well clear. Stand to one side of the spy-hole and look for a flame coming out of the hole. This small flame that burns out through the spy-hole in search of air indicates the amount of "back pressure" in the kiln. Great care must be made not to get the face or eyes too close to this flame (always wear the proper heat-proof, not plastic, goggles).

If you cannot see the flame, hold a length of rolled-up newspaper in front of the spy-hole and slowly move it toward the hole until it catches fire, thus warning you of the danger. Do not attempt to peer into the kiln at this stage through the spy-hole. When you wish to view the cones, open the back plate or vent so that the reduction eases off for a minute and the flame at the spy-hole retreats, but still keep well back from the spy-hole and wear heat-proof goggles. After looking, adjust the required degree of reduction by moving the backplate or damper in and out (or adjust the opening at the top vent) until the flame at the spy-hole is 3 or 4 cm long. This draws just enough air through the kiln to allow combustion to continue. Adjust the supply of fuel so that a balance is achieved between the fuel and the oxygen supply. Try to learn how to get a correct balance of air and fuel, so you do not have an excess of fuel burning in the flue, a wasteful method that also produces unwanted gases in the atmosphere.

The temperature should be kept rising, though the rate will be slow during reduction. The degree of reduction in the kiln may be monitored on the meter, incorporated in an oxygen-probe, which helps you to achieve repeatable results (within reasonable limits). If gas burners go out, do not relight the kiln until some air re-enters the kiln. If you do, you will get a "pop" or, at worst, a dangerous explosion. The length of time a kiln is held under reduction (i.e., with a reduced amount of available oxygen) and the temperature(s) at which this is done are a matter of choice.

4. Some ceramists find that a reduction firing is improved by opening a vent for a minute to flush oxygen briefly through the kiln before switching off (particularly for glaze colors). This prevents complete reduction of some colors which could result in an unpleasant metallic color.

5. Good reduction results may be obtained from top temperatures of 1220–1240°C/2228–2264°F; 1260–1280°C/2300–2336°F; or 1280–1300°C/2336–2372°F and over if the kiln is constructed for higher temperatures. Clays and glazes suitable for each temperature range must be used, and different qualities must be expected from the different temperature ranges. These are all discussed in the following chapters.

* * *

The Raku Firing Technique

The raku method of firing, borrowed from the Japanese tea ceremony, involves plunging biscuit-fired objects into an already-hot kiln for a low temperature glaze firing at 800–1000°C/1472–1832°F), leaving them there for 15 to 30 minutes until the glaze has matured (recognized by the red-hot walls of the objects that no longer look solid to the eye), then drawing the glazed objects from the kiln using tongs while still at top temperature. Oxidation is then maintained by allowing the work to cool in the air or even by plunging it into cold water. To achieve a good reduction the objects are taken from the kiln, passed through the air momentarily to allow slight reoxidation, and then plunged into a reduction atmosphere such as a dust-bin filled with wood shavings; these ignite on contact with the very hot ceramic objects, causing a smoky oxygen-reduced atmosphere that produces particular reduction colors and qualities.

Chapter 6
The Ceramic Process: Reversing the Natural Process

Introduction

The raw materials of ceramics consist of minerals and rocks, including clay, and chemically prepared materials of mineral origin. Clay belongs in a special category because it is used both in the plastic state to make objects and also as a dried powder to compound special clay bodies, slips, and glazes. The importance of a thorough knowledge of raw material cannot be stressed too strongly. Once this is acquired, the creative process is liberated from the constant pressure of how to achieve a particular end.

A considerable part of this chapter is devoted to frits (prefused mixtures of minerals), for two reasons. First, they form an important group of materials that are now available to modern potters for use at all temperatures, as alternative or additional materials to naturally found minerals and as colored stains. Second, understanding the nature of frits and comparing them with crystalline minerals makes it easier to understand the processes that occur during firing that convert clay to pottery and mixtures of mineral origin to glazes. Although it is not expected that students will want to make their own frits, exercises in frit making have been included to provide a better understanding of how and why they are compounded and the physical as well as the chemical properties they possess.

Phase diagrams have been included for similar reasons. They are seen not as a direct means of formulating clays or glazes but rather as a way of understanding why certain things happen.

Much refining and adjustment of the composition of clays and other raw materials is carried out by manufacturers before the potter receives a consignment. Kaolin was discussed in Chapter 4. Other clays may similarly be adjusted, for example by blending varying amounts of clays from different parts of a pit. This is usually carried out in slip form when unwanted material can be removed. Hard rocks are crushed (often after calcining which helps to loosen the structure), followed by grinding in a ball mill to a fine-grain size (see Appendix Figure A.11). The "mill-batch" is then dried to a powder.

Quality control. Most suppliers guarantee the particle size or grade by the sieve mesh through which the refined powdered raw materials pass. Usually, materials for glaze making are supplied "ground 200s mesh" (not illustrated in Figure 5.4 because it is twice as fine as 100s). Thus, with all the above processes of refining and blending, suppliers are able to offer raw materials of constant chemical composition. For example, different consignments of a particular mineral, say potassium feldspar, may differ slightly, but by blending together two or more different feldspars the composition stated in a catalog may be kept constant.

Finding Your Own Raw Materials

Some potters may not have ready access to a supplier or may prefer to find and process their own materials, accepting the impurities they contain. The use of such materials in ceramics is then established by test firings and, where possible, by comparing the results with the performance of standard materials. It may be possible to obtain a detailed analysis showing the oxide content of a particular deposit from the local Mineral Resources or Geological Department or from a chemical laboratory. Local quarries, a government department of mines, or the geology or earth sciences department of a local university are usually willing to give advice on the rocks and mineral deposits to be found in a particular locality and to tell you whether there are published analyses available. It is possible to obtain an analysis of your own found materials, but this is usually expensive, and you are advised on economic grounds not to do this unless you are satisfied with the performance of the material in test results and have a supply that will last you for several years.

A friendly stonemason may be kind enough to allow you to collect the dust that accumulates from hewing stone. In a quarry, or adjacent works, you may be permitted to collect a bagful of dust. This dust may be from granite, slate, limestone, marble, or other rocks and minerals. All may be tested for use in the pottery, and remember to wear a mask when collecting dust. Ask before leaving what sort it is likely to be. If possible take a sample, about 500 g, home to test first, before transporting a large quantity.

Preparation of Found Materials Other Than Clay

Most materials are collected in lump form, a few as sediments. Small lumps may be placed between two strong cloths or in a canvas bag and crushed with a mallet, and finally ground to a fine powder with a mortar and pestle. If you have access to a small crusher, lumps not larger than 5 cm across may be passed through it. Some hard rock (e.g., feldspars) will need to be calcined before crushing to loosen the structure. To do this most materials are fired to dull red heat, about 700°C/1292°F, but tests must be run first to assess their fusability before calcining a large amount. This is done by placing samples in individual refractory test pots and firing them to the calcining temperature. If these tests melt then a lower calcining temperature will have to be found. Mixtures of the powdered materials may be tested in this way, but keep a careful record of the proportions (equal parts, two parts to one part, and so on). Tests similar to those in Exercise 4 may also be carried out on found materials (see McMeakin, 1978).

Raw Materials Used in Ceramics

Potassium and Sodium Feldspar

Potassium feldspar ($K_2O \cdot Al_2O_3 \cdot 6SiO_2$) is used in both clays and glazes throughout the potter's firing range. Sodium feldspar ($Na_2O \cdot Al_2O_3 \cdot 6SiO_2$) is useful when soda is required for a powerful reaction, particularly at low temperature, or for the effect soda has on color. There are many regional names for potassium and sodium feldspars, which may be obtained from your supplier or from a regional government or university geology department. You should ask for their composition or formula, and choose the one with the lowest percentage of impurities.

Nepheline Syenite and Cornish Stone/Carolina Stone

Both are rocks and are used as fluxing materials, for special effects at high temperatures, and as important materials in low-temperature clays and glazes. Cornish stone, which may be considered a partially rotted light-colored granite with a variable composition and containing impurities, is often unpredictable (particularly in glazes), though manufacturers try to keep its composition constant by selling a mixed Cornish stone. The following formulas are examples. You should obtain a percentage analysis of the variety obtainable to you (see pp. 396–97).

Nepheline syenite
$0.75Na_2O \cdot 0.10Al_2O_3 \cdot 2.25SiO_2$
$0.25K_2O$

Cornish/Carolina stone
$0.40K_2O \cdot 1.30Al_2O_3 \cdot 9.00SiO_2$
$0.28Na_2O$
$0.26CaO$
$0.06MgO$

There may also be various impurities including fluorine. (Note: Unless removed, fluorine may cause blisters in work fired over 1150°C/2102°F. Also, fluorine gas is poisonous if released into the atmosphere and may harm the kiln linings and furniture. Cornish stone if defluorinated during the refining process is called D.F. stone, which is better to use.)

Limestone, Chalk, and Calcite

In this text the terms *limestone* and *chalk* are used for the natural unrefined calcium carbonate ($CaCO_3$) material derived from these rocks. The term *calcite* is reserved for the crystals and the mineral of which these rocks are composed and also the refined calcium carbonate in powdered form regularly used in ceramics. A pure iron-free precipitated calcium carbonate is also available from pharmaceutical suppliers, but it is expensive. The latter gives pure white in fired slips whereas the former may give iron spots or slight discoloration. All have the same formula $CaCO_3$.

If lumps of calcium carbonate are heated to 1100°C or over, it will decompose to calcia (CaO), commonly called *quicklime,* which (on cooling or later in use), in the presence of water will slake to calcium hydroxide $(Ca(OH)_2)$, commonly called *slaked lime,* causing swelling and possible explosion of the ceramics containing it. For this reason clay containing lumps, even very small ones, should not be used. In the fine powdered form (sieved 200s mesh or finer), the $CaCO_3$ breaks down easily during firing and the CaO combines with other oxides (e.g., silica), to make insoluble compounds that are unaffected by water.

The term *whiting* is not used in this text because it is not recognized in other languages, and also its origin is somewhat dated, having been used during the Boer War when soldiers in South Africa used chalk to whiten their belts. Further, in Britain the term refers to ground chalk but in the U.S. to ground limestone.

Dolomite

Dolomite (a calcium magnesium carbonate) is hard and requires mechanical crushing to render it down to powder form. Because it is a rock, the composition varies (see Chapter 3); hence the composition of each consignment should be obtained. Most producers adjust the composition and try to keep it at 54 percent CaO and 46 percent MgO, giving a formula of $CaCO_3 \cdot MgCO_3$.

Talc and Magnesite

Talc (also known as steatite or soapstone) is a hydrated magnesium silicate $(3MgO \cdot 4SiO_2 \cdot H_2O)$, and magnesite is a magnesium carbonate $(MgCO_3)$. Talc contains two very refractory oxides, but given the intimate combination of MgO with SiO_2 (in the same crystal structure), they react powerfully together in the presence of heat. When magnesia (MgO) is required by itself, the mineral magnesite $(MgCO_3)$, or the refined form of magnesium carbonate, may be used. The natural mineral usually contains some iron and possibly calcium or aluminum, so the refined version of both talc and magnesite may be used. Talc is used in both clay bodies and glazes.

Quartz, Quartz Sand, and Flint

These are all members of the same crystalline silica family, called the quartz family. They are the source materials for silica (SiO_2) in ceramics for clay bodies, slips, and glazes.

Quartz sand is readily available and easily mined; however, if it is used as the source (raw) material to supply silica to the ceramics market, it should be a high-purity quartz sand ground to 300s and 200s. The finer-grained (300s) sand is preferred for glazes and as a constituent in a clay body recipe for its contribution as a glass-former that is more easily drawn into the melt than a more coarse-grained crystalline silica. If the silica is to be used in white bodies or in glazes where significant iron is to be avoided, it should be obtained from manufacturers that process it in a ceramic-lined ball mill (otherwise, iron may be picked up in the milling process).

If you have bought a clay body for a particular piece of work and you wish to add grog, it is better to use an inert grog that has been pre-fired. A crystalline silica used as grog will change the chemical composition of your body (particularly with regard to cristobalite and fusibility).

Sand contaminated with salt (NaCl) (e.g., from a sea beach) should not be used. You should also test sand for $CaCO_3$ as it will probably contain shell fragments (see the hydrochloric acid test, p. 70). This will not necessarily make it unusable for ceramics, but you must be aware of the possible impurities. Never use sand from a building site. It will almost certainly be contaminated with plaster of paris (gypsum, $CaSO_4 \cdot 2H_2O$) which causes *lime-popping*: mini-explosions on firing as small lumps blow out of the walls of the ceramic.

Flint consists of microcrystalline quartz that may sometimes be collected on beaches as nodules (e.g., on the south coast of England), or found in limestone quarries. These nodules are exceptionally hard and often coated with calcium carbonate from the rock in which they are found and therefore are best prepared by industrial methods. During refining, the $CaCO_3$ coating is cleaned off by mechanically tumbling the pebbles (about 2% $CaCO_3$ remains). They are then calcined (fired) to 700°C/1292°F (dull red heat) to crack them, and finally crushed in a mechanical crusher, to render them down to powder. Calcining also burns away the small amount of carbonaceous matter that causes flints to look dark. Flint fuses at a slightly lower temperature than other forms of quartz for the following reasons:

1. Flint is microcrystalline (the crystals contained in flint are very tiny).
2. It is often associated with some calcium carbonate as described above.
3. It contains small amounts of water that help to rupture the crystal on heating.

It must be stressed that quartz, flint, and silica sand, when pure, are all SiO_2. They differ by virtue of their particle size and impurities and, therefore, the way in which they react when used in ceramics. In some countries craft suppliers market a product simply described as "silica." It would be worthwhile asking your supplier the grade (mesh size) and the crystalline source of the material and, if it is flint, whether there is any calcium carbonate impurity.

As with all materials, a new consignment should be tested against your previous consignment to see whether it gives the same result (if not, slight adjustments to your recipes may be necessary; the Exercises given in the following chapters will help you do this). Powdered crystalline silica should be stored and used slightly damp (about 5% moisture content) so that the powder does not fly through the air when being weighed out. Many manufacturers now supply it with 5 percent moisture added; this should not be allowed to dry out. The adjustment to a glaze recipe is simple: for every 20 g of silica in a recipe add one extra gram to allow for moisture content. The moisture content of your consignment may be tested by weighing out 100 g and heating it until thoroughly dry. The weight loss then represents the percentage moisture content.

Ash

Ash is obtained by burning to drive off the organic matter (carbon compounds) and leaving behind the inorganic (mineral) matter. Some excellent types are listed below:

Bone ash (calcium phosphate) is obtained by burning animal bones. Since this is a very smelly operation, bone ash is best obtained ready to use from a craft supplier.

Wood ash and other plant ash is obtained from carbonaceous (plant) matter. Plants absorb mineral compounds when they take up water from the soil, and these remain in the ash after burning. Wood, straw, or grass ash is obtained by burning in large bonfires. It must be thoroughly burned so that all the charcoal (the portion that contains carbon) is removed. If necessary, this can be completed by placing reasonably well-burned ash in a sagger and firing it to 700°C/1292°F in an outdoor knock-up kiln fired by cylinder gas and (poker style) burner. Small quantities of ash are useful for initial tests, but to maintain a bulk store of ash, ideally a ten-gallon container full should be collected. It might be a mixed wood ash, or the ash of a particular wood. Most wood ashes are high in silica and calcia as well as potassa, soda, magnesia, and phosphorus pentoxide (especially fruitwood ash) and have only 1 or 2 percent iron oxide, unless contaminated during burning or preparation. Small amounts of titania and manganese may also be present, but usually little or no alumina. Straw and grass ash have appreciable amounts of silica (hence the sharp edges on some grasses). They are therefore refractory, and some give a gray-metallic quality to glazes. The analyses of several ashes are given in Appendix Figure A.12 and the surrounding text, but remember that the soil in which the plants grew dictates the final composition of the ash. Seasonal variations in the soil also affect this. The preparation involves a considerable amount of planning and hard work, but the rewards of having a known ash to work with make it well worth the trouble. If you have a bulk supply and obtain a chemical analysis, it can be used as a standard material even in glaze formulation and calculations.

Preparation for burning ash. A large amount of wood needs to be burned in order to obtain a useful quantity of ash (see Figure 6.1). This does not

Figure 6.1. Obtaining wood ash. A full cord, or a woodpile at least twice the size of an average man, is necessary to obtain a garbage-bag-ful of ash.

mean that trees need to be cut, because the very best ash comes from the prunings of fruit trees (particularly apple trees) and some nut trees (my favorite is walnut). Orchardists are usually willing to cooperate. Also ash from a household fireplace (but not wood burned with coal) can be saved over several weeks or even months. Broken twigs and limbs may be picked up from a forest floor. A bonfire should be set on a clean area uncontaminated by iron from the soil, for instance on old broken kiln shelves or cement paving stones (the heat will be high and will probably crack them). A small outdoor fireplace, like that shown in Figure 6.2, is ideal for initial work. The same principles should be applied for larger bonfires. A windless day should be chosen for burning, and arrangements made to cover and protect the smoldering ash from rain and wind as it cools. Alternatively, the ash may be scooped into fireproof buckets of cold water and quenched. This is advisable if you must move the ash. If this is done, it may be considered as a first wash. Do not bring freshly burned ash into the studio; although it may seem to be dead cold, it is a potential fire hazard.

Wood ash contains soluble material (e.g., sodium and potassium carbonates), which many potters prefer to remove by soaking the ash in several changes of water. Any scum or rubbish should be skimmed off. The ash and water should be stirred occasionally and sieved through a coarse (60s to 80s) sieve, then left until the ash settles to the bottom. The water containing the dissolved alkalis may then be poured away, and the ash left to dry. This washing process may be repeated several times and the decrease in the degree of alkalinity of the washing water checked with litmus paper, using the manufacturer's instructions. The amount of alkalis left in the ash is the choice of the potter, and this can be made by assessing the results of test firings.

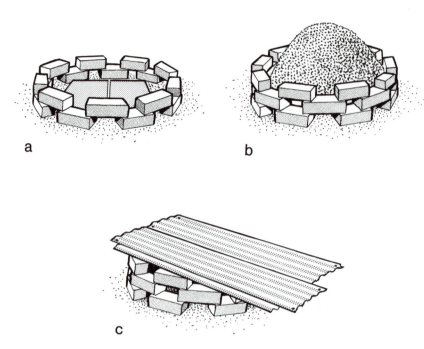

a

b

c

Figure 6.2. Stages in preparing and burning test quantities of ash. (a) Setting up fireplace. The base of old concrete blocks or kiln shelves prevents contamination from iron in the soil. (b) The possible heap of ash from a large bonfire; Figure 6.1. (c) As soon as possible, protect the ash from wind and rain with a waterproof cover. The heap should then be enclosed completely in waterproof sheeting.

In order to maintain the composition of an ash glaze and not lose the remaining soluble alkalis, some potters dry the glazes out after each glaze session (if not required for regular use) and store them dry. Other potters allow the glaze to settle, pour off the clear water, and store that, too, to be returned when the glaze is again required. Occasionally potters find that the alkalinity of the washing water and ash glazes in slip form irritate the skin; if you have sensitive skin you should try to obtain veterinarian's elbow-length gloves and wear them when hand-stirring (old cloth gloves could be placed over them so that the plastic ones last longer).

Grog

Grog (also called *chamotte*) is a grit specially prepared for addition to clay bodies. This may be done in the pottery by firing clay to convert it to a ceramic material (and therefore a material that has lost its water content and is "preshrunk"), crushing it to 0.5 cm or less, depending on the fineness required, passing it through dry sieves, and grading it according to the mesh size through which it will pass. For example, ground grog that will pass through 60s mesh but is caught on an 80s mesh will be graded as 60s down to

80s, or 60s to 80s mesh. Alternatively, grog may be bought already graded. Cheap grog may be made from waste unglazed biscuit ware, or by biscuit firing thin slabs of the chosen clay and crushing them. As a general guide, 10 percent by volume of mixed grog to plastic clay suffices for most work, and mixed grog gives a better aggregate than a single particle size.

The three grades of grog are coarse, 30s to 60s; medium, 60s to 80s; and fine, 80s to dust (see Figure 5.4). The figures quoted above are a guide only to help you to associate mesh sizes with the grades coarse, medium, and fine. If you do not have the exact grades stated in the Exercises, use the nearest grade available. Most glazes are sieved 120s, ash glazes 100s or 80s. Refined materials are generally sold 200s (silica often even finer).

Soft grog has been fired to a temperature lower than the proposed top firing temperature of the clay to which it is to be added. It opens the body, thus helping in the drying process, and if it has been prepared at a sufficiently low biscuit-firing temperature to remain porous, it can absorb moisture from sticky clays, making them more workable. It also provides some grit that helps during the making stage to lock together the slippery clay particles. During firing soft grog participates in the reactions when the temperature exceeds that at which it was prepared. It is also used for mending ware (see below).

Hard grog is made by firing above the top temperature to which the clay work is to be fired, so it remains inert during the first and any subsequent firings of the work and therefore does not shrink. Because it is hard-fired at a high temperature, it is nonporous. Many hard grogs are prepared from fireclay, porcelain body, or stoneware clay, and fired to 1400°C/2552°F. If you make your own hard grog, you should biscuit fire it, crush it, and then high-fire it. If you high-fire it first, it will be too hard to crush.

White fine-grained hard grog is prepared by high-firing kaolin to produce an aluminum silicate ceramic material, also known as "calcined china clay" (tradename *Molochite*). It is fired to well over 1400°C/2552°F to form an inert material at usual studio pottery temperatures. This material is extremely useful in the preparation of white clay bodies and refractory insulating bricks, and where the prevention of distortion on drying and firing is essential. It is also used, mixed with sodium silicate, to mend high-temperature brickwork linings of kilns, where it may be used in the same way as a mortar.

Fire clay grog is often made by industrially crushing high-temperature fire bricks. If it is made from a nearly iron-free fire clay, very pale or white grog may be obtained. However, its most popular use is as an iron-speckled fire clay grog that gives a visual and tactile texture to the fired results.

Pitchers are a special type of grog prepared from the same body to which it is to be added. Having the same composition and color as the body, it blends well with it. Usually fine-ground, pitchers are mixed with a clay body to reduce shrinkage, improve workability, and open the clay body so that it dries more easily and evenly.

Pitchers may be used to mend cracks in sculptural objects. If a small bowl of dry clay from which the object has been made is powdered and biscuit fired beside the object, it will have exactly the same fired characteristics. If required for mending, this grog can be mixed with a little sodium silicate (which does not cause the clay to shrink as water would do). The paste is packed tightly into the crack and carefully leveled off. The piece is then biscuit-fired again. After this, the piece may be glazed, if required, and taken to a higher temperature when the body and pitchers continue to mature together. In many cases, this will completely obliterate the crack. This is ideal for sculptural pieces but not advised for domestic ware or ovenware.

Frits

A frit is a prefused mix of materials. It is prepared by dry-mixing the required proportions of finely divided mineral materials, following by heating the mixture, which, as a result of chemical reaction, forms a homogeneous melt. A typical industrial fritting temperature is 1200°C/2192°F, though some mixtures need higher temperatures. The frit is then cooled quickly so that recrystallization does not have time to take place, and it remains as a noncrystalline glass on cooling. The simplest way to chill the mixture is to pour the molten frit into cold water so that it shatters into small pieces. (In modern industrial plants, a jet of cold air is directed onto the stream of frit as it pours from the frit kiln.) It may be sold in this form or finely ground. If you do not have grinding equipment, make sure the frit you buy has been ground to a powder (most craft catalogs list frits ground to 200s). In Exercise 5 below a small batch of frits will be made, and the value of frits discussed.

Reasons for making and using frits include:

1. To reduce the possibility of silicosis of the lung from crystalline silica dust. Although fine-grained, frit dust is not as sharp-edged as crystalline silica dust.
2. To render toxic material harmless. For instance, melting correct proportions of lead oxide and silica to make a frit locks the lead oxide into the glassy structure of the frit. Examples are lead sesquisilicate ($2PbO \cdot 3SiO_2$, usually stated as $PbO \cdot 1.5SiO_2$) and lead bisilicate ($PbO \cdot 2SiO_2$).
3. To render insoluble materials that would otherwise dissolve in the glaze slip, e.g., calcium borate frit.
4. To achieve blends of oxides in a proportion that cannot be found in any natural material.
5. To lower the firing temperature of a glaze recipe by prefusing a portion of the glaze constituents (see reasons below).
6. To make colored stains.
7. To use as the starting point for glazes to which various additions are made for different effects.

Disadvantages of frits include:

1. Because they do not suspend well in water, glaze slips with a high frit content quickly settle to the bottom of the container, where they form a hard layer. Frequent stirring during use helps; a little calcium chloride (not exceeding 0.1%) or an organic suspending agent, obtainable from a craft supplier, may be added.
2. Frits are not plastic; therefore, glazes containing an appreciable amount of frit do not adhere well to the surface of an object during application. To avoid this, only a portion of the glaze should be fritted. Where there is kaolin in the recipe, put only a portion of the kaolin in the *frit batch*, and add the rest of the kaolin afterward. Warming the pottery or adding a little binder also helps (see "Binders" below).
3. Frits are expensive.

Chemically Prepared Materials

A few materials, such as zinc oxide (ZnO), zirconium silicate ($ZrO_2 \cdot SiO_2$), zirconia (ZrO), and barium carbonate ($BaCO_3$), are prepared using chemical refining processes. Barium carbonate, although occurring naturally as the mineral witherite, is usually chemically prepared from barytes ($BaSO_4$). Zinc is extracted from a complex rock containing several other minerals.

Binders and suspending agents can help to suspend glaze materials that tend to settle in the glaze slip water. This is particularly useful when the frit content is high as in some raku glazes which settle too quickly. Less than 1 percent in a glaze slip is sufficient. Traditional gum binders have certain disadvantages:

1. They cause glaze slips to shrink and crack as they dry on the surface of an object before firing. As a result, the glaze crack may pull apart during firing.
2. They become moldy when stored.
3. If a gum binder is added to a glaze slip and stored, the glaze can become glutinous. This is discussed further in Chapter 10 under thixotropy. It is therefore advisable to add a gum binder only to a small amount of glaze that will be used immediately.

Types that do not cause the glaze slip to become moldy when stored include bentonite (up to 3%) with calcium chloride, and modern binders readily available at craft suppliers. Both traditional and modern binders burn away during firing.

Bat wash is a refractory mixture brushed onto kiln shelves and kiln furniture to save them being spoiled should glazes (and sometimes clay) melt onto them during firing. This is made by mixing alumina hydrate powder or zircon with china clay (in a 2 : 1 proportion) and adding water to make a slurry. This should be stirred well and immediately applied in quick strokes using a wide, strong bristle household brush. This mix may also be used as small dots (small balls) to prevent lids sticking to pots, or at the end of clay supports for sculptures (if supports are used, they should be made from the same clay used for the sculpture so the shrinkage during firing is the same). If salt glazing, use a bat wash of either alumina or silica (not a combination of them) or a mix of calcium carbonate and water.

White marking slip is made by mixing about two tablespoons of kaolin and one tablespoon of ball clay with a little water to a thick but pourable consistency. It should be sieved and kept in a tightly covered container and clearly marked. It is used to brush a small white area onto leatherhard clay or biscuit ware before marking the tests with reference numbers using the marking oxide described below. Alternatively, the reference number may be incised through the slip placed on leatherhard clay so that the mark can be seen clearly after firing (let the slip dry a little before incising).

Marking oxide is made by measuring equal parts (5 ml) of iron oxide, manganese, and cobalt (oxide or carbonate) with a little water; it is stored as above. Some kaolin may be added to give a little body, and a fine brush should be kept with it. This is used to write the reference number of each test on the test tile or object and the firing temperature.

Student Queries About Raw Materials

Students often ask why particular materials rather than oxides are prescribed for use in ceramics. The answer is that they contain the oxides that give the qualities we require. We need the oxides because of the way in which they react together in the presence of heat and, in particular, the way the metal oxides react with silica to produce glass and glazes.

The next question students ask is, "Why not use pure oxides in the first place instead of complicated materials?" The answer is

1. To acquire the purified oxides would involve prohibitively expensive chemical processes. A few have to be made but the number is kept as low as possible.
2. In a complex material containing two or three oxides, the oxides are already intimately mixed, and the job of melting them together is partly done for us (e.g., potassa, alumina, and silica are intimately combined in potassium feldspar, $K_2O \cdot Al_2O_3 \cdot 6SiO_2$).
3. Many of our natural raw materials contain minute amounts of impurities, often unidentified, that contribute subtle qualities to glazed pottery. For example, a found material may contain traces of titanium or perhaps phosphorus, which gives a subtle textured effect and "life" to matte glazes.

The Periodic Table and the Classification of Oxides into Groups

You should now refer to the *periodic table*, where the most important elements used in ceramics are listed (see Appendix 1, Figure A.2). Note the way these are grouped together, and make sure that you know the symbols of the following nine: lithium, sodium, potassium; magnesium, calcium, barium; aluminum, boron, and silicon. Hydrogen and oxygen you will already know. Lead and zinc may be added later.

To help you use this knowledge, carry out the following simple exercise: write down the oxides of each element, then check your answers with Figure 11.1, "Ceramic Table of Oxides." Make a copy of this table and enter the molar weights of each oxide, in color, and pin it over your workbench.

It is important to note that in the simplified version of the periodic table only the atomic weights of the individual elements are given. (The atomic numbers are not included as they are not needed by ceramic students, and could cause confusion and possibly the use of the wrong number.)

Calculating the Molar Weight of a Compound

Add together the atomic weights of the individual atoms, noting the digits before and after each one. This will give you the molar weight, in grams, of that material. For a quick reference, molar weights of oxides and raw materials are listed in Appendix Figures A.3 and A.4 and surrounding text. Later the transition metals will be discussed but it will be a relief to know that — except for iron, zinc, and titanium — the symbols for the rest, namely the elements which form the coloring oxides, do not have to be learned. This reduces the symbols and formulas that have to be learned to a very small number.

If those students who have not studied chemistry accept these merely as abbreviations, which they are, their studies will advance more smoothly. Also you should realize that you are not doing chemistry for the sole purpose of doing chemistry. You are doing ceramics and using chemistry as a means to an end.

A further reason for learning the formulas of these oxides is that many of the reactions taking place in the kiln depend on the ratio of the metal element to oxygen in the oxides. Knowing the formulas helps you to predict the reaction and, therefore, the contribution a particular oxide makes during firing. All this will be explained in the following chapters.

The Function of Oxides in Ceramics

Each oxide has a principal function in ceramics as well as auxiliary functions and these are discussed throughout the book.

In the presence of heat, the oxides discussed above react with one another to lower the temperature at which they melt. In particular, the metal oxides of Groups 1 and 2 and combinations of them react so powerfully with silica (which does not melt until over 1700°C/3092°F when fired alone) that melts can be achieved within the firing range of studio pottery kilns, that is, at temperatures below 1300°C/2372°F and even as low as 800°C/1472°F. Given that these oxides are powerful promoters of melting, they have been allotted a special place in ceramics and have been given the name *fluxes.*

Fluxes

As we saw in Chapter 1, the Group 1 oxides soda, potassa, and lithia form weaker bonds between the metal element and oxygen than the Group 2 oxides calcia, magnesia, and baria. Therefore, less energy is needed to break the bond in the Group 1 oxides. Because of this Group 1 oxides react with silica in the presence of heat at a lower temperature than do Group 2 oxides. Group 1 oxides are therefore referred to as low-temperature fluxes, and the Group 2 oxides are called high-temperature fluxes.

Lead oxides (PbO) and zinc oxide (ZnO) also have a similar fluxing effect. Lead oxide reacts extremely powerfully with silica at lower temperatures, and zinc oxide reacts powerfully in the middle temperature range. They are therefore also called fluxes. Besides the eight fluxes already mentioned, Hamer and Hamer (1991) cite ten other oxides that have fluxing capabilities. Of these, strontia and beryllia are expensive; one, bismuth, is better known for the mother-of-pearl luster it produces at low temperature; six are primarily used in ceramics as coloring oxides, but warrant a place in this list as some of them react strongly with other oxides during firing. Thus, although their presence in a body or glaze should be taken into account, they are not used primarily as fluxes. Of the remaining essential oxides used in ceramics, the characteristics that B_2O_3 shares with Al_2O_3 and the important function B_2O_3 shares with SiO_2 as a glass-former have already been discussed on p. 9 and are further discussed in Chapter 11.

Thus finally we come to alumina (Al_2O_3). The central and unique roles of alumina are

1. As an *essential element* in the structural makeup of *clay crystals.*
2. As a *stabilizer* in molten glazes, where it prevents the glaze flowing off the ceramic during firing. This subject forms an important part of Chapter 11.
3. In the glaze section we shall see that it also acts as a *matting agent.*

EXERCISE 4: Testing the Common Raw Materials

Testing at C.03 (1100°C/2012°F); C.8 (1263°C/2305°F); and C.9 (1280°C/2336°F) when fired at 150°C per hour (or 270°F per hour). See Chapter 5, p. 108 if firing at a different rate.

Because we are concerned here with the three important firings given above, which are regularly used in studio ceramics, Orton Cone numbers are given in this Exercise. If you become thoroughly familiar with these three cone numbers and their temperature equivalents, the others will gradually fall into place.

Aim

To test the fusibility of the raw materials commonly used in ceramics and to study their qualities after firing to C.03 in the earthenware range and to C.8–9 in the stoneware range (or the usual earthenware and stoneware firings used where you are working).

Materials

The ceramic raw materials to be tested are given in Figure 6.3. One set of three tiles is required for each firing temperature. If possible, test at C.03, C.8, or C.9 (see Plate 7).

Method

1. *Making the tiles.* Block up the prepared clay (a standard stoneware body would serve for these tests), and cut six slabs from the block of clay with a cutting harp (see Figure 5.11) or wire, or roll out slabs. Cut six tiles (about 16 cm × 14 cm × 0.5 cm thick). Leave the surface of the tile perfectly flat. *Do not make hollows* to hold the tests as this will prevent the comparison, after firing, of the fluidity of the raw materials and their reaction with the clay body, which is a planned part of this Exercise. Brush a little white marking slip across the top (see Plate 7).

2. *Marking the tiles.* When the tiles are leatherhard, mark them out, as shown in Figure 6.3. This may be done by *inscribing* circles on the leatherhard clay with an old ballpoint pen or a pencil. Do not use marking oxide as this will color the tests. (A coin 3 to 4 cm in diameter may be used to mark out the circles). Leave room to add the formula of each material after firing; putting the formula on the tiles is an invaluable way of reminding yourself which oxides each one contains. Each material must be placed, exactly covering the circle, in the exact position indicated in Figure 6.3. Leave a

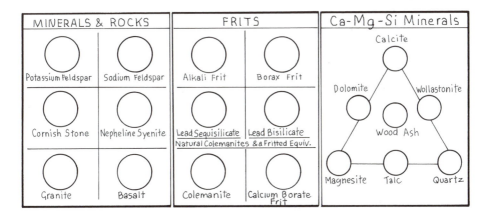

Figure 6.3. Layout of tiles for tests of common raw materials.

blank space for those that you do not have. By keeping this order you will be able to follow the assessment after you have completed and fired the tests.

3. *Drying the tiles.* The tiles may be dried and biscuit fired before applying the tests, or the tests may be placed on the leatherhard clay and the tiles once-fired.

4. *Preparing the raw materials.* Place a tablespoon of each material in a mortar with a little water and grind with a pestle, or grind on a suitable surface with a spatula, palette knife, or muller (a glass implement like a pestle but with a flat end that is grasped and held upright so that the flat grinding surface can be applied to the mix). Remember, these materials do not dissolve in water. Grinding simply reduces the particle size, giving a smooth mix. The water acts as a medium in which to grind the material and as a vehicle to carry the test mix onto the tile. The water then dries away and does not participate in the fired result. These mixes should be the consistency of thick (but not stiff) cream: that is, thicker than that usually used for glazes. Each test should be applied to give an even, smooth coat that just covers the circle, so the results may be compared with one another, particularly with regard to their fusibility and fluidity.

5. *Firing the tiles.* Fire the tiles to C.03 and C.8 or C.9 as directed above.

Assessment

The following assessment refers to the test tiles shown in Plate 7. You should assess your own tiles using these notes and the illustration as a guide. You will find small differences between your own results and those illustrated: these will be due to regional variations in materials and slightly different firing procedures, but the relative differences between the firing performance of the materials within one set of tests should be the same.

1. The tests on Tile 1 are underfired at C.03 but at C.8–9 have begun to give a glassy, though opaque, appearance, some solid still remaining in the newly formed glass. The tests, even at C.8, have not spread out beyond the circle but show, in fact, a tendency to pull in on themselves. By contrast, the frits on Tile 2 have not only fused to a clear glass so that the pottery body may be seen through it, but have flowed beyond the limits of the circles at both C.03 and C.8. The frits have produced fluid melts, whereas potassium feldspar, sodium feldspar, Cornish stone, and nepheline syenite are viscous.

2. Although the frit tests are well fused at both temperatures, there is a difference. At C.03 they are clear but pale; at C.8–9 they look "toasted," particularly the tests that have been placed over a buff or red-firing body. This is due to the greater reaction of the frit with the body at the higher temperature. Some constituents have been drawn from the body into the molten frit so that, on cooling, the glass contains a greater variety of oxides and some color. If a cross section were viewed under a microscope, it would be difficult to see where the body finished and the glass or glaze started. The very fluid alkali frit, in particular, has soaked into the body: a small amount of this gives a good bond, but too much glass in the body makes it brittle.

3. The test on Tile 2 of colemanite has fused well, though perhaps it is

not quite so fluid as the frits. However, it should be remembered that this is a crystalline mineral, not a pre-fused frit, so the crystal structures have to be broken before melting can start. The reason for its greater fusion than that of, say, granite on Tile 1, is that it contains the flux calcia combined with boric oxide, which melts to form a low-temperature glass. Colemanite may produce an opalescent bluish tinge because of bubbles or tiny crystallites in the melt that disperse the light.

4. Returning now to the first four tests on Tile 1, if you view these through a magnifying glass you will see that they are pulling in on themselves. The edges are rounded and almost seem to be lifting off the pottery as they try to roll themselves up into balls. Any cracks will have pulled apart and have rounded edges. This is a typical example of the effects of viscosity acting together with surface tension. The viscosity prevents the melt from flowing out into a thin even layer, and the surface tension pulls the blobs of molten glass in on itself. In ceramics this is called *crawling*, and in bad cases where blobs of glaze have rolled up into globules, it is called *beading*. Viscosity and surface tension will be discussed in detail later in the text; for the moment, it is enough for you to be able to recognize the faults caused by them.

5. The test of Cornish stone shows a halo of darker color around its edge. This is probably a thinner layer of Cornish stone that has reacted with the body during firing.

6. The test of *basalt* on Tile 1, fired at C.03, has not fused, though a color change indicates that some solid-state reactions have taken place. When fired to C.8, the test has fused giving a smooth shiny result, though a little tight. Very little alteration would be required to make this material into a glaze at this temperature, and it should also be useful at C.5 ($1200°C/2192°F$) with the addition of another flux-containing material. At C.9 or C.10 some basalts might give a good glaze when used alone. This is because basalt is a rock containing a variety of minerals, among them ferromagnesium minerals that decompose more readily than the potassium feldspar, mica and quartz contained in granite. The test of granite shows some glassiness and specks of color (the black specks are black mica). However, as the sample has been partially ground by hand, only the finer particles have melted, the coarser particles have remained solid with only the surface of them showing signs of melting.

7. On Tile 3 a triangle has been drawn in which the minerals at each apex contribute single oxides to the melt. Thus calcite ($CaCO_3$) contributes CaO; magnesite ($MgCO_3$) contributes MgO; and quartz (SiO_2) contributes SiO_2. Also, between each pair of these lies a mineral that contributes the two oxides contained on either side of it: dolomite ($CaCO_3 \cdot MgCO_3$) contributes CaO and MgO; talc ($3MgO \cdot 4SiO_2 \cdot H_2O$) contributes MgO and SiO_2; and wollastonite ($CaO \cdot SiO_2$) contributes CaO and SiO_2. This arrangement has been devised in order to help you learn these materials and allow you to relate them to one another. The fired results (see Plate 7) show that the three materials placed at the apices of the triangle are refractory and have remained white and powdery. The results lying between them, where the

minerals contain two oxides in intimate combination, though still under-fired, show that sintering has taken place. The wood ash in the center, which contains all three oxides discussed above plus impurities, has produced (in the sample illustrated) a glassy melt. This result will vary with different ashes; however, unless the ash is high in silica, it should give a more glassy result than the other minerals. From this we learn that while the simple oxides or carbonates of these elements are refractory, intimate mixtures of them in one mineral are more fusible.

The Value of the Calcium-Magnesium-Silicon Triangle

The layout of the triangle used on the test tile in Exercise 4 (see Figure 6.3) should help you to understand how the seven minerals on the triangle may be used in ceramics. If in a recipe you need only one of the oxides (e.g., CaO, MgO, or SiO_2), you would use the single oxide material. If you required two of them then you could select the material that contained both (and this would give you an earlier reaction during firing). It is unlikely that both oxides could be completely filled from the same material; therefore, you would fill one of them completely and fill up the other by using a single oxide material. Later, a more complex situation will be discussed, but the method remains the same.

* * *

Frit Making and Testing

All students should, where proper facilities exist, have the experience of making a frit, either individually or as part of a group. In the Exercise 5 below, a mixture of materials will be used that may be handled without difficulty or danger. The raku method of drawing tests out of a hot kiln is used; therefore, protective clothing should be worn by the operator and any assistants and the precautions regarding kilns observed; see below.

Equipment Required

Crucibles. About six. These may be bought from a chemical supplier or made from a fire clay, stoneware, or porcelain. They should be even in cross section and unglazed. Test pots thrown off the hump (i.e., a number of small pots thrown off the top of a single lump of clay) and lined with bat wash are ideal; otherwise, use thumb pots with very stable bases.

Kiln hook and tongs. A kiln hook is made from clay and biscuit fired for drawing the tests from the kiln at top temperature (see Figure 6.4). A small pair of tongs is useful for picking up the crucibles after they have been drawn from the kiln.

Clothes and gloves. Non-asbestos, heat-proof pottery gloves, thick trousers, leather apron (or similar), and proper shoes (not sandals!).

Kiln. A raku kiln or any small kiln may be used. Do not use a kiln with a large door/opening. Stringent precautions must be taken for all types of kilns. It is essential that the kiln used has only a small opening; otherwise, the operator is exposed to too much heat on opening the door to raku the tests from the kiln. If an electric kiln is used, the electricity must be switched off at the kiln and at the main switch before opening the kiln. It should be emphasized that it is not usual practice to open a hot kiln, but provided the proper safety precautions are taken, treating a kiln in this fashion for this series of experiments should not harm the kiln fabric. If a small raku-type kiln is being used, a *muffle* (ceramic box) can be incorporated or kiln bats used to prevent the flames licking around the tests. If a school demonstration is being held, it is a good idea to put up a barricade to keep students back from the kiln. One assistant should be near the kiln to open and close the kiln door for the operator and if an electric kiln is used, to double-check that the kiln has been switched off.

Bowls. A large bowl containing a little water with a smaller porcelain or pottery bowl placed inside it containing clean water for quenching the frit.

EXERCISE 5: Experimental Frit Making and Comparing a Low-Temperature Fritted Mix with a Raw Mix of the Same Composition

Aim

To test and assess the difference between the firing performance of a given composition of raw materials and that of a fritted mix of the same composition and thereby to understand the value of frits in ceramics. In order to do this the Exercise is divided into two parts:

1. Preparing a raw and a fritted mix of the same composition.
2. Making "cones" of each of these and firing them side by side in order to study their relative rates of deformation.

To ensure that the raw and fritted mixes have exactly the same composition, a double batch of raw materials should be weighed out, mixed well, then divided into two. Half should be kept as the raw mix and the other half fritted, as described on p. 132, and ground to a fine powder.

Firing note. You can make one set of tests consisting of one cone made from the raw mix and one cone made from the fritted mix; fire them side by side, viewing them frequently during firing (wearing heat-proof goggles) and recording (by sketching) their relative positions and noting the temperature. Alternatively, you can make three sets of cones and withdraw a set at stages during the firing in order to keep a permanent record of their relative rates of deformation (again note the temperature).

Materials

A *composition* of 92 percent copper oxide and 8 percent silica has been chosen because it is spectacular (when the molten frit is poured into cold water) and for the several interesting observations that can be made during assessment. As the recipe is a percentage recipe it may be weighed out in grams. You should make a double quantity of the recipe:

92 g × 2 = 184 g copper oxide
 8 g × 2 = 16 g silica (using quartz, as it has less impurity than flint).

One or two crucibles or test pots (see list above) and several small biscuit-fired test tiles or broken pieces of unglazed pottery. These are used as draw-trials, which may be drawn out of the kiln using the tongs or kiln hook (made from a s/w clay and high fired) at various stages during firing to see when a satisfactory melt has been attained.

Method

1. Make the frit mix by weighing out the ingredients to give a total batch of 200 g.

2. Prepare the mix by placing approximately 40 ml (2 tablespoons) of water in a mortar and place weighed materials in the water without raising any dust. Grind this for 5 to 10 minutes, adding more water as necessary, until a smooth consistency is achieved. A rubber kidney (a pliable flat kidney-shaped hand tool) should be used to push the mix down into the mortar and a spatula (or knife) to scrape the mix off the kidney. This mix should then be sieved through a 100s or 120s mesh sieve using the rubber kidney to wipe out the bowl and to push all the mix through the sieve. Do not use a brush, as too much of the mix will be lost on it and impurities may be introduced. The technique used is the same as in glaze making (see Figure 5.12). Thoroughly stir the mix after sieving, and place a 2 to 3 mm thick sample of the mix onto two or three draw-trials. Allow the remaining mix to dry completely, then break it up and dry-grind it until a fine powder is achieved. The purpose of making a wet mix first is to ensure that it is thoroughly blended.

3. Pile the mix up together and divide it into approximately equal halves.

4. Label one half of the mix "raw mix," and place it aside to be used later.

5. Put the other half of the mix in a crucible (which should be only half-full in case the frit is overfired and boils over). Place it in a biscuit-fired kiln tray made from a refractory clay (see Figure 6.4) and set the tray in the kiln, then the draw-trials (they will be drawn from the kiln first). The "frit kiln" should be fired to just under 1060°C/1940°F. At this temperature the kiln should show a bright orange heat color, tinged with cherry red when viewed through the spy hole, and the frit mix should be molten.

6. Turn off an electric kiln, or turn down the gas in a gas kiln before

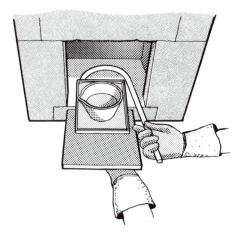

Figure 6.4. Making a frit. Frits are prefused mixtures of mineral materials. Top: frit mix placed in kiln ready for firing. Bottom left: drawing molten frit from kiln with kiln hook onto ceramic bat. Bottom right: pouring frit into cold water.

opening the kiln. Remove a draw-trial from the kiln to see whether the test placed on it has turned to a clear glass. If not, raise the temperature just a little and *soak* (hold the temperature constant) for about 5 minutes, then take another draw-trial out. Repeat, if necessary, until a draw-trial shows a clear melt. Be careful not to overfire.

7. Observing all the safety precautions described earlier, switch off an electric kiln or turn down a gas kiln, and remove the red-hot crucible from the kiln with tongs. Alternatively, slide the kiln tray plus the crucible out onto another (cold) kiln shelf using the kiln hook (have a bench or table ready to slide the tray and crucible onto it, see Figure 6.4). Heat-proof gloves *must* be worn. Immediately lift the crucible with tongs and pour the molten glass frit into the small bowl of water. It will pour like hot toffee and shatter into streamers on entering the water. If it is underfired and still too viscous to pour, place it back in the kiln, and take it to a slightly higher temperature. To save time, two crucibles, each containing some of the mix, could be heated, the second one being left in the kiln and the kiln ready to switch on again if the first frit does not pour easily, but take care that the second one is not overfired.

Grinding the Frit

Goggles must be worn when grinding frit. Frit is a glass, hence precautions must be taken to protect the eyes against glass splinters and powdered glass.

Remove the fritted particles and place them between two layers of closely woven, strong, clean cloth. Using a mallet or hammer, crush the frit as much as possible. Then empty it into a mortar containing a little water. *Place a clean cloth over the particles.* The frit may now be gently, but firmly pounded. Once the larger particles have been broken up, the cloth is removed and the frit ground further, *but keep your goggles on while you grind* the frit to a very fine powder. It is interesting to note the change of color as the powdered stage is reached (but remember that color is deceptive in powdered materials). You now have two mixes: the raw mix and a frit of the same chemical composition but different physical nature. The raw mix is a mixture of crystalline materials; the frit is a homogeneous glass.

Making Cones from the Raw Mix and Powdered Frit

Add a very small quantity of thick binder solution to the raw mix — just enough to make a stiff dough. Roll it out into a coil about the thickness of a pencil, and cut into lengths about 4 cm long. Cut the bottom of each one so that they will tilt slightly when placed upright, about 8 degrees from the vertical toward the right, as shown in Figure 6.5. (The cone will squat toward

Figure 6.5. Three pairs of handmade raw and fritted cones set up ready for firing. Photo: the author.

the direction in which it is leaning when fired.) Make three cones if you intend to draw a set from the kiln at intervals during firing. Gently lift or slide each test cone onto a smooth, clean glazed tile, and mark the tile "raw mix" with marking oxide. Do not mark the cone(s) as the marking oxide may influence the result. Set the tile aside, clean the bench and tools thoroughly, and then make cone(s) from the ground frit powder in the same way and the same size as the raw mix cone(s). The frit will be very crumbly and difficult to model, but broken cones may be remodeled if kept very clean. Place the cone(s) made from the frit on another glazed tile and label it "frit" (see Figure 6.6).

Allow the cones to dry completely; they may be hardened by placing them in a warm kiln or a cooker for about half an hour, which makes them a little easier to handle. At this point it should be possible to mount each cone in a clay support made from a coil of clay and the supports marked "R" and "F" to identify the raw cone from the frit cone. Make sure that the cones are tilting 8 degrees to the right. Set up one frit and one raw cone as a pair on a biscuit-fired tile. If you have made three cones from the raw and three from the fritted mix, set up the other pairs in the same way. These should now be placed in a kiln tray filled with alumina powder (see Figure 6.5). Do not put any alumina powder on the small biscuit-fired tiles for this experiment as you will want to see how the cones deform and flow onto the tiles. Place the cones in the kiln as shown in Figure 6.5.

Firing the Cones

An electric test kiln (as shown in Figures 6.5 and 7.1) is preferable for this test firing. If using gas, protect the cones from the direct flame, and stand a safe distance from the spy-hole when looking into the kiln. Heat the kiln slowly until a dull red color appears; if you fire too quickly you may pass right through the stages you wish to monitor without seeing them. From now on look at the cones every few minutes through the spy-hole wearing heat-proof kiln goggles with darkened lenses until one of the cones begins to bend. *Do not look at the red heat for more than a few seconds at a time.*

Viewing and Removing the Tests

Where only one set of cones have been made, the cones should be viewed through the spy-hole every 10 or 15 minutes wearing heat-proof goggles and their relative positions noted, particularly when the frit cone has bent to the three o'clock and then to the six o'clock position and finally when the frit has completely melted. At each stage shown in Figure 6.6, note the kiln color and/or temperature, and if possible make a quick sketch of the cone positions.

If three sets of cones have been made, the first set may be withdrawn (rakued) from the kiln when the frit cone has bent to the three o'clock position, the second set when the frit squats to the six o'clock position (touching the tile), and finally when the frit has completely melted (i.e.,

1. To the 1 o'clock position.
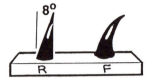

2. To the 3 o'clock position.

3. To the 6 o'clock position.

4. Finally, the fritted cone will squat completely.

5. Eventually, it will soften enough to flow onto the tile.

Figure 6.6. Expected deformation of cones during firing.

disappeared on viewing), as shown in Figure 6.6. Note the temperature and color of the kiln at each stage. Remember to switch off the electricity or turn down the gas before opening the kiln. (Reminder: you have been warned not to use a kiln with a large door opening.)

Assessment

After firing, note that the deformation of the frit cone occurs before the deformation of the raw mix of the same composition at each stage. It may therefore be concluded that a pre-fused glassy mix in which the crystal structures have already been destroyed only requires softening until it flows, whereas a raw mixture of crystalline materials first needs to be heated until the crystals are destroyed and only then will a complete melt occur. In brief, the first is a physical change only; in the second, a chemical change must precede physical deformation.

* * *

Note to Non-Advanced Students

The following section and Exercise 6 have been designed:

1. To give a deeper understanding of the different ways in which fritted mixtures and crystalline mixtures respond when fired; and
2. To use phase diagrams as theoretical devices to study what happens to different mixtures when they are heated.

Although of interest to the advanced student, or those with a science background, omission of this section will in no way impair your understanding of clays or glaze making, or prevent your making any glaze that you wish at the end of the course. A new approach to clays and glazes is given later in the text, and it is on this latter method that the formulation of clays and glazes is based. Those students not doing advanced work should go to Chapter 7.

ADVANCED SECTION

Frits and Phase Diagrams

Introduction to the Study of Phase Diagrams

In Chapter 2, a phase diagram was defined and used to illustrate the cooling history of magma in nature. It is suggested that you review this section before continuing. You should also appreciate the significant differences between the geologist's interest in phase diagrams and the ceramist's.

A geologist is concerned with a molten magma, and therefore with an intimate blend of constituents and the way in which the various minerals crystallize while cooling in geologic time. A ceramist is concerned with the heating history of crystalline materials on a much shorter time scale. It is therefore always necessary for the ceramist to realize that a reaction between two or more constituents will be completed at the temperature indicated on a phase diagram only if sufficient time at that temperature occurs. Thus, given the comparatively short time of a standard pottery firing cycle, completion is very often not possible. It should also be mentioned here that phase diagrams are based on pure materials, whereas ceramic materials contain small amounts of impurities. However, as these hasten rather than hinder reactions, the information gained from phase diagrams is still relevant.

Using a Phase Diagram to Study the Heating History of Mixtures of Two Substances Used in Ceramics

Reminder: There is no time factor in a phase diagram, only compositions and temperatures.

Let us consider first the heating history of mixes of A + B. The melting points (MPs) of these two materials and a large number of mixtures of them are plotted on a phase diagram where the compositions are marked along the base line and the temperatures on the vertical arm as in Figure 2.3. (The methods used to obtain these MPs are much the same as those used to carry out a crossover line blend, as shown in Appendix Figure A.7, though under strict laboratory conditions.) The line joining these MPs is called the *liquidus*, and the lowest point on this line is called the *eutectic point* (Figure 2.3 illustrates these, though here we are concerned with the heating, not the cooling, process).

The eutectic point represents the mixture of A and B (called the *eutectic composition*) that melts at the lowest possible temperature (called the *eutectic temperature*). More explicitly, the eutectic point is the temperature at which the eutectic composition starts to melt and will finish melting if held at that temperature until the process has been completed.

All other blends of A and B will start to melt at the eutectic temperature but will require more heat-work to continue melting the excess material (i.e., the excess above the eutectic composition). Eventually, the melting point as shown on the liquidus is reached where, if the heat is held constant, the rest of the solid will go into solution.

The System Copper Oxide–Silica

With the above knowledge, let us take a quick look at the phase diagram for the system copper oxide-silica (CuO–SiO_2) in Figure 6.7. A simplified version of the phase diagram is given showing the area in which we are interested. The pattern of melting above 1600°C/2912°F is very complex and not required for our discussion and so is omitted. Note that the composition chosen for the frit in Exercise 5 is the eutectic composition and will therefore give us a melt at the lowest possible temperature; it was with this knowledge that this composition was chosen. However, there is no indication on the phase diagram about how long the mix would have to be soaked (i.e., held) at the eutectic temperature in order to achieve a complete melt. Hence, a higher temperature was employed and draw-trials were used to monitor the melting process. The value of this diagram for our work is to indicate quickly, without undertaking a great many trial-and-error tests, the area where useful compositions may be found. The diagram also demonstrates that, by firing at a higher temperature than the eutectic temperature, a small range of compositions lying to the right and left of the eutectic composition should also melt. The significance of this is that it allows for a small margin of error in weighing out, which also applies (in most cases) to glaze making.

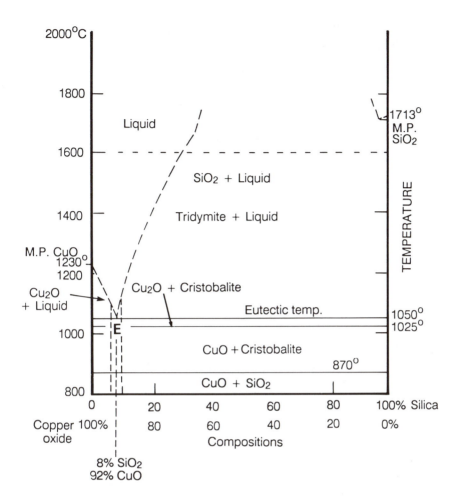

Figure 6.7. Simplified phase diagram for the CuO — SiO$_2$ system. Composition E was chosen for the test frit mixture because the melting history shows it to be the composition with the lowest melting temperature for mixes of copper oxide and silica. Areas above 1600°C are beyond the scope of studio ceramic firing temperatures, and have been omitted for clarity. From American Ceramic Society, *Phase Diagrams for Ceramists*, fig. 2142. Adapted from V. M. Ust'yantsev, L. P. Sudakova, and A. F. Bessonov, *Journal of Inorganic Chemistry* 631 (1966; originally in *Zh. Neorgan. Khim* 11, 5 (1966). Reprinted by permission of the American Ceramic Society. Note that the compilers of *Phase Diagrams* do not consider this to be an equilibrium diagram.

Solid-state reactions. Before leaving this diagram, note the changes that take place in the silica and copper before melting begins and the way in which a phase diagram illustrates this. Quartz changes its physical form but remains SiO$_2$, whereas the change in copper oxide is a chemical one. At 1025°C/1877°F cuprous oxide (Cu$_2$O) converts to CuO. Some other minerals also change their chemical and/or physical form on heating.

EXERCISE 6: Comparative Testing of Raw and Fritted Mixes at High Temperatures

This Exercise is also at the Advanced Level. Phase diagrams are considered in the Assessment, and non-advanced students are advised to go to the next chapter.

Read this Exercise right through before starting and remember to take the precautions given in the section "Making Your Own Frit" above.

Aim

To examine the firing performance of a mix of crystalline ceramic raw materials and its fritted equivalent. A high temperature (C.8–9) is used for this test.

Materials and Equipment

A 300 g batch weight of the recipe given below; two fired, unglazed, evenly potted stoneware test pots lined with bat wash to serve as crucibles (or two bought HT crucibles) about 5 to 6 cm high (make sure that they have stable bases). (It will be necessary to break these test pots during the Assessment.) The recipe given below and the equipment for frit making are the same as in previous frit tests. A small test kiln, gradient kiln, or three separate firings are required for this Exercise.

% recipe	400 g batch weight
35% calcite	35 g × 4 = 140 g calcite
28% kaolin	28 g × 4 = 112 g kaolin
37% quartz	37 g × 4 = 148 g quartz

Two important points that make this exercise different from the simple frit made in Exercise 5 must be kept in mind:

1. This mixture, although it will melt completely given the above firing cycle, forms a viscous melt and therefore will not pour after being drawn from a hot kiln.
2. A high temperature is used to frit the mix. It would therefore be dangerous to draw the frit (or the subsequently made cones) from the kiln at high temperature.

For these reasons, and because the cones are difficult to make by hand, a simple alternative method of preparing and firing the tests is given.

Method

Follow the method used in Exercise 5 to prepare the mix. Divide the mix into two, put half aside as the raw mix, and fire the other half to make the fritted mix. Make one or two small draw-trials, as in Exercise 5, if you have a spy-hole large enough to withdraw them. (You may have to design and make a special small *ceramic* kiln hook.) Put the draw-trials on a kiln shelf, or a piece of kiln shelf placed immediately behind the spy-hole, so that there is no gap between the door, when closed, and the shelf. You will still be able to see the pyrometric cones placed a little further back in the kiln, or a pyrometer only could be used for this test.

Firing the Kiln to Frit Half the Mix

Fill two test pots or crucibles not more than two-thirds full, and fire them to C.9 (1280°C/2336°F) then soak 10 to 15 minutes at top temperature. Test for full fusion by hooking out a draw-trial. If the frit mix has melted, switch off the kiln and open the top vent so that the frit will cool quickly to about 1100°C/2012°F without recrystallization. (If it has not melted, switch the kiln on again and take the second crucible to a slightly higher temperature.) At this temperature, if you are using a test kiln with a small door you can withdraw the crucible (see Figure 6.4). If your kiln is large, wait until it has cooled to 1060°C/1940°F. Quickly plunge the crucible and frit into cold water. This will freeze the frit and, hopefully, shatter it (as well as the test pot).

Making the Cones or Test Pieces

Select pieces of frit that do not have any bits of the pottery attached. As in the previous Exercise, cover the frit with a cloth and grind it (wearing your goggles), then make three cones from the powdered frit and mount them in clay supports. If it is impossible to select pieces of frit without attached pottery, select three pieces with the least pottery attached and mount these as test pieces with the pottery buried in the clay supports. Mark these clearly with "F" on the supports. Make matching cones or test pieces from the raw mix. If you have used frit with pottery attached, make the raw mix test pieces roughly the same size and shape. Mount these in the same way, and mark them clearly with "R" on the supports.

Firing the Test Cones

If using a test kiln, set up three pairs of cones or test pieces, each pair consisting of a raw and a fritted cone. Place the tests one behind the other in a test kiln (in the same or similar way to that shown in Figure 6.5). If possible, place the cone in line with spy-hole. Fire the kiln:

1. At C.03 (1100°C/2012°F) *switch off* the electricity (or turn down the gas) and draw the first pair from the kiln with the kiln hook and/or tongs using the same technique as in Figure 6.4. Then close the kiln again.

2. Turn the kiln full on, and fire to C.3 (1168°C/2134°F). *Switch off* the electricity (or turn down the gas), and draw the second pair from the kiln in the same way.

Figure 6.8. Handmade cones drawn from the kiln at C.03, C.5, and C.7–8. Photo: Peter Bramhald and the author.

3. Now fire the last pair to the top temperature of C.8 (1263°C/2305°F) or C.9 (1280°C/2336°F). Do not remove the cones. Switch off the kiln and cool as rapidly as possible—it is too hot to raku the cones from the kiln. Allow them to cool to 1060°C/1940°F or lower before drawing them from the kiln.

If using a bigger kiln, place one pair of cones clearly in front of a spy-hole, and sketch the positions or shapes of the raw and fritted "cones" at the above temperatures.

Assessment

Set up the three pairs of fired tests in the same order as before, and try to write down your own assessment of the results. Then read the assessment of the examples shown in the photograph (Figure 6.8) in which the comparative differences between the raw and fritted cones should correspond with your own firing.

At each stage in the firing, the frit is further advanced than its raw-mix partner. In the first pair (drawn from the kiln at approximately 1100 to 1150°C/2012 to 2102°F the raw cone is still standing erect while the frit cone is half way over. In the second pair, drawn from the kiln at approximately 1200°C/2192°F, both are bent over, but if you look carefully, you will see that the frit cone has lost its sharp spine and the nose of the cone is rounded, while in the raw cone it is still sharp-edged. Finally, in the third pair, taken to top temperature and cooled quickly by opening the top vent, it is still possible to see the shape of the raw cone, but the frit cone has completely melted and spread out as a glaze on the tile.

The frit, after being exposed to the heat of the kiln during the frit firing, has already completed many of the reactions that take place in the presence of heat, whereas the crystalline minerals contained in the raw mix still have to pass through these stages before softening to give a melt.

* * *

The System CaO–Al₂O₃–SiO₂

There is no published phase diagram for calcite-silica-kaolinite, but because the recipe

35 g calcite, $CaCO_3$
28 g kaolin, $Al_2O_3 \cdot 2SiO_2 \cdot 2H_2O$
37 g quartz, SiO_2

contributes 24 percent calcia (CaO), 14 percent alumina (Al_2O_3), and 62 percent silica (SiO_2) to the melt, it is of interest to look at the phase diagram that concerns these oxides (see Figure 6.9).

As there are three oxides, or *end-members*, the phase diagram has been drawn as a triangle. On it are plotted the compositions of minerals composed of these oxides or combinations of them, for example, pseudo-wollastonite (i.e., high temperature wollastonite), $CaO \cdot SiO_2$, found on the

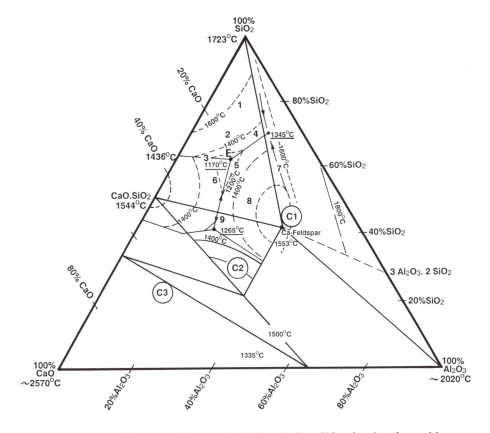

Figure 6.9. Simplified phase diagram for $CaO - Al_2O_3 - SiO_2$, showing the positions of the compositions for tests nos. C1, C2, C3, Exercise 6; and for tests 1 to 9, Exercise 28. Isotherms are shown for the relevant phase fields. Areas above 1500°C are beyond the scope of studio ceramic firing temperatures and have been omitted for clarity. Adapted from E. F. Osborne and Arnulf Huan, *Phase Equilibrium Diagrams of Oxide Systems* (American Ceramic Society and Edward Orton, 1960), fig. 630. Reprinted by permission of the American Ceramic Society and the Edward Orton Ceramic Foundation.

line joining CaO to SiO_2, and calcium-feldspar, $CaO \cdot Al_2O_3 \cdot 2SiO_2$, found in the body of the diagram and therefore containing all three oxides. Kaolinite and calcite do not appear on the diagram because they both contain other oxides — water in the case of kaolinite and carbon dioxide in the case of calcite. For this reason, the heating performance of our mix will not correlate exactly with a mix free from water and carbon, but since the water and carbon dioxide are given off early in the firing leaving calcia, alumina, and silica, the diagram will give some guidance about the course of the melting process.

The following points are pertinent to the understanding of the diagram:

1. The compositions of minerals that exist in this system (minerals consisting of CaO, Al_2O_3, and SiO_2) are marked by points on the diagram, and these points are joined together, thus dividing the large diagram into a number of smaller ones called *phase fields.*
2. There is only one eutectic point for each phase field.
3. Because a three-dimensional model would be necessary to include temperatures, these have been projected down onto the flat surface and are recorded either as spot temperatures or as lines joining all points having the same temperatures (just as heights are recorded on a geographical survey map).

Our composition (24%CaO, 14%Al_2O_3, 62%SiO_2), falls in the phase field (pseudowollastonite-calcium feldspar-silica) and lies on or very near the spot marked 1170°C/2138°F. If you look carefully at Figure 6.9 you will see that this is the lowest temperature in the phase field — it is the eutectic point for this field. All compositions in the pseudowollastonite-calcium feldspar-silica field are tied to the 1170°C/2138°F eutectic point. That is to say, on heating any composition in this field the first liquid to appear will be at 1170°C/2138°F, which will have the eutectic composition.

The patterns of melting are as follows:

1. A test mix of the eutectic composition will melt at 1170°C/2138°F *given sufficient time at that temperature to complete the melting process.*
2. All other compositions will produce some melt of the eutectic composition, at the eutectic temperature until they can no longer provide a melt of that composition. They will then require more heat to draw the remaining solid into the melt.
3. The further a composition lies from the eutectic point, the greater amount of excess material it will contain and the more heat required to draw the remaining solid into the melt.

The composition chosen for the above Exercise, which contributes 24 percent CaO, 14 percent Al_2O_3, and 62 percent SiO_2 corresponds to the eutectic composition, so we may deduce from the diagram that it will produce the first liquid on heating at 1170°C/2138°F (or very near it if we make allowances for the materials used and the breakdown and escape of the carbonate and the water) and that, if held at this temperature for a sufficient length of time, it will completely melt. This is supported by a laboratory experiment in which a test sample was taken to 1170°C/2138°F and held at this temperature until it completely melted. Fortunately, this took 24 hours, not geologic time. This laboratory experiment was a satisfactory method to use for a one-off test, but pottery kilns are not normally held at one temperature for this length of time, and you are not expected to undertake this experiment. Instead, the principle that lies behind fritting may be employed, and the mix super-heated to the temperature at which a melt may be achieved within a reasonable time. In this case, experiments demonstrated that this was 1270°C/2318°F with a short soak to clarify the melt and so give a clear glassy result on cooling.

Conclusion: Frits and Phase Diagram

1. The study of phase diagrams has highlighted the value of the concept of heat-work as a function of *time × temperature* (see Figure 6.10). That is, given sufficient heat input to enable the melting to proceed, a reaction between two or more constituents may be achieved by firing, either at low temperature for a long time, or a high temperature for a short time. A theoretical corollary to this principle is that, with experience, a modification to the above firing procedure, i.e., an in-between firing cycle, could be chosen, for example, a temperature between 1170°C/2138°F and 1270°C/2318°F with an intermediate soaking time.

2. Phase diagrams may sometimes be consulted when adjusting the composition of a frit to see in which direction the composition should be moved. This could be either nearer the eutectic point for greater fusibility or further from it to reduce the amount of abrupt melting. Or — beware — the diagram might show that even a small move in a particular direction could carry a composition into another phase field with a very high eutectic temperature.

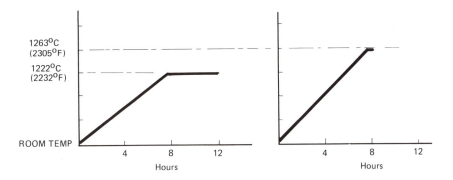

Figure 6.10. Time and temperature profiles. Heat treatment (heat work) depends on the top temperature and the length of time the work is fired.

3. In clay bodies the variable grain size and the fact that only part of the clay melts makes it impossible to predict the order in which reactions take place during firing or the composition of the melt that forms in the body. To a certain extent, this also applies to glazes, hence the marginal active use in studio ceramics of phase diagrams. Their real value to studio ceramists is as an aid to the learning process.

4. From the above observation, the conclusion must be drawn that, although phase diagrams are useful in the study of the melting process in ceramics, they have a restricted use in the formulation or alteration of compositions. An important exception to the above general statement involves the 1170°C/2138°F eutectic composition lying in the phase field: pseudowollastonite-calcium feldspar-silica of the system $CaO-Al_2O_3-SiO_2$ as described above.

Potters did not have to wait until phase diagrams were invented in order to discover this eutectic point. As Nigel Wood has pointed out, Chinese potters were using glazes that correspond closely to the 1170°C/2138°F eutectic composition in the $CaO-Al_2O_3-SiO_2$ system as early as the twelfth and thirteenth centuries. Wood's research (1978) has revealed that glazes fired in very different parts of China, and therefore made from different clays and mineral matter, have produced very similar results. This probably occurred because approximately 65 percent local clay and 35 percent limestone (or other calcia-bearing material) were used. This kind of composition falls close to the 1170°C/2138°F eutectic composition. These wood-burning Chinese climbing kilns were fired to 1200°C/2192°F or a little over with a very long firing cycle, these potters were, in fact, using the concept of heatwork as a function of time × temperature long before the scientific explanations were formulated.

■ ■ ■

1

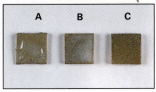

$^1/_{10}$ Alumina

2

A   B   C

4A

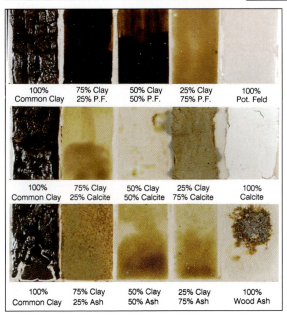

3

4B

100% Common Clay	75% Clay 25% P.F.	50% Clay 50% P.F.	25% Clay 75% P.F.	100% Pot. Feld

100% Common Clay	75% Clay 25% Calcite	50% Clay 50% Calcite	25% Clay 75% Calcite	100% Calcite

100% Common Clay	75% Clay 25% Ash	50% Clay 50% Ash	25% Clay 75% Ash	100% Wood Ash

5

6

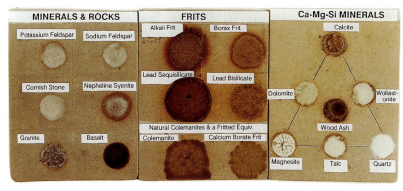

MINERALS & ROCKS

Potassium Feldspar   Sodium Feldspar

Cornish Stone   Nepheline Syenite

Granite   Basalt

FRITS

Alkali Frit   Borax Frit

Lead Sequisilicate   Lead Bisilicate

Natural Colemanites & a Fritted Equiv.
Colemanite   Calcium Borate Frit

Ca-Mg-Si MINERALS

Calcite

Dolomite   Wollast-onite

Wood Ash

Magnesite   Talc   Quartz

7

Single Materials
C.8--C.9

Blends of Two Materials.
Firing Temp. C.8-C.9

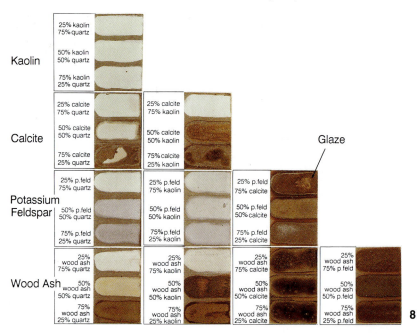

Kaolin

25% kaolin
75% quartz

50% kaolin
50% quartz

75% kaolin
25% quartz

Calcite

25% calcite
75% quartz

50% calcite
50% quartz

75% calcite
25% quartz

25% calcite
75% kaolin

50% calcite
50% kaolin

75% calcite
25% kaolin

Glaze

Potassium
Feldspar

25% p.feld
75% quartz

50% p.feld
50% quartz

75% p.feld
25% quartz

25% p.feld
75% kaolin

50% p.feld
50% kaolin

75% p.feld
25% kaolin

25% p.feld
75% calcite

50% p.feld
50% calcite

75% p.feld
25% calcite

Wood Ash

25%
wood ash
75% quartz

50%
wood ash
50% quartz

75%
wood ash
25% quartz

25%
wood ash
75% kaolin

50%
wood ash
50% kaolin

75%
wood ash
25% kaolin

25%
wood ash
75% calcite

50%
wood ash
50% calcite

75%
wood ash
25% calcite

25%
wood ash
75% p feld

50%
wood ash
50% p.feld

75%
wood ash
25% p.feld

8

Quartz   Kaolin   Calcite   Potassium
Feldspar

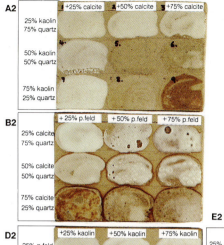

A2

+25% calcite | +50% calcite | +75% calcite

25% kaolin
75% quartz

50% kaolin
50% quartz

75% kaolin
25% quartz

Three Blends

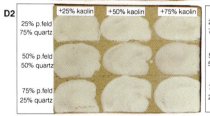

B2

+ 25% p.feld | +50% p.feld | +75% p.feld

25% calcite
75% quartz

50% calcite
50% quartz

75% calcite
25% quartz

E2

D2

+25% kaolin | +50% kaolin | +75% kaolin

25% p.feld
75% quartz

50% p.feld
50% quartz

75% p.feld
25% quartz

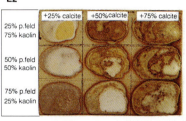

+25% calcite | +50%calcite | +75% calcite

25% p.feld
75% kaolin

50% p.feld
50% kaolin

75% p.feld
25% kaolin

9

Four Blends

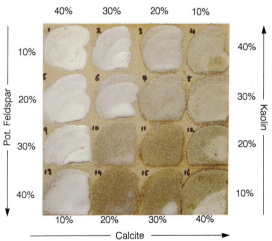

Quartz

40%   30%   20%   10%

Pot. Feldspar

10%   40%

20%   30%

Kaolin

30%   20%

40%   10%

10%   20%   30%   40%

Calcite

10

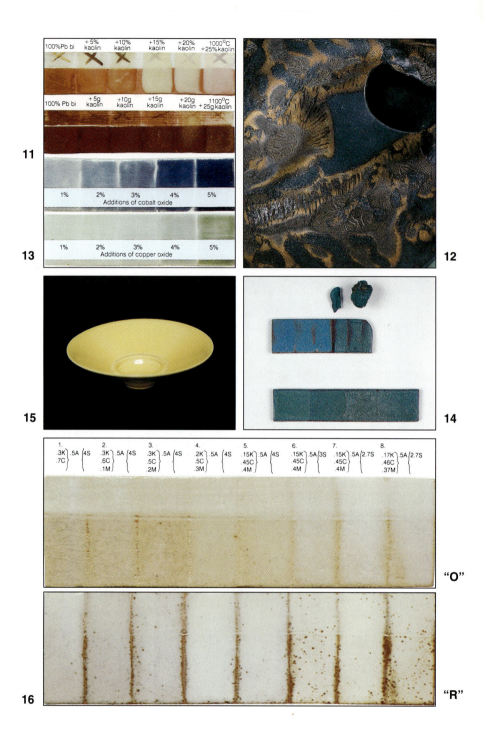

11

13

100%Pb bi	+5% kaolin	+10% kaolin	+15% kaolin	+20% kaolin	1000°C +25%kaolin

100% Pb bi	+5g kaolin	+10g kaolin	+15g kaolin	+20g kaolin	1100°C +25g kaolin

1%	2%	3%	4%	5%

Additions of cobalt oxide

1%	2%	3%	4%	5%

Additions of copper oxide

12

15

14

1. .3K .7C	.5A	4S	2. .3K .6C .1M	.5A	4S	3. .3K .5C .2M	.5A	4S	4. .2K .5C .3M	.5A	4S	5. .15K .45C .4M	.5A	4S	6. .15K .45C .4M	.5A	3S	7. .15K .45C .4M	.5A	2.7S	8. .17K .46C .37M	.5A	2.7S

"O"

16

"R"

.3K ⎫ .6A ⎫ .5Si
.7C ⎭

.6K ⎫ .6A ⎫ .5Si
.3C ⎬ .1Mg ⎭

.24K ⎫ .72A ⎫ .4Si
.22C ⎬ .54Mg ⎭

.3K ⎫ .5A ⎫ .4Si
.5C ⎬ .2Ba ⎭

.5Na ⎫ .2A ⎫ 2.7Si
.5Ba ⎭

.26K ⎫ .3A ⎫ 2.3Si
.53C ⎬ .21Ba ⎭

10% Fe₂O₃

5% Fe₂O₃

1% Fe₂O₃

0.5% Fe₂O₃

17

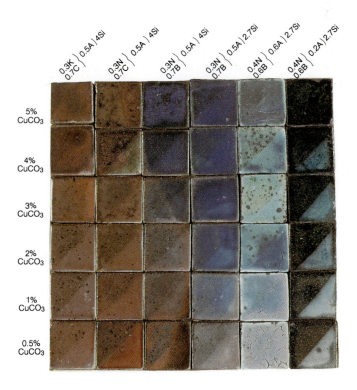

0.3K ⎫ 0.5A ⎫ 4Si
0.7C ⎭

0.3N ⎫ 0.5A ⎫ 4Si
0.7C ⎭

0.3N ⎫ 0.5A ⎫ 4Si
0.7B ⎭

0.3N ⎫ 0.5A ⎫ 2.7Si
0.7B ⎭

0.4N ⎫ 0.6A ⎫ 2.7Si
0.6B ⎭

0.4N ⎫ 0.2A ⎫ 2.7Si
0.6B ⎭

5% CuCO₃

4% CuCO₃

3% CuCO₃

2% CuCO₃

1% CuCO₃

0.5% CuCO₃

18

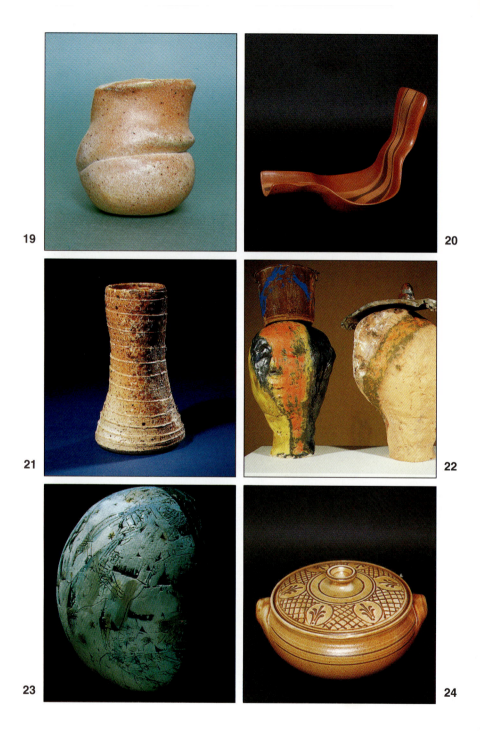

19

20

21

22

23

24

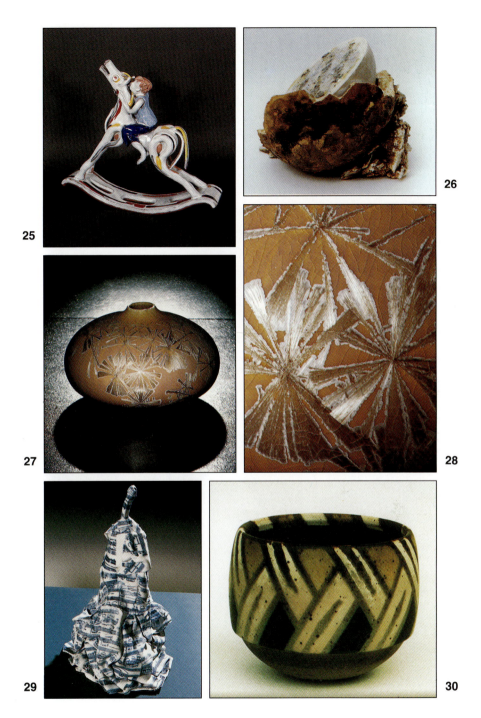

25

26

27

28

29

30

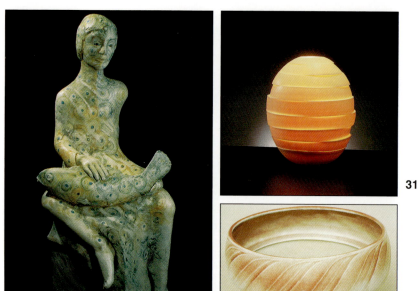

31

32

33

34

Captions for Plates 1–34

Plates 1–18. General technology and assessment of exercises

Plates 19–34. Work by ceramists with Notes on the Technology Involved.

Plate 1. A mole is the modern (SI) unit of quantity of a chemical substance. This plate shows 1 mole of lead oxide, 1 mole of alumina from which 1/10th ($0.1Al_2O_3$) has been drawn out, and 1 mole of silica. This demonstrates that a mole of a chemical substance can be seen by the naked eye whereas a molecule cannot. Photo: the author.

Plate 2. Four balls of natural clay showing some of the different colors in which natural clays are found. From left to right kaolin, La Borne s/w clay, ball clay, and a local common clay. Each ball contains 100 g (dry weight) of clay. (See Figure 7.4, "Typical colors of natural clays before and after firing.") Photo: the author.

Plate 3. An example of fired results of Exercise 8. Shown are three different natural clays fired to several temperatures. Reading from top to bottom: row 1 fired to 1116°C/2041°F; row 2 fired to 1155°C/2111°F; row 3 fired to 1189°C/2172°F; row 4 fired to 1226°C/2238°F; row 5 fired to 1259°C/2298°F; row 6 fired to 1280°C/2336°F (see "Assessment" in Exercise 8 for discussion). Photo: the author.

Plate 4A. A test to show that a formula filled by materials contributing more than one oxide increases the fusibility of a glaze. In the tests illustrated, the composition 24% CaO, 14% Al_2O_3, 62% SiO_2 was prepared using (a) calcite, alumina, and quartz (all single oxides); (b) calcite, kaolin, and quartz (kaolin containing two oxides); (c) wollastonite, kaolin, and quartz (wollastonite and kaolin both containing two oxides). It is clear from the photograph that (b) is more fusible than (a) and that (c) (with two materials containing more than one oxide) is more fusible than (a) and (b). Photo: the author.

Plate 4B. The effects of glaze constituents on color. These tests all contain nepheline syenite, kaolin, silica, zinc oxide, and iron oxide. In addition the green test contains calcite and talc; the pink dolomite; the blue dolomite, titanium dioxide, and extra zinc oxide. Tests and photo: Paola Ragni, Canary Islands.

Plate 5. An example of fired results of Exercise 20, "Triple Crossover Line Blend"; see the Assessment for further description. Tests by students of the Ceramics Department, Goldsmiths' College, University of London. Photo: the author.

Plate 6. Dry ash surface treatments on porcelain body. All consist of a mix of 33.3% kaolin + 33.3% ball clay +33.3% apple wood ash plus 1 to 5% increments of brown stain. The bottom tests contain unwashed ash, the next, ash washed once, while the top tests contain ash washed 5 or 6 times.

Plate 7. Single ceramic raw materials, example of results of Exercise 4. Photo: Mike Taylor.

Plate 8. Blends of two materials, example of results of Exercise 28. Photo: Mike Taylor.

Plate 9. Blends of three materials, example of results of Exercise 29. Photo: Mike Taylor.

Plate 10. Blends of four materials, example of results of Exercise 30. Photo: Mike Taylor.

Plate 11. Fired test results of additions of kaolin to 100% lead bisilicate frit fired to C.06 and C.03 shown over a red e/w clay body (see Exercise 32). Photo: Mike Taylor.

Plate 12. Black porcelain with luster screen print. The screen print was taken from a photograph of a cloud formation and a standard screen printing process was used to print directly onto soft leatherhard procelain. With careful handling, the clay was then modeled into shape (see Exercise 42). Screen print: the author. Photo: Derek Large. (Blyth's medium for direct screen printing, 65/101 was used in the above process; Mason Stains, Colorworks, E. Liverpool, Ohio should have a similar one; and Walkers, Australia, market a suitable underglaze meduim no. 1.)

Plate 13. Tests showing the increasing depth of color obtained from increments of 1–5% cobalt oxide and copper oxide. See Exercise 44. Photo: Mike Taylor.

Plate 14. Malachite glaze tests. See Exercise 46. Photo: Derek Large.

Plate 15. Vanadium yellow stain (containing tin oxide) in Kambalda glaze. This glaze was derived from test no. 16.8 (see Plate 16) which, with two trial-and-error tests, was adjusted to 30% potassium feldspar; 15% calcite; 15% talc; 28% kaolin; 12% quartz. To this 8% vanadium stain (containing tin oxide) was added and the pot fired in oxidation to 1300°C. Photo: Derek Large.

Plate 16. Magnesium glaze tests. A series of tests developed from the Seger C.8 test, no. 14 formula of $(0.3K_2O; 0.7CaO; 0.5Al_2O_3; 4SiO_2)$. The tests show that the addition of 0.1 and 0.2 MgO clears the glaze to transparency; with further additions the glaze becomes cloudy, then matte, with a quiet sheen at 0.4 MgO so long as the SiO_2 is kept at 4 moles. With a drop in the silica (glass) component the glaze becomes stony; with a further drop to 2.7 moles of silica the glaze is rough and unpleasant (there is too little glass). This was redressed by increasing the powerful flux K_2O by 0.02, to 0.17 K_2O, and dropping the magnesia to 0.37 MgO, to give a still stony glaze but with a hint of a sheen or shine. This is an excellent glaze for sculptural pieces, easily adapted to suit local materials (see Exercise 38). Photo: Derek Large.

Plate 17. Iron oxide tests. The effects of specific oxides in the glaze on iron oxide. See Exercise 45. Photo: Mike Taylor.

Plate 18. Copper carbonate tests. The effects of specific oxides in the glaze on copper carbonate. See Exercise 45. Photo: Mike Taylor.

Plate 19. Elisabeth Joulia, France. Made from La Borne local clay where Elisabeth Joulia lives, this pot, which fits so comfortably in the hand shows not only the superb sculptural abilities of this artist but the marvelous plasticity and good yield point (see Figure 5.5) of this local s/w clay. This is the gray clay shown in Plate 2. It was fired in a small wood burning, home-built kiln.

Plate 20. Helen Swain, UK. *Flowing Vessel.* Made from a LT terracotta, a fine grained e/w body. The form was burnished to improve the smooth surface and then coated with a mixture of red iron oxide and a LT frit. Some of the iron/frit mix was flicked off the underside when dry, giving a textural appearance, and the whole again thoroughly burnished before firing to 1046°C/1915°F. Subsequently, Helen polished the surface with antique wax. This produced an unpleasant wooden shine so she burned it off in a LT firing, leaving a smoked look on the "handle" which, fortunately, was rather pleasing. The form was then heated and oil applied very carefully, followed by a light polish with antique wax. At present on loan to the Art Gallery of Western Australia. Photo: Derek Large.

Plate 21. Janet Mansfield, N.S.W., Australia. *Flower Vase.* 33 cm high. Made from s/w clay with added crushed granite. Carved incisions were made on the surface and the piece once-fired in an anagama style kiln for three days in order to achieve a natural ash glaze (from the fly-ash in the kiln). Firing temperature 1320°C/2408°F. Photo: the artist.

Plate 22. Xavier Toubes, Spain/USA. *Exquisite Nomades.* Xavier mixes his own clay body to get the required diversity of particle size, plasticity, and strength to withstand multiple firings from e/w to s/w and raku. The sculpture is made from a clay mix of natural clays together with talc, nepheline syenite, wollastonite, and mixed grog. The form is hand-built and covered with a white slip. The dry orange-red areas have been coated with a raw lead glaze and the piece is also decorated with both oxides and stains. Xavier fires his work in gas and electric kilns, usually bisque to C.1, then fired again up to 4 or 5 times, first to C.6–7, then C.04 and C.07 and finally rakued at C.05. Photo: the artist. (*Note:* The raw lead glaze used has been applied to a sculpture and used by an expert ceramist. See p. 12 for precautions.)

Plate 23. Kari Christensen, Norway. *Day and Night.* The work is made from Dutch Wingerling clay, a high manganese clay body with a fine grog content which is excellent for surface decoration. It is compounded for 1100°C/2012°F, but Kari finds that it works well for her at 1200°C/2192°F. After the surface is carved, a white slip, made from a porcelain body, (range 1200–1300°C/2192–2372°F) is brushed on in layers so that it does not go into the carved areas unless this is wanted; it is left thinner in places where the body is to show through. The work is then biscuit fired at 960°C/1760°F. Afterward colored stains mixed with water are brushed on as a wash where required, with glaze in some areas. The piece is first fired in an electric kiln to 960°C/1760°C and then in a gas kiln to 1200°C/2192°F in reduction. Photo: Knud Larsen.

Plate 24. Janet Kovesi Watt, UK/Western Australia. The piece is made from a 50/50 mixture of two locally produced s/w bodies, one buff and fairly open textured, the other white and dense, with the addition of 10% 80s mesh grog. The pattern was trailed on when the pot was leatherhard, using a slip made from the body clay itself, minus the grog but plus 4% of red iron oxide. The pot was raw glazed when leather-hard with a satin matte glaze made from local materials including tin ore, and once fired to 1280°C/2336°F in a natural gas kiln, with moderate reduction to 1000°C/1832°F. Photo: Derek Large.

Plate 25. Esme Shorter, New Zealand/UK. *Rocking Horse Hero.* The piece was modeled in a very fine grained red-firing, LT clay body with moderate plasticity which is excellent for modeling. After being left to dry slowly and very thoroughly, it was biscuit fired to approximately C.06 (1000°C/1830°F), then glazed with white tin glaze containing 10% tin oxide and glaze fired to C.02–01 (1120–1137°C/2048–2079°F). The work was painted with enamels as soon as possible before the ceramic absorbed any moisture, and fired to 730°C/1346°F. The kiln door was left ajar for the first 400°C/752°F and the firing monitored carefully until all the medium had vola-tilized and escaped from the kiln. Esme now fires a little higher and judges maturity by inspection. Photo: Derek Large. (See p. 300 for white tin glaze.)

Plate 26. Bingul Basarir, Turkey. The form was made in two parts: one from a refrac-tory clay only, the other from a special body prepared by mixing pieces of lignite coal and adding it to the clay to create a form without losing the texture of the coal. This was very fragile but made strong enough to handle by dipping it into clay slip and a little glaze (for strength after firing) and leaving it to set. At this stage it could be modeled into shape and joined with the first part. The work was then biscuit fired to 1080°C/1976°F, and decorated where required with glaze and glass cullet (a colored glass sold in small lump form). The final firing was done by placing the work in the firebox of the solid fuel kiln and firing to approximately 1080°C/1976°F. Photo: Ozturk Basarir.

Plates 27/28. Arnold Zahner, Germany. *Crystal Glaze.* A high temperature porcelain body that fires to 1320°C/2408°F has been used (a HT natural s/w body covered with a porcelain slip, as an engobe, could also be used). The glaze consists of 40.0% frit having the chemical formula of $2ZnO \cdot SiO_2$; 7.8% lithium carbonate; 8.4% Scandinavian feldspar; 19.8% mixture of two LT frits (containing Na_2O, K_2O, and B_2O_3); 2.0% kaolin; 22.0% quartz. To this 100% recipe was added 8% manganese carbonate. For this type of glaze the firing cycle is crucial and must be monitored accurately. The piece illustrated was fired quickly to 1282°C/2339°F and the firing stopped immediately. The kiln was then cooled quickly to 1150°C/2102°F and held at 1150°C/2102°F for four hours. No special seeding agent was added to the glaze. Photo: the artist. (See p. 300 for crystalline glazes.)

Plate 29. Maria Gesler, Hungary. *The Voice of the Night.* 61 cm high, made from a porcelain body. The clay has been rolled out very thinly and silk screen printed with a cobalt oxide paste made by mixing the coloring oxide with a medium, then folded to create the form. The work was fired in a gas kiln to 1360°C/2480°F in strong reduction (note: cobalt oxide works well in "O" and "R" giving strong blues in both, but the hue may be affected by other oxides present; see Figure 13.1). Maria used antifreeze as a medium. Photo: Dallos Laszlo. (There are also commercial mediums available; see Plate 12.)

Plate 30. Ursula Scheid, Germany. The wheel-thrown vessel form was made using a pyrite-bearing s/w clay body, biscuit fired at 980°C/1796°F and brush decorated with several different colored slips. One containing iron gave a greenish color; another containing stains gave a pink where laid on thinly and white with a thicker application. The blue-black color was achieved from a slip containing cobalt. At this stage the vessel was biscuit fired again (this fixed the colors so that the surface was no longer powdery which might otherwise prevent the glaze adhering to the body). The work was then fired in a gas kiln to Seger C.12 (1360°C/2480°F) in reduction. Reduction was started at 1000°C/1832°F, and was heavy from this temperature to 1280°C/2336°F. After this a lighter reduction was used to top temperature. Photo: the artist. See Exercise 43.

Plate 31. Margaret O'Rorke, UK. Porcelain lamp, thrown 28 cm high, made from a porcelain body specially developed by Christopher Hogg of English China Clay (UK) and produced by Valentine's Clay, Stoke-on-Trent, for Audrey Blackman's rolled figures. Margaret finds this ideal for her sculpted lights. When the clay is firm but not dry (Margaret uses a blow torch to achieve the exact state of firmness required) the form is cut into rings; each ring made slightly oval and then reassembled using vinegar to moisten the joints. (The vinegar lubricates the parts without causing shrinkage problems.) The work is unglazed and fired to C.10 (1300°C/2372°F). Photo: Chris Honeywell.

Plate 32. Ann Roberts, Canada. *With a Fish in Her Lap.* Life-sized sculpture made of a LT white talc clay body with 15% added grog. The whole sculpture was covered with a high zinc matte glaze and fired to Orton C.01 in oxidation. Overglaze stains or metal oxides were mixed with a frit and used to paint on the surface before firing again to Orton C.06 to set the colors but not to disturb the surface of the matte glaze. The imagery in this work concerns an ongoing interest in women as lifegivers or players in the life cycle of the River of Life. Photo: the artist.

Plate 33. Karl Scheid, Germany. A thrown porcelain form with carved decoration. The surface was covered with a white feldspathic glaze and a blush of copper carbonate was then sprayed on with an airbrush held at a distance from the pot. Following this, another very light spray of glaze was applied over the copper carbonate layer. The copper thus developed both downward and toward the surface, giving a softer coloring. The work was fired to Seger C.12 (1360°C/2480°F) with a heavy reduction from 1000°C/1832°F up to 1280°C/2336°F and finished in a lighter reduction atmosphere. Photo: the artist. See p. 366.

Plate 34. Ken Bright, UK. *Reflective Image No. 7.* 194 x 176 cm. One of sixteen exterior wall panels based on architectural reflections at J. Sainsbury PLC Building, Bromley,

Kent. The panels are produced from handmade relief tiles with polychromatic surfaces applied by spraying, marbling, and brushing. The clay body used is Potclays "T" material, which is a refractory, low-shrinkage clay body and fires near-white. The tiles are covered with vitreous colored slips consisting of 50% Hywhite superb ball clay and 50% Wengers China clay No. 2 plus 15% addition of Ferro- (Great Britain) Ltd., Borax/zinc frit 210703 (compositions: 0.04 K_2O, 0.10 Na_2O, 0.16 CaO, 0.71 ZnO, 0.08 Al_2O_3, 0.27 B_2O_3, 1.00 SiO_2, molar weight 163.52). For the different colors, 8% to 10% additions of body stains were made and each colored slip sieved, then ball milled for 12 hours. The tiles were once fired in oxidation to C.8 (1260°C/2300°F). Photo: the artist.

Part II
Clay Bodies, Slips, and Casting Slips

Chapter 7
Preparing and Testing Natural Clay for Workshop Use

Introduction

In this chapter we consider the cleaning and preparation of raw clay, that is, clay as dug from the ground. If you have not participated in fieldwork it is possible to obtain a small amount, say ten kilograms of clay, as dug, from a potter who makes garden terracottas or flower pots, a small brickworks, or a local clay pit. Although only a small amount of clay is prepared here, the instructions can be used as a guide for those who wish to refine larger amounts at a later date. The techniques used in this chapter are used again in the preparation of clay bodies in Chapter 9. The main aim in this chapter is to instill a better understanding of clay, its constituents, and its potential in ceramics.

EXERCISE 7: Cleaning and Preparing Clay

Aim

To prepare clay for use as (1) a plastic body and (2) a dry powdered clay for future experiments to make clay bodies, slips, and glazes.

Materials

You need a bucketful of clay, a mallet (or geological hammer), mortar and pestle, and 60s–80s sieve. If you have access to a geological department a rock crusher could be used.

Method

1. Break up the dry clay into small lumps (about 2 to 3 cm across) with a mallet or geology hammer or in a small rock crusher (used in some college

geology departments) and soak in water. If your clay is slightly damp, allow it to dry completely before crushing. It is very difficult to break up damp clay, and big lumps will not reduce to a slip easily when placed in water. Soft wet clay may be soaked immediately. Pick out any sticks, stones, plant matter, or other debris that can be seen with the naked eye.

2. Let the clay slip soak for several days in plenty of water, stirring occasionally until an even slurry is achieved. Then add more water, if necessary, until it is thin enough to pour through a sieve. Common surface clay is often high in calcium. If the sample does not break down easily, make up a mixture of 5 g sodium hexametaphosphate (Calgon) to 1 g caustic soda (sodium hydroxide, NaOH). Add a little at a time to see whether it is effective, letting the clay stand for a few days between additions. If this does not work, try sodium silicate, again a little at a time. The sodium mixture can affect the plasticity of the clay, but this can be neutralized once a smooth slurry has been achieved by the addition of calcium chloride, also added a little at a time.

Warning. The sodium mixture is caustic, so do not make up a large quantity at a time, label it clearly, lock it away between applications, and throw it away when you have finished with it. *Do not leave it within the reach of children,* and *never mix it in a drinking vessel* (this also applies to household bleach).

3. Stir the slip thoroughly by hand and check that there are no lumps of clay left in it. Sieve the clay slip through a 30s or 40s mesh sieve. If you wish to check the proportion of the various grain sizes of the mineral content, you can set up a stack of sieves (with the coarsest one on the top) and note how much grit is left on each sieve after the slip is poured through the stack. If possible, note the mineral content of the grit by examining it under a microscope. Any white lumps should be tested for calcium carbonate using the hydrochloric acid test (see p. 70). Note the grit sizes present, particularly any that stay on the 30s mesh (this is too coarse for an average throwing body, but it could be sieved out using the above technique if there is not too much of it.) The grit may then be thrown away and the sieves thoroughly washed.

4. Allow the slip to settle for several days, when the clear water may be poured away gently. The remaining thickened slip may then be dried back to the plastic state by one of the methods suggested in "Workshop Practice" (see Figure 5.9). Check the slip regularly, and as soon as it reaches a workable plastic state cut it in half. Wrap half in plastic and store in a moist place (approximately 10–15°C/50–60°F). Use the other half to achieve a powdered clay as described below.

5. Preparing dry powdered clay. Do not allow the slip to dry in a solid mass. The best method to obtain dry *powdered* clay (in contrast to the above) in a small workshop is to spread the clay out thinly on a cloth-covered plaster slab or other absorbent surface in a dry, warm place. Small test amounts can be dried very quickly by placing paper-thin slabs over a hot kiln (see Figure 7.1). At this stage, it should be relatively easy to crush and reduce to a powder, but make sure that the mortar and pestle are completely dry. Other-

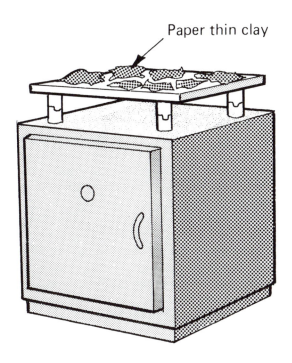

Paper thin clay

Figure 7.1. Method for drying test amounts of clay on top of a hot kiln.

wise, the clay will not grind properly. Having done this, place the powder in a jar and label it clearly as local clay with the location where it was found. Powdered local clay will be used in several experiments throughout the course of this text. You should now have a lump of plastic local clay and a jar of dry powdered clay.

*   *   *

EXERCISE 8: Firing Characteristics of Natural Clays

This is a very important Exercise that will be referred to later with respect to other clays. (A fired set is shown in Plate 3.)

Aim

To test the firing characteristics of natural clays as dug or with only a minimal amount of cleaning.

Materials

If you have brought back several clay samples from your field trip or are able to obtain samples from several different regions, they should be prepared as plastic clay as described in the previous Exercise. Three or four of the most workable ones should be selected and used in these tests (see Figures 5.5 and 5.6 for tests of workability). You will also need some firm cloths.

Method

Making the tiles from one clay type is described below. Repeat this for the other clays. Make a fat coil and cut it into four equal lengths; lay each piece in turn between two cloths together with the rolling guides (square section wooden sticks about 0.5 cm thick), so that you get all the slabs exactly the same thickness. Roll out the clay until it is just over 10 cm long. After each roll, loosen the top cloth, replace it, then turn clay and cloths over, making sure that you keep the clay slab flat. The second cloth, now the top cloth, should then be loosened, and the slab rolled again until it has the size and thickness required. Cut and mark each clay test tile as shown in Figure 7.2. Again take care to keep the clay flat.

If the particles of clay are bent out of alignment, enough of them will remain in this position to cause the tiles to return to the bent shape (i.e., warp) as the water dries off. This is, no doubt, the origin of the saying, "clay has a memory."

If you have gradient kiln facilities, then make as many tiles from each clay as the design of the kiln permits.

Measuring the wet to dry shrinkage. When the tiles are bone dry, measure the length of the incised 10 cm lines and note the wet to dry shrinkage of the four clay types. Since 10 cm = 100 mm, this gives you the amount of shrinkage per 100 mm, that is, the percent shrinkage. You should enter these figures in your notebook.

Firing

1. Make kiln test trays from refractory clay for each set of tests, and arrange the tiles ready for firing as shown in Figure 7.3. (If using a gradient kiln, make sure the kiln trays fit the compartments.) Many local clays will bloat, deform, or even melt at high temperatures, hence this precaution.

2. Fire each set to a different temperature (e.g., 1000°C/1830°F, 1100°C/2012°F, 1200°C/2192°F, 1280°C/2336°F), or temperatures near these that fit in with your own workshop firings. If the actual top temperatures reached are different from the intended firing temperature, the original temperatures should be crossed out and the correct ones entered on the tile with a permanent marking pen or fine-line brush and marking stain (see Chapter 5).

Assessment

Set up your tiles for assessment. Each clay type should be grouped together in order of firing temperature (see Plate 3). Note that the lowest fired tile is placed at the top of each group. Substitute your own data where necessary. Now assess your tiles for the following, making comparisons in each case

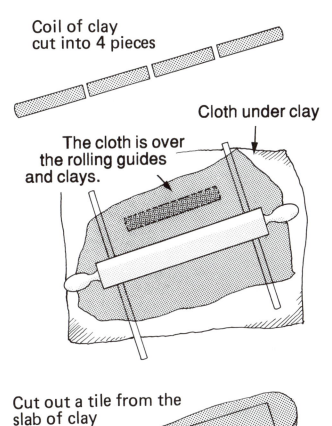

Coil of clay
cut into 4 pieces

Cloth under clay

The cloth is over
the rolling guides
and clays.

Cut out a tile from the
slab of clay

Incise a line exactly 10 cm
long and define both ends.
Mark the tile with the name
of the locality.

10 cms
Fremington

Inscribe your initials clearly
on the back of the tile and
the firing temperature.

1200c   JJ

Figure 7.2. Preparing clay tests for Exercise 8, "Firing Characteristics of Natural Clay."

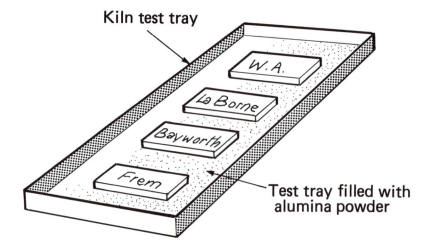

Figure 7.3. Set of tiles, one tile of each type of clay, ready for firing to the same temperature. A similar set should be made for each firing temperature tested.

between like tiles fired at different temperatures and the different clay types at the same temperatures:

1. Shrinkage
2. Fired color
3. Porosity
4. Strength and faults
5. Texture
6. Personal evaluation

1. *Percent shrinkage.* Measure again the incised line, and compare it with the original 100 mm (10 cm) length (see above) to get the overall drying and firing shrinkage. About 10 percent to 12 percent is a reasonable shrinking rate; 15 percent is too high as it is difficult to visualize the final size of a piece during the making stage and the chances of warping are high. Remember that fine-grained clays have a film of water around a very large number of particles (see Chapter 4). By the same token, if you have brought back from the field a very fine clay which you suspect might be a ball clay, a result of 15 percent shrinkage in this test could reasonably confirm that it is a ball clay. Particularly if in the initial field tests it proved to be highly plastic and if it fires near-white, it could be valuable. In the above we have discovered the shrinkage rate by practical means. For future reference:

$$\text{percent shrinkage} = \frac{(\text{original length} - \text{fired length}) \times 100}{\text{original length}}$$

2. *Fired color.* Compare the fired color of the clay with the color before firing and try to assess the reason for a change in color where this occurs. To

help you do this a table of raw and fired colors of natural clays is given in Figure 7.4, together with the likely causes of color changes during firing (see Plates 2 and 3, and descriptions in the color catalog).

Natural color (before firing)	Fired color (after firing)
Rust red. This indicates the presence of red iron oxide (Fe_2O_3).	This will change to a terracotta color after firing. The higher the temperature, the darker the color.
Dirty yellow. The clay probably contains hydrated forms of iron oxide. If the clay is fine-grained, crumbly yellow earth, it is called yellow ochre. A brighter orange-red variety is called red ochre. The important mineral in such an earth is goethite, which is the pigment, ochre.	These will fire a yellow ochre to a bright orange red ochre.
Gray to black. This indicates the presence of carbonaceous matter and/or black iron.	
1. When the color is due to black iron oxide (FeO).	On firing in an oxidizing atmosphere, the iron will take up more oxygen and convert to red iron oxide, Fe_2O_3. If the iron content is over 2%, it will fire pinkish salmon; if over 5%, a darker rust red. As the temperature rises the color darkens.
2. When the color is due solely to carbonaceous matter, i.e., decayed (carbon containing) plant matter.	The carbonaceous matter will, given careful firing, burn away. The result, in theory, is a white ceramic body. However, most clays that contain carbonaceous matter also contain some iron, as described in no. 3 below. Clays such as black ball clays are exceptions to this rule.
3. Some clays contain carbonaceous matter and a little black iron.	If these clays are given careful firing to oxidize the iron and burn off the carbon, a warm cream body may result. However, very often the carbon prevents the complete reoxidation of the iron, so some of the iron remaining as black iron oxide, causes the fired clay to fire a dirty white.
White. Clay that is considered to be iron-free.	Although called iron-free, there is always a little iron oxide present. This can be proved by firing samples in oxidation (which will give a cream tint) and in reduction (which will give a slightly bluish tint).

Figure 7.4. Typical colors of natural clays before and after firing.

3. *Porosity: Water absorption* is a convenient means to test porosity. A simple test is to touch the pottery with the tongue. If the tongue tends to stick to the pottery surface, the pottery is still very porous. The professionally accepted way of estimating porosity is to weigh the four tiles when completely dry (preferably kiln-dried and warm), and record these weights. Then soak the tiles in boiling water for 5 hours. One way to do this would be to fill a thermos with boiling water, then gently slide the tiles into it and screw down the stopper. After the tiles have soaked for 5 hours or overnight, wipe any surface moisture off them using a lint-free cloth, then reweigh the wet tiles and record their weight. Set out the figures as shown below and carry out the calculations. The calculations should be taken to three decimal places for accuracy. Example in which the percent porosity is expressed as water absorption:

Weight of soaked tile = 34.663 g
Weight of dry tile   = 34.021 g
Difference in weight = 0.642 g

$$\text{Percent porosity} = \frac{\text{difference in weight} \times 100}{\text{weight of dry tile}} = \frac{0.642 \times 100}{34.021} = 1.887\%$$

Repeat this calculation for all four tiles, and then compare their porosity. In studio pottery, 2 percent porosity is acceptable. The few pores remaining allow a little movement, giving a cushioning effect so that the body is not too brittle. Some studio potters accept up to 5 percent, and, to ensure nonabsorption, use a glaze that does not craze.

Note that, during the early stages of firing, a body is very porous up to about 600°C/1112°F, when the ceramic change occurs. Then, as firing continues, some pores close together; in others, molten "glass" accumulates. The pores begin to fill with glass, which means that, on cooling, the ceramic object has a reduced porosity; its water absorption factor is decreased. If the firing is continued until the optimum firing temperature is reached, 2 to 5 percent porosity may be expected in the cooled ceramic. If overfired, the body becomes honeycombed with tiny cavities as materials that should remain in the body begin to volatilize. Bloats and blisters appear, and the body becomes lighter and porous again. Finally, complete melting may occur.

4. *Strength and faults.* It is suggested that you read this section through before carrying out the assessment. Very simple methods of testing will be used. Here only the fired strength is tested; in industry, the greenware (prefired) strength is also measured.

Allow the fired tiles to dry overnight, then set them up in order of firing temperature. Break each tile in turn, starting with the tile fired at the lowest temperature. *Do this over white paper*, and observe whether any black powdery material falls out or is left in a cavity in the fired body. As you break the tile, try to estimate the degree of effort required to break it. It should be relatively easy to snap the first low-temperature tiles, but increasingly difficult to break the higher-fired tiles. However, if too much glass has formed in the body, it becomes brittle, and the tile will break easily.

Note: If it becomes difficult to break one of the tiles with the hands, place the tile halfway across a pencil and apply pressure on both sides.

Even listening to the sound of breaking helps: the low-fired tiles are softer and break with a dull sound, while the harder-fired tiles break with a sharper sound. Make a note of the firing temperature of the tile in each set that gave the strongest result, and examine the broken profile where you can see the internal texture of the fired body. Can you find an example where the surface is a shiny, almost glassy coat while the inside still looks like biscuit ware? Is there any black or gray core in this example, or in any other tests, where the carbon has not been burned out of the clay? Are there any empty cavities caused by trapped volatiles?

Comments on the above faults:

Shiny surface, less well-fired interior. A clay showing these features has been fired too quickly. The body will not be strong and there is a danger that, if it is glazed, the glaze will not adhere properly to the vitreous surface.

Black core. This is a fault seen particularly in common clay that has not been fired slowly enough to allow all the carbonaceous matter to burn away as carbon dioxide gas (see Chapter 5). Such clays require very slow firing in the early stages (between 700°C/1292°F and 900°C/1652°F) with the kiln vents wide open in order to allow the gas to escape.

Bloating. This may occur in association with the above fault or when iron pyrite (FeS, or iron sulfide) is naturally present in the clay. On dissociation of the FeS during firing, sulfur gas may form and expand with the heat. If it is unable to escape (firing too quickly is the classic cause), the gas may form bubbles trapped below the surface of the fired ceramic. However, remember that bloating may be due to incorrectly prepared clay. If air bubbles are left in the clay, they will expand on firing. These may not be seen until after a second high-temperature firing when the trapped air or gas expands considerably. Thus, should bloating occur, the making method, rate of firing through the early stages, and the amount of oxygen in the kiln atmosphere during the early stage of firing should be queried.

Overfired body. If a clay has been fired to a temperature above its proper firing range, it may show a honeycomb appearance inside. This may be seen by viewing the interior at a broken edge. Also, gases that would not have formed at or below the correct temperature in their rush to escape, may form mini-volcanos (see Plate 3). Overfiring in conjunction with a reduced atmosphere could cause the oxide of iron Fe_2O_3 to be reduced to FeO, which has a much lower melting point and can cause excessive melting and distortion or collapse of the work.

5. *Texture.* Examine the surface of each tile carefully and compare the tiles fired at different temperatures. Do some of them look tight and slightly shiny while others look less dense or dull and with an earthy appearance? Compare the surface textures of the fired tiles as well as the various textures at their broken edges.

6. *Personal evaluation.* Make your own assessment of the color. Part of this must be a value judgment. That is, after assessing the other fired characteristics of the tiles and establishing the optimum firing range, you may choose the temperature within this range that gives what is, in your opinion, the best color and degree of porosity for the work you wish to do. For example, if you intend to make water coolers you need a porous body so that, in use, evaporation occurs through the wall of the pottery vessels and keeps the contents cool.

*   *   *

Chapter 8
Clay Bodies: Using Blends of Natural Clays

Introduction

There are several ways in which a clay body may be compounded. In the last chapter we dealt with clay as dug. Here we shall make clay bodies by blending two or more natural clays in the plastic state (either as dug or refined). Additions of grog and plasticity are also tested. In the next chapter we shall compose bodies from dry raw materials, using natural and chemically produced materials.

The clays used in this series of tests consist of the four well-known types of natural clay. These are listed below together with the reasons for including them here. For full descriptions of each type, see Chapter 4.

EXERCISE 9: Blending Natural Clays in the Plastic State

It is not necessary to keep the test tiles made in this exercise after the fired assessment, so students in a studio class can work in groups of three. Each student can prepare a set of tiles and each set is then fired to a different temperature (e.g., 1100°C/2012°F, 1200°C/2192°F, 1280°C/2336°F). If you are working alone, make two sets of tiles, then use an earthenware and a stoneware firing or your usual temperature range.

Aim

1. To demonstrate that it is possible to make a clay body by blending natural clays, that is, clays as dug or after cleaning and refining.
2. To make you familiar with the properties of each clay type.
3. To assess the amount of water required to achieve optimum workability.

If the work is shared, it is important that everyone gets the opportunity to handle each clay type in order to obtain thorough familiarity with the characteristics of each clay and the effects of combining one clay with another. It is also important that everyone joins in the final assessment.

Materials

We shall use the term *dry weight* when referring to *dry powdered clay* (see Chapter 10).

For the tiles you will need 400 g dry weight of each of the following four clays:

1. *Common red-firing clay* is used here to introduce fluxes and color that have been well dispersed through the clay. It is also used for its plasticity.
2. *Kaolin* is used for its whiteness and refractoriness and is sometimes included solely to raise the firing temperature of a body. It may also be used to lighten the color of a clay body or to achieve pure white bodies. The degree of plasticity of the kaolin available in your area should be noted.
3. *Ball clay* is used chiefly for its plasticity.
4. *Fireclay* is included for texture and decorative effect in those fireclays that contain specks of iron pyrite. Most fireclays are refractory and are used for high-temperature bodies and many contribute plasticity. Alternatively, a natural stoneware clay could be used (see Plate 2).

As different clay types mix with different amounts of water to give optimum plasticity, it is more accurate to state and record the proportions of each clay by reference to their dry weight. Thus, if you have clays that are already in the plastic state with good workability, they are ready for use, but you must make a calculation for each clay to find the amount of plastic clay that will give the required dry weight. Calculations to achieve this are given below.

Method

Preparing the Clay

Plastic clay. The simplest way to calculate the amount of plastic clay required (in terms of dry weight) is to weigh out a 100 g sample, dry it thoroughly (see Figure 7.1), and weigh it again. For example, let us suppose that the dry weight of the sample is 70 g. We need 400 g for our experiment. The formula to use is

$$\text{weight of plastic clay required} = \frac{\text{plastic weight of sample} \times \text{dry weight required}}{\text{dry weight of sample}}$$

$$\text{plastic clay required} = \frac{100 \times 400}{70} = 571.4 \text{ g plastic clay is required}$$

Dry powdered clay, ready to use. You can weigh out 400 g dry weight of each directly, and render them down to the plastic state by the addition of water. The clay should then be allowed to rest for a week or more, if possible. If you measure the water you can record the amount added and calculate the percent water content. (For this you need to know that 1 ml of water weighs 1 g; proof of this is given in Chapter 10.) If you do this you will find that finer clays require more water and take longer to dry.

At this stage the water content may be adjusted if necessary. If too stiff, a little more water may be added; if too wet, the clay may be dried back to the plastic state by wrapping it in cheesecloth and hanging up for a short while (check it frequently). If the clay has been swamped with water, start again.

Wrap each ball of clay in plastic, and set them aside in a damp, warm place for at least a week before proceeding to allow the clay to become thoroughly and evenly wet. Plasticity may also improve, though several months would be required as a minimum time for marked improvement.

The clay may be prepared in bulk for a large group of students, but if this is done it should be by demonstration.

Now unwrap the four parcels of clay. If any are too soft, dry them back to a workable state by rolling them on a dry porous slab. You should then examine each one for plasticity. Try the finger tests for workability and plasticity (see Figures 5.5 and 5.6). If the clay cracks, add 2 percent bentonite (8 g for every 400 g dry weight of clay). Kaolin is a likely candidate for this treatment. Remember that bentonite must never be added dry. Mix it with a little water and add as a thin paste. Knead each ball thoroughly with your fingers.

Set out the balls of clay, and cut them into eight segments. This may be done by eye, but try to do it as accurately as possible.

Making the Tiles

Instructions are given for one set of tests consisting of 15 small test tiles in each set. These will be fired together to the same temperature. A set should be made for each firing temperature you intend to use. It is suggested that you use the coil method for making tiles (see Figure 7.2).

Figure 8.1 provides illustrated instructions for blending the clays. Follow these carefully. Mark the back of each tile with your initials and the firing temperature. Do not forget the 10 cm line.

Firing Instructions: Standard Procedures

Dry and place each set in a large kiln test tray (see Figure 7.3) to keep them together and in case they melt. Fire each set to a different temperature using the following temperatures or as near as possible.

Suggested firing temperatures. Reminder: Orton Cones are quoted and indicated by C (see Appendix Figure A.5).

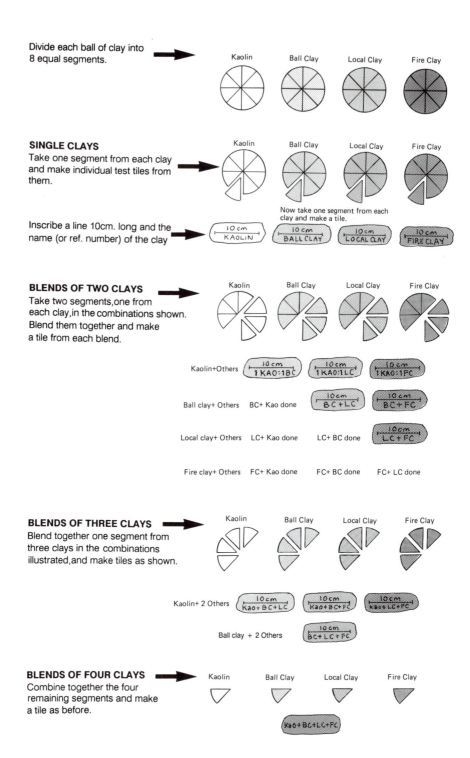

Divide each ball of clay into 8 equal segments.

SINGLE CLAYS
Take one segment from each clay and make individual test tiles from them.

Now take one segment from each clay and make a tile.

Inscribe a line 10cm. long and the name (or ref. number) of the clay

BLENDS OF TWO CLAYS
Take two segments,one from each clay,in the combinations shown. Blend them together and make a tile from each blend.

Kaolin+Others
Ball clay+ Others   BC+ Kao done
Local clay+ Others   LC+ Kao done   LC+ BC done
Fire clay+ Others   FC+ Kao done   FC+ BC done   FC+ LC done

BLENDS OF THREE CLAYS
Blend together one segment from three clays in the combinations illustrated,and make tiles as shown.

Kaolin+ 2 Others
Ball clay + 2 Others

BLENDS OF FOUR CLAYS
Combine together the four remaining segments and make a tile as before.

Figure 8.1. Blending four different natural clay types. BC = ball clay, LC = local clay, FC = fire clay, Kao = kaolin.

1. C.03–C.02 (1101–1120°C/2014–2048°F)
2. C.4–C.5 (1186–1196°C/2167–2185°F)
3. C.8–C.9 (1263–1280°C/2305–2336°F)

A firing rate of 150°C/270°F per hour should be used. If you wish to use a different rate, make a note of this and the *temperature at which the firing cone squats* (enter this in your notebook or on the back of the tiles). Keep a firing log or graph of the temperatures × time and details of the firing cycle. From this you can determine the rate of firing in that particular kiln.

Assessment

Follow the methods used in the "Assessment" in Exercise 8, making special note of the following points.

Shrinkage. Calculate the percent rate of shrinkage of all clays tested. An acceptable shrinkage rate is usually between 10 and 12 percent. If the proportion of ball clay is high the shrinkage rate can be as high as 14 percent.

Fired color. Look carefully at the variations in color among the different clay types used, and note these differences in your notebook. This information will be useful when you compound clay bodies in Exercises 12 and 13.

Texture. A coarse-grained fireclay with an appreciable iron content can give iron speckles, which are more obvious after glazing.

Porosity. Note the fired strength and any faults. If overfired, porosity can increase again.

Optimum firing temperature and use. After a thorough examination of the tests, consider which of the clay mixes can be used and the optimum firing temperature and the type of objects and making techniques for which those clays would be suitable. When making your final choice, consider the workability in the plastic state as well as the fired result. Record your observations and useful recipes.

*   *   *

EXERCISE 10: The Effect of Adding Grog to Clay

You should review Chapter 6 in conjunction with this Exercise. These tests will not be fired.

Aim

Our aim is to assess the effects of adding grog to clay on workability, texture, and firing strength.

Before adding grog to a bulk amount of clay body for a particular piece of work, the wise potter dries and fires a sample (standing it upright in the kiln) in a shape pertinent to the work to be undertaken. This will test the clay's firing strength and make sure the grog does not alter its fusibility. The grog is weighed in this exercise in order to carry out a controlled experiment (see p. 121 for "hard" and "soft" grog).

Keeping careful records of the amounts used is important for repeating results. For one-off pieces, many experienced potters put up a pile of clay and a pile of grog, judging the percentage amount of grog required by eye. They simply wet the grog and add it, little by little, wetting extra grog if necessary, until it feels right for the work intended.

Materials

You will need 1200 g of a fine-grained powdered clay or the equivalent plastic clay (see method of calculating the amount of plastic clay that will give the dry weight required on p. 160) and the grog specified below. If you do not have the exact grades specified, use the nearest ones available, and keep a record of their grades. If you wish to make your own grog, see Chapter 6. (Weights of clay refer to dry weights.)

Percent clay plus additions	*Bulk recipe*
100 g clay + 10 g coarse grog (30s–60s)	400 g clay + 40 g coarse grog
100 g clay + 10 g medium grog (60s–80s)	400 g clay + 40 g medium grog
100 g clay + 10 g fine grog (80s–dust)	400 g clay + 40 g fine grog

The mesh sizes in parentheses are only a guide to help you associate the grades: coarse, medium, and fine with the mesh sizes (see also Figure 5.4).

Method

Preparation of the Clay Body

Render 1200 g dry weight of clay down to a soft plastic state by the addition of water. Knead it with the fingers, and note the extent to which it is smooth and fine-grained and whether it yields to pressure easily (see Figure 5.5). Try forming it into a shape, and note whether it holds the shape or slumps. If you are using ball clay, note its relatively limp quality in contrast to, say, the local clay you handled in previous experiments. Divide the clay into three equal pieces by weight. Each piece will contain 400 g dry weight of clay.

Preparation of Grog

Weigh out 40 g of each of the three grogs listed above. Place each grog in a separate bowl with just sufficient water to cover each grog. Drain the water off when the grog is thoroughly dampened. Always remember that grog must be added slightly damp or it will dry out the clay too much.

Adding the grog. Add the coarse grog to the first piece of clay, the medium grog to the second piece, and the fine grog to the third. In each case you should add the grog in small amounts at a time, and stop when you feel that the amount added is satisfactory. Mark each piece clearly with the type and proportion of grog added. This may be estimated by eye or more precisely by drying the leftover grog and subtracting the weight from 40 g. Enter the percentage amount of grog added and the name or reference number of the clay body in your notebook.

The usual method of adding grog is to block up the clay and cut it into slabs with a cutting wire (see Figure 5.11). Spread the damp grog on the clay with a palette knife, pile the slabs one on top of the other, and cut through in the opposite direction. Then wedge or knead until the grog is evenly distributed.

Assessment

1. Critically examine each mix of grogged clay for texture and workability, and compare one with another. Rub a little between your finger tips to feel the grittiness that has been added. If you put it to your ear you should be able to hear the bits of grit grinding against each other as you rub. Try to make a coil of the grogged clay. Does it crack? A good clay mix will not do this. Also try the finger test (see Figure 5.6). Cut the clay through with a cutting wire, and observe the way the grit drags through the clay, scoring it. This should be particularly marked in a body containing coarse grog.

2. Make a ball of each grogged clay, and divide each one into four or eight segments (as in the previous Exercise). Try several mixes, for example, one segment containing medium-grogged clay and two segments containing fine-grogged clay. Do this until you have some idea of the effect mixtures of grog have on the workability and texture of the clay. Try to establish which textures you would require for different types of work. For example, you may think one is good for throwing and another good for coiled work. If you like a particular blend, you should enter it in your notebook for future reference. Do not let the clay dry too much during this Exercise; if necessary, wedge in a very small amount of water.

Calculating a recipe. Because each ball has 400 g dry weight of clay, there is 50 g dry weight in each of the eight segments. Since each 400 g contains 10% grog, we have 40 g in each ball of clay and 5 g grog in each segment.

Let us now suppose that the final choice from the above tests is one segment of clay containing coarse grog and two segments of clay containing fine grog. The first requires 50 g dry weight of clay and 5 g coarse grog, the second, 100 g dry weight of clay and 10 g fine grog, for total requirements, expressed in percentages, of:

150 g clay	91%
10 g fine grog	6%
5 g coarse grog	3%
165 g total	100%

Note your own calculated recipe(s) in your notebook. Because these can only be rough estimates, you should weigh out another test of the clay and the grog addition that seems satisfactory and assess it. Slight trial-and-error adjustments should then be possible and the desired recipe recorded. However, the object of this exercise is to give you a concentrated study of the tactile qualities of adding grog, so you may become familiar with its effect on the texture of clay bodies.

* * *

EXERCISE 11: Achieving Plasticity in Low-Plastic Kaolin by Adding Ball Clay

Aim

To establish how much ball clay needs to be added to kaolin to achieve plasticity.

Materials

You will need 100 g dry weight kaolin and 100 g dry weight ball clay, choosing as near-white firing ball clay as possible. You may also need some bentonite. The method used in the previous Exercise is employed here, using kaolin for the clay fraction (clay body portion) and substituting ball clay for the grog.

Method

Render both powdered clays down to the plastic state and form them into balls. Leave the kaolin in one piece and divide the ball clay into eight segments as shown in Figure 8.2. Each segment of ball clay now contains 12.5 g dry weight of clay (see Figure 8.2). Add the pieces of ball clay to the kaolin, one by one, kneading the mix thoroughly between each addition and assessing the plasticity.

One whole ball of
Kaolin = 100g

100g Ball Clay
divided into segments,

+ 3 small segments
of Ball clay =18.75g

Figure 8.2. Adding ball clay to kaolin to achieve plasticity. See also Plate 2.

You may need to cut one or two segments of ball clay in half if you are near to a workable plasticity. Once you know the amount of ball clay to add to give a good working property, record the amount of ball clay added in your notebook. You should then make and fire several test pieces to assess any loss of whiteness.

Also, to save further test firings, you should make several tests with smaller amounts of ball clay and add bentonite at the plastic state to achieve the required plasticity. Do this by adding bentonite in increments of 0.5 g dry weight, wetting the bentonite before addition, until good workability is achieved. Calculate the proportion of ball clay that gives good workability (and note the best bentonite addition) as in Exercise 9, and record the percentage recipe.

Firing and Assessment

In order to assess the possible development of color from the iron oxide introduced by ball clay, make up and fire the following mixes. For high temperature, to 50 g of the clay mix add 25 g potassium feldspar and 25 g silica. For low temperature, to 70 g of the clay mix add 25 g Cornwall stone and 5 g flint. Fire the high-temperature tests to 1280°C/2336°F and the low-temperature tests to 1101°C/2014°F.

* * *

Chapter 9
Clay Bodies for Specific Purposes Using Dry Raw Materials

It is essential to read the Introduction and General Method before attempting any of the Exercises in this chapter. Exercises 14 and 15A and B are in an Advanced Section. At the very least, students should try Exercise 12 or 13 and either 15 or 16.

Introduction

This chapter is designed to give some guidance to those who wish to compound their own clay bodies or who live in areas where bought bodies are difficult to obtain. It is equally intended for all those involved in ceramics, since a thorough basic knowledge of this most important material is essential if you are to make and fire your work successfully. The Exercises may be followed in sequence, or you may wish to select areas in which you have a specific interest. It is hoped that in studying this chapter the expertise involved in the manufacture of clay bodies will be appreciated, particularly the attention given to refining and blending different types of natural clay with one another and with other minerals and the chemically prepared materials to achieve bodies with specific, reproducible characteristics. Any adjustment to a bought body should thus be carefully considered, for it could negate the costly process involved in its production. Further, it is advisable to consult the manufacturer of the clay before attempting any change, also to carry out thorough testing before altering a bulk amount. In many cases it would be better to choose another body or to make your own.

In order to offer a quick and easy way into this subject, a standard General Method has been devised. You should follow this together with the particular information given with each type of body. In the industry, when it is wished to introduce a new body, ceramic chemists are able to start with a wide range of knowledge from previous clay bodies that have been compounded for their own works or with the expertise of colleagues. The studio ceramist new to the formulation of bodies does not have this knowledge; thus a method has been devised to meet this situation.

The Exercises start with a red-firing high-temperature (HT) body because these are the simplest to compound — the heat of the kiln does most of the work. Before starting the Exercises, two important points must be discussed.

Mechanical strength. A fired body consists of solid particles and glass. There are always some pores (spaces) left in all types of ceramics, giving a satisfactory but never perfect ceramic. Tiny, invisible fractures, or microcracks, and other flaws inevitably exist, some probably occurring in the making stage. If there is too much glass, slumping invariably occurs; on the other hand 100 percent solid is not realistic (nor would it be a ceramic fabric). Thus in judging mechanical strength in a clay body we are looking for the right balance of these two.

Resistance to thermal shock. A ceramic body transmits heat slowly. If a vessel is filled with hot water, the inside heats and expands sooner than the outside. If one part of a ceramic object is heated, it will expand while the rest does not. If an unevenly potted object is heated, thin areas will heat through more quickly than thicker areas. In such cases tension develops between the hot and the cold part, and breakage or minute cracks may occur; these may not be immediately visible but may develop and cause breakage later in use. Thus in your general assessment, all fired work likely to be subjected to significant temperature changes should be thoroughly tested (particularly, fired samples from each new batch of clay body). Test bowls (at least 15 cm high) of fired bodies required to withstand sudden temperature changes should be placed in a sink and have boiling water poured into them. These tests should be repeated over a period of time if work is to be offered for sale. For sculptural work thermal shock resistance is not usually a consideration except where outdoor sculptures are subjected to below freezing conditions, or where rapid and repeated changes of temperatures are involved. Some ceramists consider natural clays — that is natural stoneware or common clay — to work best in these conditions.

A ceramic body can withstand a certain amount of tension from mechanical or heat stress, but when the tension exceeds the *tensile strength*, cracks (usually tiny hairline ones) will occur in an attempt to accommodate the tension.

In common glass, once a tension crack forms it runs easily through the glass, breaking the object. In a porous ceramic body such as common low-temperature earthenware, tiny tension cracks may form, but the pores stop the cracks from running too far, and can also dispel the tension at least until the cause of the tension is renewed. Paradoxically, in a dense, virtually nonporous body such as high-fired porcelain that has been thinly and evenly potted, heat is transmitted very rapidly, and the body does not build up significant tension.

Resistance to thermal shock and mechanical strength are interrelated. Tiny, invisible cracks occur due to thermal expansion and contraction or to mechanical stress. These lower the mechanical resistance and form focal points should the piece be subjected to further stress. Again, since some unavoidable microcracks occur during the making stage, good technique and good design are as important for the strength of a pot as a well-compounded body. A pot of uneven thickness with poorly made corners and sharp edges will not be as resilient as a well-potted bowl with a rounded rim.

General Aim

In the following Exercises the aim is to compound bodies that have the required characteristics and a satisfactory ceramic fabric within a particular firing range. In the early stages of firing, solid-state reactions take place. Then, as firing proceeds, constituent minerals decompose, new crystals (or tiny crystallites) form, and amorphous silica is released and reacts with other constituents to give molten glass which, on cooling, glues the body together to make it a reasonably strong ceramic with a satisfactory, or acceptable, degree of nonporosity. At higher temperatures more glass forms; the body becomes tighter, denser, and more impervious. The proportion of glass to crystalline solids in the fired body is important; in porcelain the proportion of glass is higher than in stoneware and much higher than in earthenware (hence its translucence when potted thinly). Above the top temperature of the firing range for which the body has been compounded, it may be expected that too much glass will form, with the consequent collapse of the object.

Distinction Between Low-Temperature and High-Temperature Bodies

Given a correctly formulated and fired body, important distinctions between low-temperature (LT) and high-temperature (HT) bodies should be noted — namely, the degree of porosity achieved, the fired color and the amount of mullite (see below) that forms. There is a range, roughly C.3 to C.6, between LT- and HT-fired bodies where the degree of porosity is questionable. Some bodies may have a satisfactorily low level of porosity, others not. At this middle-temperature (MT) range, the warm earthy colors associated with bodies fired to high temperatures may be undeveloped, while the bright terracotta colors found in LT-fired bodies begin to darken and the bodies become tighter. Note that standard kiln shelves suffice for stoneware bodies fired up to C.10; over C.10, HT refractory shelves and kiln furniture must be used (see Figure 5.2).

Porosity is due to the spaces left as the water dries from the clay body. Given a high temperature, a sufficient number of pores are filled as the molten glass spreads through the body, making the body impervious, but in earthenware not enough pores are filled, and the body remains porous.

Mullite ($3Al_2O_3 \cdot 2SiO_2$) forms on the decomposition of kaolinite in the presence of heat. All the structural water in the kaolinite is released by about 600°C/1112°F and metakaolinite forms ("meta" simply means changed). Then, according to Lawrence and West (1982), "the metakaolin layers condense to form a new type of crystal called a spinel." Lawrence and West (1982) state this as follows.

$$3(Al_2O_3 \cdot 4SiO_2) \rightarrow 3(2Al_2O_3 \cdot 3SiO_2) \rightarrow 3SiO_2$$

metakaolin   spinel phase   amorphous silica

Small crystals, called primary mullite, which do not add significant strength to the body, form at LT. At HT long needle-like crystals develop, some of them still attached to the partially decomposed metakaolin crystals from which they grew, and these, embedded in the glassy structure that forms on cooling, bind the ceramic fabric together in the very strong structure found in both stoneware and porcelain.

It should be remembered that in any clay body, whether or not crystalline silica (quartz or flint) is added as an accessory mineral, there will be some quartz particles introduced with the clay fraction. These help to open the body and act as a filler (adding bulk to the body); they also help to balance the plasticity of the clay minerals during the making stage (see Chapter 4). During firing, once the quartz particles react with other constituents, a viscous melt begins to form, becoming the glassy matrix on cooling. Not all the quartz grains melt; some, particularly the larger grains, remain in the fired body. It is this quartz fraction that is involved in the quartz/cristobalite conversion and the inversion of cristobalite discussed on pp. 92–93. In summary, *the optimum firing temperature is that at which the body matures*, when the required characteristics of strength, color, shrinkage, porosity, and resistance to thermal shock are achieved without loss of the desired surface textural qualities and sculptural detail.

Materials Required for the Following Exercises

A refined natural clay or a blend of clays will act as a starting point in the development of each clay body. The accessory materials that may be used will be given in each Exercise. The materials chosen and the proportion of clay to accessory minerals depends on the firing temperature and the type of work and method of making. It should be noted, however, that to retain the essential qualities of clay the proportion of clay mix in a clay body is usually kept over 50 percent.

Glaze Mixes

You will need a little transparent glaze in order to see how it affects the surface and color of the fired bodies. Three simple glazes are given. Select one for your firing temperature. The bentonite (as additions to the percentage recipe) is added to prevent the glaze materials from settling too quickly.

A few drops of calcium chloride in the alkaline glaze also helps to prevent the frit from settling too quickly. (The theory behind this is discussed in Chapter 10.)

HT glaze, C.8–9	LT glaze, C.05–04	LT glaze, C.05–01
60% potassium feldspar	80% alkali frit	90% Borax frit
40% calcite	20% kaolin	10% kaolin
+3% add. bentonite	+3–4% add. bentonite	+3–4% add. bentonite

Mixing the Glazes

Grind the ingredients together with a little water to a thin but creamy consistency (about 150 ml of glaze) and sieve through 100s mesh sieve (see Figure 5.4). Place each glaze in a screw-top jar, and label clearly. Do *not* confuse the LT glaze with the HT glaze. In each Exercise, brush a strip of glaze across a portion of the test. Use the correct glaze for the firing temperature. Do not cover the whole test with glaze and make sure that there is no glaze on the back of the tile (or bottom of a test pot).

General Method

Using the Chart of Recipes. In most of the Exercises in this chapter the chart in Figure 9.1 is used; in the others specific instructions are given. The nine recipes shown in the chart represent a wide range of tests, which should be tested as Part 1 of the Exercises. Having completed them, you should select your own best result and carry out more detailed tests in that area as Part 2 of the Exercises. Tests have been shaded surrounding one of the tests in Figure 9.1. You should do likewise around your own best recipe from Part 1. *Remember, the area shaded in Figure 9.1 is an example only.*

In each recipe in Parts 1 and 2, 100 g of clay or clay mix acts as a starting point, and the quantities for the accessory materials are read off the edges of the chart. Parts 1 and 2 are used in most of the Exercises given in this chapter and Parts 3 and 4 are given for further short tests, if required.

Do not try to simplify this chart, or you will not achieve the comprehensive and logical arrangement the tests provide. Note that in every case there is at least 50 percent clay. If there is less than 15 percent flux-containing materials, the body will be a HT body, unless there is an appreciable amount of alkalis in the clay mix (oxides of Group 1 and Group 2).

In Figure 9.1, nine squares contain recipes. These constitute the first series of tests. If you are planning to fire to one temperature only, you need to make one test tile of each recipe; a 100 g dry weight of clay mix plus additions for each tile would be sufficient. If you plan to test at two or more temperatures, you will need to multiply the recipe by the number of test firings you intend to undertake, and make a larger tile from each batch recipe. Then divide each tile into the number of firings to give one test for each temperature to be tested (remember to cut the tiles so that a 10 cm line may be drawn on each one).

100g dry wt. of clay mix
plus:.............additions of A.........→

additions of B ↓ / additions of A →	5g	10g	15g	20g	25g	30g	35g	40g	45g	50g
5g	1	2	3	4	5	6	7	8	9	10
10g	11	12 100g cl. mx +10g A +10g B 120g total	13	14	15 100g cl. mx +25g A +10g B 135g total	16	17	18 100g cl. mx +40g A +10g B 150g total	19	20
15g	21	22	23	24	25	26	27	28	29	30
20g	31	32	33	34	35	36	37	38	39	40
25g	41	42 100g cl. mx +10g A +25g B 135g total	43	44 100g cl. mx +25g A +25g B 150g total	45	46	47 100g cl. mx +40g A +25g B 165g total	48	49	50
30g	51	52	53	54	55	56	57	58	59	60
35g	61	62	63	64	65	66	67	68	69	70
40g	71	72 100g cl. mx +10g A +40g B 150g total	73	74 100g cl. mx +25g A +40g B 165g total	75	76	77 100g cl. mx +40g A +40g B 180g total	78	79	80
45g	81	82	83	84	85	86	87	88	89	90
50g	91	92	93	94	95	96	97	98	99	100

Figure 9.1. General chart of recipes for compounding clay bodies. In the first stage, make test-tiles of the nine clay-body recipes. In the second stage, you should test all recipes lying adjacent to your best recipe (the shaded area in the diagram is given as an example only).

Batch weight required if testing at one temperature only	Batch weight required if testing at two temperatures		
100 g clay mix	100 g clay mix	× 2 =	200 g clay
+10 g material A	+10 g material A	× 2 =	20 g material A
+25 g material B	+25 g material B	× 2 =	50 g material B
135 g batch weight			270 g batch weight

Note. When you finally enter your recipe in your notebook, the batch recipe (including additions) should be recalculated and entered as a percent recipe.

Making the Bodies

For these small tests you need to reduce the mix to slip to make sure that a completely homogeneous mix is achieved, and then dry it back to the plastic state. The materials should be weighed out and placed in a mortar containing a little water (to prevent the powders sticking to the bottom). More water is added gradually as you mix with a pestle (see p. 102) until you have a smooth, pourable consistency. The slip must then be sieved through a 60s–100s mesh sieve, depending on the fineness you require. Any material that remains on the sieve should be reground in a mortar to separate the particles, returned to the slip, and the slip resieved using the same technique, as shown in Figure 5.12. Each test slip should then be dried back to the plastic state using one of the methods shown in Figure 5.9 or tied up in a cloth and hung up to dry. Finally, wedge and/or knead thoroughly (see Figures 5.7 and 5.8). This is possible even with such small pieces with a little practice. If grog is required, it should be added at this stage. Carry out this procedure for each of the nine recipes.

Making the Test Tiles

Unless otherwise stated, make and mark the tiles as in Figure 7.2 (the rolling guide sticks will ensure that all tiles are the same thickness — about 0.5 cm). Remember to mark the 10 cm line, the firing temperature, and the reference number of the test given in Figure 9.1. Place a small brushstroke of white slip on areas to be marked if the body is red-firing. Do not cover the whole tile with marking slip (see Chapter 5).

Firing Temperatures

A range of temperatures is suggested in each Exercise. These may be adjusted to suit firing practices in the studio in which you are working. If you are limited to one top firing temperature, then naturally your aim will be to choose the best recipe from your set of tests for that temperature. If you have access to a gradient kiln, then each tile should be divided into three or, at most, four pieces. In some cases only Orton cone numbers are given in this chapter (see Appendix Figures A.5 and A.6 for Orton and Seger equivalents). If you are firing in both oxidation and reduction, it would be valuable to use the same top firing temperature so that the characteristics produced by both types of firings at the same or similar top temperatures may be compared. If you do not have a regular reduction firing temperature, C.9 (1280°C/2336°F) is suggested. All sets of test tiles must be placed in kiln trays (see Figure 7.3) made from a refractory clay in case some of the tests melt.

Standard Assessment After Firing

Set up the fired test tiles, making sure they are in the right order. Assess them using the list below, in exactly the same way you have tested fired clay in Exercise 8 (along with resistance to thermal shock, if relevant).

1. Shrinkage
2. Fired color
3. Porosity
4. Texture (including any sculptural detail)
5. Fired strength: resistance to mechanical and thermal shock
6. Personal preference (including workability for the required making process)

Select the recipe(s) and firing temperature(s) that give(s) the most satisfactory result(s), and record these in your notebook. If the results are unsatisfactory, select the best recipe, and proceed to Part 2 (or you may decide to proceed to Part 3 directly).

On completion of the tests, make a 1000–2000 g batch of the most successful clay developed, and from it make an object and fire it to the optimum temperature for that clay. This should be done before making up a large batch. If the clay is intended for sculptural work or is to carry surface carving, the test pieces should be made to exhibit any features pertinent to the final work.

EXERCISE 12: Warm Brown Stoneware Body

Read the General Method straight through before starting.

Aim

To make the above body for the temperature range of C.6 to C.10 (1222–1305°C/2232–2381°F).

At the bottom end of this range, the fired body should be a strong ceramic fabric showing early signs of the earthy colors associated with stoneware. Toward the top temperature, the distinctive colors, sometimes like burned toast (particularly in reduction) are achieved, and the body becomes denser and hard. Given this range of qualities, it is necessary to decide on your top temperature — and whether to fire in reduction or oxidation.

Materials

Clay mix. Fireclay, kaolin, and a little common clay for color and some natural fluxing action. A little ball clay may be added for plasticity, if necessary (see Exercise 11 for guidance).

Accessory minerals. Potassium feldspar, quartz, and a little red iron oxide, if extra color is required.

Method

Part 1. Using the Chart of Recipes (Figure 9.1), make A = potassium feldspar and B = quartz. Carry out the nine recipes given in the chart, and follow the instructions in the General Method to make, mark, and cut the tiles into the number of firing temperatures to be tested.

For Parts 2, 3, 4, see Assessment section.

Firing

C.5, C.7, C.8, C.9, or C.10, or a selection of these in oxidation and/or reduction.

Assessment

Follow the standard assessment, p. 175, selecting those items relevant to your work. Repeat the assessment after Parts 2 and 3, if required.

Part 2 (if necessary, if not proceed to Part 3). Test the eight recipes lying adjacent to your best recipe from Part 1.

Part 3. If the color from the previous tests is not dark enough, a little red iron oxide could be added: try 0.5 g to 5 g in a line addition test (see Appendix Figure A.7). If, on the other hand, the color is too dark, make three or four tests in which some of the dark common clay is replaced by kaolin (e.g., in the first test replace 5 g of dark clay with 5 g kaolin; in the second test replace 10 g of dark clay with 10 g kaolin; and so on). If you feel that amounts over 10 g are required, a little extra potassium feldspar may be needed to offset the loss of flux from the common clay. This could be done (using one firing for the overall test) by using a square blend test (see Appendix Figure A.7 for layout). The kaolin replacements could be placed along the top of the chart, using increments of, say, 5 g, 10 g, 15 g, and 20 g, while the extra potassium feldspar could be placed down the side of the chart using 5 g increments up to 20 g.

Part 4. Add grog, if required, for the work to be undertaken (see Exercise 10).

After choosing your best recipe make up a batch, and test this as described in the General Method above.

*   *   *

EXERCISE 13: Buff Middle-Temperature Body, C.3–7 (1168–1240°C/2134–2264°F)

Read the Exercise through before starting.

Aim

To formulate and make a body that has some of the characteristics of stoneware (in particular low porosity) with the advantage of lower firing costs.

Middle-temperature bodies are an excellent choice for sculptural work as they give the strength and textural qualities associated with stoneware without tightening the body, which at higher temperatures sometimes changes the detail of the sculpture. The firing costs are also much lower than firings to the higher stoneware temperatures, making this also an attractive temperature range for domestic ware. Furthermore, ware produced at these temperatures has a greater resistance to chipping and moisture absorption than earthenware and compares well with stoneware. It is also worth noting that this temperature range is high enough for the popular stoneware glazes to be used with only small adjustments, and even ash glazes can be very successful.

Materials

Clay mix. Try a mix of kaolin, natural stoneware clay (fire clay if stoneware is not available), a small portion of red-firing common clay for color and fusibility, and ball clay if required for plasticity (see Exercise 11 for guidance).

Other minerals. Potassium feldspar. Nepheline syenite could be tried in place of, or as a partial replacement for feldspar for greater fusibility. If this is done, a blend of 50:50 is suggested here. If at a later date you decide to specialize in this area, a series of different proportions could be tried. Additions of calcite may be considered with caution, a little can help to bleach the red color but it starts to act as a powerful flux in this temperature range. A little ochre adds color if the body seems too pale. Talc can also be used in this body, but we shall keep this for the next Exercise.

Method

Part 1. Make the nine recipes given in Figure 9.1 with A = the feldspathic addition and B = quartz. Follow the directions given in the General Method for making the tiles. For *Parts 2–4,* see below.

Firing and Assessment (carried out after each Part undertaken)

Part 1. Fire the tiles to C.3, C.5, and C.7 (or your choice in this range).

Part 2. After firing select the best result, and note its firing temperature. Unless you are satisfied with a result from this firing, test the recipes lying adjacent to your best recipe (see the shaded area in Figure 9.1 for guidance). You should be able to select two or three test recipes from these, depending on whether you need more or less feldspathic material, and so on. If satisfied with the fired color, skip Part 3 and pass on to Part 4. If not, see Part 3.

Part 3. If the color achieved in the above tests is not dark enough, add test increments of ochre. Do this by making a fresh ball of 100 g dry weight of clay, using the recipe of your best result from Part 1 or Part 2. Add 2 g of ochre by mixing it in a very little water and kneading it into the clay; take off a button test (about the size of a small coin). Add another 2 g of ochre and take off another button test. Repeat this until you have four tests containing 2 g, 4 g, 6 g, and 8 g of ochre to 100 g clay (the small amounts of clay taken for the button tests will not affect the percentage color additions significantly). Mark the color addition to the percentage recipe on each button, on one side only of the button over a brushstroke of white marking slip. (A short form of inscription for 2 g added to 100 g, that is, to a 100% recipe, is: "2% add." and your abbreviation for the color.)

Part 4. If you wish to experiment with grog additions, you could use the remaining ball of clay from Part 3 and make your own choice of grog additions using your own results from Exercise 10 for guidance, judging the proportion of grog to clay by eye. Tests from Part 3 and 4 may then be fired together to the firing temperature of your best result from Part 1. Remember to keep a record of all you do in your notebook. Assess the final results as set out in a General Method, and as before make a 1000 g (or more) test batch of your chosen clay body, and make an object similar to the work you intend to make. Test-fire this before putting the body into general use.

Students not undertaking the Advanced Sections should proceed to Exercise 16 and/or 18.

* * *

ADVANCED SECTION

Low-Temperature White Bodies
C.06–C.03 (999–1101°C/1830–2014°F)
and C.02–C.3 (1120–1168°C/2048–2134°F).

White bodies are difficult to formulate, as it is necessary to use kaolin in order to produce them. Kaolin is refractory, so careful selection of accessory materials is necessary to produce a fusible body for the above temperatures. It is therefore essential that you review "Temperature and Crystallization of

Magma" in Chapter 2, "Changes that Occur in Crystalline Silica" in Chapter 5, and the "General Aim" at the beginning of this chapter.

Off-white natural clays have been used for centuries in many parts of the world. Although white kaolin bodies were used early in China, it was not until the seventeenth century that kaolin was discovered in Europe, first in France and in the area until recently known as Czechoslovakia, then in other locations. The kaolins from Germany, Spain, and Portugal are reasonably plastic; the English kaolins are less plastic but pure, having a very low iron and titanium oxide content, and are therefore probably the whitest-burning. Some plastic kaolins found in Georgia, in the United States, can be used to produce creamy-white or slightly gray-white earthenware. There remains to be considered the fluxing of such low-temperature bodies (given that there is no fusible clay as a starting point) and the control of cristobalite in bodies fired over C.03 (1101°C/2014°F) for thermal shock resistance to breakage at the cristobalite inversion temperature and, in bodies fired under C.03, compatibility with craze-free glazes where required.

Materials

Clay mix. Kaolin plus ball clay, the proportions depending on the whiteness of the ball clay and the degree of plasticity required (for help in achieving the right mix, see Exercise 11). If required, one to two percent bentonite may be added. Having chosen your clay mix, convert it into a percentage recipe; this then becomes your 100 percent clay mix.

Other materials. The following notes should be read in conjunction with those given in Chapter 6. The information given here is specific to this body.

Crystalline silica. Here we are concerned with the quartz particles in the clay fraction and any added to the clay mix as accessory material: some, particularly the smaller grains, react with other constituents to form compounds or enter the melt during the early stages of firing and lose their crystalline nature. However, not all the quartz melts. Some remains in the fired body, and if fired over C.03 (1101°C/2014°F), converts to cristobalite. How much forms depends on the temperature and on the length of time the body is held over C.03. Thus in a fired body we may have some quartz and some cristobalite. In bodies fired under C.03, no significant cristobalite forms. Some experienced potters add bought cristobalite to such bodies to encourage some body contraction (so that the glaze "wrinkles" on cooling) to give a good glaze fit (see pp. 94–95).

Although the centers of the remaining large grains of quartz may remain crystalline (and convert to cristobalite if fired over C.03), the surfaces soften and stick together in a process known as sintering (see p. 265), thus helping to bind the body together, a valuable role in LT bodies, which do not form as much glassy melt (to give a strong body on cooling) as do HT bodies.

Feldspar and feldspathoids. Sodium and potassium feldspar may be used for LT bodies fired over C.03, often in conjunction with nepheline syenite.

Nepheline syenite ($(0.75Na_2O \cdot 0.25K_2O) \cdot Al_2O_3 \cdot 2SiO_2$) is the principal fluxing material for bodies fired under C.03 as it reacts well with the free crystalline quartz, drawing a significant portion, particularly the finer grains, into the melt and encouraging the formation of primary mullite, which helps to bind the fabric of the body together. Further, with less crystalline quartz in the early stages of firing, the possibility of too much cristobalite in bodies fired over C.03 is reduced. Nepheline syenite also encourates sintering, thus helping to bind the fabric together. This is extremely valuable at the lower end of the range.

One word of warning. Sodium feldspar is more likely to produce warping in the body than potassium feldspar. If this occurs, sodium feldspar should be avoided. Nepheline syenite by contrast is less prone to cause warping than either of the feldspars.

In the past *Cornwall* (*Carolina*) *stone* was regularly used to fill the alkali requirements for this type of body. However, although there are still reserves of this stone, the cost of defluorination has led to its replacement by nepheline syenite. Where it is available at a reasonable cost, it can replace nepheline syenite.

Talc (steatite, soapstone), $3MgO \cdot 4SiO_2 \cdot H_2O$. When heated alone the structural water is driven off, and by 1050°C/1922°F the last traces of water are lost and talc decomposes to give cristobalite, SiO_2, and enstatite ($MgO \cdot SiO_2$), a magnesium silicate, which is a stable mineral in the fired body. Since talc (and its derivative, enstatite) has a very low rate of thermal expansion and contraction, it contributes to the resistance of the body to thermal shock. However, unless the clay mix contains good fluxing materials, talc should not be used alone as the sole fluxing material because it would in fact be very refractory. As long as it is used in small amounts with another principal flux, it works powerfully. It also helps to counteract expansion due to penetration of moisture in fired ceramics. These points are of particular value in the production of white domestic ware (and in the production of wall and decorative tiles). Further, the magnesia contained in talc has a catalytic effect on quartz, hastening the conversion of some of it to cristobalite. This has a value in glazed ware fired under C.03 (1101°C/2014°F). There are some very good American talcs; their excellence for bodies is probably due to their fine particle size and natural fibrous structure. On the whole, American-prepared bodies are higher in talc than, for example, English commercially prepared bodies.

Calcite ($CaCO_3$), a very fine-powdered carbonate, breaks down at 950°C/1742°F releasing the oxide CaO, which then reacts powerfully with silica. As calcium carbonate contributes only one oxide to the melt in contrast to three or more oxides provided by the feldspars and feldspathoids, a much smaller proportion, usually no more than 10 percent, of this raw material is needed for a good fluxing action. Calcite minerals do not have a high rate of thermal expansion and contraction, and provided that the calcium carbonate is virtually iron-free, it can also contribute to the whiteness of the body.

Wollastonite, calcium silicate ($CaO \cdot SiO_2$), may be used for its good fluxing action with other flux-containing minerals at low temperatures, and like talc, it counteracts moisture expansion in the fired ceramic (which may lead to crazing). It is gradually gaining popularity with studio potters, often used with or taking the place of talc in LT bodies.

Frits. A low-temperature frit that complements the other constituents may be used, but it should be remembered that, being pre-fused, frits form molten liquids very quickly at the deformation temperature. Frits are also expensive. Frits can be useful in bodies fired at the lower end of the earthenware range but above, say, C.05 (1046°C/1915°F) their reactions are very quick. You are therefore advised to test a series of small increments to bulk amounts. *Lead frits are not used in clay bodies because they act too suddenly.*

Grog. In order to retain the whiteness of the body, molochite or hard pitchers, a grog made from the body recipe, should be used (see Chapter 6 for making instructions). The grade of grog should be selected according to the work to be done.

EXERCISE 14: Low-Temperature White Earthenware Body

Aim

To produce a white body fired under C.03 so that no significant cristobalite is involved. This is treated as a "talk-through" exercise in which all calculations are carried out and discussed before the clay body tests are made. This method allows the assessment of each step in the calculations and selection of useful recipes. Once this is done, the tests may be made and fired together, thus saving firing time and costs and also ensuring that all tests are subjected to exactly the same firing cycle.

At each stage the recipes are converted to percentage recipes in order that they may be compared.

Materials

The selection of materials is based on the notes given above. The clay mix consists of kaolin and ball clay; nepheline syenite is chosen as the principal flux (Cornish stone or a soda feldspar could be tried instead); quartz supplies crystalline silica, and talc ($3MgO \cdot 4SiO_2 \cdot H_2O$), and wollastonite ($CaO \cdot SiO_2$) are used as auxiliary fluxes. Talc and wollastonite contribute not only fluxes but silica in a noncrystalline form, which on reaction with other constituent materials during firing passes easily into the (molten) glassy phase to become, on cooling, the chief factor in binding the ceramic body together.

Formulating the Recipes

In the calculations the following abbreviations have been used: clay mix (Cl), nepheline syenite (NS), quartz (Q), talc (T), and wollastonite (W).

If an in-depth study were undertaken, increments of, say, 5 g, 10 g, 15 g, 20 g, and 25 g of the auxiliary minerals would be carried out (with the possibility of fine adjustments by addition or subtraction of small amounts). This would involve a large number of tests. Here, for economy of space, 15 g additions of talc and 12 g additions of wollastonite are used.

Step 1. Using Figure 9.1, let A = nepheline syenite and B = quartz. Convert all recipes in the chart to percentage recipes (taken to one decimal place):

No. 12			No. 15			No. 18		
100 g Cl	=	83.3%	100 g Cl	=	74.0%	100 g Cl	=	66.6%
10 g NS	=	8.3%	25 g NS	=	18.5%	40 g NS	=	26.6%
10 g Q	=	8.3%	10 g Q	=	7.4%	10 g Q	=	6.6%

No. 42			No. 45			No. 48		
100 g Cl	=	74.0%	100 g Cl	=	66.6%	100 g Cl	=	60.6%
10 g NS	=	7.4%	25 g NS	=	16.6%	40 g NS	=	24.2%
25 g Q	=	18.5%	25 g Q	=	16.6%	25 g Q	=	15.2%

No. 72			No. 75			No. 78		
100 g Cl	=	66.6%	100 g Cl	=	60.6%	100 g Cl	=	55.5%
10 g NS	=	6.6%	25 g NS	=	15.1%	40 g NS	=	22.2%
40 g Q	=	26.6%	40 g Q	=	24.2%	40 g Q	=	22.2%

Step 2. Assess the above by comparing the *percentage recipes.* To do this we must remember that we need to maintain at least 50 percent clay mix in order to maintain the essential qualities of a clay body. It should therefore be taken into account that the addition of other accessory materials causes a lowering of the percentage amount of clay mix. It is therefore necessary to start with a recipe well over 50 percent. Hence we should start with a recipe containing sufficient clay to accommodate this.

Nos. 48, 75, and 78 contain the smallest amount of clay mix. Should it be found necessary to introduce further fluxing materials, the proportion of clay mix would be considerably reduced: almost certainly to below 50 percent.

Nos. 12, 42, and 72 are too low in fluxing material from the start, particularly for LT white bodies that need plenty of fluxing, considering the refractoriness of kaolin and the low firing temperature, even though this might be remedied by increasing the fluxing materials (which brings us back to the remaining recipes with higher levels of fluxes).

Nos. 15, 18, and 45 contain reasonable levels of both clay mix and fluxing material, so we will use these recipes as the starting point for our tests.

Step 3. In the calculations below, the percentage recipe is stated first (15a). To this recipe is added 15 g talc (T), making a new total of 115 g. Percentages are recalculated in the second recipe (15b), which now includes the talc in the percentages. To 15b is added 12 g wollastonite (W), and the percentages are recalculated to give 15c. These three recipes are the test recipes for the first batch of tests.

% Recipe 15a	Recipe 15a		% Recipe 15b	Recipe 15b		% Recipe 15c
74.0% Cl	74.0 Cl	gives	64.4% Cl	64.4 Cl	gives	57.5%
18.5% NS	18.5 NS	% recipe	16.1% NS	16.1 NS	% recipe	14.4% NS
7.4% Q	7.4 Q	of →	6.4% Q	6.4 Q	of →	5.7% Q
	+15.0 T		13.1% T	13.0 T		11.7% T
	115 g total			+12.0 W		10.7% W
				112 g total		

% Recipe 18a	Recipe 18a		% Recipe 18b	Recipe 18b		% Recipe 18c
66% Cl	66.6 Cl	gives a	58.0% Cl	58.0 Cl	gives a	51.8% Cl
26.6% NS	26.6 NS	% recipe	23.2% NS	23.2 NS	% recipe	20.7% NS
6.6% Q	6.6 Q	of →	5.7% Q	5.7 Q	of →	5.1% Q
	+15.0 T		13.0% T	13.0 T		11.6% T
	115 g total			+12.0 W		10.7% W
				112 g total		

% Recipe 45a	Recipe 45a		% Recipe 45b	Recipe 45b		% Recipe 45c
66.6% Cl	58.0 Cl	gives a	58.0% Cl	58.0 Cl	gives a	51.8% Cl
16.6% NS	14.4 NS	% recipe	14.4% NS	14.4 NS	% recipe	12.9% NS
16.6% Q	14.4 Q	of →	14.4% Q	14.4 Q	of →	12.9% Q
	15.0 T		13.0% T	13.0 T		11.6% T
	115 g total			+12.0 W		10.7% W
				112 g total		

Method

Test tiles with a 100 mm line inscribed on them should be made from each of the nine test bodies. You are also advised to make nine bowls, one in each of the clay bodies, at least 10 cm high and 15 cm in diameter. Thin, even-walled bowls would be ideal. Cover a large area of each test with a low-temperature glaze 1–2 mm thick. The simple LT glazes given on p. 172 will serve.

Firing

Fire the tests, if possible together, to C.04 (1060°C/1940°F).

Assessment

Carry this out according to the instructions given in the General Method. If you wish to carry out tests for white bodies fired over C.03, you may run out tests similar to the ones above. Soda feldspar could replace, or partially replace, the nepheline syenite and various auxiliary fluxes tried (see the notes on materials at the beginning of this Exercise). In these tests careful attention must be given to the control of cristobalite, by monitoring the content of crystalline silica and the time and temperature the work is held over C.03 (1100°C/2012°F) (see "Introduction to LT Bodies," p. 178).

* * *

High-Temperature White Bodies: Stoneware and Porcelain

The aims of Exercises 15A and 15B below are to formulate and make (1) a white stoneware body for the firing range C.8 to C.10, and (2) a porcelain body for the range C.8 to C.10, and for those who have the facilities, up to C.13 to C.15. *White stoneware and porcelain are considered together here in order to make comparisons. In the practical work they are dealt with individually.*

The body described here as white stoneware is sometimes called porcelain or a porcellaneous body. But this body is nontranslucent (the proportion of solid to glass in the fired body being much greater than in translucent porcelain) and is often a coarser-grained body to which medium to coarse white grog has been added, so the term "white stoneware" is more appropriate. These bodies are LT biscuit fired, then HT glaze-fired or once-fired so that the body and glaze mature together. This gives a good interfacial layer and therefore good mechanical strength and resistance to chipping.

The traditional firing range for stoneware is C.5 (1196°C/2185°F) to C.10 (1305°C/2381°F). However, most studio potters using modern efficient kilns that reach the upper end of this range aim for temperatures between C.8 (1263°C/2305°F) and C.10. By contrast, the range for porcelain as used by studio potters is C.9 (1280°C/2336°F) to C.13 (1346°C/ 2455°F) extending to C.14–C.15 (1366°C/2491°F–1431°C/2608°F) for "hard" porcelain. Both stoneware and porcelain may be once-fired or twice-fired, the usual firing cycle being low biscuit/high glaze firing. The extra energy supplied by a high-temperature firing enables a greater range of reactions to take place with fewer fluxing accessory materials. By C.8 or C.9 sufficient reactions should have occurred to give a strong dense body on cooling. Of particular importance are the needle-like crystals of secondary mullite, which not only help to bind the ceramic body together, but grow out of the body into the glaze. They help knit them together to give a very strong body-glaze union, or *interface,* and make the glaze less likely to chip at the edges and rims. In porcelain this is even more effective. The body-glaze interface is so well integrated that it is extremely difficult to see, even under a microscope, where the body ends and the glaze starts. Given these facts and the high-degree of vitrification of the ceramic fabric, HT porcelain is as near to glass, that is, complete vitrification, as is possible without slumping during firing. Thus it gives a clear bell-like ring when gently tapped.

The Exercises are devised for C.8–C.10 and may also be used as a starting point for hard porcelain fired at C.14 (1366°C/2491°F) and C.15 (1431°C/2608°F). Success depends on the correct assessment of the fired tests and selection from the nine preliminary tests of an area suitable for further investigation for the qualities required and the temperature to be used. It is important to decide during the first assessment at which end of this range you intend to work and to choose your best result from Part 1 with this in mind. For white stoneware these points are not so critical; translucence is not sought and the walls are often thicker. Furthermore, medium and coarse grog is commonly used for building and firing strength.

Materials

Clay mix. Kaolin and ball clay for the 100 percent clay mix if the latter is white-firing. Otherwise, use as much ball clay as possible without loss of whiteness and 1 to 2 percent bentonite to plasticize the mix. The kaolin has a considerable effect on the quality of the porcelain; hence you are advised to research the details of the kaolins (as well as the ball clays) available to you and test as many as possible (see Figure 9.2 and Plate 31). The same applies to bentonite — one that is white-firing at high temperature is necessary. In some areas fuller's earth might be obtainable at a reasonable price and considered as a plasticizer or partial plasticizer together with ball clay (see Chapter 4). It is possible that you will find a white-firing ball clay satisfactory if firing at the lower end (C.8), but over C.9 it may be necessary to use kaolin plus bentonite (or fuller's earth) as plasticizers. Micaceous/sericitic or even illitic kaolins (which are higher in alkalis than feldspars) may also prove to be useful and deserve research.

Other materials. The notes given below are directly relevant to HT white bodies. You should review the section in Chapter 6 giving details of each material.

Potassium feldspar and quartz are the traditional additions to kaolin for porcelain bodies. In some areas pegmatite may be the source material for both feldspar and quartz.

Potassium feldspar contributing potassa (and a little soda and sometimes calcia), combined with equal moles of alumina and high silica, is more refractory than the nepheline syenite used in the previous Exercise and is eminently suitable for HT fluxing.

Quartz contributes silica to the melt (particularly the finer quartz particles), while (slightly) larger particles act as a filler. Examination under an optical microscope reveals that many quartz grains (particularly 200s mesh and larger) introduced into porcelain and white stoneware are still present in the fired body, though their contours may be rounded, indicating the start of reactions. It is the amorphous silica, released during the breakup of kaolinite, and other minerals and any ultrafine crystals of quartz, many of which are distorted, that react with feldspar and contribute to glass formation. This glass is essential to the production of a hard, impervious body.

Talc ($3MgO \cdot 4SiO_2 \cdot H_2O$) acts very differently at high temperature and is therefore included here for different reasons from those given in Exercise 14. Talc supplies the very powerful secondary flux magnesia, which in conjunction with potassium feldspar assists in the conversion of the crystalline

silica to glass. At temperatures in the range C.5 to C.9, talc has a high thermal expansion and contraction, but at higher temperatures (C.10+) it reacts with clay to form cordierite ($2MgO \cdot 2Al_2O_3 \cdot 5SiO_2$), a mineral with a very low thermal expansion. Thus talc, added to a high-temperature body, helps to reduce the risk of thermal shock, particularly in hard porcelain that has to withstand constant changes of temperature in use (e.g., crucibles and casseroles).

White-firing grog is a regular addition for white HT stoneware, a white-firing one (e.g., molochite) being essential if the whiteness of the body is to be retained. If you wish to have a fine-grained texture (e.g., for throwing), 100s to dust is suggested. If you are planning to use the body for sculptural work, then the grade of grog you choose should be guided by the size of the work and the necessary building and firing strength required.

Remember: once you have decided on your top temperature, any subsequent tests should be fired to the same temperature.

EXERCISE 15A: White Stoneware Body

Aim

To compound a white-firing body that will give a satisfactory firing performance in the range of C.8 (1263°C/2305°F) to C.10 (1305°C/2381°F) using the materials discussed above.

Method

Part 1. Prepare the nine clay body tests by following the instructions given in the General Method in conjunction with the Chart of Recipes (see

Figure 9.2. Margaret O'Rorke, UK. *Porcelain Light.* 38 cm high. Thinly thrown in one piece, fluted and carved, with a transparent porcelain glaze made from a special porcelain body formulated by Dr. Christopher Hogg at English China Clay, UK (produced by Valentine Clay, Stoke-on-Trent, UK) and initiated by Margaret and Graham Gould. "The kaolin used in the body is ECC Super Standard Porcelain, which is unusually strong and white firing for a kaolin (needing only 3 percent Bentolite H bentonite — a sodium bentonite from Texas for optimum plasticity). It gives a strong, white translucent body because of its low light absorption (due to low iron and titanium) and low light scatter (due to reflections from crystalline materials and bubbles). There is some scatter from the small proportion of crystalline material, mostly crystals of mullite. If there were no tiny crystals, the body would be no longer porcelain but glass and would slump during the firing process, given the high firing temperature (O'Rorke fires to Orton C.10 in oxidation) and the thinness of the potting" (Christopher Hogg, quoted by permission). Photo: John Woroniecki. (Author's note. "Super Standard Porcelain" is a kaolin. As the name implies, it is ideal for making porcelain bodies.)

Figure 9.1) making A = potassium feldspar and B = quartz. If you wish to add white-firing grog use the grades and proportions appropriate to the work you intend to make (see Exercise 10 for guidance), adding the same amount and type to all tests. Remember to make the correct batch weight for the number of test firings to be undertaken (see suggested firings below) and to dampen the grog before adding it to the mix. Make and mark the tiles as shown in Figure 7.2, and inscribe the chosen firing temperature. Brush a band of the HT glaze across the front of each test (e.g., glaze no. 14, p. 285). The glaze application should stand proud of the tile and not look like a thin wash (see Figure 11.5).

Firing

The standard stoneware firing range of C.8 to C.9, and/or C.10, should be tested. If you have a gradient kiln, C.6 or C.7, as well as C.12, could also be included, which would give you a good overview of the heating history of the body in this range. For each firing temperature place a set of tests (consisting of a sample of each clay body) together on a piece of old kiln shelf covered with batwash or in a kiln tray, and fire one set to each of the above temperatures. If you carry out Parts 2 and 3 these should also be glazed in the same way and fired in kiln trays.

Assessment

Examine the tiles for color and other qualities as described in the General Method above. Choose the best result and decide whether you have a satisfactory test result or whether you need to proceed to Part 2.

Part 2. Make and test-fire those recipes lying adjacent to your best recipe (selecting those you feel will be useful, that is, those with more or less flux as required). If grog has been added in Part 1, repeat the same addition in these tests. Select the best overall recipe.

Part 3. If you still need more fluxing power, a little nepheline syenite could be added, using a line addition test (see Appendix Figure A.7) to assess the amount required. The reason for such an addition is to draw excess cristobalite into the melt. If frits are used it must be remembered that they act very quickly and may cause excess melting, i.e., overfiring.

Final Assessment

Carry this out in accordance with the General Method above. After choosing the best result, make a batch large enough for several larger test pieces, maquettes of the type of work you intend to make, and examine the fired results carefully.

*   *   *

EXERCISE 15B: Porcelain Body

Aim

To compound a dense white-firing body that gives a clear ringing sound when gently knocked and is translucent when thinly potted and fired at C.10 and higher. The clay mix and other raw materials for this body are discussed in the introduction above; also see "ECC Grolleg and Standard Porcelain" in Chapter 4 (see p. 65).

Method

Part 1. Carry out the nine test recipes (see Figure 9.1), selecting your clay fraction as described in "Raw Materials" and making A = potassium feldspar and B = quartz (these accessory additions are the same as for white stoneware minus the grog). Follow the instructions given in the General Method for the preparation, making, and recording of the number of test tiles required.

Firing

Studio porcelain is often fired in the range of C.9 to C.10. For translucent porcelain C.10 to C.12 should be considered. (Some experienced ceramists fire even higher, up to the region of C.14 or C.15. If you kiln is constructed to fire above C.10 and you wish to use these high temperatures, the same set of tests will serve, but a more refractory recipe must be selected from your test results.)

Assessment

Assess the fired results paying attention to those characteristics relevant to the work you intend to undertake. Enter your findings in your notebook.

Part 2. After choosing your best result from Part 1, it is important that you test the recipes lying adjacent to it to ensure that you arrive at the best possible recipe for porcelain (see Figure 9.1). Again assess the results as in Part 1.

Part 3. For porcelain fired above C.10 (especially for hard porcelain), additions of talc (to generate cordierite) may be tested by a line addition test of increments to your best result from Part 2 (e.g., 100 g best result +5 g, +10 g, +15 g, +20 g, +25 g, and +30 g increments). If you have the use of a gradient kiln, the tests could be tested at several temperatures; otherwise, you are advised to choose one particular temperature. For this you will need six tests each carrying a different increment of talc.

Final Assessment

Carry this out as before and enter your best result(s) in your notebook with comments.

Make a batch of the body (or bodies) giving the best result(s) large enough to make three or four objects. If you wish to evaluate the translucence of the body, make the thickness of each object slightly different (carving could also be used). Ensure that these tests dry very evenly, otherwise you may introduce faults (e.g., vertical rim cracking), which may be thought to be a fault of the body or of the firing but which is, in fact, caused by poor workshop practice. Glaze a large area of each test piece with one of the following glazes.

For C.8–9 in oxidation or reduction (matte white, translucent at C.10) (the author)

30% potassium feldspar
15% calcium carbonate
15% talc
28% kaolin
12% flint

For 1350°C in reduction (Beate Kuhn, Germany) (matte white)

22% potassium feldspar
12% calcium carbonate
10% kaolin (using china clay)
40% flint
16% magnesium carbonate

For 1400°C/2552°F in reduction (Carl-Harry Stalhane, Sweden)

27% feldspar
33% kaolin
 8% nepheline syenite
30% flint
 2% bentonite

The glaze by Stalhane is quoted from Peter Lane. Further glazes suitable for white stoneware and porcelain are discussed in Chapter 12 (see Lane, 1980).

*   *   *

■   ■   ■

EXERCISE 16: A Clay Body for Raku Firing and Similar Firing Techniques

You should review "Raku Firing," p. 112, and the instructions and precautions in "Making a Frit," p. 130, before attempting this Exercise. Since a raku clay body must be judged on its raku firing performance, this Exercise considers the whole process.

Aim

To produce a body that will withstand the raku method of withdrawing the fired work from the kiln while red hot.

A body for raku firing must be able to withstand considerable thermal shock. The following helps to achieve this:

1. An open porous texture (see "Resistance to Thermal Shock," p. 169).
2. A making technique that produces objects of even cross section throughout for even heat transmission. A thin cross section also helps.
3. Constituent materials with low rates of expansion and contraction.
4. The addition of an inert coarse-grained to medium-grained material that causes the body to remain open during firing thus assisting in heat transmission.

You should work, at least initially, with coarse-grained clays biscuit fired to about C.09–06 (923–999°C/1693–1830°F). This should be a standard slow firing to burn out the carbon and other volatiles and to make the body strong enough to handle during glazing and setting in the kiln for the glaze firing. The LT raku firing means that raku wares are easily broken and water can penetrate the body. To overcome this some ceramists high bisque-fire at about C.5 (1196°C/2185°F) and then low glost-fire in the raku range of C.09–06 (923–999°C/1693–1830°F) in order to use typical raku glazes, though some of the subtle raku glaze effects are considered to be due to the texture of low-fired bodies. Another problem with high bisque ware is that it is difficult to handle when glazing and setting in the kiln. Warming the object before glazing and adding a binder (see p. 123) to the glaze helps, but does not eliminate the problem. Also, if persistent cracking ocurs in high bisque-fired pieces where the clay has proved satisfactory when fired under 1100°C, excess cristobalite might be the cause.

Results similar to raku are obtained by firing in a one-off paper kiln, literally made from paper with a minimal structural framework, or by placing the work in the fire box of a solid-fuel kiln (see Plate 26).

The top temperature for the raku glaze firing is usually judged by eye: at red-heat when the work is glowing red-hot and looks almost transparent, it is ready to be drawn from the fire with long-handled tongs. However, draw tiles or rings (see p. 132) and/or cones or a pyrometer should be used, and once you have established the ideal top temperature, you should fire by these means as much as possible. Always remember to wear kiln-goggles or a heat-proof face shield and not risk damaging your eyes. The following Exercise deals with standard raku practice.

Materials

Clay mix. All types of natural clays "as dug" or "with minimal cleaning" or a clay body developed in the previous Exercises. The former should be tested for sufficient fluxing content to give a reasonably strong body at the low raku firing temperature. Some will need the addition of grog to open the body for quick heat transmission thus reducing the possibility of thermal shock. Fireclay and coarse stoneware clay are particularly useful as they remain porous and are thereby able to resist thermal shock. Kaolin may be added to lighten color.

Grog. In most cases an addition of grog is essential. You should choose a mixture in accordance with the work to be done (see Exercises 10, 12, and 13 for guidance). Initially, grog with a mesh size 40s–60s is suggested (see p. 81 for sizes in microns). Later on, you may like to experiment with even coarser grog for some types of hand-built work. Sand is used by some raku potters; if this practice is followed and firings are taken over 1100°C/2012°F, remember that the quartz grains will convert to cristobalite and too much cristobalite may cause cracking. Other materials similar to those listed for sculptural bodies on p. 198 may also be employed. Some of these burn away during firing leaving the body full of vesicles (tiny empty cavities). This serves the purpose of good resistance to thermal shock and also makes the ceramic lighter in weight.

The correct grog addition may be assessed by trying a wide range of increments of grog, e.g., additions of 10 g, 15 g, 20 g, 25 g to each 100 g dry weight of clay body. For the technique of adding grog, see Exercise 10, "The Effect of Adding Grog to Clay." Loss of plasticity may be redressed by the addition of bentonite.

Other materials. A little potassium feldspar or nepheline syenite can be added if more fusion is necessary, particularly if your first-fired tests are crumbly, that is, insufficiently sintered. Talc, petalite, and lithium carbonate may be included as these have low rates of expansion and contraction. However, you are advised to keep the body recipe as simple as possible initially.

Equipment. It is essential that you use the safety clothing and equipment listed on p. 130. You will also need a container of water and a metal lidded container of sawdust.

Method

Choose not more than three or four bodies to test, and from each of these make four test pieces at least 6 cm high (thrown or hand-built bowls or objects similar to the work you intend to make). Biscuit fire them to 1000°C/ 1832°F. Draw them from the kiln at top temperature, and immediately plunge into cold water.

Select one clay body that exhibits good thermal resistance, and make up a batch sufficient to make six test bowls or objects, again at least 6 cm high. The walls of all these tests must be of even cross section and not too thick. If these are closed forms, remember to pierce the clay wall to enable the air to escape. At least six tests should be made in order to carry out the three after-firing techniques described below (two tests for each technique).

If required for the final work, part of the tests should be covered with white slip before the biscuit firing, and before the raku firing a large area should be covered with glaze, applied partly over the slip and partly over the bare body. This will give you a useful range of results.

The glaze. One or both of the following simple raku glazes may be used on each test with 2% to 3% bentonite for glaze suspension and a few drops of binder solution (see p. 123).

95% high alkali frit	or	85% colemanite (or calcium borate frit)
5% kaolin		15% kaolin
+4% add. bentonite		+4% add. bentonite.

Note: You should make at least 1000 g bulk dry weight of glaze. Do not add binder to the bulk amount of glaze; instead, take out a small amount needed for current work and add binder to that.

Partial replacement of the kaolin by a little ball clay might assist suspension in the glaze slip and adhesion to the body. If the alkaline glaze is applied thickly, a good crackle glaze may be had: try 3 mm or experiment with 1 mm to 4 mm thicknesses on the same test piece so that you see the outside limits. If test bowls are used, the degree of glaze flow and pooling may be assessed. For a smoother, craze-free glaze, a borax frit might be substituted. Interesting color results may be had by the addition of 0.5% copper oxide (use the oxide rather than the carbonate as carbonates need to break down before being effective), black iron oxide, or a light overspray of iron sulfate.

Firing

For the first experiment, the test pieces should be biscuit fired to C.09 to C.06 (923–999°C/1693–1830°F) in the usual way. The tests should then be glazed and thoroughly dried and set to warm near or on top of the raku kiln. Then with the kiln at top temperature, the tests should be placed in the kiln using long-handled tongs (see Figure 6.4). Remove the work at glowing red heat about C.07 (984°C/1803°F). For further information, see p. 112.

Cooling Treatment

After drawing from the kiln at top temperature, either a full oxidation, partial oxidation, or reduction state may be achieved. Two tests should be subjected to each type of cooling. You should draw the tests from the kiln one at a time so that they do not cool before treatment.

For full oxidation, allow the object to cool in normal atmosphere.

If objects have been fired in reduction, in a gas or solid-fuel kiln, and partial reoxidation is required, they may be plunged into cold water — thus preventing full reoxidation from occurring. If you have used an alkaline glaze thickly, this sudden quenching can produce a crackle glaze.

For reduction, hold the object in the atmosphere with the tongs for three seconds. This allows a glaze to smooth out and clear the piece of complete reduction, which could leave it unpleasantly dark. Then plunge the object into a container of sawdust (the sawdust will ignite). Cover the container quickly with a flame-proof lid and let the pieces cool. On removing them from the sawdust, the tests may be scrubbed clean. Take care that two pieces do not touch in the sawdust or they may stick together. The tests subjected to the water treatment give a further indication of the resistance of the body to thermal shock (see p. 169).

Assessment

Set up the test pieces, each one clearly marked with the cooling technique used. Examine them closely for breakage or cracks and select the most satisfactory clay body results. Remember that a porous underfired texture is acceptable for raku ware, though not an essential characteristic. Even high bisque-fired porcelain can be raku glaze fired, provided the walls are thinly and evenly potted so that heat transmission to all parts of the body can occur quickly and evenly. The addition of pitchers or molochite to the body as grog should help.

If most of the tests break during firing, then you should reconsider your clay body recipe *and* making techniques. Do the clay bodies contain materials with high rates of expansion and contraction? If so you could replace the offending materials with those with lower rates of expansion and contraction.

Has the firing been taken over C.03 (1101°C/2014°F) for any length of time? If so, steps could be taken to reduce the cristobalite content by firing lower or for a shorter time over C.03. Remember that you are reducing cristobalite because you are moving the work from a hot to cold environment very quickly. The design of the work may also affect the firing performance and should be considered where cracking happens repeatedly.

*   *   *

Lithia may be used in raku bodies to increase resistance to thermal expansion and contraction, but it is expensive. Thus it is not used in commercially produced raku bodies and is only recommended for research into specialized raku work in studio ceramics. If you wish to consider trying this material you should read "Lithium-Clay Bodies" in the following section.

ADVANCED SECTION

Ovenware: A Theoretical Discussion

The superb cooking pots very simply made by hand and low-fired in open bonfire firings in Africa, Central America, and elsewhere stand as exemplars of this type of ware. Of even section, open body, and little if any cristobalite formation, they have truly stood the test of time. This type of ware is highly porous, but this is accepted as it is the pores that give the body the ability to resist the stress caused through expansion and contraction with sudden change in heat, and to stop tiny tension cracks, which inevitably form, from running too far. Thus the ware has a reasonably long life.

Against all these favorable features must be set the fact that, being porous, they are unhygienic. So modern industrial ovenware is often made in hard porcelain, while many studio potters use stoneware. There are pros and cons for all categories which may be summarized as follows (R.T.S. = resistance to thermal shock):

1. LT earthenware (under C.03): high porosity, good R.T.S., low mechanical strength, low production cost, low hygienic factor.
2. MT ware (C.5–C.6): medium to low porosity, moderate R.T.S., moderate to good mechanical strength, moderate production cost.
3. HT stoneware (C.8–C.10): very low porosity (1–2%), moderate R.T.S., good mechanical strength, high production cost. Firing care is necessary: if overfired, too much glass forms making the ware brittle with a loss of mechanical strength.
4. Hard porcelain (C.12–C.15): no porosity, good R.T.S. if thinly and evenly potted, good mechanical strength, very high production cost.

Given the above ratings, it is hard to choose among types of ware. The top temperature to which your kiln will fire and/or the cost of firing may rule out 4; the unhygienic and cleaning problems of 1 may restrict your choice to 2 and 3. If 3 is chosen, great care must be exercised that the cristobalite balance is adjusted (by the body composition and the firing cycle used) to give both good glaze fit and satisfactory R.T.S. The choice largely depends on the aspects of ceramics you like and the problems you are interested in solving as well as the quality and character you wish to achieve. It should also be added that this holds true whether you make your own clay body or buy a prepared one.

Modern ovenware fired C.8 to C.10 or over, using grogged bodies, is either first biscuit fired (at a low temperature) then glaze-fired, or once-fired, the latter giving better integration of the body and glaze.

Where it is necessary to reduce the quartz content of a body and thereby the cristobalite content, high alumina (and thereby low silica) kaolins should be found and used. Further, Lawrence and West (1982) advise that materials containing lime or iron should be as low as possible as these promote the change of quartz to cristobalite. They also suggest the use of nepheline syenite instead of feldspar for greater reaction with quartz so that it is drawn into the melt. Trial-and-error testing needs to be conducted therefore to find the optimum amount of quartz.

EXERCISE 17: White or Near-White Ovenware Body

Potters who have access to high-temperature kilns and wish to undertake research involving firings over C.10 and up to C.14 should investigate two types of bodies: high alumina (low silica), and lithium-clay bodies. A cordierite body is also discussed in this section.

High Alumina Bodies

If you study the analyses of kaolins available to you, you should be able to find one that has a high alumina (lower silica) content and is therefore a more refractory clay body, which may be fired to a higher temperature without incurring adverse crystal changes. If you study the heating history of kaolinite (see Chapter 5), it may be seen that, provided plenty of alumina is present, mullite and glass should develop in the fired ceramic fabric, thus taking up a significant fraction of the crystalline silica present in the kaolin used or added as quartz.

Lithium-Clay Bodies

Spodumene ($Li_2O \cdot Al_2O_3 \cdot 4SiO_2$) or petalite ($Li_2O \cdot Al_2O_3 \cdot 8SiO_2$) is recommended.

There are also a *lithium carbonate* and a lithium mica called *lepidolite*, containing soda, potassa, and fluorine, which can produce contra-effects in bodies. These and eucryptite (another lithium mineral) are *not* recommended.

Spodumene and petalite may contain a small amount of iron as a replacement of aluminum in the crystal structure (see Deer, Howie, and Zussman, 1986). Where this occurs, even small amounts can give color, hence it is advisable to obtain a detailed analysis or test samples before bulk buying.

At 1080°C/1976°F spodumene goes through a crystal inversion: alpha-spodumene becomes beta-spodumene. The beta-spodumene crystal has a lower thermal expansion than the alpha form, therefore it helps to reduce the risk of thermal shock. It should, however, be noted that the low rate of expansion and contraction refers to *crystalline* lithia minerals. If they are taken into the glass-structure by overfiring or by using the wrong composition, this characteristic is lost. It is therefore important that the top firing temperature is carefully monitored. Additions of potassa and soda are therefore kept to a minimum or omitted altogether, as they encourage the breakdown of the spodumene and its subsequent participation in glass formation.

With the discovery of large reserves of spodumene, associated with tin at Greenbushes, Western Australia, research has been carried out into the physical properties of mixes of spodumene and kaolin and also the importance of spodumene in heat resistant bodies. See Kusnik (1988), and Terry (1989).

Lawrence and West (1982) suggest that a composition ranging between 35% spodumene + 65% clay, and 65% spodumene + 35% clay should prove useful. Tests could be carried out by using a crossover line blend of recipes ranging between these two end members as in previous Exercises. See Appendix Figure A.7 for a guide to the layout, but change the increments, using (35 + 65); (40 + 60); (45 + 55); (50 + 50); (55 + 45); (60 + 40); and (65 + 35).

Although a series of simple initial tests of the type given in this chapter could be undertaken and assessed, it must be emphasized that repeated trials should be carried out in which full-sized items of ovenware are used instead of test tiles in order adequately to assess their resistance to thermal shock and their mechanical strength. It should also be remembered that all the above information will be canceled out if the clays are not properly prepared and the test pots unevenly potted. Further, after firing and after cooking, it is essential that items of ovenware be subjected to a series of rigorous tests, for example, plunging them into cold water from a temperature of 150°C/302°F, then 175°C/347°F, then 200°C/392°F, and finally 250°C/482°F, and by putting samples of the ware into normal domestic use to test durability through regular cooking sessions.

In order to get a good glaze fit, the glaze must not shrink on cooling as much as the body; it will thus be put under a little compression. Using our previous analogy, the glaze must be able to "wrinkle" a little so that in all subsequent heating and cooling it can expand and contract with the body.

The following glaze by Paul Rado (1988) may be used for temperatures over 1380°C/2516°F:

$$0.7CaO \quad Al_2O_3 \quad 10SiO_2$$
$$0.3K_2O$$

The conversion of formulas to recipes will be studied in Chapter 12.

Cordierite Body

The formula for cordierite is $2MgO \cdot 2Al_2O_3 \cdot 5SiO_2$. In the ceramic industry a cordierite body is used for heat-resistant ware. Magnesia, MgO, introduced by talc, combines with alumina and silica in the temperature range 1360–1450°C/2480–2642°F, to form crystals of cordierite ($2MgO \cdot 2Al_2O_3 \cdot 5SiO_2$) which has extremely low expansion and contraction rates. The raw materials usually used to produce such bodies are talc, clay, and grog. Apart from the high-temperature firing required, cordierite bodies, until recently, had a very limited firing range, but after considerable research this has been extended. With the addition of potassium feldspar (about 10%), the firing temperature can be reduced to 1300–1350°C/2372–

2462°F, but these temperatures are still beyond the reach of many studio potters. Those who wish to fire in this range should consult Lawrence and West (1982).

* * *

■ ■ ■

EXERCISE 18: Clay for Large Sculptural Work

Aim

To make a clay body suitable for large sculptural work.

Introduction

Many of the points raised in the previous Exercises are relevant here, and the bodies already discussed could serve various types of sculpture. Sculptures do not have to be resistant to thermal shock in the same way as domestic ware, but sculptures may well be placed in an outside environment where temperatures are likely to drop well below freezing, in which case local experience should be taken into account. Most sculptural works should be fired and cooled extremely slowly, as they are often of uneven thickness. Consequently, the kiln should not be opened until the temperature drops to near room temperature. LT-fired bodies are advised for sculptures that are to be brightly colored, and a white body or white slip over the body is a good background for color work. Having decided on the type of work you wish to produce, it is essential to check the space available in the kiln. There is no point in making a large sculpture and then finding that it is 6 cm too large to fit into the kiln. If you are working in a college studio, you should discuss this and the work in general with the technicians. (See also Figure 9.3.)

Materials

As in previous Exercises the clay body may be made from natural clays and accessory minerals. As for other bodies, workability for the making technique you intend to use should be considered. Plasticity is important if the form or sections of the form are to be thrown, and the finger test can be used to test clay for coiled work (see Figure 5.6). For slab work the ability to hold shape during making, without slumping, is important, therefore less plasticity is usually required than for throwing (see Figures 5.5 and 9.3).

Tests pieces of similar construction to the finished work should be fired (standing in kiln trays) to make sure that the grog added will stay inert at the firing temperature you intend to use.

A number of other materials, such as straw, rice, perlite, animal hair,

Figure 9.3. Maria Kujunski, Poland and Australia. *Torso.* 50 cm high. Stoneware clay. Slabs of clay, 3 mm–1 cm thick, were used to build the sculpture, and the work was once-fired to 1240°C in an electric kiln for 10 hours. Photo: the author.

and other fibrous materials, may also be included. These give structural strength during making and burn away during firing (see also Figure 9.4).

A long slow biscuit firing with open vents in the early stages of firing is necessary to ensure that organic additions are burned away (for this reason they need not be included in the percentage recipe). You should also make sure that the materials used do not give off toxic fumes (if so, they must be controlled or not used). Some materials, for example, wood shavings, sawdust, or straw, leave an open, light-weight ceramic fabric that is a valuable asset in a heavy sculptural piece, but it should be noted that they leave a rough, pitted, or sponge-like texture and surface which may not be suitable for glazing unless covered with a smooth clay slip.

Method

The testing and preparation of a clay body may be carried out by following the General Method in conjunction with one of the previous Exercises. For the first series of tests Figure 9.1 should be used. Then a line addition test should be made to estimate the amount of grog required (see Exercise 10, if further guidance is needed regarding the addition of grog). A sufficient batch for each test should be made to demonstrate the qualities and strength required. Either in the initial tests or after you have selected what look like one or two suitable bodies, one or more maquettes of the work to be undertaken should be made with applied glaze or surface treatment, if these are to be used, and then fired and thoroughly assessed before embarking on an ambitious project.

Firing

The top temperature and type of firing (reduction or oxidation) is your choice. Color of the body may be controlled by the firing. For example, in unglazed work a toasted look could come from a reduction firing, whereas oxidation gives more neutral tones; in both cases, color deepens with increasing firing temperature. If a body is fired to the top end of its firing range, a high

Figure 9.4. Colin Pearson, UK. Porcelain jug, 37.5 cm high. Pearson writes: "I have for some time been adding 0.1 percent by weight of 3 denier chopped polyester in 12 mm lengths to both porcelain and stoneware throwing bodies. It is kneaded in at the plastic stage. The most notable effect is on plasticity, especially with the porcelain. The characteristic soft rubbery yielding feel disappears, and it stands up and retains its shape when being wheel thrown and does not slump. A much thinner section can be obtained. There are certain other advantages: a stronger leatherhard and dry strength, and an ability for the body to be bent without cracking. The latter is particularly advantageous in facilitating the twisted and convoluted strip handles I am using in my current work. Similarly, the joining of attachments is easier, and with far less, if any, cracking when drying. The fibres burn out easily during firing. There are disadvantages: turning and trimming are a little more difficult as the tool picks up the fibres, similarly it is not advisable to introduce to a pug mill" (quoted by permission). For Pearson, the advantages outweigh the disadvantages. Photo: Colin Pearson.

proportion of glass forms, the maximum amount of shrinkage occurs, and the body becomes tight and dense. Some types of work will look splendidly strong when hard fired; other pieces will look shrunken or compressed, and detail may be lost. If the work is underfired, a rough or rugged quality may be achieved. On the other hand, the texture of a body fired in the middle of the firing range for that body may look looser and more gentle and may, because of this, help to manifest the aesthetic sense of the piece. The size of the finished object will be nearer to the size "as made," and some potters feel that more of the freshness and verve of the "hands-on" making of the work remains.

Assessment and Observations

Follow the General Method Assessment with reference to those characteristics important in sculptural work. If the tests do not exhibit the textural quality or color you require, it is sometimes possible to correct this by lowering or raising the firing temperature by one or two cones (e.g., if the piece looks too tight or too "burned looking" at C.9, the firing temperature could be lowered to C.7 or C.8). If firing in reduction, the amount of reduction could be controlled to give the effect required. The sculptor should also consider whether there is an intrinsic value in having the same quality of material and color throughout the body, or whether surface treatment suffices.

There are a host of surface treatments that may be used, from bright shiny multicolored glazes and enamels (see Plates 25 and 26), to quiet stony or matte effects (see Plate 20). A white slip may be applied to the leather-hard clay to give a neutral base or to reduce or eliminate a rough surface, particularly if a glaze is to be applied (a glaze does not sit well on a rough surface). If necessary, a fine-grained red-firing clay with added iron oxide could be used to make a slip and be applied at the leatherhard stage and burnished before firing to 800–1000°C/1472–1832°F.

Another useful surface treatment is to use an iron wash with a little added flux (test 2% add. to 10% add.) and perhaps a little kaolin or ball clay for body. This may be applied by brush or daubed on where required with cotton wool. To test proportions follow Parts 3 and 4 in the General Method.

Any of the shiny or matte glazes discussed in Chapter 11 (e.g., the magnesium or barium matte glazes) may be used. Of special interest for middle- and high-temperature sculptural pieces are dry ash surface treatments such as that seen in Figure 10.2, *Quarter Horse*, sculpted by Ken Bright, which has a dry ash slip glaze containing wood ash, kaolin, and ochre over a near-white, low-shrinkage refractory clay, fired at the lower end of the stoneware range. See also "Blends of Two Materials," Exercise 28, and Plates 5, 6, 8 (H, I, and J) and 22.

In such dry "glazes" the clay fraction used may be kaolin or any of the natural clays or clay bodies, and the ash may be unwashed or washed wood or grass ash (see p. 118). Katherine Pleydell-Bouverie's now historic ash glaze is one part ash + one part feldspar + half a part of Pike's clay (a siliceous ball clay). Stated in modern terms, this is 40 g wood ash + 40 g potassium feldspar + 20 g ball clay (or kaolin could be tried) for C.6 to C.10. For C.5 to C.6, the feldspar should be replaced by nepheline syenite with exciting effects for middle-temperature sculptures. A light spray of either glaze over another glaze of the same firing temperature may be used. For specialized work or exciting highlights, there are many other ashes that may be prepared, for instance, orange peel, tobacco, or tea leaves. Straws of various kinds give metallic finishes but are refractory and therefore need a high temperature. The author's favorites are apple wood, walnut wood, and also orange peel (which gives unusual highlights).

For subtle variations in combinations of three materials, such as those mentioned above, you should use the method and layout shown in Appendix Figure A.8 and surrounding text, using hexagonal tiles.

*   *   *

Chapter 10
The Clay-Glaze Relationship, Clay Slips, and Casting Slips

Introduction

In the first two Exercises in this chapter we seek to establish the subtle difference between a clay slip and a glaze. In these it is shown that, with the correct additions to a clay slip we first achieve a *slip-glaze*, and with further additions, *a glaze*. Clay slips and casting slips are placed in the same chapter as they require the same technological knowledge (e.g., density of slips). They are, however, used in very different ways; a clay slip is applied to the clay surface, whereas a casting slip becomes the body of the ceramic form or sculpture.

Remember to use your mask and to turn on the extractor fan to reduce dust when handling powdered materials.

Terminology for Stating a Recipe

The required weight of dry powdered constituents is referred to as the dry weight of raw materials. Even after mixing with water, reference is made to the "dry weight" of raw materials *suspended* in the water (they do not dissolve). If the water were evaporated, a homogeneous cake of mixed dried powders would be left and could be broken up into powdered form again.

Clay Slips

Clay slips are used for the following reasons:

1. To cover an unwanted body color or to provide a white base for colored decoration.
2. To enhance the surface with a smoother or slightly vitreous finish or to use as a colored surface decoration (see Plate 34).
3. To render the body less absorbent, i.e., to reduce the porosity.

4. To achieve a dense, smooth surface (by using a finer-grained slip) over a coarse-grogged body which is to be glazed. If the rough surface is left, the grit will stand out from the glaze and a glaze may soak into the body at the molten stage resulting in a thin glaze with a sugary appearance.

A clay slip can be made from a single natural clay or a mixture of clays selected according to the color, firing temperature, and grain size required. Flux containing materials, fillers, alumina, and silica may also be included.

In small test amounts (e.g., 100 g dry weight), it is essential that all materials be evenly distributed through the slip. This can be done by pouring about 20 ml water into a 16 cm (diameter) mortar, placing the weighed powders on top of the water and grinding with a pestle to a smooth paste and then adding more water to achieve a pourable consistency, using the same technique as that used for glaze making (see Figure 5.12). Test quantities could be mixed with a laboratory mixer (a "jiffy mixer" is obtainable from some American craft suppliers). For larger quantities, sprinkle the powders onto, say, half a bucketful of the water. Once all the powder becomes moistened, the slip may be mixed by hand or with a blunger (see Appendix Figure A.11) and the rest of the water added. For a fine slip, sieve through 120s mesh sieve; for a standard slip, sieve through 80s–100s mesh. A quick check on the thickness (technically speaking, the density) of the clay slip may be made by dipping a finger into the mix. For most purposes, the slip should be thick enough to coat a finger but not so thick as to obscure the outline of the finger nail or the hairs on the back of the finger (see Figure 5.13). Later in this chapter scientific methods are discussed. If the slip is too thin, allow it to settle, pour the clear water into another container, stir the clay slip thoroughly, and return some of the water until the required thickness is obtained.

Making Test Additions to a Clay Slip

The best method of making additions is to use a percentage recipe and add regular increments. Additions may be carried out in one of the following ways:

1. Mix each test separately. In terms of grams this would be 2 g added to a 100 g recipe, 4 g added to another 100 g recipe, and so on. This method is exact but expensive. The following is advised for most cases.

2. Make up one 100 g recipe, and to this make the first addition, e.g., 2 g; sieve after mixing, take out a sample of the slip, and place it in the first space on the test tile. Add another 2 g to the 100 g slip, giving a total of 4 g added, and place a sample in the second place. Then add another 2 g, and so on. Remember to *mix thoroughly after each addition*. If you are careful, the small amount lost by taking out samples will be minimal.

The increments do not always have to be those given above. Depending on the range you wish to cover, they could be multiples of 3 (3 g, 6 g, 9 g) or multiples of 5 (5 g, 10 g, 15 g) additions, and so on. An advantage of using regular increments is that you need weigh out only the total amount, block it up, and divide it, by eye, into the number of equal portions required (see "Layout," Appendix Figure A.7). If the added material is to become a permanent part of the recipe, a new percentage for the recipe should be calculated. If the addition is a color it is sensible to leave it outside the 100 percent recipe; this simplifies your work if you wish to try another color, or several colors.

Applying a Slip

Generally speaking, slip should be applied to the surface of leatherhard clay objects by dipping or brushing. If it is applied too thickly, it will shrink and pull away from the body as it dries; it will obscure carved or textural features. As an initial guide, 1–2 mm thickness is adequate.

If the clay mix used for the slip has a potentially good *plasticity*, there will be adequate adhesion to the clay body. The tiny clay particles align themselves to the body surface so that, as the water dries out, they are drawn onto the surface "gluing" the slip to the body. This close contact also assists interaction during firing of the finer particles of slip and body, thus helping to fuse them together.

Precautions. Do not apply a slip over a dusty surface. If this is done, the wet slip will not adhere to the body surface and it will flake off either while drying or during the early stages of firing. This also applies to glazes.

EXERCISE 19: Common Clay as Body, Slip, and Glaze

Aim

To show the relationship between a clay body and a clay slip that has been made increasingly more vitreous by the addition of a fluxing material. A LT firing will be used.

Materials

You will need five leatherhard thin-walled test pots or objects (test pots thrown off a hump of clay or pinched pots are ideal). These should be made from a red-firing common clay, 100 g dry weight of slip prepared from the *same* clay, and 80 g of alkali or borax frit (note the catalog number of the frit used).

Method

After completing each pot, mark it clearly by incising "Ex.19" and the test number.

For the first leatherhard test pot, apply the slip (without additions) by pouring or dipping. Cover only part of the surface so that you can compare the body and slipped areas after firing.

Weigh out four 20 g lots of the frit, or weigh out 80 g and divide it into four equal portions by eye.

For the second test pot, add the first 20 g portion of frit to the slip, mix well, sieve, and apply the slip.

For the third test pot, add the second 20 g portion of frit to the slip (this makes a total addition of 40 g of frit). Mix, sieve, and apply.

For the fourth and fifth test pots, repeat the above, adding the remaining portions of frit one at a time.

You now have test additions of 20 g, 40 g, 60 g, and 80 g of frit to 100 g dry weight of clay. If these are percented out the recipes become 83% clay + 17% frit, 71% clay + 29% frit, 63% clay + 37% frit, and 56% clay + 44% frit. At this early stage in our studies, it is worth averaging these out as follows: 80% clay + 20% frit, 70% clay + 30% frit, 60% clay + 40% frit, and 55% clay + 45% frit.

Drying the tiles. Make sure that the test pots are thoroughly dry before setting them in the kiln. A spot of water placed on the clay should dry immediately, and the surface of the pots should feel warm against the cheek.

Firing

Once-firing to C.03 (1101°C/2014°F) at the rate of 150°C/270°F per hour is recommended, but if you know the optimum firing temperature of the clay you are using (when used as a clay body), you should fire to that temperature. If once-firing is not possible put the pots through a standard biscuit firing and then a low-temperature (earthenware) firing. Whichever method is used, the pots *must be placed in a kiln tray made from a refractory clay* (see Figure 7.3).

Assessment

Set up the fired test pots in the order first to fifth. If you now look along this line you should see increasing vitrification of the applied slip and the rim becoming smoother; maybe the last one or two clay pots have completely melted. This Exercise demonstrates that a red-firing common clay slip only needs a small addition of fluxing materials to make a useful nonshiny, non-dusty slip; and with further additions a *vitreous slip*; and then, if a highly fusible clay has been used, a shiny opaque *slip-glaze,* or a *complete melt.*

The establishment of the technical relationship between a clay and a glaze supports the principle that a slip or glaze should be seen as an extension of the body on which it is applied. Applying a slip or glaze to a pot or object should not be done as a matter of course but rather should serve a specific purpose, which may be functional or aesthetic.

* * *

EXERCISE 20: Triple Crossover Line Blends

Aim

To produce three crossover line blends that will show:

1. The subtle change from clay to clay slip to glaze as the mix becomes more fusible.
2. The different qualities obtained by using different fluxing materials:
   a. red-firing common clay and potassium feldspar
   b. red-firing common clay and calcite
   c. red-firing common clay and wood ash (see Figure 10.1 and Plate 5).

Materials

About 200 g dry weight of the four materials listed above (see Chapter 6 for the preparation of wood ash).

One white or buff-firing tile, 15 cm × 15 cm, in a bought stoneware clay or one you have compounded and tested yourself. Make two tiles if you are firing in oxidation and reduction. Usually, high-clay mixes are applied to leatherhard clay. Here it is suggested that you place the tests on biscuit-fired tiles so that you can see the fault caused by placing a clay slip onto a pre-shrunk surface. For further interest, apply the 100 percent clay tests in different thicknesses on the three left-hand spaces.

1	2	3	4	5
100% (thin) Common clay	75% Common clay	50% Common clay	25% Common clay	
	25% Pot. Feldspar	50% Pot. Feldspar	75% Pot. Feldspar	100% Pot. Feldspar
1 100% (medium) Common clay	2 75% Common clay	3 50% Common clay	4 25% Common clay	5
	25% Calcite	50% Calcite	75% Calcite	100% Calcite
1 100% (thick) Common clay	2 75% Common clay	3 50% Common clay	4 25% Common clay	5
	25% Wood ash	50% Wood ash	75% Wood ash	100% Wood ash

Figure 10.1. Plan for triple crossover line blend.

Method

Mark the tiles with the numbers only (or at least mark the first square with a "1" (one) and *place an arrow on the back of the tile pointing to the top of the tile.* Work from left to right across the tile starting with the top row. There is no need to weigh the 100 percent tests. Simply grind a little material with water to a smooth paste and apply the three 100 percent common clay tests first. Allow each test to dry a little before applying the next test or they may run together. Weigh out the mixes of two materials and make a creamy slip. Since only a small amount of each mix is required, divide each percentage by 5, giving the following amounts for the top row, as shown below (where pot.feld = potassium feldspar)

| clay only | 15 g clay | 10 g clay | 5 g clay | |
| | 5 g pot.feld. | 10 g pot.feld. | 15 g pot.feld. | pot.feld. only |

The same amounts should be weighed out for the clay + calcite and clay + wood ash tests. Ash is a particularly difficult material to sieve, but it should be possible to pass *all* of it through a 60s or 80s mesh sieve after a thorough grinding. If the ash still contains much carbonaceous matter, it should be calcined in a temporary (or raku) outdoor kiln fired by a gas poker. This can be done by placing the ash in a saggar or tall loosely lidded biscuit-fired pot (so that the air can escape but not the fly ash) and taking it to just over 717°C/1323°F.

The tests (other than the 100% clay tests) should be applied as an even layer, and for such small tests it is necessary to apply them a little thicker than usual, say, 2–2.5 mm. Otherwise, you do not get a full-bodied result (see Figure 11.5). Remember, once the water has dried off, the applied test will be much thinner. Clean around each test before applying the next one. Finally, apply the 100 percent tests of potassium feldspar, calcite, and wood ash.

Firing

Fire the tests to your standard stoneware workshop firing temperature or C.8–9, but remember to make a note of the actual top temperature used. If you have a test for reduction firing, it should, if possible, be fired to the same temperature as above so you can compare the fired results. After firing, label the tile as in Plate 5, and write the actual top temperature used on the back of the tile.

Assessment

The following assessment should be studied in conjunction with Plate 5 and your own results.

100 Percent Tests

On the fired test tile (Plate 5), you will see that 100 percent clay has cracked and pulled apart, particularly where it is thick. This is called *crawling*, and it demonstrates what happens when a slip is applied too thickly or to a preshrunk biscuit-fired body.

In the top row, 100 percent clay has a slight sheen, but the surface is still rough to the touch. Your own tests should have the same tactile quality. Run your finger across the top row from left to right, and you will feel the surface of the tests getting smoother as you approach the feldspar end.

The 100 percent feldspar gives a smooth and glassy, though tight, result, while 100 percent calcite and 100 percent wood ash display a refractory character.

The Blends: Clay + Calcite and Clay + Wood Ash

In the three blends of clay and calcite in the middle row, and those of clay and ash in the bottom row, we have combinations of materials that are all calcia-rich. There is little chance of obtaining a balanced oxide content from them. The 75 percent common clay + 25 percent calcite in the middle row has fused sufficiently to give a surface that is smooth to the touch, but the rest are rough. A similar result has been obtained from the 75 percent common clay + 25 percent wood ash.

The other results containing wood ash look very thin and have disappeared in parts. Wood ash contains appreciable amounts of carbonaceous matter unless thoroughly burned off; hence tests containing wood ash must be applied more thickly than those without ash. This also applies to ash glazes. The tests with 50 percent common clay + 50 percent wood ash and 25 percent common clay + 75 percent wood ash have a rather sugary result on the test tile illustrated; this is no doubt due to the type of wood ash used and perhaps to the mode of collection. (Sometimes coarse sand is picked up with the ash, and remains as grit during firing.) In your own test you may find that 50 percent common clay + 50 percent ash gives interesting results, particularly if you have used a highly fusible ash with a significant amount of K_2O and Na_2O (see Appendix Figure A.11).

The Blends: Potassium Feldspar and Common Clay

Probably the biggest surprise for you, on seeing fired results, will be the rich brown obtained from combinations of red-firing clay and potassium feldspar. The latter contributes alkali oxides (K_2O and usually some Na_2O). These complement the calcia in the clay, giving a well-fluxed mix, and, together with the high proportion of silica, react with the iron contained in the clay to produce this color. This contrasts with the results in the other rows where CaO (from the calcite) has a bleaching effect on iron, hence the results in the second crossover line blend are paler, giving a light yellowish ochre or warm brown. In the final blend, ash that also contains a high percentage of calcia again has a bleaching effect, but as the ash contains a number of other impurities which also affect color, a variety of different effects can be achieved, depending on the wood ash used.

Degree of Vitrification

Turn your tests in the light and study the comparative degree of shine or sheen on the tests. Feel them and assess which are smooth and glassy and which are rough. You will find several very different types of surface treatments contained in this set. Pick out some of the results that appeal to you and think how they could be used.

Useful Combinations

Depending on the proportions used, mixes of common clay and feldspar are particularly useful as common clay is usually rich in calcia while potassium feldspar is rich in potassa and soda. Common clay with wood ash may also give interesting effects; these are often matte or dry and are popular for sculptural work. Another interesting combination comes from wood ash + potassium feldspar + common clay. Later we shall come to a similar mix where kaolin replaces common clay.

*   *   *

EXERCISE 21: Developing a White Clay Slip

Introduction

Making a white slip is relatively easy, but it is very important to get it right. A simple white slip such as a marking slip (see Chapter 6) made from kaolin and a little ball clay is regularly used in ceramics, but as a finished surface or as a layer of slip to be covered by a glaze, before or after biscuit firing, it requires some care.

Aim

To make a white slip that will:

1. Mask the color of the clay body, provide a white foundation for colored clay slip decorations, and be usable as a starting point for colored slips.
2. Adhere to the clay body during the drying and early stages of firing and is not powdery after the biscuit firing. A slip that is too powdery will rub off, get dirty, and prevent a glaze adhering.

3. Produce various degrees of matteness or sheen in the slip. Here the degree of vitrification is important.
4. Be suitable for clay slip decoration (see Plate 24).

If a glaze is to be placed over the slip, the finished color has to be taken into consideration, as different constituents affect color. This will be dealt with in the chapter on color, but, to give you an idea, calcia has a bleaching effect on color (greens and browns are "yellowed"), whereas soda and potassa encourage more turquoise hues.

These tests may be prepared for any firing temperature or firing cycle, but the results *must* be assessed in relation to the purpose for which the slip is to be used and the firing temperature (the higher the temperature the greater the vitrification).

Materials

Slip

You will need some potassium feldspar, quartz, and your best recipe of kaolin + ball clay from Exercise 11, one that gave reasonable plasticity (and therefore adhesion) without loss of whiteness. You will also need one beaker (about 250 ml), four smaller identical transparent or translucent containers, and a medium (80s–100s) sieve.

Because the refractory clay kaolin must form the basis of a white slip, the addition of a feldspathic raw material introduces the fluxing oxides that promote fusion producing a satisfactory fired slip. It is worth noting at this point that the trio of alkali frit, nepheline syenite (rock), and sodium or potassium feldspar (mineral), can be used as partial replacements for one another to modify the fusion of a slip to suit the firing temperature. However, the usual feldspathic material employed is potassium feldspar, and this should be used initially in these tests. A further point is that the introduction of such materials decreases the proportion of kaolin and thereby offsets the loss of bulk caused by the shrinkage of the kaolin fraction as its water content dries off.

The addition of quartz also increases the bulk of the nonclay material; when introduced for this purpose, both materials are called *fillers*. Quartz also adds brilliance to a white slip and helps to produce a harder fired surface. Thus such additions give a good "cover-coat." When an appreciable proportion of these materials is incorporated, it is sometimes possible to use them on biscuit-fired ware, thus providing scope for developing techniques useful to ceramic sculptors. However, for general use, the application of slips to leatherhard clay is more likely to give the best results and should be considered as the normal procedure.

Test Tiles

Twelve hexagonal tiles made from clay suitable for the firing temperature you wish to use (see Appendix Figures A.8 and A.9). Six of the tiles will be used for the first test, and the second lot, for more detailed testing. If you make the tiles about 5 cm wide and not too thick (0.5 cm is sufficient), a complete set will not be too heavy. Score the back of the tiles in case you wish to fix them with adhesive leaving one area smooth for marking. A red-firing body is recommended so that you may judge the slip as a cover-coat.

Preparing and Firing the Tests

The six initial recipes numbered 5, 12, 14, 23, 25, and 27 in Appendix Figure A.8 should be tested, using A = potassium feldspar, B = quartz, and C = a clay mix of kaolin and ball clay. These should be mixed as in previous Exercises and applied to the tiles by pouring or dipping. Mark the back of each tile very clearly (by incising) with the number of the tile (the small number on top of each "tile" given in the chart). You will then be able to identify each one after firing by referring to the chart.

Fire the tiles to your chosen temperature and enter this in your notebook and/or on the back of the tiles. After firing, replace each tile in its correct position and assess them using the guide below. After you select the recipe nearest the quality you are looking for from this firing, the six that surround the selected recipe on the chart should be tested. For example, if no. 12 on the chart is your best recipe, then nos. 7, 8, 13, 18, 17, and 11 should give the recipes for the second lot of tests. You should then select the best recipe from these six plus the best recipe chosen from the first group. (The alternative is to make all thirty-six tiles initially.) Ideally, you should keep all the tiles on a chart drawn on hardboard with each tile placed in its correct position. If later you wish to explore another area, you can carry on from this point without repeating any tests.

Assessment

Observe whether the particles have adhered to one another and to the body, or whether the slip is still powdery; also make sure there is no tendency for the slip to flake off the body surface. Note carefully the increase in vitrification and smoothness produced by increasing the feldspathic additions and the extent to which the quartz has improved the whiteness and quality of the slip as a cover-coat. These tests form a catalog of results at your firing temperature, and, depending on the type of work to be undertaken, you may choose a slip that shows no signs of dusting or flaking and that would be suitable under a glaze or one with a slight sheen for colored slip decoration without a covering glaze. Again, you may choose one that gives a matte look useful in sculptural work, but even here, the slip should not be powdery because the surface will not be durable and will get dirty quickly. As long as this condition is met, many popular dry effects may be achieved, for example, with added wood ash or color (a crossover line blend will indicate the proportions) to give excellent finishes (as in Figure 10.2).

If a slip has flaked, the application may be too thick or the shrinkage between the body and the slip may be incompatible. A different proportion

Figure 10.2. Ken Bright, UK. *Quarter Horse.* 36 cm h × 41 cm l. A directly modeled horse study, hollow formed with clay slabs on a removable armature. The sculpture was fired with an independent supporting clay bridge made at the same time as the sculpture (so it would dry and fire at the same shrinkage rate as the horse), to prevent collapse or distortion. The horse is made in low-shrink refractory clay, and the surface covered with a dry slip glaze containing wood ash, china clay, and ochre. The work was fired in oxidation to 1260°C/2305°F. Private collection, Mrs. James Mason, Switzerland. Photo: Ken Bright.

of kaolin and ball clay could be tried, or you may need to run tests in which the slip is applied to the clay at various stages of drying (thereby equalizing the shrinkage on drying), but these steps are rarely necessary.

After useful recipes are selected, they should be placed in your notebook with a description of the character of the slip at the firing temperature used. This helps avoid repeating the same tests later.

Further suggestions.
1. For increased vitrification or for a lower temperature, nepheline syenite could be used as a partial-replacement of feldspar, or a frit such as a borax-zinc frit for middle temperatures.
2. Calcia, introduced by the addition of calcite, or precipitate calcium carbonate free of iron impurities may be used for specialized work.

This is used by Rosemary Wren (England) on her ceramic birds and animals where pure white markings are required.

3. Zirconia may be added for extra whiteness on work fired at C.8–9.

*   *   *

Measuring and Adjusting the Density of a Slip: Trial-and-Error Method

The methods discussed here apply to glaze slips as well as clay slips.

It is useful to be able to measure the density of a bucket of slip so that you may always keep it constant (see Figure 10.3). There are several good reasons for this:

1. A definite measure is a great help to the beginner who is unsure how dense or "thick" a slip should be. This may save a lot of failures initially.
2. It enables you to retain consistency in your work. Each time you come to slip a batch of pots you can measure the density and then, if necessary, adjust it to its original density.
3. By employing this principle it is possible to monitor the amount of additions made to a slip with reasonable accuracy.
4. It is essential basic knowledge for slip casting.

Density and Specific Gravity

The *density* of a material is defined as the relationship between its *mass* and its *volume*. Put more simply, it is the amount of matter in a given volume (see Figure 10.3); it may be calculated by dividing the mass (expressed in grams) by the volume it occupies (expressed in milliliters).

The density of water is 1 g per ml. To check this is interesting and a good introduction to the practical work that follows. To do so, weigh 100 ml of water standing at room temperature (remember to subtract the weight of

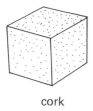
cork
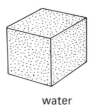
water
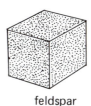
feldspar

Figure 10.3. Densities and specific gravities of cork, water, and feldspar, illustrated by cubes with a volume of 1 cc (= 1 ml).

the beaker). You will find that 100 ml of water weighs 100 g; hence 1 ml weighs 1 g. So *the density of water is 1 g per ml.*

In ceramics, a slip consists of solid particles of mineral matter held in suspension in water (they do not dissolve but remain suspended as tiny particles). The more solid particles in the suspension, the greater its density. A thin suspension might have a density near 1 g per ml, that of water; a suspension that is nearly all solid might have a density near 2.5 g per ml, the average density for most solid ceramic materials. We can encounter a wide range of densities between these two limits.

The density of a material relative to that of water is often expressed as its *specific gravity* (SG), the number of times it is denser than water (or less dense like cork), as shown in Figure 10.3. For example, if 100 ml of slip weighs 170 g, then the density of the slip is 170 g per 100 ml or 1.7 g per ml. Its density relative to that of water (1 g per ml) is 1.7. So its SG is 1.7 (note that SG carries no "units" like weight or volume).

Density of a slip can be *measured* in two ways: with a float or hydrometer, or by calculation using the slip weight as in Exercise 23. A simple way to use the first method is to place a small fishing float in a suitably adjusted slip and make a permanent mark on the stem where it cuts the surface. On all future occasions when you wish to ensure that this or any other slip has the same density, the water content can be adjusted so that the float cuts the surface at the same level.

Hydrometers are calibrated commercial equivalents of the fishing float, designed to measure density. Small hydrometers about 12 cm long are now obtainable from some craft suppliers. Bigger ones are useful for a bucketful of slip but not for small test amounts. When placed in a well-stirred slip the hydrometer should sink to a level between 1.4 and 1.6 SG. If it is not marked, you can place it in an adjusted slip and mark it in the same way as the fishing float above.

Adjusting the Slip: Trial-and-Error Method

If the slip is too thick, gradually add more water. If it is too thin, allow the slip to settle and pour off about two-thirds of the clear water into another container. Then return this water, a little at a time, stirring the slip thoroughly and, at regular intervals, check the SG until you have the required density. Exercise 22 illustrates how to adjust slip weight by calculation.

EXERCISE 22: Adjusting the Density of a Slip Using the Slip Weight

Aim

To adjust the density of a bucketful of slip to the standard density of 150 g/ 100 ml, using the slip-weight method.

Materials

1. A narrow glass or other transparent graduated cylinder, not more than 7 cm wide (the narrower, the more accurate), marked with a 100 ml level (see Appendix Figure A.11). Weigh the cylinder empty and write the weight permanently on the side.

2. A weighing balance or scales and some slip. If you do not have a suitable workshop slip, prepare a slip as described in Exercise 21, adding sufficient water until a pourable consistency is reached.

Method

1. Check that none of the slip is stuck to the bottom of the bucket and mix well. It is a good idea to tip the slip into another bucket to check this.

2. Put some slip into a smaller container and pour it into the cylinder up to the 100 ml mark, using a funnel so that the slip does not stick to the sides and give an incorrect reading of the level.

3. Weigh the slip together with the cylinder, and subtract the weight of the cylinder to find the slip weight.

For example,

$$
\begin{aligned}
\text{if the weight of cylinder} + 100 \text{ ml slip} &= 257 \text{ g} \\
\text{and the weight of cylinder alone} &= 98 \text{ g} \\
\text{then the slip weight} &= 159 \text{ g}
\end{aligned}
$$

This slip has a density of 159 g/100 ml; therefore, it is thicker than the standard density of 150 g/100 ml.

Adjusting the Slip Weight by Calculation

Note: the following formula has been devised using water at 4°C. Ordinary tap water usually serves, provided the slip and water are approximately the same temperature.

A slip that is too thick. To find the amount of water to add to every 100 ml of slip in order to reduce its density, the following formula may be used, where A = the weight per 100 ml of the (old) thick slip and B = the desired weight per 100 ml of the (new) slip.

$$
\text{amount of water to add per 100 ml of slip} = \frac{(A - B) \times 100}{(B - 100)}
$$

For example, if the slip weight of the (old) thick slip A is 160 g/100 ml, and the desired weight of the (new) slip B is 150 g/100 ml, then the amount of water to add per 100 ml of slip is

$$
\frac{(160 - 150) \times 100}{(150 - 100)} = \frac{1000}{50} = 20 \text{ ml.}
$$

So a bucket containing 200 ml of (old) slip would require 40 ml (or 40 g) of water.

A slip that is too thin. The same formula as above may be used. It will give a negative answer, the amount of water that must be *removed*.

For example, if A, the old slip weight, is 140 g per 100 ml and B, the desired new slip weight, is 150 g per 100 ml, then

$$\frac{(A - B) \times 100}{(B - 100)} = \frac{(140 - 150) \times 100}{(150 - 100)} = \frac{-10 \times 100}{50} = \frac{-1000}{50} = -20 \text{ ml.}$$

In other words, 20 ml water must be *removed*.

To remove the excess water, allow the slip to settle and pour off 20 ml of clear water into another container. Check the slip weight again in case you have removed a little too much; if so, return some of the water slowly until the slip weight is the desired new slip weight (in this test 150 g/100 ml).

* * *

Using the Slip Weight

The slip weight may be used to check the density of a slip, so that you can keep it constant. This may be the standard, 150 g/100 ml, or you may wish to use a slightly thicker or thinner slip. It is important to remember that, once you have chosen a slip weight, the thickness of the coat of slip applied to your work will change if you change the slip weight.

The slip weight may also be used to check a slip density before adding another material, for example, color. This can be carried out in two ways:

1. By making trial gram additions to 100 ml of slip with a particular slip weight, say 150 g/100 ml. For example, additions of 10 g, 20 g, and 30 g of a required color or other ceramic material (e.g., potassium feldspar) to 100 ml of slip of, say, 150 g/100 ml, i.e., a line addition test.

2. By using the slip weight to estimate the amount of raw material present in the slip and then making additions relative to their dry weight.

The first method is a quick one when your materials are already in the form of a slip and is satisfactory *if you regularly work in this way.* This is the method used in the next Exercise. The second method must be followed when you wish to use published percentage additions stated in terms of dry materials, e.g., Daniel Rhodes' color additions (see Rhodes, 1989). These methods will be considered in the following practical work.

EXERCISE 23: Simple Line Addition Color Test Using the Slip Weight

The following technique may be used with your own choice of slip and firing temperature, but keep a record of the slip recipe and top temperature used, and whether oxidation or reduction.

Aim

1. To use the slip weight to make color additions. In this Exercise we shall use a wide range of increments: +10% add., +15% add., +20% add., and +25% add. red iron oxide added to 100 ml white slip.

2. To test the effect of placing a transparent glaze over part of the colored slip tests and to compare this with the color of the slip in an unglazed area. For the purposes of this Exercise we shall use a slip-weight of 150 g / 100 ml.

Materials

You will need 400 ml of your chosen white slip; 70 g of red iron oxide; two 15 × 5 cm leatherhard test tiles, one in an earthenware clay body for LT firing and one in a stoneware body for HT firing. If firing in oxidation and reduction, make two stoneware tiles. You will also need a small mortar and pestle, one graduated beaker (preferably 250 ml), and four smaller identical transparent beakers.

Method

Note. In the Advanced Section following this Exercise a quick method is given. Here the longer but more straightforward method is used so that you are totally clear about what you are doing.

Stir the slip thoroughly and make sure that it has a slip weight of 150 g / 100 ml. If not, adjust it before you start (see Exercise 22).

Place a test of the slip (no color addition) in the first square. Stir the slip again thoroughly, and immediately divide it equally among the four small beakers; each beaker now contains 100 ml slip. You should make the following additions to each 100 ml slip, following the mixing instructions given below:

To the first lot, add 10 g of red iron oxide (place a test in space 2 on each tile).

To the second lot, add 15 g of red iron oxide (place a test in space 3 on each tile).

To the third lot, add 20 g of red iron oxide (place a test in space 4 on each tile).

To the fourth lot, add 25 g of red iron oxide (place a test in space 5 on each tile).

Preparing the Tests

Mixing test quantities of color. Place a little of the 100 ml white slip in a mortar (preferably a glass one), then the required amount of coloring oxide. Grind well until evenly dispersed, and add the rest of the 100 ml of slip. Sieve through a fine (120s) mesh sieve using a pliable rubber kidney to wipe out all the colored slip from the mortar. It is also suggested that you use a rubber or plastic kidney or a nylon kitchen sink brush to push the mix through the sieve. If you do not do this, you may lose some color. Now add the rest of the slip and stir thoroughly. Carry out these steps for each color addition.

Apply a strip of transparent glaze across the bottom of each tile by pouring. Do this after biscuit firing if twice-firing. If applying glaze to the unfired slips, take out just sufficient glaze from the bulk glaze, hold the test tile over the sink (or waste glaze bucket) and pour on the glaze, using a glaze-test spoon. Do not return the waste glaze to the bulk glaze, as it may be contaminated with iron. Use a glaze appropriate to the firing temperature you intend to use. If you do not have a stock workshop glaze, use the glaze recipes given in Chapter 9, pp. 172, 190.

Enter only the Exercise number, your initials, and the name of the colorant on the back of the tile (over a brushstroke of white slip) with an arrow pointing to the top of the tile. Do not enter color additions on the back of the tile, or you may get them back-to-front. With this method you may enter the color additions on the front after firing by reference to the figures given above. Thoroughly clean the color from the mortar, dampen the mortar, and rub in a little *ball clay* to absorb any remaining color. The rest of the Exercise and assessment is carried out as described in the previous section.

Firing

$$\text{LT: C.04–C.02 } (1060–1120°\text{C}/1940–2048°\text{F})$$
$$\text{HT: C.8–C.9 } \quad (1263–1280°\text{C}/2305–2336°\text{F})$$

If possible, use the same temperature for oxidation and reduction so you can compare the effect of the two types of firing. After firing mark the top temperature reached on the back of the tiles and the color additions, for example, 10% add. (and the name of the color).

Assessment

1. Note the depth of color produced by the increasing amounts of iron oxide.

2. Note how very pale the color is from the LT firing and that it darkens considerably in the HT firing.

3. Note also that the color in the slip does not fully develop until sufficient glass forms. This may be seen in the small strip where you have applied the simple glaze mixes. Because slips do not fully fuse, about three times the amount of color is required for a slip than a glaze.

4. Note any effect the addition of color has on the fusibility of the slip. If you do see a difference, how much oxide must be added before any significant effect is seen?

Remember that, in order to produce repeatable results, the same slip weight must be used every time. If you do not use the standard slip weight (150 g/100 ml), but prefer a slightly denser or thinner slip, then it is essential that the slip weight you use be recorded for future reference. The above technique could be used for other colors (see Plate 34). The Advanced Section below gives another method of carrying out this Exercise.

* * *

ADVANCED SECTION

Quick Method by Dilution
(requiring only 100 ml of slip and 20 g of color)

The technique of dilution provides a quick and cheaper method of carrying out a line addition color test. A slip weight of 150 g/100 ml is again used. The resulting percent color additions will be slightly different but will still serve the same purpose.

A sample of the well-stirred slip (no added color) is placed in the first square. The slip is then stirred again and 100 ml is measured out and immediately divided into four equal portions (giving four 25 ml lots of slip). Then 5 g of color is added to one of the 25 ml lots, mixed thoroughly, and sieved as described in the first part of Exercise 23. This is the only time you need to sieve. A sample of maximum strength of color is then placed in the *last* square on a test tile. The color is then diluted by adding the second 25 ml of white slip, mixing thoroughly, and placing a sample in the *second last* square. The process is continued by diluting the color by adding the third and then the fourth lot of white slip and taking out a sample after each addition. This gives you:

5 g color in 25 ml slip (equals 20 g color in 100 ml slip), Test 5
5 g color in 50 ml slip (equals 10 g color in 100 ml slip), Test 4
5 g color in 75 ml slip (equals 6.6 g color added to 100 ml slip), Test 3
5 g color in 100 ml slip (equals 5 g color added to 100 ml slip), Test 2

Test 1 will be the plain white slip you first placed on the tile, Test 1.

Mark the tile with the Exercise number, firing cycle, and top temperature on the back, and the color additions on the front. The preparation of the tests, firing, and assessment should be carried out in the same way as previously described, and Figure 10.4 consulted for layout. Once completed, the method used to carry out the tests may be forgotten and the color additions on the tile read from left to right as 0% color, 5% color, 6.6% color, 10% color, 20% color.

■ ■ ■

We now study the alternative method of making additions to the solids suspended in a slip where the proportions of solids to water are unknown. This situation often occurs in a busy workshop where a large bulk supply of slip is kept in stock and has been used several times, or where some of the water may have evaporated. The first thing to do is to stir the stock slip thoroughly, making sure that none is stuck to the bottom or sides (check this by pouring the slip into another container) and immediately take out 100 ml of slip. Next find the solid content of the 100 ml slip, from this you can quickly calculate the weight of solids in the bulk amount, or in another portion of it. For example, you may wish to add color to, say, 500 ml of white slip taken from your bulk stock of slip, for a particular piece of work or test additions of a fluxing material to make the slip more vitreous. Three steps are involved in this study:

1. To find the weight of solids in 100 ml of slip.
2. To use this to calculate the amount of solids in a bulk amount.
3. To calculate the amount (dry weight) of colorant (or other material) to add to the bulk amount of solids in the slip to give the required percent addition.

Steps 1 and 2 are carried out in Exercise 24, step 3 in Exercise 25.

EXERCISE 24: Dry Weight of Solids Suspended in a Slip (a) by Evaporation (b) Using Brongniart's Formula

Aim

To find the dry weight of solids suspended in 100 ml slip and to use this to calculate the amount of solids in a bulk amount.

There are two ways of finding the amount in 100 ml slip, one very simple but slow, the other quick, using Brongniart's formula.

1. Simple (but Slow) Method by Evaporation

Stir the slip thoroughly, and immediately put 100 ml into a weighed container; evaporate the water from this sample in a warming cupboard or over gentle heat, weigh the dry residue plus container and then subtract the weight of the container. This gives you the weight of solids in 100 ml of the slip. Divide this figure by 100 to get the unit factor (the weight of solids in 1 ml of slip).

Next, measure in milliliters the volume of the bulk amount (or your chosen smaller batch weight taken from the bulk amount) that you wish to color and multiply the weight of solids in 1 ml slip by the bulk volume in ml.

The bulk volume of slip may be found by pouring the slip into a container of known volume up to the marked level (any excess over this could be measured in a standard measuring jug). Many buckets are still marked as two-gallon buckets: these hold 7570 ml (U.S. measure) or 9080 ml (UK measure). For example,

Weight of dry solids in 100 ml after evaporation + container =	153.33	g
weight of container =	70.00	g
therefore, weight of solids alone =	83.33	g
unit factor (weight of solids in 1 ml slip) =	0.833	g
therefore, weight in say, 1550 ml is: 0.833 × 1550 =	1,291	g
(to the nearest whole number)		

2. Quick Method Using Brongniart's Formula

The weight of solids in a slip might appear to be the slip weight minus the weight of the same volume of water, but this would not be accurate because the specific gravity of the solids held in suspension is significantly higher than that of water (SG of water = 1; see "density of water" above). The traditionally accepted specific gravity for ceramic materials is 2.5 if you regularly use kaolin, potassium, feldspar, and silica. If you include other materials (e.g., calcite, SG 2.8; alumina, 3.8; talc, 2.8; typical colorants, 2.6 or higher), an average specific gravity of 2.6 would be more accurate. (*Note.* Oxides of lead also have high specific gravities, but they are used only in glazes, not in clay slips.)

Brongniart's formula deals with these problems. It states:

$$\text{true dry weight of solids suspended in the slip} = \frac{\text{apparent dry weight} \times \text{SG of solids}}{(\text{SG} - 1)}$$

where apparent dry weight = weight of slip – weight of same vol. of water. Griffiths and Radford (1965) give a proof of this formula.

Example: Using 100 ml slip with SG = 1.5 (i.e., a slip weight of 150 g/100 ml)

weight of 100 ml slip	=	150 g
weight of 100 ml water	=	100 g
apparent dry weight	=	50 g

Putting this figure in Brongniart's formula gives:

$$\text{true dry weight} = \frac{50 \times 2.5}{2.5 - 1} = 83.3 \text{ g}/100 \text{ ml} = 0.833 \text{ g}/\text{ml}$$

So we can use the unit factor of 0.833 g solids in 1 ml slip to calculate the weight of solids in bulk amounts of slip (e.g., 0.833 × 7570 = 6306 g solids in 7570 ml slip).

The calculations can also be carried out using the bulk amount directly in Brongniart's formula.

Example: Using 1550 ml of slip with SG 1.5

$$
\begin{aligned}
\text{weight of 1550 ml bulk slip} &= 2325 \text{ g} \\
\text{weight of 1550 ml water} &= 1550 \text{ g} \\
\text{apparent dry weight} &= 775 \text{ g}
\end{aligned}
$$

The formula gives:

$$
\text{true dry weight} = \frac{\text{apparent dry weight} \times \text{SG}}{\text{SG} - 1} = \frac{775 \times 2.5}{2.5 - 1} = 1291.2 \text{ g}
$$

So we have 1291 g solids in 1550 ml slip.

* * *

EXERCISE 25: Adding a Colorant (or Another Material) to a Slip with Respect to the Dry Weight of Ceramic Materials in the Slip

Warning: do not undertake the second part of this Exercise unless you have tested a 100 ml sample first and are completely satisfied with the results.

Aim

To add 15 percent coloring oxide to the dry weight of solids contained in: (a) 100 ml white slip; (b) 2000 ml bulk amount. You should try to carry out this calculation yourself, looking at the following steps if necessary.

Cobalt oxide or carbonate or an oxide of iron is suggested for initial practical work (note which you use; remember that black iron oxide and cobalt oxide will be stronger than the carbonate or oxide of other colorants).

Method

First find the weight of the container (this should be written on the side of it). If you are using an electronic balance, press "tare"; this will eliminate the weight of the container. If not, then you must weigh the 100 ml of slip and subtract the weight of the container.

For the purposes of this Exercise let us suppose that 100 ml slip weighs 155 g (with SG = 2.5 for the solids). Brongniart's formula gives

$$
\text{true dry weight of solids} = \frac{(155 - 100) \times 2.5}{(2.5 - 1)} = 91.66 \text{ g in 100 ml slip}
$$

That is, there are 91.66 g solids in 100 ml of slip. To make a 15% add. of coloring oxide to the slip, we must add 15% of 91.66 g, or $(0.15 \times 91.66) = 13.7$ g (rounded) coloring oxide to 100 ml slip. For an addition to a bulk of slip, for example, 2,000 ml, since 13.7 g/100 ml = 0.137 g/ml, we need 2,000 × 0.137 = 274 g color.

Preparing and Firing the Test Tiles

The color addition tests should be prepared and added to the slip in the same way as in Exercise 23 and fired to the temperature you intend to use for your finished work. This must be done before making additions to the bulk amount. You may fire to one or several temperatures, noting these on the test tiles and using the correct body for each firing temperature. When the results of this test firing are satisfactory you may safely add the colorant to the bulk amount.

* * *

EXERCISE 26: Line Addition Color Tests Using the Technique of Dilution

Aim

To run line addition color tests using a technique in which the maximum amount of color to be used is added to a portion of the slip, and the color diluted by further additions of (equal) portions of slip.

This is a quick method involving only one sieving but the method requires concentration. In this test we shall use a slip with a SG of 1.5 (if you do not have a hydrometer, adjust the slip weight to 150 g/100 ml, the slip will then have an SG of 1.5, see above explanation). Having carried out this test and selected the depth of color you prefer, you may, by using Brongniart's formula, find the dry weight of raw materials contained in a 100 ml of slip and establish the amount of color to add to a particular bulk weight to achieve the color you prefer. The advantage of this method is that you need only carry out the calculations for the color result in which you are interested. A further advantage of this technique is that the minimum amount of color is used; the method is therefore economical.

Materials

1. A set of five leatherhard test tiles, about 7 cm × 5 cm, with a small hole at the "top" of the 7 cm length (to thread string through later). For the tiles use your standard earthenware clay if firing at LT. If firing at HT use a stoneware or porcelain body. Make two HT sets if testing in oxidation and reduction (see Figure 10.4 for layout and method). You should note that the type of clay body and the firing cycle chosen may affect the resulting colors. For this reason the catalog or your reference number for the clay used should be inscribed on the back of the tile and in your notebook.

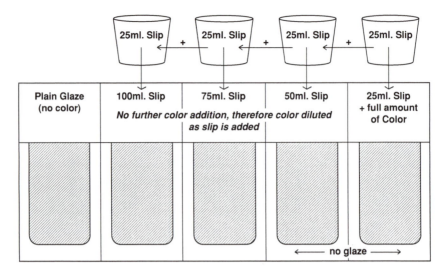

Figure 10.4. Layout for testing additions of color using a dilution technique.

2. Five grams of the following five commonly used coloring oxides or carbonates (note whether you use the oxide or the carbonate): copper, cobalt, manganese, iron (use red iron oxide), and chromium oxide (strictly speaking, this is chromium sesquioxide, common name, chromia).

3. For each color tested you will need 100 ml of the white slip used in the previous Exercise.

4. A transparent beaker marked with 100 ml and four smaller transparent or semitransparent identical beakers (paper cups may be used *and thrown away immediately afterward*).

5. A mortar and pestle for grinding the color with the slip.

Method

One color test is described below. You should treat each color oxide (or carbonate) in turn, in exactly the same way.

Stir the slip thoroughly and check the SG at 1.5 (if you use a different SG, record this in your notebook). Take out a sample of the slip (no color) and place it in the first square on the test tile. Then stir the slip again, immediately measure out 100 ml, and divide it equally among the four small beakers, 25 ml each. Soak the 5 g color, just covered with hot water, for a few minutes (this helps to break up any lumps: the color does not dissolve); then add all of it to one of the beakers containing 25 ml slip; mix thoroughly and sieve. This is the only time you need to sieve, but it must be done here. Take out a sample and place it on the *last* square on the tile (the opposite end from the test without color).

Now dilute this colored slip by adding a second lot of 25 ml slip. This gives 5 g color in 50 ml slip. Mix thoroughly and apply a test to the second to last square on the tile. Dilute the color again by the addition of the third lot of 25 ml slip, and so on until all the slip has been used. Remember to take out a test after each addition. When the slip is dry, carefully pour a strip of glaze across the bottom of the test tile in order to study color development after firing. Do not cover the whole test and be careful not to get any color into the bulk glaze (if contaminated with color, pour it into the waste glaze bucket or throw away). Finally, thoroughly clean the color from the mortar using a little moistened *ball clay* (this absorbs the color and is a very good cleaning agent).

You now have:

5 g color in 25 ml slip which is equal to 20 g color added to 100 ml slip
5 g color in 50 ml slip which is equal to 10 g color added to 100 ml slip
5 g color in 75 ml slip which is equal to 6.6 g color added to 100 ml slip
5 g color in 100 ml slip which is equal to 5 g color added to 100 ml slip

Enter only the Exercise number, the color addition, and your initials on the back. Do not enter color addition on the back of the tiles or you may get them back-to-front. These should be entered on the front of the tile after firing, again using a permanent marker over a patch of quick drying liquid correction fluid.

Firing

If you are twice-firing, the tiles should be biscuit fired (to about 1000°C), assessed (note the color strength), and returned to the kiln for the second firing, otherwise, once-fired to your standard earthenware or stoneware firing temperatures (approx. C.03 to C.04 or C.8 to C.9), noting the exact top temperature used.

Assessment

Examine the tests for the degree of vitrification and the increasing depth of color as the proportion of coloring oxide is increased and as the firing temperature is raised. If you have fired in reduction, you will notice that the colors are less brilliant, more earthy than those fired in oxidation. You should now choose the depth of color you prefer, and calculate the percentage color addition to the dry weight of solids in the slip and enter this information in your notebook. See Exercise 24 for method.

*   *   *

Flocculated and Deflocculated Slips

It is very important that you review the discussion on ion-exchange, calcium clays, and sodium clays (see pp. 18, 47, and 48), as well as the section "Methods of Measuring Density," above, before proceeding to the following section.

Flocculated Slips

Where particles of clay are able to aggregate to make larger particles, or flocs, the slip becomes "thicker" and gradually more difficult to pour: it becomes *glutinous* or *viscous*. The slip is said to be *flocculated*.

If a slip needs to be flocculated, a little calcium chloride (CaCl) may be added (a few drops to a 4 gallon bucketful of slip plus a little bentonite should be sufficient). This goes into solution in the water and releases calcium ions which attach themselves to the broken edges of the clay particles (see Figure 3.4).

The standard flocculant is calcium chloride. Other flocculants include calcium sulfate, calcium hydroxide, magnesium sulfate, magnesium chloride, and hydrochloric acid. Vinegar, gelatin, or a polymer adhesive may also be used, but their effects are temporary (a few hours for gelatin, a week or two for vinegar).

Uses of Flocculated Slips

1. In clay slips with a very fine particle size, a small degree of flocculation is useful for forming slightly larger clay flocs that will physically support and keep in suspension mineral particles such as feldspar.

2. When a slip is too thin, the addition of a flocculant promotes the formation of flocs of clay large enough to settle by their own weight to the bottom of the container. The clear water may then be poured into another container, the slip stirred, and if necessary, some of the water returned little by little, until the required consistency is achieved.

3. Flocculation is used in filter pressing to aid the dewatering process, and can make the body more plastic.

4. Flocculants are added in order to make the slip denser for brush decoration or slip trailing. One or two drops plus a little bentonite are usually sufficient in a two-gallon (9080 ml (UK), 7570 ml (U.S.)) bucket of slip.

Deflocculated (More Fluid) Slips

Where the particles are not able to aggregate but in fact repel one another, they slip past one another with ease. In such a situation very little water is required to reduce the clay to a fluid slip. A deflocculated slip may be obtained by the introduction of one of the deflocculants listed below or one of the new commercially prepared deflocculants. These dissolve in the water and provide sodium ions, which, when adsorbed onto the clay, cause the particles to repel one another.

Traditional Standard Deflocculants

Sodium silicate ($NaSiO_2$, water glass) is used in ceramics in gel or liquid form; it is hydroscopic and therefore takes up water when exposed to a damp atmosphere. It should never be stored in glass or ceramic containers as it attacks them chemically. Sodium silicate is sold in different grades of density. These are discussed at the end of the chapter.

Sodium carbonate ($NaCO_3$, soda ash, washing soda) may be used in either powdered or crystal form. Other deflocculants include potassium carbonate, sodium tannate, and various humates. Calgon (sodium hexametaphosphate), a household product, may also be used.

Modern deflocculants, for example the polyacrylates based on sodium and ammonia, give improved stability, making aging superfluous and the casts less likely to distort (Alston, cited by Rado, 1988). These have various proprietary names from different manufacturers. Probably the best known proprietary deflocculant, based on sodium, is Dispex (an ammonium polyacrylate, its new number is N.400 replacing no. 42). It has a worldwide distribution. It is used to fine-tune a casting slip to which sodium silicate has already been added. When you have very nearly arrived at a satisfactory state of deflocculation, Dispex can be added drop by drop until the exact fluidity is obtained. Some of the newer deflocculants have been specially prepared to prevent some of the adverse effects on the plaster mold caused by attack from the alkalis.

Provided the clay in the slip does not already have calcium ions adsorbed onto it, only a small amount of deflocculant is needed. This is the case with a slip made from known raw materials that do not release calcium or sodium ions. However, if a natural clay other than kaolin or ball clay is used, it is likely to be a calcium-clay and should be dealt with as explained below.

Uses for Deflocculated Slips

1. To assist in the breakdown of clods of natural clays so that they may be more easily prepared for use in the pottery. Many common clays are calcium clays, so they have the tendency to form large lumps that do not disperse easily in water. The addition of sufficient sodium compounds is required to force the calcium ions to float off the clay and allow the sodium ions to take their place (see "ion exchange," p. 18). This will produce a situation in which the clay particles repel one another, the aggregates break down, separate and produce lots of very fine particles: the tiny particles of Na-clay repel each other and therefore slide past each other with ease, producing fluidity. Hence only the minimum amount of water is necessary and, on drying a satisfactory cast is achieved.

2. To deflocculate a clay in the preparation of a casting slip. This is discussed under a separate heading below.

Rado (1988) suggests a very simple experiment to demonstrate the effect of deflocculants: mix some clay with just enough water to make a stiff paste, then add a few milliliters (literally, a few drops) of calgon or sodium silicate and stir.

Thixotropy

A *thixotropic* substance behaves like a jelly when still but like a liquid when stirred. This is the property of slips by which they change their physical state when stirred or left standing. It may occur in clay slips or glaze slips, but is particularly important in casting slips. Stirring increases the agitation already present in varying degrees in slips by virtue of sodium ions that may be introduced by the local water used or by the breakdown, or partial breakdown, of sodium/potassium-bearing minerals or frits. When such slips are left to stand for more than a few days, the natural attraction of like particles seems to overcome the ionic repulsive forces and the slip starts to coagulate or flocculate. It gradually forms a gel and in this state is not capable of taking up the detail of a mold. There is a great temptation to add more water to a slip that looks too "thick." Should this happen, *don't add water. Stir it vigorously!* A little thixotropy is good as it gives extra firmness to the cast, but beyond this, it is harmful as described below.

Casting Slips

Casting slips fall into a separate category because, though formulated as slips, they are used as clay bodies. Further, because of the casting process they need to have a greater density than standard slips. For this reason you need to be thoroughly familiar with the first part of this chapter, especially the sections dealing with density, flocculation, and deflocculation, before attempting this section. As the preparation of casting slips is very different from the preparation of other clay bodies, the important factors in the development of a casting slip are dealt with first, then an Exercise is given.

Briefly, in slip casting the clay object is made by pouring a fluid slip into a porous hollow form, called a mold, and left until a layer of clay partially dries against the mold, the water being drawn into the plaster mold. The mold is then turned upside down and left to drain (propped slightly). As soon as the form, called the *cast*, is firm enough and has shrunk a little from the mold, it is turned out to become the clay wall of the object. Because the level of the casting slip drops as the water in it is drawn off, a collar added to the top of the mold would hold a little extra slip. As soon as the slip is drained from the piece, the collar can be trimmed off.

From this point onward, in studio pottery, the object may be treated like any other leatherhard clay work (modeled, carved, cut and joined, burnished, or glazed).

Some of the earliest molds were thrown pots carved on the interior and biscuit fired to give a porous form or "mold," so that once the cast was turned out the carved areas became relief decoration. Today most molds for ceramics are made from plaster of paris. Exciting ideas such as pressure casting, battery casting for large items, and microwave drying are being explored and used by the ceramic industry and may have spin-offs for studio technology.

For methods of making plaster molds and the techniques of making slip cast objects, you should refer to Frith (1985), Cowley (1978), Norton

(1974), and Kenny (1953). What is of concern here is the demand made on the casting slip by the plaster mold and the technical means of meeting it.

Characteristics Required of a Casting Slip with Reference to the Molds

The water from the layers of slip nearest the plaster mold is drawn into the mold by capillary action. These dewatered layers then become the clay walls of the pot or object. Calcium ions in the plaster react with the sodium deflocculated slip and a cation exchange takes place. The layer of slip lying near the plaster mold "re-flocculates" and the resultant open structure helps allow the water to pass through quickly. (The slip further away remains deflocculated and can be poured away.) The process is self-regulating as the build-up of the clay wall eventually seals the mold and prevents more water from being absorbed.

Therefore:

1. The plaster mold needs to be able to draw the water from the slip lying near it so that the cast becomes firm enough for the mold to be emptied and dried ready for re-use. This is an important economic consideration.
2. It follows that the slip needs to have a minimum water content so that the mold does not have to absorb more water than absolutely necessary.
3. The slip must be sufficiently fluid to flow into every part of the mold, make good contact with it and take up the form and surface features in detail.
4. The cast must shrink sufficiently for satisfactory release from the mold.
5. The slip must be capable of forming a thin but dense cast which is firm and strong enough for the subsequent demolding, any hand-building that you may wish to undertake, handling in the dry state and use as a fired object.

Whereas a standard clay slip has a density of 150 g/100 ml, a casting slip has a density of 170 to 180 g/100 ml; it is this factor that enables it to form a dense cast against the mold in a relatively short time and before the mold becomes saturated. However, an ordinary slip of this density would not make good contact with the mold (see no. 3 above), hence some other means of gaining fluidity must be sought, and this brings us deflocculation.

A deflocculated slip, in which the clay body fraction has all the qualities of a good clay body including porosity, meets all these requirements. Given that the studio potter or sculptor may wish to manipulate the body after it is released from the mold, some plasticity is desirable but the degree of plasticity required for throwing is not necessary.

Deflocculants produce fluid slips for pouring into the mold. A deflocculated slip also stays fluid in that part not in contact with the mold. This means that it can be poured away easily when the cast has formed. Only a minute amount of deflocculant is necessary, and success in making a good casting slip depends very much on the care and attention given to this. This point is dealt with in the following Exercises.

Generally speaking, when the water is drawn from the clay layer nearest the mold, the fine flat crystalline particles of clay minerals are sucked onto the mold. They align themselves parallel to the surface, packing close together to give a strongly bonded cast that takes up the fine detail and prevents warping, cracking, and excessive shrinkage. Too much water or over-deflocculation negates this; the latter results in loss of fine detail and may "glue" the cast to the mold.

A good clay remains sufficiently porous to allow the water to continue to pass through the firm layers, already formed against the plaster mold, and so increase the thickness of the clay wall. The thickness aimed for by most studio potters is about 3 to 4 mm. After this, the rate of buildup of the clay cast (the clay wall) gets slower and slower; the limit is reached when the cast is about 1 cm thick.

A properly deflocculated slip will contain just sufficient moisture to allow the clay cast to shrink away from the plaster as it dries and so facilitate its removal from the mold.

Types of Casting Slips

The term *clay body* is used below because, although initially we are making a slip, at the end of the casting process this will be the body of the object. The following discussion will be dealt with under two headings: the type of body used for bone china and the type used for standard casting slips.

Clay Body for Bone China Casting Slips

The material that distinguishes bone china from other ceramic bodies is animal bone ash. Experiments could be based on the standard commercial combination of kaolin, animal bone ash, Cornish stone, or a similar feldspathic material (see p. 115) varying the amount used to suit the material available to you. The recipe given below illustrates the type and proportions of (clay + accessory materials) used for industrial bone china casting slip (from Paul Rado, 1988).

50% animal bone ash
25% kaolin
25% Cornwall stone

Here, a bone ash content of not less than 46 percent is advised.

Clay Body for Standard Casting Slips

The clay fraction plus the added accessory minerals should meet the requirements of a standard body for the work to be carried out (though not necessarily the degree of plasticity required for throwing), as well as the fired properties and the fired qualities you envisage. You are advised to use a powdered clay body, at least initially, as it is easier to keep track of the water added to the powdered materials. Below is given a simple recipe for the clay body fraction of a casting slip, quoted from David Cowley (1978). It is stated here as a percentage recipe. This makes it easier to compare with other recipes and to calculate bulk amounts when required. For example, for a batch weight of 500 g multiply each item by 5, for a batch weight of 1000 g multiply by 10, and so on. The addition of water and deflocculants are dealt with later.

Earthenware: C.03 (1101°C/2014°F):
  40% ball clay
  15% kaolin (using "English China Clay")
  17% Cornwall stone (or an equivalent feldspathic material)
  <u>28% flint (see below)</u>
100% recipe

Materials Used in Making Casting Slips

These are considered under three headings: the clay body, water, and deflocculant.

The Clay Body

As for clay bodies and ordinary clay slips, materials such as feldspar, Cornwall stone, or nepheline syenite, together with quartz, are the chief accessory minerals added to the clay fraction. Talc is also often included. Commercially produced slip-cast ware is made from the traditional combination of refined and blended kaolins, ball clay, feldspar or bone ash, and quartz. (The flint variety of quartz, if available, is finer and therefore enters the melt more readily during firing.) Studio experiments could be based on these materials.

Given that the forming of a firm layer of clay (the future cast) against the mold depends on water passing through the clay layer to the plaster mold until the "cast" reaches the required thickness, the cast must remain porous. The casting slip must therefore contain a sufficient proportion of accessory minerals to keep the body open and allow the water to pass. Furthermore, the proportion of clay minerals to accessory minerals in the body should lie between the limits for a good body, for once the shape has been formed the cast body is in every respect the same as other leatherhard clay forms. For both standard casting slips and bone china it should be noted that 0.5 percent of bentonite may be added to give plasticity and strength at the greenware stage (USA Wyoming bentonite is recommended). Though the clay bodies used for standard slips and bone china are different, the method of treating them thereafter (the combination with water and the addition of deflocculant) is the same.

Other Materials

The experimental work that appeals to studio potters has led them to include many of the materials listed on pp. 198 and 201 for addition to clay bodies. A word of warning is not inappropriate at this point. Grog and other coarser materials settle quickly in the fluid casting slip. You are therefore advised to start your experiments with a casting slip that will pass through a 120s mesh sieve, then ball milled if required. If you wish to add grog, this should be done after sieving through 120s. A grog not coarser than 80s is advised (e.g., 80s to dust) and after addition, the grogged body resieved through 80s mesh.

As stated above, it is possible to use a plastic clay body, but if you do you will have to calculate the dry weight of the clay body fraction in order to correlate it with the deflocculant and the water content; for this you should refer to Exercise 24.

If coarse-grained clay bodies are used, some features such as strength and density, as well as definition of (surface) detail, may have to be forfeited.

Water

Just enough water is needed to give a thick creamy slip and also to enable the cast to shrink a little on initial drying so that it releases from the plaster mold. Your usual tap water may suffice, but not in hard water areas. If you have problems when you assess the final slip it is suggested that you make a comparative test using purified water and/or obtain an analysis. If the water contains excess calcium, de-ionize; if excess sodium, use rainwater.

The water should be taken from a measured amount so that afterward you may record how much you have used. If you have used a burette or pipette in your tests, any unused water must be returned to the "measured amount."

In industry the water content has been reduced so dramatically that there is only 30 percent (and in some cases even less) water in the slip. In studio ceramics, where the quick turn-around of plaster molds is not such a vital economic concern, a little more water is used and a slightly longer casting time while the cast sets in the mold is accepted. Thus a range of proportions are stated below as "reasonable limit proportions" for initial experiments. Once you have experience in selecting and handling your materials you may be able to reduce the water content further.

Best:	72% clay body	limit for water content:	60% clay body
	28% water		40% water

Deflocculants

Deflocculants affect the prefired slip-state of the body. They are not concerned with other stages in the process (their proportions are therefore chosen irrespective of firing temperature). Once a fluid slip is achieved and the cast made, the deflocculants may be forgotten.

The traditional deflocculants sodium silicate and sodium carbonate are generally used between the proportions of 1 : 1 and 3 : 1, with a total proportion of under 1 percent addition to the clay body (dry weight, i.e., under 1 g to every 100 g clay body). As a starting point, equal parts could be tried and these proportions adjusted after initial tests, or several comparative tests could be carried out testing, say, three proportions at the same time. This technique will be used in Exercise 27. Any adjustments to these proportions will depend on the clay body and water used, in particular the ball clay and sodium or calcium ions contained in the water and clay (some potters have found sodium carbonate alone suits their materials).

The following guides are offered so that you may see what problems are involved and the importance of a proper balance of sodium silicate and sodium carbonate.

If only *sodium silicate* is used, the slip will be able to be fired but the cast (the slip-cast object) will be brittle when dry, and difficult to *fettle* (see Glossary). It does, however, sometimes work when a bone china slip is being prepared.

If casting slip containing too much sodium silicate is left to stand without stirring for several days, too much viscosity develops. This can usually be corrected by stirring briskly (without resorting to the addition of further water).

If only *sodium carbonate* is used, the slip casts quickly but tends not to support itself and is flabby. In other words, there will be a fluctuation in the viscosity of the slip. Leaving the slip to stand to mature before use helps a little but does not remove the problem (see "Aging" below).

If you decide to proceed to advanced slip cast work using commercial deflocculants, the correct one for the recipe should be obtained from your craft supplier. In this case the manufacturer's instructions should be followed (see also "Modern Deflocculants" above).

Two important points should be noted.

1. Use as little as possible of the deflocculant, add it slowly and give it time to react. As you add it there will come a sudden change from a viscous to a very runny slip. *Stop adding the deflocculant immediately and note the exact amount added.*

2. If too much deflocculant is added, your casts will be flabby: they will distort when turned out of the mold or rapidly form dense, thin casts that will not thicken further. If this happens you should start again, using a fresh sample of slip, with the foreknowledge of where the change occurred. As you approach this point add extremely small amounts until fluidity is achieved.

For repeat tests, use the same slip and the same water (clays vary in their own natural calcium or sodium content and certainly the water does also). What you are trying to do is neutralize the effect of calcium (causing the slip to flocculate) by adding sufficient sodium to drive off the adsorbed calcium. If you add too many sodium ions you get further problems, called "over-deflocculation." Perhaps at this stage you should review "ion exchange," as well as "Flocculated and Deflocculated Slips" (see above). These seem to be complicated issues but in reality just a little trial-and-error testing is needed.

To ensure accurate measurement and recording of the amount of this mix added to the clay body it should be added drop by drop from a measured amount. A burette is recommended, or, failing this, a pipette (Appendix Figure A.11); each addition should be carefully recorded and the slip stirred well and the fluidity tested. In industry and large specialist potteries the viscosity may be tested by a "viscometer."

Important adjustments. You may need to alter the proportions of sodium silicate and sodium carbonate slightly. If the cast is flabby, add more sodium silicate to the next test; if it is too brittle, add more sodium carbonate; keep a record of the adjustments.

The usual method is to make up a solution of the deflocculants, then add it to the water or very gradually to the thick, creamy clay-water mix until it changes to a fluid consistency. This usually happens quite suddenly: the viscosity changes quickly from a thick to a runny slip. If the suggested limit for deflocculants is reached without attaining fluidity, a few milliliters of water will have to be added. If this does not work, a different deflocculant could be tried. Before doing this you should throw away the 100 ml sample already tested and start with a fresh sample. As a last resort the local water supply could be analyzed or a test carried out using purified water. All else failing, sodium tannate or one of the deflocculants listed on p. 229 may be tried. If this does not work the clay should be questioned for suitability.

To prepare sodium tannate, 10 g of soda ash (sodium carbonate) and 10 g of tannic acid are added to 100 ml of boiling, preferably purified water. This mixture is particularly useful for deflocculating common clays as they are high calcium clays and therefore difficult to reduce to fluidity. However, only some of them respond to this treatment.

Aging

Traditionally, after the preparation of the casting slip has been completed and sieved (through 120s mesh), it should be left to stand *covered with a lid* for 24 hours before use. Some advocate leaving it for 4 to 5 days. Stir gently with a paddle now and then to prevent a thixotropic reaction, but do not allow bubbles to form, as these spoil the cast; the container may be knocked gently on the side to persuade these to rise to the surface. Finally, it should be sieved again before use through 120s and then 80s mesh if coarser particles have been added after the first sieving. If a modern sodium polyacrylate is used, aging is not necessary.

Mixing the Slip

A small mixer attachment that fits an electric drill may be used to mix small amounts but see that no bubbles are left in the slip (knocking the side of the container or gently stirring will release them). A blunger or one of the sophisticated slip mixers with pump attachment is advised for larger quantities, especially if using plastic clay (see blunger, Appendix Figure A.11).

A bulk amount of slip should be blunged for several hours, then left to rest and paddled at least every few days. Using a wide blade paddle will stir the slip without creating bubbles.

Firing

The casts may be fired to any of the pottery temperatures suitable for the clay body being used. The industrial method of high bisque, low glost, or standard pottery firings may be employed (see Chapter 5, "Firing Cycles").

EXERCISE 27: Making a Casting Slip

Aim

To carry out tests to develop a casting slip in such a way that the contribution of each of the three components, clay body (clay + accessory minerals), water, and deflocculant, may be understood. Thus the preparation of each is stated separately and then the three put together.

Remember: the clay body you use will dictate the top firing temperature. Conversely, if you wish to use a particular top temperature this will dictate the type of composition, a greater fluxing action being required for lower temperatures. The aim here is to achieve the most clay body with the least amount of water. Use deflocculants to render the clay body fluid instead of the usual procedure with ordinary slips of adding lots of water.

Materials

The proportion of each material plays a vital part in the success of slip casting. In the following discussion, percentage figures are given.

You will need a burette or pipette to control very accurately the addition of water (see Appendix Figure A.11). There are three parts to the casting slip.

1. *Clay body* suitable for the top firing temperature to be used and the ceramic characteristic you wish to achieve. Use a dry powdered clay body mix for this Exercise (either a purchased powdered body or one of your own recipes from Chapter 9); by doing this you will be able to monitor accurately the proportion of solids to water used. Again, for this Exercise, a simple white body using kaolin and ball clay together with flux-containing material and quartz is suggested. Ideally you should use a recipe for a clay body that you have already tested as a body.

Purchased powdered porcelain or bone china bodies are ideal for casting slips, and so are some of the stoneware or earthenware bodies if you take into account the texture (from added grog and coarse materials) for the work to be undertaken. When buying a clay body for slip cast work, you are advised to buy it in a powdered form checking that the grade/particle size is smaller than 80s mesh.

2. *Water.* The water used must be taken from a measured (or weighed) amount. At the end of the Exercise, you can find the total amount used by subtracting the amount left. This is important if you are to record your recipe.

3. *Deflocculants.* Sodium silicate and sodium carbonate are used in this Exercise to enable you, in the assessment and adjustment, to become familiar with the nature of casting slip. For the same reason we shall start with a 1 : 1 proportion of sodium silicate to sodium carbonate and adjust these proportions, if necessary, using the "Important Adjustments" guide on p. 236.

The goal is to find the best proportions of (clay body : water) to give a thick creamy slip. Given the percent limits for (clay body + water) stated on p. 234, a series of tests are given as 100 percent recipes. These have been set out as a crossover line blend ranging from proportions with very small amounts of water to limit proportions (much beyond this limit there would be too much water). Dry weights of clay body are given.

| clay body: | 72% | 71% | 70% | 69% | 68% | 67% | 66% | 65% | 64% | 63% | 62% | 61% | 60% |
| water: | 28% | 29% | 30% | 31% | 32% | 33% | 34% | 35% | 36% | 37% | 38% | 39% | 40% |

Method

Note: The following procedures refer to the preparation of *test amounts.* The preparation of a bulk amount once a satisfactory recipe is found will be dealt with under "Batch Weight," below. Two methods are suggested for dealing with test quantities.

1. The simple way would be to start with, say (72% clay body + 28% water), and see whether this gives you a thick creamy slip. If not, try the next proportion (69% clay body + 31% water), and so on.

2. The quick method needs care. A measured amount of water is gradually added to 100 g clay body until a thick creamy slip is obtained. The amount of water *added* + the 100 g clay body is then converted to a percentage recipe. Preparation and mixing instructions for this method are given below.

Preparation

1. Weigh 100 g dry powdered clay body (clay + accessory materials) and mix thoroughly by rolling round in a firmly closed plastic bag. Leave until the dust settles.

2. Measure 50 ml (or weigh 50 g) water. This becomes your "measured amount of water."

3. Dissolve 1 g sodium carbonate in just enough hot water to cover the powder (taken from the measured amount of water and heated). Add 1 ml sodium silicate. This becomes your measured amount of deflocculant (you

will not be using all of this). Return any remaining heated water to the measured amount.

Mixing

1. Place half the water in a bowl.

2. Gradually sprinkle about half to one third of the powdered clay body onto the water, stirring constantly until powder is evenly dispersed in the water. From time to time add a little more of the clay mix, also water (from the measured amount) to keep the mix at a mixable consistency.

3. When all the powder has been entered and you have a thick paste-like consistency *note how much water you have added at this stage.*

4. Now continue adding water from the measured amount of water, drop by drop, preferably using a burette or pipette, until the paste turns to a thick (but not fluid) slip. At this point you must stop adding water and prepare to add deflocculant: if you added more water the slip would not be dense enough to make a good cast.

5. Return all the unused water in the burette, or pipette, to the measured amount of water and subtract the amount of water left from the original "measured amount of water" to find the exact amount added to the clay body. Enter this result in your notebook and discard the test material.

This is now your (clay body : water) recipe. For example, if you have added 43 ml (43 g) of water to your 100 g clay body, your (clay body + water) recipe is equivalent to (70% clay body : 30% water). It is quite a good idea to double check this recipe by weighing out another 100 g clay body + 43 g water, adding the last amount of water slowly to ascertain that the full 43 g is required. You could also add a little more water to see what effect this has. Discard this test material.

Adding Deflocculant to 1000 g Test Slip

Testing with 100 percent clay body makes for easy understanding of the proportions but leaves the deflocculant addition as a very small amount to be weighed out. Hence it is suggested that, having understood the method and the proportions, you carry out the remaining tests using a bulk weight of 1000 g. For example, using the recipe in the list above with the lowest water content, we have:

% Recipe	1000 g Batch weight
72% clay body	720 g clay body
28% water	280 g water
100% total	1000 g total
+0.2% add. deflocculant.	+2 g deflocculant (maximum).

It should be appreciated here that the deflocculant is added *in addition* to the recipe of (clay + water). During testing this makes it easier to keep track of what you are doing, given that varying amounts of deflocculant are tested before a final recipe is chosen.

Adding the deflocculant, you will need a 1000 g mixture of your best (clay + water) recipe and your prepared solution of deflocculant (see Preparation, item 3 above). This mix should be added drop by drop from a burette to the 1000 g (clay body + water) until a fluid mix is obtained. By noting the amount of deflocculant left in the burette you can, by subtraction, find the exact amount of deflocculant used. This amount should then be written into your recipe as an addition to the percent recipe of (clay body + water). See example given above, p. 239. Finally, sieve 80s, then 100s.

Testing the Performance of the Slip

This must be carried out before and after firing. In order to assess the prefired performance you should pour the slip into one or more small test molds to see whether it conforms to the "characteristics required with reference to the mold" set out above. If necessary, consult "Important Adjustments," p. 236. Leftover slip should be poured onto a plaster slab and when firm cut into tiles and biscuit or bisque fired ready for future glaze tests. One of these test tiles should be incised as soon as the slip has set with a 100 mm line and fired to assess the shrinkage. This is especially important for slip cast ware when you wish to make a finished object of a particular size (see Chapter 8).

Measure the wet-to-dry *prefired shrinkage* by measuring the incised line again when dry and ready for firing. A reasonable total drying plus firing shrinkage would be 10 to 12 percent shrinkage for studio ceramics.

Firing Cycle for Slip-Cast Objects

The tradition of high bisque, low glost is a satisfactory process in an industrial situation except for hard porcelain where low-biscuit, high-glaze firing is used (see p. 184). High bisque, low glost means that there is less breakage when handling objects before and during glazing. It also means that defective ware may be thrown out before wasting a more expensive glaze-firing on them. It does, however, have disadvantages. It is difficult to glaze bisque fired work; also, the clay has completed its transformation to ceramic material and there is not very much reaction between clay and glaze during the second firing. By contrast, by once-firing, or low biscuit plus high glaze firing, both the clay and glaze pass through the final stages of their transformation to ceramic materials at the same time. They therefore bind together, mainly in the higher temperature range. This produces a much harder and less chippable ware. Despite this, there are justifiable reasons for a studio potter to follow the industrial method. For example, if the product is to be a ceramic sculpture, the higher bisque firing could give a strong impervious body while the low glost could enable many brilliant LT glaze colors to be used for the surface treatment.

Assessment After Firing

Carry out the standard assessment for fired qualities (shrinkage, strength, color, and so on). Further questions have been added below with particular reference to casting slip. Record the answers to them and try to improve on your results next time.

1. How long did you leave the poured casts before tipping out the excess slip? If you used different times which time seemed to be the best?
2. How thick was the most satisfactory cast?
3. Was the surface spoiled by bubbles in the finished surface? Do not stir the slip too vigorously just before pouring it into a mold.
4. Critically examine the surface. If you plan to leave your work unglazed, is the surface satisfactory, should it be smoother/more textured?
5. Has the cast shrunk sufficiently (but not too much) to come away from the mold easily? If not, have you sufficient water in your slip to promote shrinkage away from the cast on drying? In rare cases you may have de-watered your slip so efficiently that there was not enough water to cause sufficient shrinkage when the clay dried out.
6. Has the cast come out easily, or has it been caught by undercuts in the mold? If so, correction to the mold must be undertaken.
7. Has the cast picked up the fine detail from the mold? If not, the slip is either too coarse or too thick or the mold questionable.
8. Is the color of the cast satisfactory? If not, question (i) the clay body; (ii) the cleanliness of your mixing or the mold; (iii) the firing. A reduction firing sometimes causes dark blotches on porcelain and overfiring white bodies may make them gray.

* * *

Bulk or Batch Weight, Test Pieces, and Storage of Casting Slips

When you have achieved a satisfactory casting slip recipe, a batch weight of 3000 g or 5000 g dry weight of casting slip should be made. As you will, at this stage, be using a tested recipe, the deflocculant could be added to "the exact measured amount of water" to be used. When preparing a bulk amount of slip a blunger may be used, or it may be stirred by hand or with a paddle. Apart from this, the method of mixing is as for test amounts. Several test objects similar to the work to be undertaken should be cast from this batch. These should be marked with your reference number for slip casting tests. From now on the body may be treated as a standard greenware or leatherhard clay form and biscuit fired at C.06 (ready for an HT glazing) or bisque fired at C.5 (ready for a LT glazing) and placed in a dust-free container ready for glazing (if used). Casting slip should be stored in a container

Figure 10.5. Sandra Black. *Lace Bowl*, 1989. Slip cast porcelain pierced at the leatherhard stage, biscuit fired to 850°C, sanded and polished, then fired unglazed to C.8 in oxidation. See text for full description of technique. Photo: John Austin.

with a narrow opening. If necessary a film of polythene should be placed covering and touching the complete surface of the slip and an air-tight lid placed on the container so that the slip is not exposed to air. This should be a regular routine procedure with casting slip.

A slip-cast unglazed bone china bowl is shown in Figure 10.5. It was made by Sandra Black using the following recipe developed by Owen Rye, with materials available in Australia.

Clay mix	plus additions of	Deflocculant
30.0% Eckalite no. 1 kaolin		+2% Dispex
45.0% bone ash, natural		+1% sodium silicate
22.8% potassium feldspar		water (60 ml per 100 g
2.2% silica		dry weight of clay body)

Eckalite no. 1 kaolin has a percentage analysis of SiO_2 46%, Al_2O_3 38%, FeO 0.45%, CaO 0.03%, MgO 0.01%, Na_2O 0.05%, TiO_2 0.7%, l.o.i 14.76%. It would be an interesting exercise to convert this to a unity formula (see p. 397) and also to compare it with those of the American and English kaolins given on p. 65 together with the comments on fired qualities.

Sandra Black adds the deflocculant to the measured amount of warm water, then sprinkles the clay body mix onto the water. It is left to slake overnight and then blunged (for about twenty minutes to half an hour) until the bone ash breaks up and a smooth slip achieved. Following this the deflocculated slip is sieved 80s and finally 120s mesh.

The work is pierced at the leatherhard stage and the ragged surfaces trimmed by scraping with a fine steel kidney, then steel wool. It is then biscuit fired at 850°C and at this stage polished: to do this it is soaked in water (to eliminate dust), then sanded with wet and dry paper (300 and 600 grade) and rinsed again under running water to get rid of the deposit from the sanding paper (which might otherwise cause specking). Care is taken that the biscuit firing does not go over 850°C, as this would make the surface too hard to polish. After thorough drying, the final firing of this unglazed work is then taken to C.7 to C.9 in oxidation. This body is not fired in reduction as during tests graying has been found to occur. The wide firing range gives scope to adjust the actual heat-work used: if the firing is a little longer than usual the lower end of the range is used, if a shorter time, then the high temperature is selected.

Degrees Twaddell (°TW): A Note Regarding the Specific Gravity of Slips

Your craft supplier may catalog the SG of sodium silicate and ready-made suspensions and casting slips, quoting the SG as "degrees Twaddell" abbreviated °TW. This is done because the SG of most slips falls between 1 and 2 (e.g., 1.5, 1.55, 1.6, 1.7) and the important differences between them might not be readily comprehended. Degrees Twaddell were derived by taking that portion of an SG in excess of 1 (e.g., where the SG is 1.5, taking the 0.5;

where the SG is 1.6, taking the 0.6; etc.) and multiplying the excess by 200 (i.e., 0.5 × 200; 0.55 × 200; 0.6 × 200; 0.7 × 200), thus giving an expanded scale of differences and whole number figures.

The formula is $°TW = (SG - 1) \times 200$. The SGs listed below therefore have the following values:

SG		°TW
1.3	=	60°TW
1.4	=	80°TW
1.45	=	90°TW
1.5	=	100°TW
1.55	=	110°TW
1.6	=	120°TW
1.7	=	140°TW
1.8	=	160°TW
1.9	=	180°TW

Thus a standard slip of 1.5 SG could be quoted as 100°TW. *Note:* as water has a SG of 1.0, its value in degrees Twaddell is 0°TW.

If you find the above difficult to remember, the following limerick may help:

> There were once some young men in a Twaddle
> Whose minds decimal points did boggle.
> With a scheme they had fun,
> From SG they took one,
> Then times two hundred untangled their muddle.

This is not just twaddle: Bill Twaddell devised the first hydrometer (in the nineteenth century) and it was decided that this scale should be named after him.

Part III
Glaze and Color

Chapter 11
Introduction to Glazes
and Glaze Development

Introduction to Glazes

It is now taken for granted that you will use your mask and turn on the extractor fan, or take other precautions when handling powdered materials.

By now you should know the temperature equivalents for cones 06, 04, 03, 5, 8, 9, and 10. Temperature equivalents of these cones will not be stated from now on unless necessary. A full list of temperature equivalents is given in Appendix Figure A.5 and surrounding text.

Glaze is chemically related to glass, but there are significant differences. First, a glaze forms an intimate association with the ceramic body to which it is fused; that may affect the finished surface. Second, a glaze requires a more viscous melt than those used in most glass-making processes, because the glaze has to remain on the vertical surfaces while in the molten state. However, an understanding of the nature of glass is essential to the understanding of glazes.

Glass may be defined as a noncrystalline mixture of silicates, borates, and oxides of sodium, potassium, calcium, and other metals. That is to say, in the process of glass-making, the mineral constituents are melted down so that their crystalline structures collapse and the melt reverts to the form found in molten magma. If the melt is then cooled rapidly, so that crystals do not have time to grow again, the noncrystalline structure remains, and a clear transparent glass results.

Glaze consists of glass or a mixture of glass and crystalline material. When a glaze, applied to a pottery surface, has completely melted at top temperature and has remained in the noncrystalline state on cooling, the pottery surface, or a decoration placed upon it, may be seen clearly through the glaze. If a glaze has been compounded to include raw materials that combine readily to form crystals and the initial cooling is slow enough for this to occur (the first 100 to 200 degrees are important), the glaze will be a mixture of glass and crystals. Where there are sufficient tiny crystals (crystallites) in a glaze to reflect the light from their fresh, newly formed crystal faces in a multitude of directions, various degrees of shiny to matte and opaque glazes may be achieved. These are sometimes referred to as microcrystalline glazes. Where crystallites aggregate to produce large crystals that are visible to the naked eye, they may be referred to as macrocrystalline glazes.

Categories of Oxides Required

There are three essential categories of oxides required to make a satisfactory glaze: glass-formers, stabilizers, and fluxes (see Figure 11.1).

Glass-Formers

The two important glass-forming oxides are silica (SiO_2) and boric oxide (B_2O_3).

Silica is the chief glass-former, giving a hard durable glass. It is easily available to the potter in various forms of quartz and in combination with other oxides in raw materials such as clay, feldspar, talc, and wollastonite, and also in pre-fused frits (see Chapters 1 and 6).

Silica is capable of forming a glass by itself, but a very high temperature, 1710°C/3110°F, is required to melt it, and even then, it is an extremely viscous melt. In ceramics the use of silica alone to make glazes is neither financially viable nor practical, as the clay body would melt long before the silica glass. In glaze-making, as in clay body composition, fluxes lower the temperature at which silica fuses.

Boric oxide (B_2O_3) plays a complex part in glaze-making. Here we are concerned with it as a glass-former. It may be introduced into the mix in the form of frits or via one of the natural minerals such as colemanite. Several other well-known minerals contain boric oxide, such as borax (a compound of sodium and boric oxide), but they are soluble in water and are only of value for frit-making. In the melt, boric oxide joins with silica to form the

CERAMIC TABLE OF OXIDES Arranged according to their use in ceramics

FLUXES		STABILIZER	GLASS-FORMERS
Group 1 Alkali oxides potassa K_2O soda, Na_2O lithia, Li_2O	**Group 2** Alkaline earth oxides calcia, CaO magnesia, MgO baria, BaO strontia, SrO	alumina, Al_2O_3	silica, SiO_2 boric oxide, B_2O_3
Others: Lead oxide, PbO Zinc oxide, ZnO			

Figure 11.1. The twelve most important ceramic oxides grouped according to their chief use in glazes.

Characteristics	Advantages	Disadvantages
MP 741°C	Enables a low temperature glass to be made (B_2O_3 has a M.P. of 741°C compared with 1710°C for silica). Thus the inclusion of a little B_2O_3 lets glass formation take place at a lower temperature.	Given this low M.P. it cannot be used in large amounts in H.T. glazes. Further, it tends to volatilize at high temperatures. Gives very shiny glazes which are not always acceptable.
Solubility and durability	Boro-silicate glasses resist chemical attack and are therefore valuable in the glass and high temperature ceramic industry.	Boric oxide and pure borate glasses are soluble in water; therefore the bulk of the glass in glazes must consist of silica.
Viscosity	Very small amounts can reduce the viscosity of a melt considerably, letting a more fluid melt flow out and give a smooth and even surface.	Too much B_2O_3 has the opposite effect, causing the melt to be more viscous.
Thermal shock	Small amounts introduce good resistance to thermal shock: B_2O_3 reduces the amount of expansion and contraction of glass and glazes when they are subjected to changes of temperature. Thus, like silica, boric oxide is said to have a low "coefficient of thermal expansion and contraction."	Large amounts seem to reverse this. Glazes containing high proportions of B_2O_3 tend to expand and contract when exposed to sudden heat changes. The glaze may crack or craze as a result.

Figure 11.2. Advantages and disadvantages of boric oxide (B_2O_3).

glassy structure. However, it may replace only a small part of the silica glass in a glaze for a number of reasons. These reasons bring both advantages and disadvantages, as shown in the table in Figure 11.2.

From this table we can see that small amounts of boric oxide are beneficial, while large amounts cause defects. Its great advantage is that, with a melting point of 741°C/1365°F, as opposed to 1710°C/3110°F for silica, even small amounts of boric oxide will considerably reduce the temperature at which a glaze melt is achieved. The possibility of being able to fire a glaze at such low temperatures makes many ceramists want to group boric oxide with the fluxes. Indeed, many glaze chemists regard it this way. Hermann Seger in his original research in the late nineteenth century placed boric oxide with silica in his formulas. Later Felix Singer placed it with alumina.

From these observations we can see that boric oxide is indeed a curious substance, and it is not surprising that there is some disagreement over whether potters should group it with the fluxes, with alumina, or with silica. However, these are niceties of classification. In reality, a potter considering whether to include B_2O_3 in a glaze mix, takes many factors into account, but the amount of glass formed in the melt at the intended firing temperature will be of paramount importance. Thus, when potters wish to make a glaze, the reasons for their choice of glass-former(s) involve the following characteristics. Silica, the chief glass-former, gives a hard durable surface and is easily available in a number of cheap raw materials. It is also very refractory, so we must add:

1. Fluxes (which ones and how much will be discussed later); or
2. Low-temperature glass-former boric oxide (B_2O_3) so that, on firing, the mix will fuse at a lower temperature; or
3. Boric oxide and some fluxes.

After studying the above, we shall obviously choose either no. 1 or 3; otherwise, the disadvantages of boric oxide will be introduced into the glaze. Whichever decision is taken, remember that, since silica is the chief glass-former, as much of it as possible should be included as its refractory nature will allow.

Stabilizer

As mentioned at the beginning of this chapter, glazes must be stabilized so they will remain on vertical surfaces during firing. To achieve this, alumina is added and the proportion adjusted to give the required degree of viscosity. Alumina also prevents the glaze from soaking too much into the body at top temperature. A reasonable union of body and glaze is desirable because it prevents the glaze from chipping and makes a harder ware. However, it is vital that not too much glaze soaks into the clay, because a rough unattractive surface would result and the extra glass could make the pottery too brittle. Alumina may be introduced into a glaze by using kaolin or one of the feldspathic materials.

The proportion of alumina in a glaze is crucial; this will be dealt with in several places in the text. For the moment the following general information is sufficient:

1. Just enough alumina is essential to prevent the glaze flowing off the pot.
2. A little extra alumina may contribute to the formation of minute crystals producing a nonshiny, or matte, glaze.
3. An excessive amount of alumina causes the glaze to become too thick, too viscous, and too refractory. In bad cases the alumina will prevent reactions taking place, and the "glaze" remains powdery and underfired.

Fluxes

Although fluxes are primarily used to hasten fusion, ceramists must realize that these oxides also contribute to the formation of other characteristics in glazes, such as texture and color (discussed later). Here we are concerned with their ability to influence the fusion of a glaze and the materials used to introduce them. The principal fluxes are discussed here.

Lead oxide (PbO) is a powerful flux at low temperatures, giving a very fluid melt, so it is often used as the sole flux in low-temperature glazes. However, it begins to volatilize at temperatures over 1100°C/2012°F. Thus, if fired above this temperature, it can cause a fired glaze to be too thin or so fluid that it soaks into the body, leaving little or no glaze on the surface. Moreover, it can produce so much glass in the body that the fired ceramic becomes brittle. When the correct amount of lead oxide has been included in a glaze and it has been fired to the correct temperature, a brilliant shiny glaze with a very smooth surface results.

Lead oxide and lead carbonate are toxic and should only be used as a lead sesquisilicate or lead bisilicate frit (see p. 12). The fired glaze should be tested for lead release before selling or using (see Bibliography under "Health and Safety," p. 399).

The Alkali Metal Oxides

Potassa (K_2O) is a very useful flux through the potter's entire range of firing temperatures. It may be used at low and medium temperatures as the principal flux, or in smaller amounts in high-temperature glazes where it may be considered an auxiliary flux (e.g., to calcia).

Soda (Na_2O) is very active from approximately 800°C/1472°F upwards, but it has a tendency to volatilize over 1200°C/2192°F with the same drawbacks described for lead.

Potassa and soda perform best when used together. However, they are never used as the only fluxes in a glaze, not even at low temperature, as the cooled glaze would be soluble. A little calcia is included as a stabilizer to prevent this. The following examples give you an idea of the proportions of these oxides that could be used to flux a glaze.

LT glaze	*HT glaze*
5 moles soda	2 moles potassa
3 moles potassa	1 moles soda
2 moles calcia	7 moles calcia
10 moles total	10 moles total

As the mole is now accepted as our standard unit of amount, the ceramic convention of not stating it in formulas or calculations is adopted here (see Lawrence and West, 1982). Further, as the ceramic convention is to make the fluxes add up to 1, the above fluxes would be expressed as

LT glaze	*Ht glaze*
0.5 soda	0.2 potassa
0.3 potassa	0.1 soda
0.2 calcia	0.7 calcia
1.0 total	1.0 total

Lithia (Li$_2$O) resembles soda in its effectiveness at low temperature, but it is like potassa in its wide firing range from about 800°C/1472°F to over 1200°C/2192°F. It has several advantages over soda and potassa. The addition of 1 percent lithium carbonate increases the gloss of a glaze and improves the resistance to wear. Higher amounts promote crystallization (more so than potassa or soda); with 2 to 3 percent a mistiness appears and increases with higher amounts. Again, very small amounts decrease the thermal expansion of a glaze, which is useful in LT glazes. In larger amounts this is reversed.

At higher temperatures lithia can be included for its particular color response with copper oxide and cobalt oxide (see Chapter 13). If too much is used at high temperature it tends to cloud the glaze, in contrast to calcia's brilliantly clear glazes. Lithium minerals are expensive but since lithia is the lightest of the metal oxides (mole weight 29.9 g as opposed to potassa 94 g, soda 62 g, and calcia 66 g) less lithia need be used.

As Paul Rado (1988) points out, "It seems a paradox that lithia, present in the crystalline form as in lithia bodies, has a very low (even negative) thermal expansion, whereas in the molten form, as in glazes, it causes a very high thermal expansion."

The Alkaline Earth Metal Oxides

These include calcia, magnesia, baria, and strontia. All the oxides listed in Group 2 of the Ceramic Table of Oxides (see Figure 11.1) are extremely refractory by themselves (none of them melt under 2000°C/3632°F), yet in suitable combinations with silica and other oxides melts may be produced at temperatures well within the reach of studio pottery kilns.

Calcia (CaO) is the principal flux in HT glazes firing over C.5 and is nearly always included in one form or another. At C.10 and above, it may be used as the sole flux. Under C.5 calcia becomes an auxiliary flux, or shares the work of fluxing equally with other fluxes, usually potassa. Its ability to act as a flux diminishes at lower temperatures, and under C.03 it is used to stabilize K$_2$O and Na$_2$O as already described, or to make the glaze opaque and matte (a "lime matte glaze").

Magnesia (MgO) in small amounts performs vigorously at high temperature as an auxiliary flux, but it is of little use as a flux under C.5. When talc (3MgO $\cdot$ 4SiO$_2$ $\cdot$ H$_2$O), or a frit is used to introduce magnesia, fusion occurs more readily. Its most useful firing range as a flux is C.5 to C.7. In the ceramics industry MgO is never used as the sole flux; CaO is preferred as it gives a stronger glass, and therefore, the whole piece is stronger.

Baria (BaO), like magnesia, is a good auxiliary flux over C.3 (1168°C/2134°F) if used in small amounts. Its firing range may be extended below this temperature if it is incorporated in a frit containing potassa and soda. Again, combinations of baria and boric oxide in a glaze or frit give extremely fluid melts at a lower temperature than when one of them is used without the other (see Exercise 31).

Strontia (SrO), another Group 2 fluxing oxide, introduced into a glaze via a frit, acts as a flux throughout pottery firing temperatures. In this form it can be used to replace lead oxide, thereby removing the risk of lead poisoning. It can be introduced as strontium carbonate though a higher temperature is required to break down the carbonate and release the oxide. Once released, however, it is more fusible than calcia. Thus, though more expensive than calcia, it may be used where a more fluid melt is required. Much used in Russia, there is new interest in strontia as a glaze material in other countries and some students working in the lower temperature range may like to carry out some research work on this flux after completing the course.

Other Oxides

Zinc oxide (ZnO) is an important auxiliary flux in the middle-temperature range (especially C.4 to C.6). About 2 to 4 percent by weight of zinc oxide in a glaze recipe is sufficient to give a good fluxing action. Below C.03 it does not act directly as a flux, but up to 1 percent can stimulate other fluxes and so increase the rate of fusion. In the higher temperature range (over C.5) small amounts can act as a starter flux, but it is always an auxiliary flux, the usual proportions of zinc to calcia stated in moles being: 1 mole of zinc oxide to 2–3 moles of calcia.

Lead oxide (introduced in a frit), *boric oxide,* or some zinc oxide can be included to improve the quality of the glass at low temperatures and to counteract shrinkage. Zinc also plays an important role in its ability to replace lead in low- and middle-temperature glazes in situations where the toxic nature of lead could be harmful. The famous Bristol glaze is an important example where lead has been replaced by zinc.

Types of Glazes

Glazes may be classified into six general types: transparent, opaque, matte, dry, crackle (or craquelle), and crystalline; within these categories there are a number of varieties. In the following description of glazes two further terms, underfired and overfired, have been included in order to describe fired glazes adequately.

Transparent Glaze

It is important to note that, where a completely transparent glaze is required, the correct proportion of oxides, and therefore of the raw materials that provide them, must be used so that everything will be drawn into the melt at the required firing temperature. It must also be cooled quickly through the first 100 degrees to prevent crystals from reforming. (Usually a normal cooling suffices, but if the kiln is extremely well insulated, it may be necessary to open the top vent slightly for a short while. Do *not* create a draft.) A transparent glaze is used so that the character of the ceramic body, or a surface decoration placed upon the body, may be seen through it.

Transparent glazes that do not *craze* (see below) are often used for domestic ware (see test no. 14, Plate 10; and test nos. 1 to 3, Plate 16).

Opaque Glaze

Ceramic raw materials, called opacifiers, that do not dissolve or only partially dissolve in the melt and crystals that form during cooling remain suspended in the cooled glaze scattering and reflecting the light in all directions. If sufficient opacifier is used, the body cannot be seen through the glaze and the surface presents a solid white (or colored) glaze. Tin oxide (3% to 7%) is the traditional LT opacifier; zircon ($ZrSiO_4$) (up to 16%), and refined zirconium dioxide (ZrO_2, zirconia) and its commercially produced derivatives, with or without zinc, are the HT opacifiers. This, however, is not a rigid ruling as both may be tried at LT and HT (though not tin in reduction). Mixes of the two are also used to reduce the high cost of tin, though the zirconia gives a duller quality than the brilliant, shiny tin glazes (see Plate 25).

The addition of a little zinc to zircon opacified glazes acts as a flux, offsetting the refractoriness of zircon silicate and also assisting opacification. This, however, does not occur in the presence of boric oxide (see Exercise 31).

Colloidal material and bubbles trapped in the glaze can give a cloudy or mild opaque quality: phosphorus released from fruit wood ashes is an example, giving a bluish milky opalescence. The scientific explanation is that substances with different refractive indices have different angles of reflection (see pp. 364, 367).

Matte Glaze

All the constituents enter the melt on firing, but on cooling some recrystallization occurs, and the minute invisible crystals thus formed are held within the glassy fraction to give a silky smooth but opaque glaze with a soft sheen (not the high gloss derived from tin or zircon). These are examples of supersaturated solutions from which some constituents precipitate on cooling. To achieve a satisfactory glaze, the proportions of the excess oxides have to be judged accurately for the firing temperature used. Simple methods of estimating these amounts will be given later. Baria, magnesia, and alumina are examples of HT matting agents (see Plate 16), calcia an example of a LT agent.

Underfired Glaze

This is not a true glaze, and where it is deliberately used for, say, a sculptural piece, it could more correctly be described as a "surface treatment." It is not fully matured, and some of the raw material may still be present in a rough-ground state. On the other hand, it may be sufficiently vitreous to feel smooth, though visibly opaque and often tight. If the glaze has been applied by brush, it may resemble house paint. Sometimes a viscous underfired glassy glaze is used effectively as a thick roll on a vertical surface. Alternatively, it may be rough and dry, in which case it may be called a dry glaze.

Dry Glaze (or surface treatment)

This type of surface treatment is often used for sculptural pieces when a rough weathered quality is sought. Many excellent finishes may be had from mixes of wood ash and kaolin (with or without coloring oxides or stains). A dry glaze is useful if quiet colors, which have not been fully developed by the presence of sufficient glass, and the qualities of a well-adhered textured surface are desired (see Plate 6).

Overfired Glaze

This occurs when a glaze has been fired above the temperature for which it has been compounded. It may also occur if the glaze has been soaked for too long at or near the top temperature. Although the first cause is the most common, the second should not be overlooked. An overfired glaze may run off the object onto the kiln shelf or form a pool of glaze inside a pot. In some cases overfired glazes look thin because some of the glaze constituents have volatilized, or because the glaze has become so fluid that it has soaked into the body. Sometimes the glaze disappears altogether; in other cases, it may have a volcanic appearance. This happens very often when a glaze has been soaked at top temperature but accidentally has been allowed to rise above this temperature for a short period so that new reactions start but do not complete. Very often this occurs without the potter knowing it has happened. Careful monitoring of the kiln is the answer.

Crackle Glaze

This type has been referred to in several places of this textbook. Here only a short summary is given. These are alkali glazes that shrink more than other types of glazes on cooling and therefore crack or craze. If this effect is desired, the glaze is usually called a *crackle glaze*; if it is not wanted, but occurs, it is called a *crazed glaze*.

Crystalline Glaze

This consists of a glassy matrix containing crystals which are large enough to be seen with the naked eye. The crystals may result from the precipitation and recrystallization during the cooling stage of firing of some of the constituents from a supersaturated solution (see Plate no. 27/28) or by seeding the glaze (see Figure 11.3). An oxidation firing is recommended for this type of glaze.

Crystal structure and growth around a nucleus are considered in Chap-

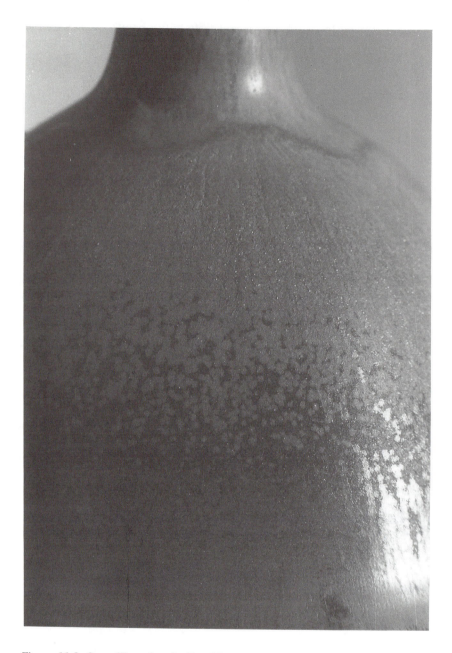

Figure 11.3. Crystalline glaze by Ray Silverman, showing a mass of small crystals. Photo: Geoff Kenward.

ter 1. In order to produce macrocrystals, the glaze is nucleated, or "seeded," by including such materials as titania, ilmenite, zirconium silicate, or zinc oxide in the glaze. Alternatively, a frit may be used that includes the required constituents, for example, zinc and silica. The glaze is then fired high enough to produce a fluid melt. The firing is stopped and in the initial stages of cooling tiny crystals (crystallites) form which can act as nuclei around which larger crystals can grow. The number of nuclei that form depends on the rate of cooling. If a lot of nuclei form, many small crystals will result. For macrocrystals, only a few nuclei are required, hence the glaze is cooled rapidly to at least 100°C/180°F lower, where nucleation does not occur, but constituents are still able to move in the glassy matrix. At this point the temperature is held constant for three or four hours and must not be allowed to fluctuate; during this time large crystals, sometimes 8 cm across, can form. The majority of crystal glazes are fired to C.10 or higher, but they may be achieved as low as C.09. If large crystals are to grow, the melt should be sufficiently fluid to allow constituents capable of forming large crystals to aggregate. For this reason the glaze must have an unusually low alumina content. The body used is also important: a fine grained clay without added sand or grog that gives a smooth surface and does not hinder crystal formation, e.g., a porcelain body, is excellent. For further reading see Norton (1974), Sanders (1974), and Hopper (1983).

Method Used in the Study of Glazes

Glaze development is dealt with in this chapter concentrating on glaze materials and combinations of them. In the next chapter we consider the oxide content of glazes and the way materials are chosen to fill glaze formulas.

Here, the Exercises are carried out in the following order.

1. High-temperature glazes, consisting of blends of two, three, and four materials: potassium feldspar, calcite, kaolin, and quartz.
2. Middle-temperature glazes, concentrating on three useful middle-temperature materials: colemanite, barium carbonate, and zinc oxide.
3. Low-temperature glazes, in which emphasis is placed on frits, tin and zirconia; clear glazes, opacified glazes, and the techniques of maiolica and enameling are also studied.

The Exercises are interspersed with relevant theoretical discussion. Although photographs of the fired tiles are given, you are advised to carry out 2-blends and 4-blends so that you may follow the assessment with respect to the materials available to you in your region. The tests of 3-blends are optional, though you should read the assessment. We begin with high-temperature tests for C.8–9, as the heat of the kiln in this range provides considerable energy enabling us to start with simple compositions of common and inexpensive raw materials.

Clear Transparent Glaze as a Norm

In Exercises 28 to 32 the principal aim is to produce clear transparent glazes without blemishes, that is, glazes in which all constituents are fully involved in the melt. Once you understand how a clear transparent glaze is achieved, this glaze will act as a norm (a standard or "normal" glaze) and, when things go wrong, a glance back at it may set you on the right track again. Having followed through this rather strict program of tests, you will be able to apply the knowledge gained to a wider field.

Visual Recall

By undertaking tests in which the number of materials used is gradually increased, we can, by visual means, create a store of knowledge about the effects the various materials have on one another. These tests will help you to develop an ability that may be labeled "visual recall." This visual recall is invaluable in glaze-making. Eventually, you will be able to imagine in your mind's eye exactly what the addition of a certain raw material will do to a glaze and have some idea how much to add to achieve the effect you desire. It is in this visual recall that the art of glaze-making lies.

Glaze Development

Exercises 28 and 30, on blends of two and four materials, are essential exercises. Note that minerals are described by their generic (or family) names, not as specific or regional varieties.

EXERCISE 28: Blends of Two Materials

Aim

To study the fusibility of mixes or *blends* of potassium feldspar, calcite, kaolin, quartz, and wood ash and to try to discover the reason why some mixes fuse while others do not. This is an essential Exercise.

Materials

About 100 g each of quartz, calcite, potassium feldspar, kaolin, and wood ash is needed. You should use the purest type of each family available in your area (e.g., for quartz use the purest SiO_2 mineral available; for potassium feldspar use one with the highest proportion of potassa, low calcia and soda, and carbon-free ash if possible). Note the name or catalog number and composition or formula of each material you use. You will also need ten leatherhard tiles, 9 cm × 9 cm in a stoneware clay. Make one or two extra tiles in case of breakage.

Method

Making and Marking the Tiles

Most of the fired tests carried out in glaze development should be kept for reference purposes and will be invaluable for anyone teaching, or planning to teach. You are therefore advised to prepare them as shown in Figure 5.11. The tiles illustrated are specifically designed for this Exercise (see also Plate 8).

1. Apply a thin coat of white slip on the front of the tiles in the white areas indicated in Figure 11.4 and a brush stroke of slip on the back. *Do not* put white slip on the areas where the glaze tests will be placed. Prop up the tiles a little until the slip has set.

2. As soon as the glistening water has evaporated, mark the front of the tiles as shown in Figure 11.4, using a very fine brush and marking oxide. If you wish, you could simply mark or score the letters A to J on the tiles at this stage and fill in the recipes with a waterproof permanent marker after firing.

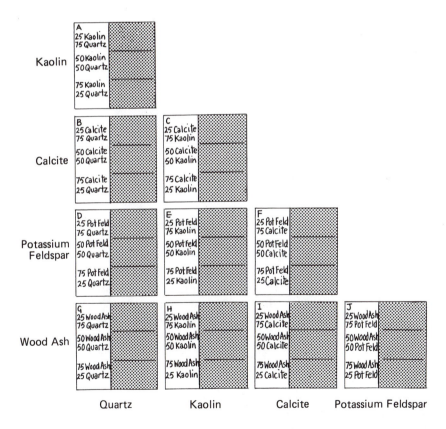

Figure 11.4. Layout for Exercise 28, "Blends of Two Materials," fired at C.8–C.9, 1260–1280°C/2300–2336°F.

3. Dry the tiles thoroughly and biscuit fire them if you are twice-firing (see p. 96).

4. Find a piece of hardboard, large enough to enable you to draw a chart approx. 35 cm × 35 cm. Paint the board with white household emulsion paint, and draw the outline positions (full size) for the ten tiles, marking them A to J. Do this in pencil. Write the rest of the information given in Figure 11.4 on the board surrounding the tiles, and place each leatherhard (or biscuit-fired) tile on the chart in the correct position before and after applying the glaze tests. This will help to prevent mistakes. After firing and the initial assessment, the tiles may be glued to the card and the remaining information written in with a permanent marker.

Making the Test Glazes

If several students are working together, the full amount could be weighed. For example, 25 g kaolin + 75 g quartz for the first test. The mix could then be shared by the group. If only one set of tiles is involved, a smaller batch of mix could be made. A reasonable quantity would be a total batch weight of 20 g, 5 g kaolin + 15 g quartz.

If you use the small batch weights, simply grind each test with a little water to a smooth paste on a glazed tile using a muller or a spatula/palette knife (if each test is well prepared, it should not need sieving). Add just sufficient water to apply the mix to the test tile. If you are making a full 100 percent recipe, place about 50 ml of water in a small mortar, and gently pour the mix on top of the water. Grind with a pestle until all the lumps have disappeared and you have a smooth paste. Then gradually add more water, mixing all the time until a finger dipped into the glaze is completely covered, but not thickly (see Figures 5.12 and 5.13). The specific gravity or the slip weight may be tested in one of the ways used for clay slips (see p. 216).

The specific gravities and slip weights for glazes are

Standard (leadless) glazes:
   SG = 1.45–1.5, slip weight = 145–150g/100ml
Glazes containing lead frits:
   SG = 1.55–1.6, slip weight = 155–160g/100ml

Sieve the test through a 100s or 120s mesh sieve. Any lumps left on the sieve should be returned to the mortar with a little of the glaze mix and reground until all the material passes through the sieve. When sieving ash tests, you should use a coarser sieve mesh, say 60s or 80s, or sieve the slip containing the other materials through a finer sieve (say 120s or 100s) and then add the ash and pass through a 60s/80s mesh.

Make sure that you do not leave any of the mix in the mortar. Use your rubber kidney to scrape it out. As glaze tests are mixed in small quantities, even 0.5 g of one material spilled or left on a sieve or in the mortar can make a difference to the result. This is very important in every glaze test you mix.

Figure 11.5. Applying glaze to a tile using a glaze mop. Photo: Ken Bright.

Applying the Glaze Tests

Use a full-bodied glaze mop or brush to apply the glaze test to the tile. Draw the brush, well-loaded with the mix, smoothly across the test area on the tile to give an even thickness (see Figure 11.5). If the deposit is not thick enough, wait a second or two until the glaze has stopped glistening with water but is not completely dry. Then recharge the brush, and draw it again lightly across the tile (if you wait until the glaze is "white dry" you may lift the first stroke off with the second). Make absolutely sure that each test tile is replaced in the right position.

Testing the Glaze Deposit for Thickness

While you are learning, check the thickness of your glaze by poking a thin pin or a needle through it. Better still, clean off a profile perpendicular to the edge of the glaze, particularly if you are raw glazing. This should be done when the glistening water has gone off but before the mix is "white-dry." The glaze tests should be about 2 mm thick (ash glazes 3 mm). It is better to apply these tiny test glazes a little on the thick side, rather than too thin, so do not be too sparing.

Throw away the remains of the test mix (or place it well aside if you plan to keep the mixes). It is essential not to confuse materials at this stage. Wash the glass and other equipment thoroughly, and quickly finish the other two tests for Tile A: 50% kaolin + 50% quartz, and 75% kaolin + 25% quartz.

Weighing and Mixing the Rest of the Glaze Tests

Figure 11.4 shows the proportions and the materials to mix together for each test on the remaining tiles. They should be mixed and applied in exactly the same way as described above.

Assembling the Tiles for Checking

As soon as each tile has been completed, clean any glaze off the back of the tile and replace it on the chart in the correct position to avoid confusion. If you do not do this, the tile will stick to the kiln shelf.

Firing

Make sure that all the tiles are placed together and fired in the same kiln. Fire the tile(s) in oxidation to C.8–9 or your standard workshop stoneware temperature, noting accurately the temperature reached, and switch off. *Do not soak on this occasion.* You will then see the exact stage the tests have reached at this temperature. Be careful not to overfire, or all your efforts will have been wasted. It is a good experience to fire the kiln yourself, or at least be present during the firing so that you can monitor the rate of temperature rise and the exact top temperature of the firing. This data should be recorded on a graph or in your notebook for future reference.

Results of Trials and Questionnaire

After arranging your fired tiles on the chart, try to answer the following questions. Do this in conjunction with the set in Plate 8. In the first attempt, answer them quickly and write down the answers. Then study the tiles again, using the assessment given at the end of these questions.

1. Is there any difference between the results on Tile A (kaolin and quartz) and quartz fired alone, as seen in the tests of single materials?
2. Quartz is common to tiles A, B, and D, but combined with kaolin on Tile A, with calcite on Tile B, and with feldspar on Tile D. After studying these three tiles, can you say what effect the feldspar has on quartz that is not achieved by kaolin or calcite? In general terms, how much feldspar has been needed to influence the degree of melting?
3. Write down the oxides contained in quartz, potassium feldspar, and calcite, and try to work out why quartz combined with feldspar gives a better reaction than quartz combined with calcite or kaolin.

4. a. Which of the three tests on Tile E (feldspar and kaolin) is the most satisfactory?
   b. How does it compare with the test of feldspar fired alone in the trials of single materials?
   c. How does it compare with the test on Tile D of 75% feldspar and 25% quartz?
5. a. Describe the appearance of the three tests on Tile F (feldspar and calcite), and compare them with the results on Tile I (wood ash and calcite) and Tile J (wood ash and feldspar).
   b. What characteristics do the tests on these tiles have in common?
   c. In what ways are they dissimilar? The differences will be subtle; it may be necessary to pick up the tiles and turn them in the light to evaluate them. Remember also that your results will depend on the particular ash used.
6. Make a list of the three test results which in your opinion are the best, and note the amounts and names of the raw materials in each one.
7. Pick out from the dry glazes (more accurately, surface treatments) one that might be useful, say, for a piece of ceramic sculpture (see Figure 10.2).
8. Which tests, if any, show crazing? Is there a common material that seems to be the cause of the crazing? If so, did this material craze when it was tested alone in the previous tests?
9. Looking at the complete set of tiles, can you see an overall pattern of increasing fusibility? If so, why is this?
10. Cut out ten small pieces of paper, and place them each on a tile. Write down the oxides contained in each test. How does the oxide content of each test correlate with the visual results of the tests? You are now advised to stick the tiles onto the chart in the correct order as a permanent record.

These questions have been designed to make you observe closely and think about the results. Go through the questions again, study and compare the fired results.

*   *   *

Although the following is marked as an Advanced Section, many of you will be able to follow it. Otherwise you should proceed to "Blends of Three Materials" (p. 275).

ADVANCED SECTION

This section discusses eutectic mixtures, that is, how particular proportions of two or more materials react together to produce the lowest possible melting temperature for such mixtures.

Remember that experiments to produce phase diagrams have been carried out by many investigators over the years, and therefore small differences sometimes appear in publications. Further, it should be noted that different experiments often give different results for eutectic temperatures. This could be due to improved techniques or because of the problems of achieving perfect equilibrium. For example, the author of phase diagram 4373 (1968), in the system SiO_2–Al_2O_3, states that the eutectic temperature is 1546°C, whereas the author of phase diagram 6443 (1975), quotes it as 1587°C plus or minus 10°C (see Figure 11.7, p. 267).

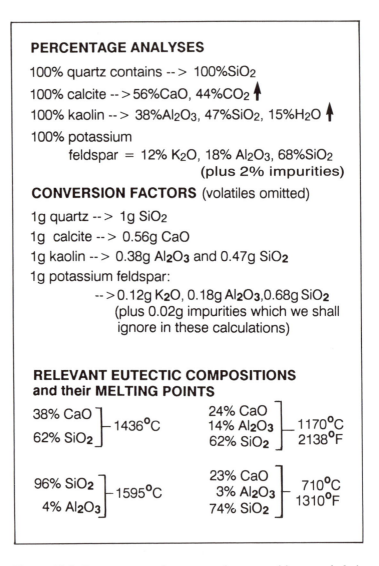

Figure 11.6. Percentage analyses, eutectic compositions, and their melting points, with conversion factors.

We shall now look at the tiles in greater detail, and, bearing in mind our reservations about using phase diagrams, as outlined in the section on frits, we shall support our visual evidence with data supplied by ceramic chemists. Figure 11.6 gives the percentage analyses of the four materials used on tiles A to F together with relevant conversion factors and some published eutectic compositions. We shall use all of these in the next few pages. (Ash is not included as it is a highly variable material.)

Percentage Analyses

Each percentage analysis states the proportions of oxides contained in the raw material. This is broken down further by dividing the percentage figures by 100 to give the amount of each oxide in 1 g of the material. These unity figures, or conversion factors, are very useful as they save lengthy, repetitive calculations. Since our concern is with the oxides *that enter the melt*, we shall not include in the conversion factors any oxide that volatilizes and is therefore a "loss on ignition" (usually expressed as l.o.i). For this reason water (H_2O) and carbon dioxide (CO_2) have been excluded.

Eutectic Compositions and Their Melting Points

A eutectic composition is the particular combination of two or more materials in a simple system that melts at the lowest possible temperature for a mixture of those materials.

In the following calculations it may be argued that the impurities in our raw materials affect our results. However, since the impurities lower the possible fusion temperatures and not raise them, the discussion is still valid.

We have already seen in Chapter 2 how geologists illustrate the way two minerals crystallize out of a cooling magma (see Figure 2.3). It has also been shown in the section on frits in Chapter 6, how phase diagrams are used in order to understand the heating history of ceramic materials. You are advised to review both of these sections before proceeding.

Tile A (Kaolin and Quartz) (see Plate 8)

It is clear from the results in Exercise 4, "Testing the Common Raw Materials," that silica by itself does not melt at temperatures normally used by the studio potter, so only a little improvement is seen on Tile A when quartz is combined with kaolin. We no longer have a powdery mass. The mineral grains have *sintered* (stuck together at points of contact), and all three tests of quartz and kaolin on Tile A have adhered to the pottery body. However, the result is a long way from the glassy state normally associated with a glaze.

Using the conversion factors given above (see Figure 11.6), we may calculate the proportion of oxides present in the fired test results on Tile A. Let us consider the first test on Tile A of 25 percent kaolin + 75 percent quartz. Since this is a percentage recipe, it may be quoted as 25 g kaolin +

75 g quartz, and by using the conversion factors we may convert this very quickly to a percentage of oxide content:

Calculations. For those who have not previously studied chemistry, the first line of the calculations should be read as follows:

1 g of kaolin *gives* 0.38 g Al_2O_3 plus 0.47 g SiO_2 to the melt.

(The water contained in the kaolin will vaporize during firing and is therefore omitted from this statement.) This method is used for all similar statements.

$$1 \text{ g kaolin} \rightarrow 0.38 \text{ g } Al_2O_3 + 0.47 \text{ g } SiO_2, \quad \text{therefore}$$
$$25 \text{ g kaolin} \rightarrow (0.38 \times 25) \, Al_2O_3 + (0.47 \times 25) \, SiO_2$$
$$= 9.50 \text{ g } Al_2O_3 + 11.75 \text{ g } SiO_2.$$

$$1 \text{ g quartz} \rightarrow 1 \text{ g } SiO_2, \quad \text{therefore}$$
$$75 \text{ g quartz} \rightarrow 75 \text{ g } SiO_2.$$

Adding up the total amount of Al_2O_3 and SiO_2, we have

9.50 g Al_2O_3 and 86.75 g SiO_2 = 96.25 g total oxide content.

Converting these figures to percentages gives

$$\frac{9.50 \times 100}{96.25} = 10\% \, Al_2O_3 \quad \text{and} \quad \frac{86.75}{96.25} \times 100 = 90\% \, SiO_2.$$

The list of eutectic compositions (see Figure 11.6) shows that this composition lies very near the eutectic composition of 96 percent silica plus 4 percent alumina (taken from the phase diagram, no. 6443, for SiO_2–Al_2O_3, published in 1975; see Figure 11.7). This would give a clear glassy result if soaked long enough at the eutectic temperature. However, you will also see that this eutectic composition does not melt until 1587°C, plus or minus 10°C. Because glazes fired in pottery kilns receive far less heat treatment than eutectic tests, it is no wonder that our glaze test does not show signs of fusion.

A phase diagram shows the melting history of combinations of SiO_2 and Al_2O_3 under laboratory conditions. Provided you bear in mind the observations made in the section on frits and phase diagrams in Chapter 6, a study of this diagram may act as a guide to the understanding of the melting history of combinations of kaolin and quartz.

Let us look at a eutectic mix of 95 percent SiO_2 and 5 percent Al_2O_3. The phase diagram for Al_2O_3–SiO_2 (Figure 11.7) tells us that, on heating, this mix will remain solid until 1587 (plus or minus 10°C), the eutectic temperature. At this point it will completely melt to give a liquid of the same composition, provided that the mix is held at this temperature long enough for the reaction to be complete. If we now consider the composition on the phase diagram which is slightly richer in alumina, 90 percent SiO_2 and 10 percent Al_2O_3 (comparable to our fired mix of kaolin and quartz), we shall see that,

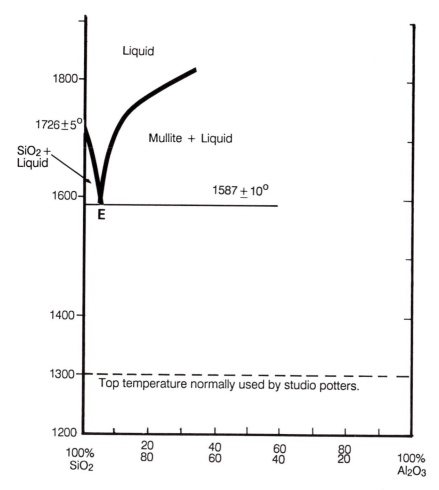

Figure 11.7. Simplified phase diagram for Al_2O_3–SiO_2, showing melting histories in the area near the eutectic composition. Other areas are beyond the scope of studio ceramics and have been omitted for clarity. Adapted from I. A. Aksay and J. A. Pask, *Journal of the American Ceramic Society* 58, 11–12 (1975): 507–12, fig. 6443. Reprinted by permission of the American Ceramic Society.

on heating, it remains solid until the eutectic temperature is reached. At this point some liquid of the eutectic composition forms, and will continue to form until all of the solid that can supply a liquid of the eutectic composition has been used up. If the temperature is now further increased, the excess material (in this case, alumina) will be drawn into the melt.

Tile B: Calcite and Quartz (see Plate 8)

The results are no better on Tile B. Sintering has occurred, but each test result still consists of an unfused mass. Here again we have only two oxides, CaO and SiO_2, left in the fired result after the CO_2 has burned away. The test result: 75 percent calcite + 25 percent quartz has hardened a little more than the other two tests, so we may consider this to be the best result and calculate the fired oxide content.

Calculations using conversion factors (see Figure 11.6).

$$1 \text{ g calcite} \rightarrow 0.56 \text{ g CaO,} \quad \text{therefore}$$
$$75 \text{ g calcite} \rightarrow (0.56 \times 75) \text{ g CaO} = 42 \text{ g CaO.}$$

$$1 \text{ g quartz} \rightarrow 1 \text{ g SiO}_2, \quad \text{therefore}$$
$$25 \text{ g quartz} \rightarrow 25 \text{ g SiO}_2.$$

Thus in the glaze we have 42 g CaO + 25 g SiO$_2$ = 67 g total oxide content. Converting these figures to percentages, gives

$$\frac{42}{67} \times 100 = 63\% \text{ CaO} \quad \text{and} \quad \frac{25}{67} \times 100 = 37\% \text{ SiO}_2$$

The phase diagram that contains these two oxides (Figure 6.9, p. 143), shows that one side of the triangle joins SiO$_2$ and CaO. You will also see that both oxides have exceptionally high melting points and that the lowest temperature at which a combination of CaO and SiO$_2$ can melt is 1436°C (and then only by holding the mix at this temperature for a long soak or by prefusing the mix). Given these facts, we have no hope of obtaining a melt under normal pottery firing conditions of temperature and soaking time. These results may be considered with those on Tile C.

Tile C, Calcite and Kaolin (see Plate 8)

The first test on this tile, C1 (25 percent calcite + 75 percent kaolin) shows little difference from the results on Tile B. Only the tests C2 (50% calcite + 50% kaolin) and C3 (75% calcite + 25% kaolin) are beginning to show some advance in the melting process. In the test result of C2 on Tile C, it appears that a large part of the mixture has disappeared during firing. This is due to the carbon and water burning off, leaving only a pitted remnant of the original glaze mix. This conclusion is supported by the calculations given below.

Calculations using conversion factors

$$1 \text{ g calcite} \rightarrow 0.56 \text{ g CaO} \quad (0.44 \text{ g CO}_2 \text{ volatilizes}), \quad \text{therefore}$$
$$50 \text{ g calcite} \rightarrow 28.00 \text{ g CaO} \quad (22.00 \text{ g CO}_2 \text{ volatilizes}).$$

$$1 \text{ g kaolin} \rightarrow 0.38 \text{ g Al}_2\text{O}_3 + 0.47 \text{ g SiO}_2 \quad (0.15 \text{ g H}_2\text{O vaporizes});$$
$$50 \text{ g kaolin} \rightarrow 19.00 \text{ g Al}_2\text{O}_3 + 23.50 \text{ g SiO}_2 \quad (7.50 \text{ g H}_2\text{O vaporizes}).$$

Total oxides in original mix	Total oxides after firing
28 % CaO	28.0 g CaO
22 % CO$_2$	0.0 CO$_2$
19 % Al$_2$O$_3$	19.0 Al$_2$O$_3$
23.5% SiO$_2$	23.5 SiO$_2$
7.5% H$_2$O	0.0 H$_2$O
100 % total	70.5 g total

The loss-on-ignition (l.o.i) = 29.5 g: over one-fourth of the original recipe has volatilized. (Note: The H_2O in the above list represents the water present in its various forms.)

Concentrating now on the total oxides left in the test glazes after firing, we may convert the fired test results for C1, C2, and C3 into our percentages. Note that we are concerned with the contents of the *fired glaze, not* the *unfired glaze mix.* Many students overlook this point!

C1: 25 g calcite → 14.00 g CaO
75 g kaolin → 28.50 g Al_2O_3 and 35.25 g SiO_2
total oxides = 77.75 g
% analysis: = 18% CaO; 37% Al_2O_3; 45% SiO_2

C2: 50 g calcite → 28 g CaO
50 g kaolin → 19 g Al_2O_3 and 24 g SiO_2
total oxides = 71 g
% analysis: = 40% CaO; 27% Al_2O_3; 34% SiO_2

C3: 75 g calcite → 42 g CaO
25 g kaolin → 9 g Al_2O_3 and 12 g SiO_2
total oxides = 63 g
% analysis: = 66% CaO; 15% Al_2O_3; and 19% SiO_2

On the simplified version of the phase diagram for CaO–Al_2O_3–SiO_2 (see Figure 6.9), the approximate positions of the three compositions C1, C2, and C3 have been plotted. It may be seen that all three compositions lie outside the triangle, or "phase field" containing the lowest possible eutectic temperature, 1170°C. At first glance, it might be thought that C2 could be useful, as it is tied to the next best eutectic temperature of 1265°C. However, this is only the temperature at which liquid of the eutectic temperature appears. Since C2 does not lie at or near the eutectic point, considerable superheat would be required to draw the excess material into the melt. The isotherms (lines of temperature) on the diagram indicate that this temperature would be about 1500°C. Compositions C1 and C3 similarly lie too far from a useful eutectic point.

Therefore, compositions suitable for firing under normal pottery conditions should lie in the phase field: SiO_2–$CaO \cdot SiO_2$–$CaO \cdot Al_2O_3 \cdot 2SiO_2$ (the field of cristobalite–pseudowollastonite–calcium feldspar) and as near to the 1170°C/2138°F eutectic point as possible. If we calculate the recipe of materials needed to fill the eutectic composition, it will be seen that it cannot be achieved by using calcite and kaolin alone; a third material has been added.

Proof. Convert the eutectic composition of 24% CaO + 14% Al_2O_3 + 62% SiO_2 to a recipe, using the conversion factors given in Figure 11.6 but in the reverse order:

0.56 g CaO is supplied by 1 g of calcite,   therefore
24.00 g CaO is supplied by $\dfrac{1 \times 24.00}{0.56} = 43$ g calcite.

$$0.38 \text{ g } Al_2O_3 \text{ is supplied by 1 g kaolin, therefore}$$
$$14.00 \text{ g } Al_2O_3 \text{ is supplied by } \frac{1 \times 14.00}{0.38} = 37 \text{ g kaolin.}$$

The 37 g of kaolin will also supply some SiO_2:

$$1 \text{ g kaolin supplies } 0.47 \text{ } SiO_2, \text{ therefore}$$
$$37 \text{ g kaolin supplies only } 0.47 \times 37 \text{ g} = 17.40 \text{ g } SiO_2.$$

But the eutectic composition requires 62 g SiO_2. We only have 17.40 g, so we need a further 44.6 g, which has to be supplied by a material containing silica alone. In this case 44.6 g quartz (or another member of this family) has to be added, thus carrying this composition beyond the scope of Exercise 28, "Blends of *Two* Materials." We shall deal with this in Exercise 29, "Blends of *Three* Materials." This does not mean that it is impossible to make a glaze using two natural materials, as seen in the blends of clay and ash on Tiles I and J (see Exercise 28 and Plate 8).

The purpose of this investigation has been to show that a balance of all the oxides is essential for the production of a satisfactory glaze. It should now be clear that an excess of any one of the oxides that carries the composition too far from a eutectic point in any direction will require too much superheat, and quickly places it beyond the reach of pottery kiln firing temperatures.

Tile D (Potassium Feldspar + Quartz) and Tile E (Potassium Feldspar + Kaolin)

Let us look at Tile E first. The tests on Tile E show no improvement on potassium feldspar alone, as seen in Exercise 4 and on Plate 7: "Testing the Common Raw Materials." The addition of kaolin serves only to increase the amount of alumina and silica, which proportionately lowers the only flux, potassium oxide. A temperature much higher than 1300°C would be needed to fuse completely the test of 75 percent potassium feldspar + 25 percent kaolin. The evidence of the phase diagram supports this. E1, E2, and E3 have been plotted on the triaxial phase diagram for $K_2O–Al_2O_3–SiO_2$ (Figure 11.8) where it can be seen that they all lie in the phase field called mullite ($3Al_2O_3 \cdot 2SiO_2$). Although tied to the reasonable eutectic temperature of 985°C, they are so far from it that an extraordinary amount of superheat would be required to fuse them.

On Tile D the fired results show that combinations of potassium feldspar and quartz are ineffective if the proportion of quartz remains high. Even the third test D3 (75% potassium feldspar + 25% quartz), which is slightly glassy, is still not as good as potassium feldspar alone, as seen in Exercise 4. However, the phase diagram for $K_2O–Al_2O_3–SiO_2$ seems to tell us a very different story. From this we learn that there is a eutectic point in this system at approximately 58% potassium feldspar + 42% silica. This composition fuses at the temperature of 985°C. For this reason, it might be

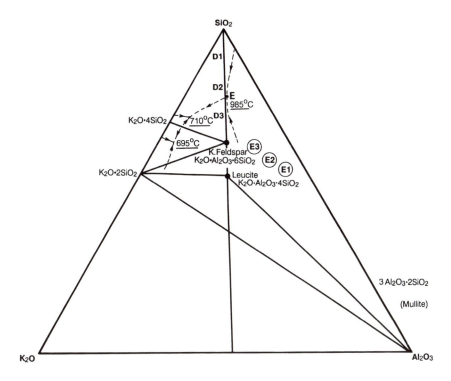

Figure 11.8. Simplified phase diagram for $K_2O-Al_2O_3-SiO_2$, showing the positions of the compositions D1, D2, D3 on Tile D and E1, E2, E3 on Tile E, Exercise 28. Adapted from E. F. Osborne and Arnulf Huan, *Phase Equilibrium Diagrams of Oxide Systems* (American Ceramic Society and Edward Orton, Jr., Ceramic Foundation, 1960), fig. 407, Plate 5. Reprinted by permission of the American Ceramic Society and the Edward Orton, Jr. Ceramic Foundation.

expected that the tests D2 (50% potassium feldspar + 50% quartz) and D3 (75% potassium feldspar + 25% quartz) would give a good result. Certainly these two results indicate the presence of some glass by a moderately shiny surface, but neither has cleared to a transparent glaze, and D2 is still rough to the touch. Even the more detailed line blend of potassium feldspar–quartz (see Figure 11.9), which was taken up to 1250°C (over 250°C above the published eutectic temperature) and held at this temperature for three hours has not produced a better result than potassium feldspar alone (see Exercise 4). How may we resolve the conflict between these two sets of evidence?

On the triaxial phase diagram in Figure 11.8, D1 lies very near the silica apex and therefore would be refractory, but D2 and D3 lie quite near the eutectic point of 985°C and therefore deserve closer study. In order to do this a biaxial phase diagram for leucite–silica that shows blends of potassium feldspar and silica is given in Figure 11.10, and D1, D2, and D3 have been plotted on it. (Note that the author of Figure 11.10 expresses the eutectic

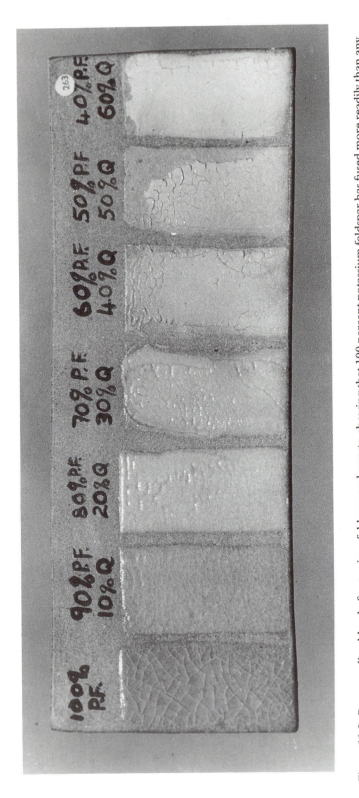

Figure 11.9. Crossover line blend of potassium feldspar and quartz, showing that 100 percent potassium feldspar has fused more readily than any mixture with quartz. Photo: the author.

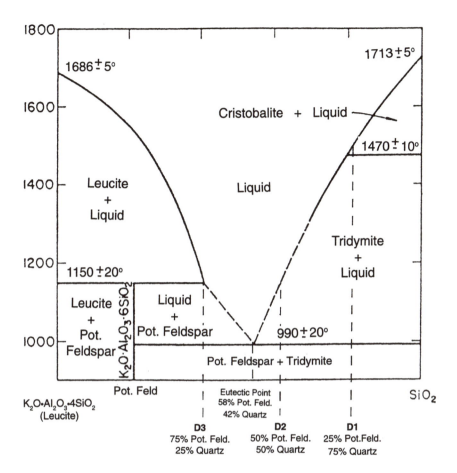

Figure 11.10. Biaxial phase diagram for $K_2O \cdot Al_2O_3 \cdot 4SiO_2$ (leucite)–SiO_2, showing the melting history of mixtures of potassium feldspar and quartz. Superimposed on the diagram are the compositions D1, D2, D3 on Tile D, Exercise 28. From the American Ceramic Society, *Phase Diagrams for Ceramists*, fig. 412, after J. F. Schairer and N. L. Bowen, *American Journal of Science* 240 (1947), fig. 4. Reprinted by permission of the American Ceramic Society.

point at 990°C (±20°C) compared with 985°C in Figure 11.8. The reason for this is given above, p. 264.)

If you study this diagram, you will see that 100 percent potassium feldspar and mixes containing more than 75 percent of it start to decompose at 1150°C. Some of the silica released from the decomposing feldspar enters the melt, leaving the remaining constituents to re-form into crystals that contain a smaller portion of silica, namely, leucite ($K_2O \cdot Al_2O_3 \cdot 4SiO_2$). As these will be tiny newly formed crystallites with fresh faces, they will not obstruct the passage of light to the same extent as rough ground particles of feldspar. The leucite will still affect the quality of the fired result, making the glaze slightly cloudy and sometimes milky, but not as opaque and white as in the case of mixes that still contain particles of ground feldspar. With this knowledge the melting history of compositions D3, D2, and D1 can be traced on the phase diagram.

In *Composition D3*, liquid of the eutectic composition forms at 990 ± 20°C; with further heat increase above this temperature, more and more solid would be drawn into the melt. D3 meets the liquidus at 1150°C and would only thereafter complete its conversion to the liquid phase at that temperature (given time to complete the melting process).

For *Composition D2*, on heating to the eutectic temperature, liquid of the eutectic composition forms, which takes up all the feldspar in the mix and some of the silica. The excess silica is gradually drawn into the melt until on reaching the liquidus just under 1200°C, either with a long soak or with superheat in lieu of a long soak, the last of the silica melts.

The heating history of *Composition D1* is similar to that of D2, but there is a considerable amount of excess silica and more heat treatment (heat-work) would be required to convert all of it to the liquid phase. It should also be noted that, as the heat input increases, a conversion of the crystalline silica from tridymite to cristobalite occurs.

All the above has been described on the basis that at the top temperature the mix has been held at the necessary temperature long enough for the conversion from solid to liquid to be completed. In practice, this is usually not possible under normal pottery firing conditions, which leads us to the next topic.

Investigating the Extra Heat Required to Replace a Long Soak

It is now necessary to discover the time, or the amount of superheat in lieu of a long soak, required to allow the melting process to be completed. We have already seen the tests on Tile D and the repeat detail tests (see Figure 11.9), which when taken 100°C higher to 1250°C (260°C above the eutectic temperature) and soaked for three hours, became more glassy but did not produce complete melts. Given these results, a mix of the eutectic composition was tested under laboratory conditions to discover the amount of superheat required in lieu of a long soak at the eutectic temperature, 985°C, to complete its conversion from the solid to the liquid phase. This mix was chosen because, being the most fusible mix, it would establish the minimum soak time and/or superheat required to complete the melt.

The mix was first taken to 1450°C/2642°F, and still the test sample was white, tight, and opaque. It was then taken higher still. Not until 1660°C/3020°F, plus a four-hour soak did the sample clear to a transparent complete melt.

In these experiments we have used materials that contribute at most three oxides. In practice many glazes contain at least four or five oxides as well as impurities, making it extremely difficult to identify eutectics or to trace the course of melting.

Before leaving this topic it is worth mentioning again that, although a theoretical consideration of the subject is useful for teaching purposes, it has little value when composing a glaze. This does not mean that eutectics do not play an important part in the firing of ceramics. On the contrary, they are of great value in bringing the initial fusion of a body or glaze down to a reasonable temperature. The problem lies in their complexity, especially when more than three oxides are present in a mix.

■ ■ ■

EXERCISE 29: Blends of Three Materials

Firing temperature: C.8–9 in oxidation

The traditional method of running triaxial blends has not been used here. Instead a format is used that relates directly to the previous tests. By doing this and using the same refined materials, comparisons may be made more readily between the tests of blends of two materials and blends of three materials.

It is suggested that you study Plate 9, together with the oxide content of the tests given in Figure 11.11, and try to follow the arguments set out in the assessment. In Figure 11.11 both the percentage analyses and formulas of each test are given; it is useful to be able to read both these forms of expressing the chemical composition of materials and glazes as they enable the potter to compare a glaze with the oxide content of minerals and also make use of knowledge gained from other areas of science. (It would be a good idea to photocopy Figure 11.11 so that you can place it beside the assessment while studying it.) After this you may decide whether to undertake any of the tests. If you do, tiles 9 cm × 16 cm will be adequate, and you should follow the method used in Exercise 28.

Assessment of Blends of Three Materials

Looking at Plate 9 and surveying the test tiles as a whole show that all the tests on Tile D2 are white and none are shiny. It is clear that there would be little value in carrying out these tests, but it is worth considering why they have resisted the heat of the kiln and remained underfired. If you look at the materials used, you will see that the only flux is potassa, contained in potassium feldspar. Since potassium feldspar has the theoretical formula $K_2O \cdot Al_2O_3 \cdot 6SiO_2$, only a small fraction of the feldspar consists of K_2O. Even in the recipe with 75 percent potassium feldspar, the K_2O is far outweighed by the Al_2O_3 and SiO_2 introduced with it and the SiO_2 introduced by quartz. (Check the formula of your own feldspar, and you should find this statement rings true, that is, there is proportionally much less flux than the other constituents). Therefore adding kaolin increases the silica content and brings with it increasing amounts of the very refractory oxide alumina, and no further flux. The solution is to add one of the fluxes that react

TILE A2

25% kaolin / 75% quartz	+ 25% calcite	+ 50% calcite	+ 75% calcite
unity formula	$1CaO$ $0.4Al_2O_3$ $6SiO_2$ [1:15]	$1CaO$ $0.2Al_2O_3$ $2.9SiO_2$ [1:14]	$1CaO$ $0.1Al_2O_3$ $2SiO_2$ [1:20]
analysis	$12\%CaO$ $10\%Al_2O_3$ $78\%SiO_2$	$22\%CaO$ $8\%Al_2O_3$ $70\%SiO_2$	$31\%CaO$ $7\%Al_2O_3$ $62\%SiO_2$

50% kaolin / 50% quartz	+ 25% calcite	+ 50% calcite	+ 75% calcite
unity formula	$1CaO$ $0.8Al_2O_3$ $5SiO_2$ [1:6]	$1CaO$ $0.4Al_2O_3$ $2.4SiO_2$ [1:6]	$1CaO$ $0.26Al_2O_3$ $1.6SiO_2$ [1:6]
analysis	$13\%CaO$ $18\%Al_2O_3$ $69\%SiO_2$	$23\%CaO$ $17\%Al_2O_3$ $60\%SiO_2$	$31\%CaO$ $15\%Al_2O_3$ $54\%SiO_2$

75% kaolin / 25% quartz	+ 25% calcite	+ 50% calcite	+ 75% calcite
unity formula	$1CaO$ $1.2Al_2O_3$ $4SiO_2$ [1:3]	$1CaO$ $0.58Al_2O_3$ $2SiO_2$ [1:3]	$1CaO$ $0.4Al_2O_3$ $1.3SiO_2$ [1:3]
analysis	$13\%CaO$ $29\%Al_2O_3$ $58\%SiO_2$	$24\%CaO$ $25\%Al_2O_3$ $51\%SiO_2$	$32\%CaO$ $23\%Al_2O_3$ $45\%SiO_2$

TILE B2

25% calcite / 75% quartz	+ 25% potassium feldspar	+ 50% potassium feldspar	+ 75% potassium feldspar
unity formula	$0.15K_2O$ $0.15Al_2O_3$ $5SiO_2$ $0.85CaO$ [1:33]	$0.3K_2O$ $0.2Al_2O_3$ $5SiO_2$ $0.7CaO$ [1:25]	$0.35K_2O$ $0.35Al_2O_3$ $5.4SiO_2$ $0.65CaO$ [1:15]
analysis	$4\%K_2O$; $13\%CaO$; $4\%Al_2O_3$; $79\%SiO_2$	$7\%K_2O$; $10\%CaO$; $7\%Al_2O_3$; $76\%SiO_2$	$8\%K_2O$; $9\%CaO$; $8\%Al_2O_3$; $75\%SiO_2$

50% calcite / 50% quartz	+ 25% potassium feldspar	+ 50% potassium feldspar	+ 75% potassium feldspar
unity formula	$0.08K_2O$ $0.08Al_2O_3$ $2SiO_2$ $0.92CaO$ [1:25]	$0.15K_2O$ $0.15Al_2O_3$ $2.3SiO_2$ $0.85CaO$ [1:15]	$0.2K_2O$ $0.2Al_2O_3$ $2.6SiO_2$ $0.8CaO$ [1:13]
analysis	$4\%K_2O$; $27\%CaO$; $5\%Al_2O_3$; $64\%SiO_2$	$7\%K_2O$; $22\%CaO$; $7\%Al_2O_3$; $64\%SiO_2$	$8\%K_2O$; $18\%CaO$; $9\%Al_2O_3$; $65\%SiO_2$

75% calcite / 25% quartz	+ 25% potassium feldspar	+ 50% potassium feldspar	+ 75% potassium feldspar
unity formula	$0.06K_2O$ $0.06Al_2O_3$ $0.86SiO_2$ $0.94CaO$ [1:14]	$0.1K_2O$ $0.1Al_2O_3$ $1SiO_2$ $0.9CaO$ [1:10]	$0.15K_2O$ $0.15Al_2O_3$ $1.4SiO_2$ $0.85CaO$ [1:9]
analysis	$4\%K_2O$; $46\%CaO$; $4\%Al_2O_3$; $46\%SiO_2$	$7\%K_2O$; $39\%CaO$; $8\%Al_2O_3$; $46\%SiO_2$	$9\%K_2O$; $29\%CaO$; $10\%Al_2O_3$; $52\%SiO_2$

TILE E2

25% p.feld. / 75% kaolin	+ 25% calcite	+ 50% calcite	+ 75% calcite
unity formula	$0.15K_2O$ $1.14Al_2O_3$ $3SiO_2$ $0.85CaO$ [1:2.6]	$0.1K_2O$ $0.6Al_2O_3$ $1.6SiO_2$ $0.9CaO$ [1:2.6]	$0.06K_2O$ $0.4Al_2O_3$ $1SiO_2$ $0.94CaO$ [1:2.5]
analysis	$4\%K_2O$; $13\%CaO$; $33\%Al_2O_3$; $50\%SiO_2$	$4\%K_2O$: $23\%CaO$; $28\%Al_2O_3$; $45\%SiO_2$	$4\%K_2O$; $33\%CaO$; $26\%Al_2O_3$; $37\%SiO_2$

50% p.feld. / 50% kaolin	+ 25% calcite	+ 50% calcite	+ 75% calcite
unity formula	$0.3K_2O$ $0.8Al_2O_3$ $2.7SiO_2$ $0.7CaO$ [1:3]	$0.15K_2O$ $0.5Al_2O_3$ $1.6SiO_2$ $0.85CaO$ [1:3]	$0.1K_2O$ $0.34Al_2O_3$ $1SiO_2$ $0.9CaO$ [1:3]
analysis	$9\%K_2O$; $13\%CaO$; $26\%Al_2O_3$; $52\%SiO_2$	$7\%K_2O$; $23\%CaO$; $24\%Al_2O_3$; $45\%SiO_2$	$7\%K_2O$; $33\%CaO$; $22\%Al_2O_3$; $38\%SiO_2$

75% p.feld. / 25% kaolin	+ 25% calcite	+ 50% calcite	+ 75% calcite
unity formula	$0.3K_2O$ $0.6Al_2O_3$ $2.6SiO_2$ $0.7CaO$ [1:4]	$0.2K_2O$ $0.36Al_2O_3$ $1.6SiO_2$ $0.8CaO$ [1:4]	$0.15K_2O$ $0.26Al_2O_3$ $1SiO_2$ $0.85CaO$ [1:4]
analysis	$10\%K_2O$; $14\%CaO$; $21\%Al_2O_3$; $55\%SiO_2$	$9\%K_2O$; $23\%CaO$; $19\%Al_2O_3$; $49\%SiO_2$	$10\%K_2O$; $32\%CaO$; $18\%Al_2O_3$; $40\%SiO_2$

Figure 11.11. Layout and recipes for Exercise 29, "Blends of Three Materials," showing the unity formulas and percentage analyses of tests on Tiles A2, B2, and E2, fired at C.8–9.

particularly well at temperatures over C.5 (1200°C/2192°F), i.e., the Group 2 fluxes and, in particular, CaO. We may therefore put aside Tile D2 and concentrate on the other three tiles: A2, B2, and E2.

Tile A (Quartz and Kaolin) and Tile A2 (with Calcite Added)

Comparing blends of two materials on Tile A with blends of three materials on Tile A2 where calcite has been added, reveals that again there is only one flux. In this case, it is the high temperature flux calcia which begins its fluxing action over 1100°C/2012°F. (Its role below this temperature is discussed on p. 252.)

If you compare the results at the top of Tile A with the top row of Tile A2 (see Plate 9), you will see that the addition of calcite produces a slight improvement. The results look less white and powdery than the test (25 g kaolin + 75 g quartz) on Tile A, and the last test in the top row of Tile A2 shows the first signs of fusion. Increased fusion may be detected along the bottom row but they still feel rough.

(In Plate 9, note how the last two tests have lost their whiteness. This is because they were applied too thinly and have merged with the surface of the clay.)

In the middle row of Tile A2, a marked change is seen where 50 g calcite has been added to 50 g kaolin + 50 g quartz in test no. 5, giving us a recipe of:

50 g calcite	or	33.3% calcite
50 g kaolin	or	33.3% kaolin
50 g quartz	or	33.3% quartz
150 g total		100.0%

This test result is so clear that you may have difficulty seeing it in the illustration. It is a completely transparent glaze. Notice how the light reflects off the shiny surface — a startling contrast with the other results. We have chanced on a mix that gives a transparent, glassy result. It is clear from this examination that test no. 5 is the best result on this tile and is the test referred to in the assessment of Tile C, "Blends of Two Materials." If you look back to the assessment of Tile C (kaolin + calcite), you will see that we could not fill the total requirement of silica in any of the tests without adding a third material. This has been accomplished by adding quartz in test no. 5, Tile A2.

If there are other usable compositions consisting of these three materials, their recipes must lie very near test no. 5 and toward tests nos. 6 or 3, but not toward nos. 1, 4, and 7, the very dry white results to the left.

Students not following the Advanced section should proceed to p. 279 for a short discussion of Tile B2.

Advanced students should proceed to the following discussion that involves phase diagrams.

ADVANCED SECTION

Given that the three materials used on Tile A2 contribute the three oxides CaO, Al_2O_3, and SiO_2 let us examine the fired results shown in Plate 9 (and your own results if you have carried out the tests) in conjunction with the positions of their compositions on the phase diagram for CaO–Al_2O_3–SiO_2 (see Figure 6.9). The proportions of these oxides in each test are critical: a small excess of any one of these oxides can throw the glaze out of balance.

Let us examine this in conjunction with the chart showing the formulas and percentage analyses of each glaze (see Figure 11.11). In this chart, you will see that test no. 5 (50 g kaolin + 50 g quartz + 50 g calcite), contributes the following proportion of oxides to the melt:

stated as a percentage analysis: 23% CaO; 17% Al_2O_3; 60% SiO_2
stated as a formula: 1CaO 0.4Al_2O_3 2.4SiO_2

The calculation converting the percentage composition to a formula is not given here as this subject is dealt with in detail in the next chapter.

Assessment

Using the formula of our test glaze, stated above, let us compare the test glaze with the formula of calcium feldspar:

Calcium feldspar = $CaO \cdot Al_2O_3 \cdot 2SiO_2$
Test no. 5. = $CaO \cdot 0.4Al_2O_3 \cdot 2.4SiO_2$

Reminder: Calcium feldspar has only 2 moles of silica and not 6 moles as in potassium feldspar. Which do you think will melt sooner?

We can make use of the *percentage analysis* to plot the position of test no. 5 on the phase diagram. For practical reasons this has been done for you (see Figure 6.9), but make sure that you know how to carry this out (see p. 144 for help). Now study the position of test no. 5 in relation to the position of the eutectic point for this phase field, marked E in the figure, and the position of calcium feldspar. The eutectic temperature is 1170°C/2138°F; the MP for calcium feldspar is 2570°C/4658°F. Find these points on the phase diagram. Can you estimate the temperature at which test no. 5 is able to fuse completely?

The *answer* to this question must be approximately 1180–1200°C/2156–2192°F, if given enough time at this temperature for reactions to complete. Furthermore, if there is one composition lying near the eutectic point (i.e., test no. 5) that is able to give a complete melt within our firing capabilities, then there is reason to expect that there are others, certainly those lying between no. 5 and the eutectic point.

If you now look at the plots for the other tests on Tile A in the triaxial phase diagram for $CaO-Al_2O_3-SiO_2$ (see Figure 6.9), you will see that test nos. 1, 4, and 7 lie a long way from the eutectic point. Test no. 1 lies very near the silica apex, and no. 7, being in another phase field, is tied to a different eutectic point with a eutectic temperature of 1345°C/2453°F. Thus the underfired results of these tests on Tile A2 correspond with the theoretical findings. The compositions for test nos. 8 and 9 are similarly distant from the eutectic point, E. Only the compositions of test nos. 3 and 6 lie near the eutectic point, but not as near as no. 5, confirming the suggestion given above that further experiments be carried out to the right and above test no. 5 on Tile A, that is, toward test nos. 3 and 6 but clearly not extending beyond them as the phase diagram and the test results show that the limits have been reached or passed.

We now come to the value of phase diagrams in this study. If you consider any of the compositions in the phase diagram, you will see that a move in any direction rapidly changes the proportions of the oxides to one another, and a different temperature will be required to melt them. Thus, when composing a glaze it is not just a matter of a little more or a little less of a certain flux but the balanced *proportions* of all the oxides that contribute to the melt. The other point revealed by this study, which is a comfort to know, is that there are always a few compositions lying near a successful one that should give good results, and this allows us a margin of error in weighing out. On the other hand, it also reveals that if a composition lies near the border with another phase field a slight error in composition (or in weighing out) may carry the composition over into another phase field with a possible considerable change in results, for example, in refractoriness or even color.

Superheat Versus Holding the Glaze at the Temperature at Which Melting Begins

The phase diagram shows that the eutectic mix of 24 percent CaO, 14 percent Al_2O_3, 62 percent SiO_2 is capable of melting at 1170°C/2138°F if held at this temperature. Experiments were therefore carried out by the author to find the time required to complete the melt at this temperature. This proved to be 24 hours. The tests carried out in this Exercise and illustrated in Plate 9 demonstrate that it melted by 1260–1280°C/2300–2336°F without this long soak. Clearly, it requires only 100°C of superheat in lieu of a 24-hour soak to melt it.

Just because this diagram shows so clearly what is happening on this tile, it does not follow that phase diagrams can be used with ease in every case in ceramics. Nor can it be inferred that, because the above eutectic composition required only 24 hours to complete the melt at 1170°C/2138°F, other eutectic compositions will melt at the eutectic temperature within a reasonable period. In fact, many compositions would probably take many years or even geologic time. Further, other triaxial phase diagrams are not as useful as this one, which is relatively easy to illustrate because there is only one flux, thus giving a glaze consisting of only three component oxides which can be represented on a triangle. It is fortunate for ceramists that the one for $CaO–Al_2O_3–SiO_2$ serves our purpose so well.

■ ■ ■

Tile B2 (Calcite and Quartz) plus Potassium Feldspar

Comparing the results on Tile B2 with the white and still powdery results on Tile B, we can see that the addition of potassium feldspar has had a significant effect. In test no. 1 on Tile B2, which only has 25 percent potassium feldspar, the improvement is minimal and the results rough to the touch. However, as we look along the top row of Tile B2, we see the development of a shiny glassy surface, though it remains tight and white and full of bubbles and craters. These indicate that the kiln must have been switched off at a stage when the glaze was boiling (and the volatiles escaping). Craters have been formed by the escaping gases and have remained in the cooling glaze because the melt at this temperature was too viscous to flow in and fill up the crater or allow the glaze to smooth out into an even surface.

The results are worse in the middle row where the bubbles are only just forming. These tests contain far too little silica, giving an unbalanced ratio of alumina to silica. Similarly, in the bottom row there is an imbalance between the fluxes and alumina + silica. Only in the last test, no. 9, is there some semblance of a glaze, and even here, there is too little of the essential glass-forming silica to form a clear transparent glaze.

The Alumina: Silica Ratio

If you look at the formulas of the tests in Figure 11.11, you will see that there is 1 mole of flux in each formula. This gives us a constant against which we may compare the proportions of the other oxides and their effects on the results.

The proportions of silica in the majority of the tests on Tiles A2 and B2 lie between 1.4 and 5 moles of silica. Again, excluding test nos. 4 and 7 on both tiles and no. 8 on Tile A2, the range of alumina content lies between 0.1 and 0.4 of a mole. These are reasonable levels for both alumina and silica, and tests confirming this will be included in the next chapter. However, if the proportions of alumina to silica in each test are compared, a very different picture emerges. Two examples are taken:

$$\text{test no. 5 on Tile A2:} \quad 0.4\,Al_2O_3 : 2.4\,SiO_2$$
$$\text{test no. 5 on Tile B2:} \quad 0.15\,Al_2O_3 : 2.3\,SiO_2$$

To simplify these proportions so that we may study them, we can reduce the alumina to *unity*, thus giving a constant from which to make comparisons:

$$\text{test no. 5 on Tile A2:} \quad \frac{0.4\,Al_2O_3}{0.4} : \frac{2.4\,SiO_2}{0.4} = 1\,Al_2O_3 : 6\,SiO_2$$

$$\text{test no. 5 on Tile B2:} \quad \frac{0.15\,Al_2O_3}{0.15} : \frac{2.3\,SiO_2}{0.15} = 1\,Al_2O_3 : 15\,SiO_2$$

We now see that there is six times more silica than alumina in the first glaze, and 15 times more silica in the second glaze. These tests alert us to the fact that the ratio of alumina to silica is very important. Because this concept is very important, and because it is used in the glaze calculations, these proportions are placed in square brackets, e.g., [$Al_2O_3 : 6SiO_2$] or simply [1:6].

The best result on Tile A2, no. 5, and no. 6 as second best, have alumina : silica ratios of [1:6]. Comparing this ratio with the alumina : silica ratio in the top row shows that in each case the ratio is well above [1 : 10], namely from [1 : 14] to [1 : 20]. This proportion of alumina : silica gives poor results. Along the bottom row, on the other hand, the ratio of [1 : 3] gives a dry result. A satisfactory alumina : silica ratio must therefore lie somewhere between them (lower than [1 : 15], higher than [1 : 3]). These findings are supported by the results on Tile B2, where the only tests producing reasonable results are nos. 8 and 9, with alumina : silica ratios of [1 : 10] and [1 : 9] respectively (in contrast to the other results where ratios are [1 : 15] up to [1 : 33]). Again, tile E2 shows that a proportion of [1 : 4] is only just beginning to give a reasonable result. Thus it is seen that where the proportion of silica is more than 10 times that of alumina, the result is underfired at the temperature used. Where the proportion of silica is less than 5, the result is dry and, again, underfired. This leads us to the conclusion that, given sufficient flux to promote melting, a proportion of [1 : 5] up to [1 : 10] is a satisfactory proportion of alumina : silica at the chosen firing temperature.

If a glaze contains this proportion but still does not give a clear transparent result, it means that either:

1. the amount of silica is so small that not enough of this important glass-forming oxide is present to provide sufficient glass in the glaze, or
2. the amount of alumina as well as silica present, if the alumina : silica ratio is kept within the limits, is too much for the flux(es) at the firing temperature used.

A good example is seen in test no. 4, Tile A2, where the alumina : silica ratio is [1 : 6] but the total amount of the refractory oxides (alumina and silica) is much too high for the amount of the single flux (calcia) present. The percentage analysis tells us that there is only 13 percent CaO in contrast to 23 percent CaO in test no. 5 and similar high proportions of calcia in the other reasonable results.

The only other test result that is difficult to assess in the photograph is no. 8 on Tile A2. This has lost its whiteness and may appear to be transparent, but in reality it is rough to the touch. This roughness may be accounted for by the high proportion of alumina in relation to the silica, namely 0.58 Al_2O_3 to 2 SiO_2, giving an alumina : silica ratio of [1 : 3], thus denoting a dry glaze.

Tile E2 (Potassium Feldspar and Kaolin) plus Calcite

You should now try to make your own assessment. For those who have not carried out the tests, a brief description of each test is given below.

Top row: 1, rough, underfired; 2, and 3, slight shine, underfired.
Middle row: 4, smooth but stony no shine, still white; 5, and 6, same as 2 and 3.
Bottom row: 7, glassy but crazed where thick; 8, slight shine, smooth; 9, the same.

The photograph of the fired results shows that the glazes improve toward the bottom left, where tests 4, 7, and 8 have very satisfactory fluxes. So why is the result of test no. 7 more glassy than no. 4? How can the alumina : silica ratio help to answer this question? The answer is that no. 7 with a ratio of [1 : 4] has a higher proportion of glass-forming silica. This ratio also tells us that the three glazes in this corner (4, 7, 8) could do with a little more glass-forming silica (e.g., raising the silica in no. 7 to 3.5 moles to give an alumina : silica ratio of [1 : 5.8] would improve the glaze considerably). This and similar questions will be studied in the next chapter.

Although the assessment of this Exercise is complicated, it will help to develop a critical sense of the proportions or balance of oxides that contribute to a clear glaze. Further, when you try to formulate a special glaze such as a matte glaze or a crystalline one, you will know how to adjust the balance (or proportions) of the oxides to achieve these effects. This aspect of the subject will become much clearer after you have studied the section on *the melt*.

*   *   *

EXERCISE 30: Blends of Four Materials

This is an essential Exercise.

Aim

To gain as swiftly as possible a general idea of the type of glazes produced by varying the proportions of four important materials. We shall continue our quest for a clear transparent glaze; in addition, other qualities will be noted.

A set of sixteen recipes will be made. The leftover glaze should be dried and stored as powders (small labeled polyethylene bags serve well, but secure them tightly). When you start to use a new clay body, these sixteen tests may be repeated, and the results compared with the first set in order to assess the glaze potential with the new clay. For this reason a 100 g batch will be made of each recipe.

Materials

You will need 400 g each of potassium feldspar, calcite, kaolin, and quartz (record the reference number of each material in your notebook); sixteen jars with lids; a waterproof marker; and one red-firing tile, 15 cm × 15 cm for a C.8–9 firing (two tiles if firing in oxidation and reduction). Mark the tiles, by scoring, into sixteen squares, daub a tiny brushstroke of white slip in the left-hand top corner of each square on the front, and number the squares 1 to 16 (see Figure 11.12). Brush a patch of white slip on the back of the tile,

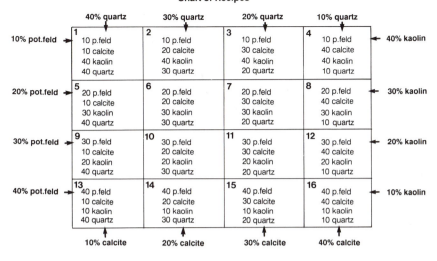

Figure 11.12. Layout and recipes for Exercise 30, "Blends of Four Materials," fired at C.8–9.

and when dry, write with marking oxide, Ex.30, C.8–9, and "O" or "R" according to the type of firing. Also draw an arrow pointing to the top of the tile. The tiles should then be biscuit fired if you are twice-firing.

Recipes

The sixteen recipes are given in Figure 11.12, which also shows the way the recipes have been constructed.

Preparing the Test Glaze Mixes

Follow the instructions given in Exercise 28 for making and applying the glazes. This should be carried out in two separate stages. The first stage, weighing out the sixteen recipes, requires a two-hour session without interruptions. Store the sixteen mixes in the screw-topped jars, and label them clearly. You need only weigh the dry mixes at this stage, and then reduce each one to slip form in another session in the pottery. Remember to use your waterproof marker. A foolproof method of weighing is suggested.

Set up sixteen squares of paper, number them 1 to 16, lay them out in the same order as the tiles (four rows of 4), and write the relevant recipe on each one. Instead of weighing out each glaze individually, you may work more systematically by first weighing out all the feldspar requirements, next the calcite, then the kaolin, and finally the quartz. For example, you may lay out four lots of 10 g feldspar, placing one amount in each of the four squares in the top row, four lots of 20 g for the second row, four lots of 30 g for the third row, and four lots of 40 g for the fourth row. You have now weighed out all the feldspar required. Repeat this for the calcite required, this time working in columns: four lots of 10 g calcite in the first column, 20 g in the second column, and so on for the kaolin (from the bottom upward) and the quartz (from right to left). *Place each weighed amount separately* on the papers so that you can make a quick check when all have been weighed. Finally, weigh each test: it should weigh 100 g (if not, repeat it). Place each completed recipe in its labeled jar.

Applying the Glazes

After mixing each recipe with water, and sieving, replace it in its correct jar. Apply the glazes systematically from test nos. 1 to 16 checking each recipe carefully. In these tests it will be useful to see the results of different thicknesses of glaze. To do this lay on several brush strokes, gradually building up the thickness toward one corner (see Plate 10).

Reminder: when overbrushing, apply the first stroke, and wait until the glistening water has gone off. However, before the glaze is white-dry, immediately apply the second stroke of glaze.

Storing the Glazes

If you intend to use the mixes again quite soon, they can be left in the wet state. Otherwise, they should be dried out and stored as powders until required again. When required for use again, all that is needed is to add water, mix, and sieve each one.

Firing

See Exercise 29 for detailed instructions. Fire the tiles to C.8–9 or your standard workshop stoneware temperature (noting accurately the temperature reached), and switch off. Do not soak on this occasion. If firing in oxidation and reduction, fire both to the same top temperature. You can then compare the difference between the results from the two types of firing cycles to the same top temperature.

Assessment After Firing

Read the following and try to answer the questions. When making assessments always feel the fired tests as well as looking at them.

1. Can you, in your set of tests, name one result which is: (a) underfired and dry; (b) just beginning to mature (has reached the glassy stage but is still white and tight); (c) is starting to clear to a transparent glaze but still retains some cloudy patches; (d) has cleared to a transparent glaze?

2. Do the results help you to decide which of the four materials are likely to cause underfiring when present in large amounts?
3. Are there areas on the tile where the glaze seems to have either soaked into the body or was too thinly applied?
4. Is there any result which, in your opinion, is a true matte glaze? That is, one that has reached maturity on heating, so that a complete melt has formed and, on cooling, sufficient recrystallization to act as a barrier to the passage of light without making the glaze rough (one that has a smooth sheen, not a high gloss)? If there is such a glaze on the tile, which oxides (supplied by the materials used to make the glaze) do you think may have contributed to the matte quality of the glaze? For example, an excess of calcia giving a lime matte glaze or an excess of alumina giving a high alumina matte glaze.
5. Study the layered brush strokes of glaze tests, and try to decide how thick you think a glaze application should be.
6. Do you think that you now understand the meaning of the expression *maturing*, and *firing range*, of a glaze? If not, consider the dry, powdery-looking results and compare them with the glassy but milky ones, those that are beginning to clear and those that have cleared to a transparent glaze (if any). These are all stages in the maturing of a glaze. The firing range defines the firing temperatures between which the glaze develops a satisfactory surface to the stage where an optimum quality is achieved (e.g., from a smooth but slightly cloudy glaze to full transparency).

Selecting a Clear Transparent Glaze

Finally, you should select a result that gives a clear transparent glaze at C.8 (or the one that comes nearest to this description). Where you cannot decide between two or more glazes, choose the one with the maximum amount of glass-forming silica. Your choice will probably be narrowed down to the block of tests in the middle of the tile, test nos. 7, 10, 11, 14, and 15. You may have to turn the tile in the light to study the glassiness and compare the results.

In the tests used for the photograph, there is little to choose among test nos. 10, 11, 14, and 15. Since no. 14 contains the greatest amount of glass-forming silica, it has been selected as the best result, and for the purposes of the next Exercise, recipe no. 14 will be used as a starting point.

Selected recipe,
glaze result no. 14   *Firing cycle*
40% potassium feldspar   Oxidation to C.8–C.9
30% quartz
20% calcite
10% kaolin

Glaze formula (taken to one decimal place)

0.3 K$_2$O   0.4 Al$_2$O$_3$ 3.7 SiO$_2$
0.7 CaO   [Al$_2$O$_3$: 9.25SiO$_2$]

The figures in square brackets express the proportion of Al$_2$O$_3$ to SiO$_2$. In order to arrive at this proportion, divide through by the amount of alumina (in the above case, divide the alumina by 0.4, bringing the alumina to 1; divide the silica by 0.4, giving you the proportion of silica to one unit of alumina). The method of calculating a glaze formula is dealt with in the next chapter.

Potters will be interested to learn that this recipe is exactly the same as Bernard Leach's famous Cone 8 glaze, which is often referred to as the 40–30–20–10 glaze. Leach (1945) remarked of this glaze that at C.8 (Seger) it gave him a slightly cloudy, soft glaze and that when fired to C.9 (Seger) it cleared to a transparent glaze. (*Note:* C.8 and C.9 Seger are approximately 20°C higher than Orton cones, see Appendix Figures A.5, A.6.)

This is a very useful glaze. It uses cheap and easily available materials, gives a hard and durable surface, and does not involve handling any toxic materials. It is also very near the most important formula postulated by Herman Seger (1902) in his endeavors to set up a series of recipes for making pyrometric cones. Seger's formula is

0.3 K$_2$O   0.4 Al$_2$O$_3$ 4 SiO$_2$
0.7 CaO

In this formula the Al$_2$O$_3$ to SiO$_2$ ratio is [1 : 10].

* * *

Comparative Study of Glazes from Two-, Three-, and Four-Blends

We can now review the glaze results from the Exercises that gave the nearest results to a clear transparent glaze, that is, to our *norm*. The glazes chosen are listed below and the following points will guide you in this assessment (no. 5 on Tile A2 has already been discussed and is excluded here).

1. The fluxes in the three glazes are remarkably similar:

Test no. 3, Tile F, in two-blends:

Recipes	Formulas		
75% potassium feldspar	0.35 K$_2$O	0.35 Al$_2$O$_3$	2.1 SiO$_2$
25% calcite	0.65 CaO		[1 : 6]

Test no. 7, Tile E2, in three-blends:

75% potassium feldspar	0.3 K$_2$O	0.6 Al$_2$O$_3$	2.6 SiO$_2$
25% calcite	0.7 CaO		[1 : 4.3]
25% kaolin			

Test no. 14, in four-blends:

40% potassium feldspar	0.26 K$_2$O	0.4 Al$_2$O$_3$	3.7 SiO$_2$
30% quartz	0.74 CaO		[1 : 9.25]
20% calcite			
10% kaolin			

2. Given previous observations that a favorable alumina : silica ratio seems to lie between [1 : 5] and [1 : 10], test nos. 3 and 14 lie within these limits, while test no. 7 lies just outside and is, in fact, slightly matte. (There is too much alumina to the amount of glass-forming silica to give a clear transparent glaze.)

3. Test no. 14, with almost 4 moles of glass-making silica and only a tenth the amount of alumina, gives the most glassy result. Thus, although nos. 3 and 7 approach the qualities required of our norm, it is test no. 14 that gives the most glassy transparent glaze, though requiring the upper limits of the firing range C.8–9 to clear the glaze. A little frit should clarify the glaze for the lower end of the range: a line addition test (see Appendix Figure A.7) would enable you to find the correct amount to add.

4. If we now compare test no. 5 on Tile A2 in three-blends with test nos. 3 and 7 in four-blends, we again see a similarity, even though in test no. 5 there is only one flux. Although in the above discussion we have concentrated on the alumina : silica ratio, it is of equal importance to note the ratio and type of fluxes to alumina and silica to achieve, or approach, our norm. This is a major concern of the next chapter.

Middle Temperature Glazes

In this section glazes maturing in the middle-temperature range (C.4 to C.6) will be considered. Test no. 14 from Exercise 30 will be used as a starting point, and the three flux-containing materials colemanite, zinc oxide, and barium carbonate will be introduced singly and in combinations. If colemanite is not available, ask your supplier for a crystalline mineral of similar composition. Failing this, use a calcium borate frit (and record the catalog number and composition in your notebook). Remember, if you use a frit, that it is prefused (see p. 122). Colemanite, barium carbonate, and zinc are extremely useful in this temperature range, but this does not mean that they cannot be used at other temperatures, as we shall see later. As these three materials are almost always chemically refined, their formulas will be the same as their theoretical formulas: barium carbonate (BaCO$_3$); zinc oxide (ZnO); and colemanite (2CaO·3B$_2$O$_3$·5H$_2$O). Notes on these materials are given below. Many students find it more interesting to carry out Exercise 31 then, having critically observed the fired results along with the assessment, to study these notes.

Colemanite

The origin of this crystalline mineral salt (calcium borax) is discussed on p. 46. This should be reviewed. It is the least soluble of the borax minerals and has a further value in that it also contains calcia. This intimate association of the low-temperature glass-former boric oxide, B_2O_3 with the refractory oxide calcia brings this otherwise refractory oxide into early fusion. Although the solubility of colemanite is low, a glaze slip containing large amounts of it should not be left standing in the wet state too long. If left longer than a few days some of it may go into solution and deflocculate the glaze (see p. 228). If this happens, it assumes a thick, gel quality. Students tend to add more water in order to overcome this and make the glaze pour properly, but this increases the problem as the extra water gives a false impression that the glaze has the correct density. Once applied, the glaze shrinks excessively as the water dries out, causing the glaze to crack ("craze") or even spit off (sometimes explosively) in the early stages of firing. If it manages to stay on the pot, the already cracked glaze layer may crawl during firing.

This means that a glaze containing over 10 percent of colemanite should be made only in sufficient quantity for immediate use, or dried off after each glazing session to avoid this problem. To do this, let the glaze settle and pour the clear water into a storage container. This should then be returned when the glaze is again required.

Despite these problems, many potters use up to 75 percent colemanite with careful firing. Some report that, whereas one consignment of colemanite works well, another spits and flakes off. This may well be due to differing amounts of water in the mineral salt, or perhaps the presence of impurities in the form of other mineral salts with a high water content.

If spitting persists, you could try preheating the glazed object slowly until the water has gone off before committing it to further firing. If raku firing, the object could be placed in the cold kiln and heated slowly with it.

Potters continue to use this material because they feel that it gives a pearly quality to raku glazes. A cloudiness may also be seen in colemanite glazes of the earthenware and middle-temperature range, and it may also appear in some high-temperature glazes. In the latter case, a little cloudiness appears in an otherwise transparent glassy glaze during slow cooling. This results from a small amount of recrystallization together with the formation of millions of small bubbles that scatter the light and give the glaze a slightly opalescent appearance.

Apart from the special effects described above, colemanite glazes are associated with brilliant, shiny surfaces. These are usually achieved by using colemanite in association with one or more of the other fluxes. In the middle-temperature range, with which we are concerned in the current practical work, these include barium carbonate and zinc. At lower temperatures, colemanite may be combined with lead oxide, giving lead borosilicate glazes, potassium or sodium feldspar, or their alkali frit equivalent.

These combination glazes have a very special benefit, for boric oxide does not expand or contract during heating and cooling as much as other oxides. Thus the problem of cracking may be prevented or reduced. However, given the adverse effects of large proportions of boric oxide, one or more middle-temperature fluxes are used. It is here that the double role of boric oxide may be seen: it is a low-temperature glass-former and complements silica at the same time it complements the fluxes but does not replace them. Used in this way boric oxide can help to produce transparent glazes that do not craze.

In low-temperature glazes with lead frit and colemanite, the calcia (from the colemanite) and the lead frit, once fused together in the melt, contribute to a smooth, clear glaze, while the boric oxide (again from the colemanite) encourages a brilliant color response.

Barium Carbonate

This compound is found in the mineral witherite ($BaCO_3$) and is also produced from barytes ($BaSO_4$) by chemical processing. As a raw material, it is *poisonous* and should be handled with care (see "Health and Safety" in Bibliography). Once fused into the glaze it is safe.

Although all the Group 2 (alkaline earth) oxides are considered to be relatively insoluble compared with the high solubility of Group 1 (alkali) oxides soda and potassa, a little baria may go into solution if calcium chloride is in the glaze slip. The extent to which this happens is usually insignificant. But should blemishes appear on the fired glaze in the form of scum marks, the possibility of barium salts precipitating should be considered, and the practice of putting calcium chloride in that particular glaze slip to assist suspension should be discontinued. Add a little bentonite instead.

During firing it is a little more difficult to break down barium carbonate than calcium carbonate. There are two stages of disintegration, and a little reduction at 900°C/1652°F assists this:

$$900°C + \text{"R"}$$
$$\text{Step I:} \quad BaCO_3 + CO \rightarrow BaCO_2 + CO_2\uparrow$$
$$\text{Step II:} \quad BaCO_2 \rightarrow BaO + CO\uparrow$$

Baria contributes to a hard, durable surface, though not as hard as that achieved with calcia. The usual plan is to make calcia the principal flux with just sufficient baria to promote a more vigorous fluxing action. Remember that a mix of fluxes is better than one. However, even a slight excess of baria over the amount required to give a clear glaze will quickly render the glaze matte and then opaque.

This works as follows. If the excess is not drawn into the melt during firing but stays as a solid in the glaze, it will give a dull, somewhat stony, lifeless quality. If all the excess is drawn into the melt and subsequently precipitates as the glaze cools, recrystallization occurs. A number of tiny new crystals form, often with other constituent oxides, particularly crystals of barium feldspar, and these remain suspended in the glass, giving the soft pearly sheen with which barium glazes are associated. Later, we shall see that baria has a considerable effect on color and may be introduced for this reason.

Although general guidelines may be given (e.g., 10% barium carbonate for high-temperature glazes), the exact amount of the addition of baria that makes the change from a very clear glaze to a cloudy one and then to a matte glaze depends on the firing temperature and the type and proportion of the other components of the glaze. This will be seen in the results of the current Exercise and will be referred to again in several places.

Note for those firing hard porcelain in the region of 1400°C/2552°F. Baria in glazes fired in this region can cause discoloration.

Zinc Oxide

Zinc oxide is obtained from minerals such as sphalerite (zinc sulfide, ZnS) and, like barium carbonate, is poisonous in the powdered form in which it is supplied. Raw zinc oxide shrinks during the early stages of firing; it also tends to splatter and pin-hole, hence the calcined version should be used. Most suppliers will send you this form, but if in doubt, you should make a specific inquiry. It should also be remembered that zinc oxide should only be used in oxidation. In reduction it grays the glaze (for pin-holing, see Glossary, also Fraser, 1986).

Zinc oxide works powerfully in the middle-temperature range, C.2 to C.6, and is therefore considered to be an important middle-temperature flux. It is also used throughout the pottery firing range. The precise amounts are discussed in the assessment of Exercise 31 and in the next chapter. Here it is sufficient to say that, when used in low-temperature glazes in amounts of approximately 5 percent by weight or 0.2 moles, it has a considerable fluxing effect, and may be used at temperatures as low as 800°C/1472°F. Again, amounts of roughly 2 percent by weight or as low as 0.01–0.02 moles are often used at high temperatures as a starter flux or to give a boost to a sluggish glaze. In the middle-temperature glazes we shall see that amounts between 5 percent and 10 percent are adequate to produce brilliant glazes. The exact amount, however, depends on the other oxides present and their proportions. It is never used as the only flux, or even as the major flux in large amounts, as its action is thereby reversed. However, a moderate excess may be used in conjunction with titanium dioxide to produce macrocrystalline glazes, which will be studied later.

If too much zinc oxide is used, the excess quickly causes considerable viscosity, and the glaze will crawl, or "bead," leaving bare patches on the body. On the other hand, it does not contract on cooling as much as potassa or soda and may replace some of these oxides in low-temperature glazes to reduce or prevent crazing. This apart, the usual practice, when introducing zinc oxide into a glaze, is to replace a little of the calcia that would otherwise have to be used, but never all of it. It is also wise to reduce the alumina a little to offset the refractory nature of zinc oxide. Even when the correct amount has been used, it is advisable, when firing zinc glazes, to give them a good soak at top temperature so that the glaze can release all the gases bubbling through it. The glaze will then be able to smooth out and so prevent pin-holing, crawling, or pitting.

Zinc oxide gives a high gloss and, like calcia, helps to produce hard glaze surfaces in transparent glazes and is especially useful for its resistance to attack by acids which is of particular value for glazes on vessels used in the chemical industry. It was introduced into the ceramic industry in the nineteenth century and called the Bristol glaze, to replace lead oxide glazes which were causing many deaths by lead poisoning.

It is a useful oxide, but a number of tests should be run to make sure that the zinc does not cause any of the faults mentioned above before using it on a final piece of work. It is also important that tests should be carried out on the same body as used for the final work and the test tiles (or objects) should be much larger, preferably maquettes (models), of the final work. Unless you are experimenting with crystalline glazes, the chief guideline to follow is to introduce zinc oxide in as small an amount as possible that will give the effect you desire. Never adopt the attitude that a little more might be more effective: it may result in quite the opposite effect!

EXERCISE 31: Colemanite, Zinc, and Barium Carbonate for Middle-Temperature Glazes

Aim

To develop a series of glazes maturing in the C.4 to C.6 firing range by additions of the above materials to a starting recipe chosen from the previous Exercise. In these tests we hope to find a clear transparent glaze (corresponding to our norm) and, in addition, translucent to matte glazes. Besides studying the contribution these materials make to the fusibility of a glaze, the effect each one has on the character of the glaze will be noted.

As in the previous Exercise, a little frit may be added after assessing the results of the firing of the first part of this Exercise. The frits recommended are high-alkali frit or borax frit. This is not the only way of producing a glaze for a particular firing range, as we shall see in the next chapter. However, working by trial and error as a preliminary study will make you familiar with the materials and the effects they have on the character of the glaze. It will also be seen in the final chapter how the different oxides, and therefore the different materials, affect color.

If this is to be your main temperature range, test firings should be carried out at three temperatures in this range.

Materials

Glaze. You will need 1200 g bulk dry weight of Glaze 14 (see below) and the three materials listed above: colemanite, zinc oxide, and barium carbonate.

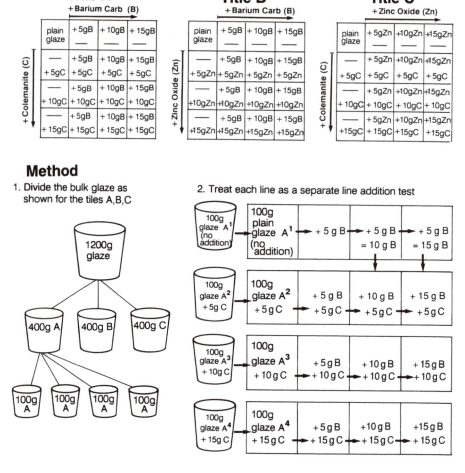

Figure 11.13. Layout and method for tests of combinations of colemanite, barium carbonate, and zinc oxide.

Test tiles. You will need three tiles, about 15 cm × 15 cm, in a buff or red-firing stoneware clay, each tile divided into sixteen squares on the front and inscribed clearly on the back: Tile A, Tile B, and Tile C, along with the Exercise number, type of firing ("O" or "R"), and proposed firing temperature. You may, if you wish, make the tile a little larger so that you have a margin (unglazed) along the top and down the left side where you can enter the additions of materials used; this could be done before or perhaps more neatly after firing (see Figure 11.13 for layout).

Equipment. In addition to your usual equipment for glaze-making, you will need three 250 ml identical straight-sided beakers (or similar containers) and four smaller identical containers. These should be sufficiently transparent for the glaze level to be seen through the side of the container. Paper cups are suitable, but remember, once they have been used to hold glazes they should be broken and thrown away.

Method

Preparing the Glaze

By using the following method, the addition of single materials as well as combinations of them may be achieved.

1. Weigh out 1200 g dry bulk weight of Glaze 14:

$$40 \times 12 = 480 \text{ g potassium feldspar}$$
$$20 \times 12 = 240 \text{ g calcite}$$
$$10 \times 12 = 120 \text{ g kaolin}$$
$$30 \times 12 = \underline{360 \text{ g quartz}}$$
$$100\% = 1200 \text{ g total batch weight of Glaze 14.}$$

The order of stating this recipe has been reorganized to place the flux-containing materials first. This convention helps us when we come to compose our own recipes and will be discussed in the next chapter.

2. Stir the glaze thoroughly and check the density (see Chapter 10); stir again and immediately divide the batch glaze equally among three identical containers marked A, B, and C. Each container now contains 400 g dry weight of glaze. Set aside glaze mixes B and C together with Tiles B and C, and prepare to glaze Tile A with additions of colemanite and barium carbonate (see Figure 11.13).

3. Label the four small containers A1, A2, A3, and A4. Stir Glaze A thoroughly, and divide it equally among them. Each small container now holds 100 g dry weight of raw materials. Line up these four containers against the chart for Tile A1 as shown in Figure 11.13. Each of these 100 g portions of glaze will be used to glaze one row.

Adding Dry Materials to a Glaze Slip

When adding increments of dry materials to a glaze slip, remember to place a little of the glaze slip in a mortar, weigh the powders, and gently pour the dry powder onto the slip. Mix to a smooth paste, gradually add the rest of the glaze slip (and an extra few drops of water if necessary), and sieve.

Glazing the Tiles

Remember to stir the glaze thoroughly before applying to the tile. Glaze each tile in the order shown in Figure 11.13. The following notes are given in case you need them. Divide the glaze A equally among four beakers, A1, A2, A3, and A4. Make the additions of colemanite as follows. *Note:* Do *not* add colemanite to Glaze A1.

Beaker A1:   plain glaze, *no* addition
Beaker A2:   add 5 g colemanite
Beaker A3:   add 10 g colemanite
Beaker A4:   add 15 g colemanite

Mark the beakers A2, A3, and A4 clearly with the correct colemanite addition. Now put the colemanite away (you do not need it any more for this tile), and carry out the following steps using each beaker in order, as follows:

A1: Place a sample of A1 (plain Glaze 14) in the first square of the tile. This gives a test of the starting recipe, *with no additions.*

A2: Place a sample of glaze A2 in the first square of the second row. This gives a test of Glaze 14 + 5 g colemanite.

A3: Place a sample of glaze A3 in the first square of the third row. This gives a sample of Glaze 14 + 10 g colemanite.

A4: Place a sample of glaze A4 in the first square of the last row. This gives a sample of Glaze 14 + 15 g colemanite.

This completes the glazes in the first column (tests with colemanite additions only). We shall now complete the tests by working across the tile, treating each row separately. To the first row:

1. Add 5 g of $BaCO_3$ to A1, using the above mixing instructions, and apply a glaze test to the *second* square in the top row of Tile A.

2. Add a further 5 g of $BaCO_3$ to the glaze, for a total addition of 10 g. Apply a test to the third square on Tile A1.

3. Add a further 5 g of $BaCO_3$, making a total addition of 15 g. Apply a test to the last square in this row. You now have a row of tests with additions of $BaCO_3$ only. Glaze A1 may now be thrown away; you will not need it again. This completes the glaze tests in the top row.

The procedure for row 2 (using glaze A2), row 3 (glaze A3), and row 4 (glaze A4) is exactly the same as that given above, except that you will start with a glaze containing colemanite. The remaining tests will therefore have additions of colemanite and barium carbonate, as shown in Figure 11.13. This achieves a series of miniature line-addition tests. Across the top and down the left-hand side, there are additions of single materials. Each remaining square contains additions of two materials. Across the diagonal from top left is a line blend containing equal increments of $BaCO_3$ and colemanite.

Tile B and Tile C

These are glazed up in exactly the same way as Tile A. Be very careful that you use the correct combinations for each tile.

Marking the Tiles

Mark the back of each tile with the Exercise number and the tile identification (A, B, or C), and *place an arrow to indicate the top of the tile.* Do not mark the increments of the additions on the back of the tiles. It is very easy to make a mistake. Details may be taken from Figure 11.13 and written around the edge of the tile when you mount the results.

Firing

The three tiles should be fired to C.4–C.5 (1180–1200°C/2156–2192°F) with no soak or as short a soak as possible. This helps to give greater distinction between the individual tests. (Fire at lower end of range if using calcium borate frit.)

If, after firing, the top row of Tiles A and B are smooth and glassy, then you have overfired the tiles, and the rest of the tests will not serve the purpose of testing glazes fired to C.5 to C.6.

Assessment

After firing, set up Tiles A, B, and C as before. By putting them in this order you will be able to follow the remarks made below. Remember that the body affects the overall results of the tests but not the relative differences between one test and another within the same set.

Tile A and Tile B

1. The first thing to observe on Tiles A and B is that those tests to which only barium carbonate has been added are white, dry, and cracked. Barium carbonate added to Glaze 14 by itself has done nothing to improve the fusibility. If you run your finger along the top row of these two tiles, you can feel how rough the test results are.

2. Now look down the first columns of Tiles A and B (colemanite has been added on Tile A and zinc oxide on Tile B). A different picture is seen. Even with the first addition of 5 g colemanite on Tile A and 5 g of zinc oxide on Tile B, there is a considerable increase in fusibility. In both may be seen a glassy if still tight glaze. With the next addition (a total of 10 g), tests on both tiles are smoother, but we may now detect a difference between those with colemanite additions and those to which zinc oxide has been added. The tests with zinc oxide additions are very glassy and increasingly transparent, but those with the additions of colemanite alone have remained cloudy.

3. Despite the refractoriness of barium carbonate seen along the top row of Tiles A and B, an addition of it to the glazes containing colemanite on Tile A, makes rapid improvements. If you look across rows 2, 3, and 4, you will see a clearing of the glaze that increases with an increase in barium carbonate, thus demonstrating that barium carbonate does contribute to the fluxing of a glaze when combined with another fluxing oxide. On Tile B, zinc by itself rapidly gives increasing transparency, and it may seem that the addition of barium carbonate is unnecessary, but bearing in mind the problems arising from zinc as described above, the usefulness of baria in these glazes must be recognized. Further the transparent and particularly the semitransparent glazes derived from zinc with baria give a softer quality that is often desired by studio potters and sculptors.

Tile C

The first test with Glaze 14 is white and rough, that is, underfired at this temperature. However, with the additions of colemanite, the results become smooth and shiny, though they remain cloudy and viscous. In the first column (test nos. 1, 5, 9, and 13), the results indicate that there is too much of each of these refractory materials. The increase in B_2O_3 helps to improve the transparency but does not clear the cloudiness completely. By contrast, the tests containing zinc oxide rapidly become glassy and transparent. The last result in the top row looks very shiny but contains quite a large proportion of zinc oxide. This glaze could be tried on a larger test object, but bearing in mind the problems caused by too much zinc oxide, let us look at the combined additions of zinc oxide plus colemanite.

All the combination tests (those with both colemanite and zinc oxide) show signs of a clear melt. This indicates that further research in this area might be worthwhile.

Comparing the tests overall, clearly zinc oxide is an extremely powerful flux, and only small amounts are required for a considerable effect. Colemanite comes next, and barium carbonate is of little use as a flux by itself, although when combined with colemanite which contains boric oxide, a powerful reaction is obtained. A similar reaction is seen on the second tile between zinc oxide and barium carbonate, the result being even clearer.

Other Qualities

A considerable amount of time has been spent looking at fusibility and the combinations of oxides that produce a clear transparent glaze. In doing this a starting point has been established from which to study other qualities of the glazes. On Tile C, for instance, there are a number of very shiny transparent glazes, while Tile B has several transparent glazes that do not have quite such a high gloss. Finally, on Tile A, we find a range of much "quieter" glazes with increasing degrees of translucence, some with a soft, semiopaque quality that ranges from complete opacity to a slight cloudiness. You should pick up the tiles and turn them in the light in order to evaluate and compare these characteristics.

*   *   *

Low Temperature Glazes

Introduction

Here we are concerned with glazes containing frits and the use of tin oxide and zirconia. Frits were discussed in detail in Chapter 6 and should be reviewed, particularly the reasons for making frits. Because frits are glasses, they only require softening in order to make them flow and do so readily when heated in a kiln. In Exercise 4, "Testing the Common Raw Materials" (see Plate 7), it was seen that alkali, borax, and lead frits spread out considerably on the flat surface of the test tile when heated to stoneware temperatures. In order to assess this flow at lower temperatures and the effect of adding more refractory materials, tests in Exercises 32 and 33 must be fired standing upright, supported, if necessary, by kiln props and standing in a bed of alumina or alumina hydrate powder in a kiln test tray.

The method of making the tiles, mixing, sieving, and applying the glaze will not be described as these topics have been dealt with adequately in previous Exercises (in particular Figures 5.11 and 7.2). Remember to mark the back of the tiles with the Exercise number, the reference number, and firing temperature.

The tests may be either raw-glazed and once-fired, or biscuit fired before glazing. The extra amount of reaction with the clay body when raw-glazing is remarkable; hence if several students are working together, a comparative study of once-fired and twice-fired tests would be interesting. However, if you are working alone, it is best to fire in the manner in which you intend to work.

The glazes in Exercises 32 and 33 are excellent for maiolica and enameled ware; see below.

EXERCISE 32: Low-Temperature Glazes Containing Frits

Aim

To carry out a line addition test in order to compare the performance of the following frits alone and with increasing additions of kaolin.

Materials

You will need two test tiles, 19 cm × 6 cm, in a red-firing earthenware clay for each frit tested. Divide the tiles into six sections as shown in Plate 11 by incising, as this helps to keep the tests separate. Dip half of the tile lengthwise in a white marking slip. Reserve a narrow strip at the top for writing the kaolin increments and, when dry, brush a cross over the white slip in each section with red iron oxide. A little gum arabic may be added if raw-glazing. After firing, the crosses will help you observe the degree of opacity with increasing kaolin additions and also the degree to which 100 percent frit takes the iron into solution.

For each line addition test you will need 100 g dry weight of the following frits mixed to a slip and 25 g of kaolin, blocked up and divided into five equal portions:

for Tile A, an alkali frit
for Tile B, lead bisilicate
for Tile C, borax frit

Method

1. Apply a 100 percent frit test to the first square with a glaze mop (see Figure 11.5), or dribble the "glaze" from a straight-edged spoon held against the tiles and moved down the tile as you pour the glaze. Each test application should cover the red iron oxide crosses and part of the red body. It is not advisable to glaze right to the bottom of the tile because of the fluidity of some of the tests. Clean off any glaze below the mark indicated (see Plate 11). Do this before the glaze becomes white-dry.

2. Add 5 g kaolin to the glaze slip, and apply a test to the second square.

3. Continue the additions, in increments of 5 g, giving additions of 5 g, 10 g, 15 g, 20 g, and 25 g kaolin to the 100 g frit.

4. Check that the thickness of the glaze application is the same for each test. If necessary rub down any high spots *with a clean finger for each test* (if extremely thick, very gently scrape with a knife). Do this over a sink (wearing a mask) when the tests are powder dry, and wash your hands immediately afterward, but do not get the tile wet. Better still, try to apply the glaze evenly.

Apply the remaining tests in the same way.

Firing

One tile of each frit should be fired to C.06 (1000°C/1830°F), the other to C.03 (1100°C/2014°F). Use your own firing temperature (near these temperatures) if more convenient, but remember to change the inscription on the tiles. Do not soak the tiles at top temperature, this will enable you to assess the state of activity at top temperature after firing. See Plate 11 for lead frit tests fired to C.06 and C.03.

Assessment

From each frit tested, select your own best recipe. Below are two examples:

100 g alkali frit	100 g lead bisilicate
15 g kaolin	10 g kaolin

giving percentage recipes of

87% alkali frit	91% lead bisilicate
13% kaolin	9% kaolin

C.06 (1000°C/1830°F)

The alkali frit results remain transparent throughout the tests with only a little cloudiness, marked by a slight blurring of the crosses in the last three tests. All the tests are crazed extensively, and change in character with increasing kaolin. By contrast, the lead bisilicate frit results become opaque as the kaolin increases and the crosses become difficult to see. However, the tests remain glassy and smooth to the touch until, with the addition of 25 g of kaolin, the result becomes dry and rough.

C.03 (1100°C/2014°F)

The alkali frit, though transparent and glassy (even with 30% kaolin added) is crazed and pin holed throughout. The pin-holing is caused by the escape and attempted escape of volatiles (the maximum effect having been captured by not soaking the tests at top temperature). The lead frit tests at C.03, however, give extremely shiny transparent glazes throughout and it is only with a 15 g addition of kaolin that a few pin-holes indicate the arrested escape of volatiles. There is a little crazing in the 100 percent lead frit test where the application is too thick. The rest of the lead glaze tests are craze-free.

In these glazes there is only a small amount of the very refractory alumina (supplied by the small proportion of kaolin), but there is an extremely large amount of silica, causing an excess of this oxide. The melt must therefore be due to the powerful fluxing ability of the lead oxide and the fact that this is in frit form and therefore prefused such that it becomes molten early in the firing and reacts with the less active silica.

Further Testing (optional)

Additions may be made to a chosen recipe from the above results by a second line addition test, or you may wish to develop a glaze composed of both lead and borax frits. This could be done by using a layout very similar to the one in Exercise 29, illustrated in Plate 9, making the materials down the left margin borax frit and lead frit with additions of kaolin across the top.

A more detailed layout is suggested, using increments of ten for the frits (ranging from 90% borax frit + 10% lead frit to 10% borax frit + 90% lead frit) with additions of kaolin chosen from your results of the previous exercise (or increments of 5 g ranging from 5 g added to 15 g added). Lead bisilicate is recommended for this test. You should draw a rough plan of this layout (giving 27 tests) and then make an initial selection, as we have done in previous tests. For example, 30% + 70% to 70% + 30% for the frits. This gives 15 tests (these can be supplemented, if necessary, by a second set of tests using intermediate proportions). After firing to C.06 and C.03, as in previous tests, a satisfactory test result should be repercented. Let us suppose that the following batch recipe was found to be the most satisfactory. This may be repercented as follows:

Batch recipe	Percentage recipe
70 g borax frit	64 % borax frit
30 g lead bisilicate frit	27 % lead bisilicate frit
10 g kaolin	9 % kaolin
110 g total	100 % total

This recipe can be recognized as being very similar to Harry Fraser's (1974) transparent low-solubility earthenware glaze for C.05–C.01, thus illustrating the value, for comparative purposes, of recording glazes as percentage recipes.

Fraser's low-solubility glaze for C.05–01
65% borax frit
25% lead bisilicate frit
10% kaolin (china clay quoted)

*   *   *

EXERCISE 33: Opacifying a Glaze for Low-Temperature Firing

Tin oxide is the traditional material for opacifying a glaze, giving a shiny white glaze, but zircon, zirconium silicate, or commercially prepared zirconium compounds are cheaper. Titanium dioxide (TiO_2) may be included to improve the opacity of tin or zircon glazes. If the titania available to you makes your glaze creamy, it contains a little iron and should be omitted if pure white is required. Opacification may also be obtained by adding calcia, with or without zinc oxide. Zinc silicate crystals form on cooling from the melt, giving opacity with a matte quality. In this Exercise we shall concentrate on tin oxide and zirconia.

Your supplier may have several opacifiers marketed under brand names. If you use one of these, note the type, the constituents, and the recommended amounts to use.

Aim

To opacify a transparent low-temperature glaze chosen from one of the previous Exercises by the addition of tin oxide and/or zirconia (zirconium dioxide, ZrO_2) to obtain a white glaze.

Materials

You will need a test tile about 15 cm × 4 cm in a red-firing earthenware body (biscuit fired if twice-firing), divided into five sections with a thin strip along the length of the tile dipped in white slip on which to write the percentage additions (see Appendix Figure A.7 for layout, but use the increments given here). Do not cover the tile in white slip. You will also need 100 g dry weight of your chosen glaze recipe from the previous tests (rendered down to glaze slip) and 9 g of tin oxide or 16 g of zirconia. If using a commercial opacifier, follow the maker's recommended additions. If you wish to undertake two tests, one with tin additions, the other with zirconia, the qualities of the fired results can be compared.

Method

1. Convert your glaze recipe into a percentage recipe. This is essential as you will be making additions to the percentage recipe.

2. Using a line addition test (see Appendix Figure A.7), make additions of the opacifier in increments of 3 g (3 g, 6 g, and 9 g) of tin oxide, or increments of 4 g (4 g, 8 g, 12 g, and 16 g) of zirconia, as additions to the percentage recipe. (Some zirconia goes into the melt, hence larger amounts are required.)

3. Use the method given in Exercise 28 to make and apply the glaze tests. (Be careful not to obliterate your reference number by the opacified glaze.) Take out a test after each addition and place it on the test tile.

4. After the test piece is glazed, 5 g of coloring oxide may be added to the glaze mix and a test placed in the last section.

5. Dry and fire the tiles to C.05 (1046°C/1915°F).

Glazes should be stored in either the wet or the dried state and labeled carefully. This especially applies to the tin glaze, which is expensive.

Assessment

1. Assess the tiles for the degree of opacity, the extent to which the color of the body is masked. You are advised to use the minimum amount necessary to give a satisfactory opacity.

2. If you have tested both opacifiers, note the sheen on the two glazes, and make a personal choice about which you like better.

3. If you have dipped a corner in a colored tin glaze, note how the opacifier makes the color milky.

4. If the body shows through the glazes, does this give a warmth to the glaze, or do you prefer the result that gives complete opacity?

*   *   *

Maiolica, or In-Glaze Decorated Ceramics

The traditional form of this decoration is achieved by covering the body with a tin glaze and, before firing, decorating by painting with coloring oxides mixed with a little water, (e.g., oxides of iron, cobalt, and copper). Alternatively, the color may be mixed with a little of the tin glaze, in which case the color needs to be stronger. This type of pottery is also called tin-glazed earthenware, Hispano-Moresque ware, faience, and Delft ware (see Caiger-Smith, 1973). Before using this method on a finished piece of work, you should make color samples by testing a range of coloring oxides and strengths of color on the tin glaze to be used (the samples should be kept for future reference). If you pierce a hole through each test tile, they can be strung together.

Enameled, or On-Glaze Decorated Ware

Enamels are pre-fused mixes of colors, fluxes, and other oxides that influence the color or the stability of the enamel. An advantage of enameling is that the fired color is the same as the pre-fired color of the enameling stain, which is a great help to the artist.

In this type of decoration, the glaze is first applied and fired. Then the decoration is painted on the fired surface using on-glaze enamel colors mixed with oil (e.g., linseed oil, oil of lavender, light vegetable oil) or a commercial medium. The work is then fired to a temperature that slightly softens the glaze (but does not remelt it) so that a good union of decoration and glaze is achieved. Plenty of ventilation is necessary: usually the kiln door is left ajar (and guarded for safety reasons) until the oil has burned off (at about 400°C/752°F). Various new commercial on-glaze products are available that use water as a medium. The colors can be applied by brush or used with an airbrush or pen. The ware is then refired to temperatures between 700°C and 830°C/1292°F and 1526°F. Different enamels require different temperatures, so the manufacturer's instructions must be observed.

Some colors contain lead and should not be used on food or drink containers. However, colors obtained commercially will be formulated according to worldwide health regulations.

The ware must be very dry at the time it is decorated and fired as soon as possible. If moisture gets into the ware, it will dry out again through the glaze and the enamel and may cause blistering.

On-glaze enamels may be applied to both low-temperature and high-temperature ware (and sometimes to vitreous biscuit ware). However, in all cases, the firing must be conducted at the temperatures given by the manufacturer of the enamels. (See Plate 25 and the corresponding information in the Catalog of Color Work.)

Chapter 12
The Life History of a Melting Glaze and Glaze Formulation

Introduction

Once more let us begin by considering a clear transparent glaze, that is, our norm (see p. 258). In the early stages of heating, a glaze passes through many of the solid-state reactions already described, such as the breakdown of the carbonates and sintering. However, because glazes are only thin layers, they are not subject to the escape of volatiles to the same extent as clay bodies. As the temperature increases, the bonds between the ions are stretched slightly, causing a loosening of the structure (this may be likened to swelling from heat). Gradually the crystals become distorted and lose their characteristic form, and a disordered structure results.

If we tried to make a glass of pure crystalline silica (quartz), we would require a temperature of 1710°C/3110°F to melt it (i.e., to destroy the regular crystalline structure). Even then we would have an extremely viscous melt, for the bonds between silicon and oxygen are very strong. Some of the bonds would rupture, and the structure would be considerably distorted, but in any ceramic melt there is still a structure, even though it is a distorted one. Silica does not boil until over 3000°C/5432°F and remains viscous (because of the slow breakage of the bonds) throughout its liquid phase. As a result of the high viscosity of silica, all glazes high in silica have viscous melts.

Because of the presence of fluxing oxides, considerable interaction takes place between them and the more fusible materials. The fine-grained particles of more resistant materials, particularly silica, are involved and a molten mass begins to form. As the temperature is increased, this molten material attacks the surrounding larger grains and the more refractory constituents. Gradually, the crystals disintegrate; only remnants of their structures remain, and the mass reverts to the form found in magma as polymer chains, rings, and perhaps a few single entities, develop. There is constant change as the glaze matures: entities form, break up, exchange partners, and generally change their positions in relation to one another. As soon as sufficient structural breakdown has taken place, movement occurs: the molten state, or "melt," has been achieved, and the glaze will flow. The important thing to remember is that, though the characteristic crystal forms are lost, *some bonds remain: some structure is left.* If no structure remained and if, at this stage, the glaze consisted of monomers (single molecules), there would be nothing to hold them together, and they would fly off into the atmosphere, that is, volatilize. The fact that some residual structure remains brings us to an interesting sidelight (and provides an area for research), which may answer the question why two glazes with exactly the same oxide composition, placed on the same clay body, and fired side by side in the same kiln but using different minerals to fill the formula (for example, using dolomite instead of calcite or magnesite, to fill the requirement for calcia and magnesia), are different in character after firing. No doubt, impurities and perhaps differing grain size play a part, but this does not seem to be a sufficient answer. Another interesting example is the different gloss (and sometimes color) achieved from talc and dolomite.

As the molten stage of the glaze is reached, escaping gases from both the clay and the glaze help to stir the latter as they bubble through it. The molten glaze will also start to react with the surface of the body. In low-temperature glazes this will not amount to very much, but in glazes fired above C.5 considerable interaction may take place, giving a strong interfacial layer. If the kiln is held or "soaked" at top temperature (30 minutes to one hour is usual in studio ceramics), an equilibrium is reached in which no further reactions take place. This state of equilibrium can only be maintained if the kiln is *kept at the required top temperature throughout the soak period and not allowed to go above it*; otherwise new reactions may start to occur. If firing is done correctly, the little craters left by the escaping gases will be infilled by the molten glaze, and the glaze smooths out to cover the surface evenly.

Suppose that the kiln has been correctly fired and soaked, but just before switching off, the temperature accidentally rises, by just 20°. Some compounds that were perfectly happy to exist as they were at the intended firing temperature (and this refers to constituents in both the clay and the glaze) may suddenly become activated. New gases may be given off and new craters formed that are not infilled; moreover, the loss of these volatiles may leave the glaze looking thin, clearly having lost some glaze constituents. The glaze may become so fluid that it either soaks into the body or flows too much, a disaster if it flows onto the kiln shelf.

A closer look at the way in which glaze constituents interact in the presence of heat will tell us a great deal about the composition of glazes and guide us in formulating them. The interaction of glass-formers and fluxes will be considered first, then the effects of adding alumina. The study of viscosity and surface tension will also be dealt with in this section.

Before heating, the crystalline silica has a tightly packed, well-ordered structure. With increasing heat the structure "swells"; the silica bonds are stretched (their oxygen now relatively far away). Fluxing oxides released from minerals or chemically prepared materials mingle with the silica. Their bonds now also stretched, they react with the silica. The silicon atoms break with their own oxygen and grab the oxygen of nearby fluxing oxides, which give up their oxygen more readily, and the melting process begins. What this description reveals is that it is the *oxygen* that is required to act as a structure breaker and promote melting.

This is an over-simplification; in reality, complex reactions take place in the molten mass between the released ions. Other oxides (e.g., tin or zircon) play their part. Alumina helps to hold the structure together, giving a degree of viscosity that prevents the melt flowing off the ceramic surface.

With their function as fluxes completed, the metal ions, together with any metal oxides in excess of the fluxing requirements (i.e., those not used as structure breakers), now fill a further role to modify the character of the glaze. Each metal oxide brings with it special qualities to affect the texture, opacity, formation of new crystal or the color of the glaze. It is also important to realize that, although the original structure has been destroyed, some structure remains, if this were not so the whole glaze might very well volatilize.

In Chapter 1 we saw that the Group 1 metal oxides are weakly bonded to their oxygen partners and therefore do not require high temperatures to release their oxygen. By contrast, the Group 2 metals have stronger bonds with oxygen and more energy is required, in the form of heat, before they will dissociate and release their oxygen to act as structure-breakers. The optimum temperature ranges in which the various metal oxides act in this way are set out in Figure 12.1.

Producing a Melt

In practice it has been found that, taking the above optimum fluxing temperature range for the various fluxes into consideration, one mole of flux(es) to one mole of silica is required to produce a melt at low temperature. This will be demonstrated in Exercise 34, test A. With increasing heat-energy, one mole of suitable flux(es) and two moles of silica are capable of reacting together to produce a melt. At temperatures approaching C.10, one mole of flux(es) to four or five moles of silica is capable of producing a melt. These are average figures and not exact ratios for every situation. The materials used, the type of firing, and the top temperature as well as the soak period mean that slight adjustments to these figures are required, which may be assessed by specific testing, but even given these considerations generalized ratios may be stated as follows:

Low temperature, under Orton C.03,
   1 mole flux : 1 mole glass-forming silica

Medium temperature, Orton C.4 to C.6,
   1 mole flux : 2 moles glass-forming silica

High temperature, Orton C.8 to C.10,
   1 mole flux : 4–5 moles glass-forming silica

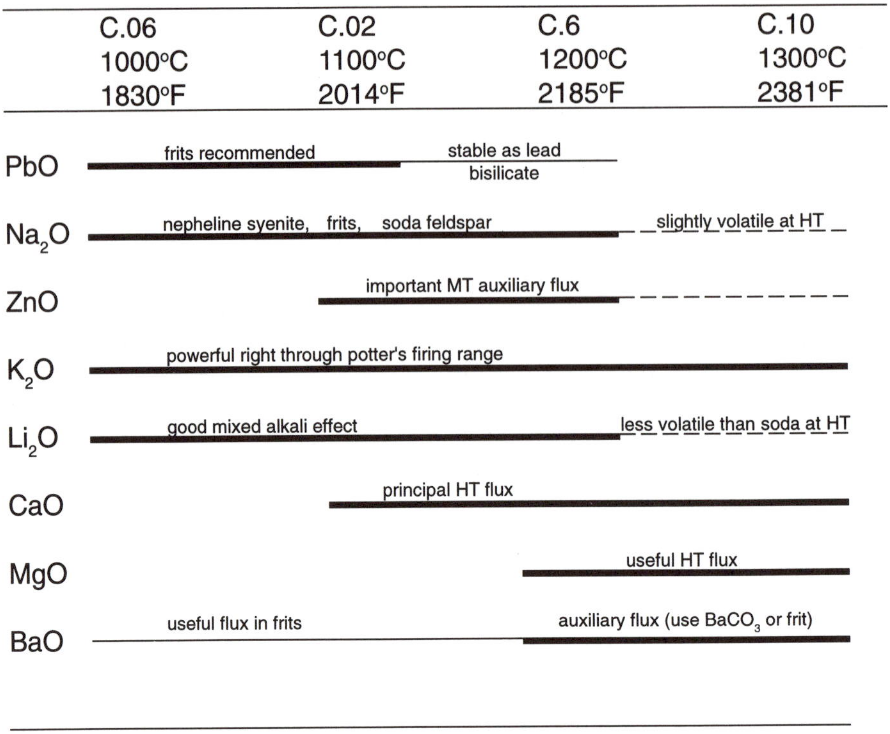

C.06	C.02	C.6	C.10
1000°C	1100°C	1200°C	1300°C
1830°F	2014°F	2185°F	2381°F

PbO — frits recommended · stable as lead bisilicate

Na_2O — nepheline syenite, frits, soda feldspar · slightly volatile at HT

ZnO — important MT auxiliary flux

K_2O — powerful right through potter's firing range

Li_2O — good mixed alkali effect · less volatile than soda at HT

CaO — principal HT flux

MgO — useful HT flux

BaO — useful flux in frits · auxiliary flux (use $BaCO_3$ or frit)

Figure 12.1. Optimum firing ranges for fluxing oxides in glazes. These oxides also perform other functions discussed elsewhere in the text.

These ratios are relevant to the production of a melt. However, this would be too runny for our purposes. This leads us to a study of viscosity and surface tension, and the part played by alumina in a glaze.

Viscosity and Fluidity

Viscosity is the resistance of a molten glaze to flow due to internal friction. The constituent molecules, oxides, and silicates of the melt resist change in their position relative to one another. A very viscous glaze on melting will have very little movement even on a vertical surface, where it may form thick sagging rolls of glaze. It will prevent the escape of gas bubbles from both body and glaze and make the glaze look thick, opaque, and unctuous. A reasonably mobile, or fluid, glaze flows out and covers the ceramic surface smoothly. It infills any deficiency in the application of the glaze; it also allows the volatiles to escape and infills the craters left behind as the bubbles burst. On vertical surfaces, the forces of gravity assist by placing a stress on the bonds holding the glaze together, thus lessening the viscosity. On horizontal surfaces, this is not such an important factor. What is important here is that the glaze has sufficient fluidity to spread out and cover the flat surface evenly. The degree of viscosity may be measured accurately in a laboratory. The unit of measurement is the *poise* and is described by Parmelee (1973) and Hamer and Hamer (1991). Most studio potters and sculptors judge this by results.

Surface Tension

The forces of attraction within a liquid cause a tension at the surface and encourage a tight smooth surface. An understanding of this may be gained by studying drops of water on a sheet of glass. Small blobs pull in on themselves, making as tight a ball as possible. Isolated blobs of glaze do much the same thing on melting. Larger blobs, on melting, are distorted by the pull of gravity and flatten out, but the edges remain smooth and rounded (see Figure 12.2). The reason for this is that, within the glaze, the forces of attraction act in all directions, but at the surface, they act sideways and downward only.

A satisfactory tension permits good contact between glaze and body. If the glaze can creep into crevices and get a good hold on the body, it is said to wet the body. If the tension is high, this does not occur; instead, the glaze pulls itself into balls. The interaction between glaze and body is also influenced by the composition of the body, not just of the glaze. If, as a result of the interaction between the body and the glaze, a layer of fluid glaze develops next to the body, it is impossible to produce a satisfactory glaze. The rate of glaze flow next to the body will change, and bubbles will keep coming through from the more fluid layer as more body material is drawn into the melt. Longer soaking or raising the firing temperature does not help as it only encourages the production of more liquid and more gas bubbles.

Viscosity and Surface Tension

Viscosity and surface tension acting together influence the qualities of a glaze enormously. Viscosity affects the extent to which the molten glaze flows over the surface, and surface tension pulls the resulting glaze into as smooth and tight a cover as the composition and the firing temperature allows. Viscosity and surface tension can be seen to act on one another in an important way: if the glaze is viscous and a crack exists in the unfired glaze, which is a little too wide for the viscous glaze to flow into and mend, the surface tension pulls the parts in on themselves and forms separate pools or globules of glaze. The glaze will *crawl* or form beads of glaze.

Viscosity and surface tension can be *adjusted* in several ways:

1. Adjust the amount of alumina present (decrease it slightly to make the glaze more fluid, or increase it to make it more viscous).
2. Raise or lower the silica content in the same way. This affects the flux : silica ratio, and therefore the amount of fluxing action that can occur.

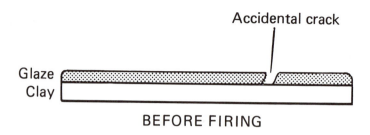

Accidental crack

Glaze
Clay

BEFORE FIRING

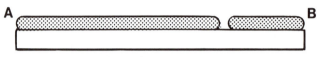

A   B

AFTER FIRING
At the edges (A&B) and at the crack
the glaze pulls in on itself forming
rounded edges.

If the glaze is very viscous it can
pull in very tightly leaving large bare
patches on fired body.

Figure 12.2. Effects of surface tension on cracks in glazes.

3. Examine the alumina : silica ratio. Under [1 : 5] the glaze will be viscous; ratios near [1 : 10] will be more fluid, given a satisfactory proportion of fluxes (see p. 280).
4. Consider the fluxes.

These oxides can be arranged as follows to show their effect on surface tension.

magnesia, zirconia, calcia, baria ↔ lead oxide, soda, potassa

(See Hamer and Hamer, 1991 and Shaw 1971 for a complete list.) To make the glaze more fluid, decrease those at the left in proportion to those at the right, and reverse this procedure to make the glaze less fluid/more viscous.

All these points should be taken into consideration together when making an adjustment.

Alumina

In a molten glaze a few of the aluminum ions released from ceramic materials can enter the glassy structure. There the aluminum ions can replace up to 1 in 4 silicon ions. They can also combine with other constituents to form new crystals. Aluminum ions are capable of going into six-fold coordination with oxygen (linking with six oxygen ions); they then sit straddled between the glassy polymers like six-legged "spiders" that reach out and grab the sagging glassy strands and stiffen the melt. In a glaze with a satisfactory viscosity (fluid enough to flow out and cover the surface, yet not too runny), there is a break-and-make system: the aluminum atoms hold the glaze steady for a short while and then break from one oxygen and grab another as the polymer slips past, thus controlling the rate of flow (see Figure 12.3). Too many spiders and this make-and-break system would be sluggish: the glaze would be viscous. This is the theory behind the idea that, if bonds are broken and new bonds made almost immediately, there is a slight movement so the glaze can spread out in an even layer. In a melt where there are too many aluminum spiders, this break-and-make system does not work,

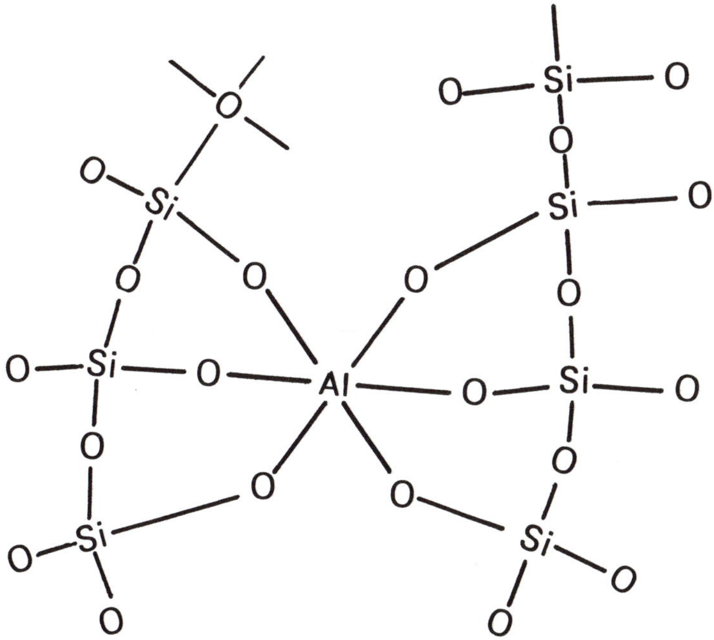

Figure 12.3. Alumina acting as stabilizer, linking the polymers across the strands.

or works with difficulty, and the viscosity will be high. Conversely, with too few spiders the viscosity will be low.

Alumina and Crystal Formation

Used in excess of requirements for a stabilized transparent glaze, alumina can give increasing opacity and matteness to a finished surface. If this addition is done on a haphazard basis, resulting in an excessive amount of alumina, the glaze may be underfired and the surface may get dirty quickly and be difficult to clean. However, with the correct amount, alumina combines with other oxides to form tiny crystals that produce very beautiful matte glazes. Hamer and Hamer (1991) say that most glaze melts contain 5–15% alumina; over 15% will precipitate on cooling to form fresh faced crystals which produce satisfactory alumina matte glazes. Where more than 25% of alumina is present the glaze will be too refractory to melt at studio pottery temperatures.

What must be explained here is the paradox that alumina can contribute to the formation of tiny crystals in a matte glaze and at the same time prevent excessive devitrification (recrystallization). The explanation lies in the structure of a glaze melt. Figure 12.4 shows an artist's impression of how

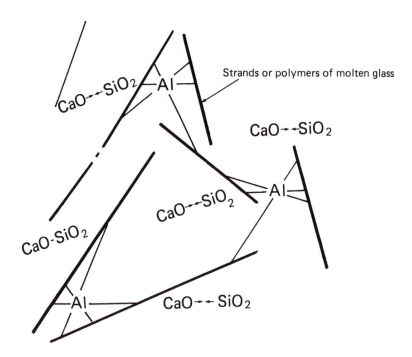

Figure 12.4. The "paradox of alumina." Scattered throughout the melt are released ions that may form crystallites or small visible crystals if they are able to migrate together.

scattered through the melt are small amounts of elements and oxides that can get together and form minute crystals because they lie near to one another in a suitable proportion. At the same time, the glassy structure forming in the cooling melt prevents large-scale movement so that large crystals or aggregates of crystals cannot form. In a high-alumina glaze, excess alumina (alumina that does not participate in the glassy structure) can participate in the formation of millions of tiny crystals to produce matte glazes. The types of crystals that are most likely to form with alumina as a component are

calcium feldspar $(CaO \cdot Al_2O_3 \cdot 2SiO_2)$
barium feldspar $(BaO \cdot Al_2O_3 \cdot 2SiO_2)$
mullite $(3Al_2O_3 \cdot 2SiO_2)$

The part played by mullite in glazes is very different from its function in bodies, for there is not the room for its long thin crystals to grow in the glaze itself. However, in high-temperature glazes where the mullite grows out of the body into the glaze layer, it gives an extremely strong body-glaze interface. Again, the ends of the needle-like crystals projecting into the glaze can act as seeds or nuclei around which other crystals may grow. Tiny mullite crystallites may also act as nuclei for crystal formation.

Selecting the Correct Proportions of Alumina for Stability

In the previous pages the average proportions of flux : silica required for various firing temperatures to give satisfactory melts on cooling were established. We must now consider the proportions of alumina that stabilize such glazes. Potters have always made glazes by trial and error, judging the proportions that worked for them. In more recent times ceramic chemists have carried out a vast number of tests, though basically still working by trial and error, and have arrive at the optimum proportions of oxides in glazes. Herman Seger in the late nineteenth century was among the first to make such carefully recorded tests.

As a result of all this testing, it can be stated that a satisfactory ratio of alumina to glass-forming silica for a clear transparent glaze would be in the region of one mole of alumina to ten moles of silica, $Al_2O_3 : 10SiO_2$. This proportion may now be coupled with the proportions for flux : silica stated above, thus giving us a list of generalized proportions of the various oxides required for different firing temperatures (see Figure 12.5). You should review "The Alumina : Silica Ratio," p. 280.

Glaze Formulation

The generalized formulas given in Figure 12.5 are used as the starting points for our glaze formulation. In this way the information and Exercises given here will link directly with the explanation of the structure of melts and the

Firing Temperature	Flux		Stabilizer		Glass-former
C.06 (1000'C/1830'F)	1 mole	:	0.1 mole	:	1 mole
C.03 (1101'C/2040'F)	1 mole	:	0.2 mole	:	2 moles
C.5 (1196'C/2185'F)	1 mole	:	0.3 mole	:	3 moles
C.8 (1263'C/2305'F)	1 mole	:	0.4 mole	:	4 moles
C.9 (1280'C/2336'F)	1 mole	:	0.5 mole	:	5 moles

Figure 12.5. Table of generalized proportions for fluxes : stabilizer : glass-former.

types of glazes that result. After these exercises are completed, it does not matter which method you use to calculate your glazes — from formulas or percentage analyses to recipes and vice versa or by feeding your data into a computer and letting it run the calculations from a program written by yourself or a software company. The important point to note is that you have a method that permits you to introduce the correct compositions of the regional materials available to you. Given this, it would be pointless to burden students, at least at the outset, with a seemingly endless maze of figures. Thus in the initial Exercises we shall use the theoretical compositions for the materials required, and calculations will be rounded off to one decimal place. There is another good reason for using a simplified formula: if a large number of very tiny amounts of trace minerals and/or impurities are included, you are far more likely to make a mistake. It is better to have an average result for the major constituents rather than one that is a long way off through miscalculation.

A further observation is made from experience: if you use the same materials consistently (bulk buying is advised once you have tested and selected the best available materials for your work) and if you have noted the impurities present, you will, by using the theoretical and shorter formulas for all calculations, get the same relative differences appearing. You will become used to recognizing these and taking them into account intuitively.

Initial Low-Temperature Exercises: Exercises 34, 35, and 36

In the following Exercises, lead oxide fluxed glazes are considered first in Exercise 34, then soda and potassa fluxed glazes in Exercise 35. This is followed by the introduction of calcia and finally tests of the partial replacement of silica by boric oxide in Exercise 36.

Do *not* undertake the lead glaze tests unless you have the proper facilities of a research laboratory or glaze room (see Chapter 5). Instead, each Exercise should be read carefully. All students should undertake, or participate in, Exercise 35 (alkali-fluxed glazes) and Exercise 36 (where calcia is added to stabilize the alkali glazes).

Aim

The aim of these exercises is to introduce an organized method of gradually building glaze formulas so that the effect of each addition of an oxide may be fully assessed. Single oxide materials are used in order to simplify the initial glaze calculations. Calcined alumina powder (though not a regular glaze material) is used to fill the very small amounts of alumina required in this group of tests that cannot be filled by kaolin as the latter would introduce too much silica.

Materials

You will need lead oxide, using litharge, and calcined alumina if undertaking Exercise 34. Sodium carbonate, potassium carbonate, calcined alumina, kaolin, colemanite (alternative name, borocalcite), and quartz are needed for Exercises 35 and 36. The amounts required are given with each Exercise.

You will need three curved test tiles that will stand up during firing for Exercise 34 (soft leatherhard tiles bent around a broom handle serve, see Figure 12.6), and two flat tiles, approximately 10 cm square, for Exercise 35 and 36. Use a red-firing clay for all of them and hard biscuit-fired tiles for Exercises 35 and 36. The lead oxide fluxed tests may be once-fired or twice-fired.

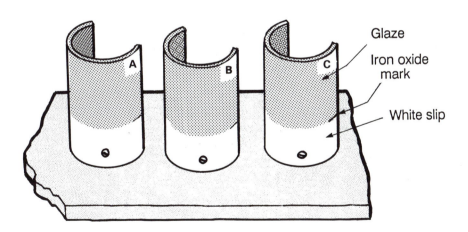

Figure 12.6. Lead oxide tests ready for firing. If leatherhard tiles are bent around a broom handle, they make excellent self-supporting test tiles and the fluidity of the glazes during firing can be noted. An unglazed area is left at the bottom of the tiles and the kiln shelf covered with bat wash or alumina powder to protect it and prevent the tiles from sticking to it.

Preparing and Applying the Tests

The soda and potassa tests are soluble and should be mixed with the minimum amount of water or a spirit medium and placed on high biscuit-fired tiles. The other test glazes may be weighed out, mixed with a little water to a smooth paste on a glazed tile with a palette knife, and then have more water added to give a creamy consistency. Alternatively, they may be mixed using a mortar and pestle. All glazes must be sieved and then applied by dipping or pouring (best with a flat-edged glazing spoon).

EXERCISE 34: Lead Oxide Fluxed Glazes

Test 34A. Here we aim to show that the following proportions of oxides make a glass, but that this is too fluid at top temperature to be considered as a satisfactory glaze.

The *formula to be tested* is

$$\text{1 mole of PbO : 1 mole of SiO}_2$$

Of the four oxides of lead, litharge (PbO), which has a molar weight of 223 g, has been chosen (i.e., 1 mole of litharge weighs 223 g). If another oxide of lead is chosen, the correct molar weight must be used. The only other oxide required is silica, which has a molar weight of 60 g. We may now convert our formula into proportions by weight:

$$\text{1 mole PbO } + \text{ 1 mole SiO}_2$$
$$(1 \times 223 \text{ g}) + (1 \times 60 \text{ g})$$
$$223 \text{ g PbO } + \text{ 60 g SiO}_2$$

For a reasonable amount of glaze mix, we may divide the amounts by 10, to give a "glaze" recipe of 22.3 g PbO + 6.0 g SiO_2. This recipe should be mixed and applied to the first curved test tile as stated above in "Preparing and Applying the Tests." It should be marked clearly as 34A and set aside, and then tests 34B and 34C prepared. As soon as you finish preparing these tests, throw away leftover mix and clean everything thoroughly.

Test 34B. In this test our aim is to show that alumina stabilizes the glaze. Following the generalized proportions, add alumina as one-tenth the amount of silica present in the previous test. As there is 1 mole of silica in the previous test, we must add 0.1Al_2O_3.

The *formula to be tested* is

$$\text{1 mole PbO : 0.1 mole Al}_2\text{O}_3 \text{ : 1 mole SiO}_2$$

The above formula has been written in full. This format will be retained for complete clarity in the first few formulas (with the "1" expressed and "mole" written in full); then taken for granted, and the formula written in the conventional way, as PbO : 0.1Al_2O_3 : SiO_2.

Materials	Formula	Molar weight
Lead oxide (litharge)	PbO	223 g
Calcinated alumina	Al_2O_3	102 g
Quartz	SiO_2	60 g

Calculating the recipe from the formula:

In order to weigh out the required quantities, the amount of each material must be multiplied by its molar weight (i.e., the weight of one mole of the material):

$$1 \text{ mole PbO} \quad : 0.1 \text{ mole } Al_2O_3 \quad : 1 \text{ mole } SiO_2$$
$$= (1 \times 223) \text{ PbO} : (0.1 \times 102) \, Al_2O_3 : (1 \times 60) \, SiO_2$$
$$= 223 \text{ g PbO} \quad : 10.2 \text{ g } Al_2O_3 \quad : 60 \text{ g } SiO_2$$

Using calcined alumina to fill the requirement for Al_2O_3, we have a recipe for Test 34B of:

223.0 g lead oxide (litharge)
10.2 g calcined alumina
60.0 g quartz
293.2 g total

For our small test, we may again divide all the amounts in the recipe by 10 so that we only have a small batch to weigh out:

22 g lead oxide (PbO)
1 g alumina (Al_2O_3)
6 g quartz (SiO_2)
29 g total

Mix and apply the test to the second curved tile as in test 34A, and set it aside with the first one. Make sure the tiles are marked.

Test 34C. We aim to show in this test the effects of increasing the alumina content. This is achieved by simply increasing the alumina to 0.2 moles of Al_2O_3.

The *formula to be tested* is

$$1 \text{ mole PbO} : 0.2 \text{ mole } Al_2O_3 : 1 \text{ mole } SiO_2$$

Materials	Formula	Molar weight
Lead oxide (litharge)	PbO	223 g
Calcined alumina	Al_2O_3	102 g
Quartz	SiO_2	60 g

Calculating the recipe from the formula gives

$$1 \text{ mole PbO} \quad : 0.2 \text{ mole } Al_2O_3 \quad : 1 \text{ mole } SiO_2$$
$$= (1 \times 223 \text{ g}) \text{ PbO} : (0.2 \times 102 \text{ g } Al_2O_3) : (1 \times 60 \text{ g}) \, SiO_2$$
$$= 223 \text{ g PbO} \quad : 20.4 \text{ g } Al_2O_3 \quad : 60 \text{ g } SiO_2$$

This may now be stated as a *batch recipe*:

Batch Recipe	or	Small Batch Recipe
223.0 g lead oxide		22 g lead oxide
20.4 g calcined alumina		2 g calcined alumina
60.0 g quartz		6 g quartz.

Prepare the test mix as before; apply the test to the third test tile and mark it 34C. This completes the set of tests for Exercise 34.

Firing

The three lead oxide glaze tests for 34A, 34B, 34C should be set up as shown in Figure 12.6, standing on a bed of calcined alumina powder and fired to 1000°C. They may be fired when completed or set aside to be fired with the next group of tests, which also require the same firing temperature. *But do not get into a muddle!*

Assessment

Make your own assessment of your fired results. You should find that the first test is shiny and transparent but has run badly, flowing off the bottom of the tile and solidifying in the alumina powder used to protect the kiln shelf. You should find that the second test is smooth, transparent, and shiny and has not run, while the third test is smooth, has not run, but is no longer shiny.

From these observations we may conclude that lead oxide is a powerful flux with the ability to flux silica at a very low temperature. Furthermore, only a very small amount of alumina is needed to stiffen the glaze to prevent it running without loss of gloss. You should find that 0.1 moles is sufficient. Finally, when an excess of alumina is used, the glaze loses its shine and becomes matte.

*   *   *

Introduction to Exercises 35 and 36

These are essential tests. Photographs cannot do them justice. For reasons that will be explained below, you will not necessarily want to keep these tests. If several students are working together, only one set need be made (or carried out as a demonstration). However, it is important that every-one should study them while they are hot from the kiln and again after several days and, if possible, months later. Study the calculations for Exercise 35, and then prepare the tests. Do the same for Exercise 36. Since the materials used to supply the soda and potassa are soluble, these tests must be mixed to a stiff paste and applied to hard (near impervious) biscuit-fired or warmed tiles to drive off the water quickly. Alternatively, the tests could be mixed with a spirit medium that evaporates quickly. The test mixes should be spread onto the tiles in even layers (about 3 mm thick). They may then be set aside until all the tests are ready and fired together. Before you start, study the formulas given below, and see how they are grouped together and gradually developed. If a class or group are working together it is suggested that two sessions are organized: first, to study the calculations and collect together the recipes; second, to prepare, fire, and assess the tests.

Reminder. From now on the standard convention is followed of not stating the 1 (one) where only one mole is required and the word mole is also omitted. Thus in the following calculations 1 mole $Na_2O : 0.1$ mole $Al_2O_3 : 1$ mole SiO_2 is written $Na_2O : 0.1Al_2O_3 : SiO_2$.

The formulas for all the tests in Exercises 35 and 36 are set out here as a group so that you can see how the formulas are gradually developed.

Tile 1. For Exercise 35

Test 35A: soda as the only flux
Na_2O $0.1 Al_2O_3$ SiO_2

Test 35B: potassa as the only flux
K_2O $0.1 Al_2O_3$ SiO_2

Test 35C: using alumina
$0.5 Na_2O$ $0.1 Al_2O_3$ SiO_2
$0.5 K_2O$

Test 35D: using kaolin
$0.5 Na_2O$ $0.1 Al_2O_3$ SiO_2
$0.5 K_2O$

Tile 2. For Exercise 36

Test 36A: introducing calcia
$0.5 Na_2O$
$0.3 K_2O$ $0.1 Al_2O_3$ SiO_2
$0.2 CaO$

Test 36B: introducing boric oxide
$0.5 Na_2O$ $0.9 SiO_2$
$0.3 K_2O$ $0.1 Al_2O_3$ $0.1 B_2O_3$
$0.2 CaO$

Test 36C: increasing silica
$0.5 Na_2O$ $1.5 SiO_2$
$0.3 K_2O$ $0.1 Al_2O_3$ $0.1 B_2O_3$
$0.2 CaO$

Test 36D: using a frit
with the same formula as 36C.

Special Firing and Assessment Techniques for Tests on Tile 1 (35A–35D)

Tests 35A–D must be assessed while they are still hot. It is therefore necessary to draw them from the kiln using the raku technique (see Chapter 5), so they should be placed at the front of the kiln. A raku kiln or a small electric kiln can be used, do not use a kiln with a large door opening, which is dangerous. Fire the tests to C.06 (1000°C/1832°F) and soak for 10 minutes. Do not overfire. *The kiln should then be switched off* and allowed to drop to about 800°C/1472°F and the tests drawn from the kiln by the "raku" technique and examined immediately. The tests 36A–D may be fired with the above tests and also rakued from the kiln or left in the kiln to cool in the normal way.

EXERCISE 35: Soda and Potassa as the Only Fluxes

Where necessary sodium carbonate, potassium carbonate, and barium carbonate will be abbreviated to sod.carb., pot.carb., and ba.carb.

The goals of Tests 35A–D are

1. To demonstrate that soda and potassa, singly or together, are capable of acting as fluxes at the low temperature of C.06, but that a "glaze" so formed quickly devitrifies as it takes up water from the atmosphere.

2. To introduce kaolin in 35D to fill the alumina and part of the silica required in the formula. In each test in this series the generalized formula for low temperature, 1 flux : 0.1 stabilizer : 1 glass-former, is used as a starting point.

The materials for tests 35A–35D are

Material	Formula	Molar weight
Sodium carbonate	Na_2CO_3	106 g
Potassium carbonate	K_2CO_3	138 g
Calcined alumina	Al_2O_3	102 g
Kaolin	$Al_2O_3 \cdot 2SiO_2 \cdot 2H_2O$	258 g
Quartz	SiO_2	60 g

Note. On heating, Na_2CO_3 and K_2CO_3 dissociate. The released CO_2 escapes as a gas and is therefore not included in the calculations. In books containing technical data and in catalogs this is referred to as a loss-on-ignition (l.o.i.):

$$Na_2CO_3 \overset{heat}{\to} Na_2O + CO_2\uparrow$$

$$K_2CO_3 \overset{heat}{\to} K_2O + CO_2\uparrow$$

where the ↑ indicates that the CO_2 is l.o.i.

This is also the case with the H_2O associated with the kaolin. The other two materials are single oxides that do not contain any material lost during firing.

Calculations

In the following calculations the instructions are given on the left with the mathematical calculations on the right together with a checklist to make sure that all the oxides required in the formula are supplied. In 35A these are set out step by step and each step is repeated and gradually added to in order to show how the required formula is filled. This method will be used where necessary and then, when you are thoroughly familiar with the method, all calculations will be placed together. For simplicity the batch and percentage recipes are stated corrected to the nearest whole number.

Test 35A: Soda as the Only Flux

Formula to be filled:

$$Na_2O \quad 0.1Al_2O_3 \quad SiO_2$$

Step 1

One mole of sodium carbonate supplies one mole of soda (Na_2O). This is entered opposite. All the soda required has been found.

Materials		Oxides supplied		
		Na_2O	Al_2O_3	SiO_2
1.0 sod.carb.	$\rightarrow$	1.0		

Step 2

Next, 0.1 mole of alumina gives all the alumina required.

Materials		Oxides supplied		
		Na_2O	Al_2O_3	SiO_2
1.0 sod.carb.	$\rightarrow$	1.0		
0.1 alumina	$\rightarrow$		0.1	

Step 3

One mole of quartz supplies all the SiO_2 required. All oxides have now been found. Make sure of this by comparing the totals in the checklist with the oxides required in the formula. After this is done the checklist is no longer needed.

Materials		Oxides supplied		
		Na_2O	Al_2O_3	SiO_2
1.0 sod.carb.	$\rightarrow$	1.0		
0.1 alumina	$\rightarrow$		0.1	
1.0 quartz	$\rightarrow$			1.0
total oxides found		1.0	0.1	1.0

Step 4

Now we must find out the weight of each material we require in grams. To do this, we multiply the number of moles of each material required by the weight of 1 mole of this substance.

Material		$\times$ Molar weight	= Batch weight
1.0 sod.carb.	$\times$	106 g	= 106 g
0.1 alumina	$\times$	102 g	= 10 g
1.0 quartz	$\times$	60 g	= 60 g
total oxides found			176 g

Step 5

The list showing the weight of each material required is called the batch recipe.

Batch recipe
106 g sodium carbonate
10 g alumina
60 g quartz
176 g total batch weight

Step 6. You will find it helpful to have all recipes add up to the same figure. The most convenient is 100, a percentage recipe. Divide each weight by the batch weight and multiply by 100:

$$\frac{106}{176} \times 100 = 60\% \qquad \frac{10}{176} \times 100 = 6\% \qquad \frac{60}{176} \times 100 = 34\%$$

Percentage Recipe for Test 35A:

60% sodium carbonate
6% alumina
34% quartz

Test 35B: Potassa as the Only Flux

By now you should begin to understand the method and the reasons for the steps taken to convert the formula to a recipe of ceramic raw materials. It is therefore suggested that you draw up your own chart and try to do the calculations yourself, referring to the data given below when necessary. You are advised to use this layout in your own work (no matter how roughly) so that the figures do not get muddled and so that you can see at a glance whether all the oxides have been filled (particularly feldspar and clay).

Formula to be filled:

K_2O $0.1Al_2O_3$ SiO_2

Calculation:

Step 1. 1.0 mole potassium carbonate supplies 1.0 K_2O

Materials		Oxides supplied		
		K_2O	Al_2O_3	SiO_2
1.0 pot.carb.	→	1.0		

Step 2. 0.1 mole alumina supplies 0.1 Al_2O_3

Materials		Oxides supplied		
		K_2O	Al_2O_3	SiO_2
1.0 pot.carb.	→	1.0		
0.1 alumina	→		0.1	

Step 3. 1 mole quartz gives 1 mole silica, SiO_2

Materials		Oxides supplied		
		K_2O	Al_2O_3	SiO_2
1.0 pot.carb.	→	1.0		
0.1 alumina	→		0.1	
1.0 quartz	→			1.0
total oxides	→	1.0	0.1	1.0

Step 4. Having checked that all the oxides have been filled correctly, write down the list of the number of moles of each material required and multiply each one by its molar weight.

Material		× *Molar weight*	=	*Batch weight*
1.0 pot.carb.	×	138 g	=	138 g
0.1 alumina	×	102 g	=	10 g
1.0 quartz	×	60 g	=	60 g
		total batch weight	=	208 g

Step 5. The final step is to convert this to a percentage recipe.

$\dfrac{138}{208} \times 100 = 66\%$ $\dfrac{10}{208} \times 100 = 5\%$ $\dfrac{60}{208} \times 100 = 29\%$

Percentage Recipe for Test 35B

> 66% potassium carbonate
> 5% alumina
> 29% quartz

Test 35C: Two Fluxes

In this formula there are two fluxes, Na_2O and K_2O, but they are still dealt with in the same way. Again, the carbonate fires away.

$$0.5Na_2CO_3 \xrightarrow{\text{heat}} 0.5Na_2O + 0.5CO_2\uparrow$$

$$0.5K_2CO_3 \xrightarrow{\text{heat}} 0.5K_2O + 0.5CO_2\uparrow$$

Formula to be filled:

> $0.5Na_2O \quad 0.1Al_2O_3 \quad 1SiO_2$
> $0.5K_2O$

Calculation:

		Oxides supplied			
		Na_2O	K_2O	Al_2O_3	SiO_2
Step 1. 0.5 sodium carbonate contributes 0.5 soda, Na_2O.	0.5 sod.carb.	0.5			
Step 2. 0.5 potassium carbonate contributes 0.5 potassa, K_2O.	0.5 pot.carb.		0.5		
Step 3. 0.1 alumina supplies 0.1 Al_2O_3.	0.1 alumina			0.1	
Step 4. 1 quartz contributes 1 SiO_2.	1.0 quartz				1.0
	total oxides	0.5	0.5	0.1	1.0

Step 5. Look at the check list and make sure that all oxides have been found. This done, the checklist is no longer required.

Step 6. We now have a list of materials required. This tells us how many moles of each material we require. Convert this to a recipe in grams by multiplying the number of moles required by the weight of one mole of each material.

Material	× Molar weight	= Batch weight
0.5 sod.carb. ×	106 g	= 53 g
0.5 pot.carb. ×	138 g	= 69 g
0.1 alumina ×	102 g	= 10 g
1.0 quartz ×	60 g	= 60 g
	total	= 192 g

Step 7. Convert the batch to a percentage recipe.

$$\frac{53}{192} \times 100 = 28\% \qquad \frac{69}{192} \times 100 = 36\% \qquad \frac{10}{192} \times 100 = 5\% \qquad \frac{60}{192} \times 100 = 31\%$$

Percentage Recipe for Test 35C

> 28% sodium carbonate
> 36% potassium carbonate
> 5% alumina
> 31% quartz

Test 35D: Introducing Kaolin

In this test the same formula is used as in the previous test, but kaolin ($Al_2O_3 \cdot 2SiO_2 \cdot 2H_2O$) is used to fill the required amount of alumina (Al_2O_3). For the first time we have to deal with a material that supplies more than one oxide to the melt.

Formula to be filled:

$$0.5Na_2O \quad 0.1Al_2O_3 \quad SiO_2$$
$$0.5K_2O$$

Calculation:

Step 1. 0.5 sodium carbonate gives 0.5 Na_2O; 0.5 potassium carbonate gives 0.5 K_2O

Materials	Na$_2$O	K$_2$O	Al$_2$O	SiO$_2$
	\multicolumn{4}{c	}{Oxides supplied}
0.5 sod.carb.	0.5			
0.5 pot.carb.		0.5		

Step 2. Dealing with the kaolin. 1 mole of kaolin → Al_2O_3 + $2SiO_2$ + $2H_2O$ (the H_2O evaporates), so 0.1 kaolin gives 0.1 Al_2O_3 and 0.2 SiO_2. Thus from 0.1 kaolin we get all the alumina we need and some of the silica.

Materials	Na$_2$O	K$_2$O	Al$_2$O$_3$	SiO$_2$
0.5 sod.carb.	0.5			
0.5 pot.carb.		0.5		
0.1 kaolin			0.1	+ 0.2

Step 3. Dealing with the silica. The formula requires 1 mole of silica. The kaolin has already supplied 0.2 silica, so we still need 0.8 silica. This can be supplied by 0.8 quartz.

Materials	Na$_2$O	K$_2$O	Al$_2$O$_3$	SiO$_2$
0.5 sod.carb.	0.5			
0.5 pot.carb.		0.5		
0.1 kaolin			0.1	+ 0.2
0.8 quartz				0.8
total oxides	0.5	0.5	0.1	1.0

Remember that a glaze formula represents the oxide content of the glaze after firing and therefore does not include those oxides which disappear during firing. Thus the water is not included in the calculations.

The checklist now shows that all the oxides required by the formula have been filled. The checklist may be ticked off, it is no longer required.

Step 4. The number of moles required for each material is now multiplied by the molar weight to find the amount in grams that must be weighed out. This is then converted to a 100% recipe.

Material		× *Molar weight*	= *Batch weight*
0.5 sod.carb.	×	106 g	= 53 g
0.5 pot.carb.	×	138 g	= 69 g
0.1 kaolin	×	258 g	= 26 g
0.8 quartz	×	60 g	= 48 g
		total batch weight	= 196 g

Step 5.
Converting the batch to a percentage recipe

$$\frac{53}{196} \times 100 = 27\% \qquad \frac{26}{196} \times 100 = 13\% \qquad \frac{69}{196} \times 100 = 35\% \qquad \frac{48}{196} \times 100 = 25\%$$

Percentage Recipe for Test 35D:

> 27% sodium carbonate
> 35% potassium carbonate
> 13% kaolin
> 25% quartz

*　*　*

EXERCISE 36: Adding Calcia and Boric Oxide

These tests should be placed on Tile 2 (see p. 317).

Aim

Our aim here is to study (1) the value of including calcia (CaO) in soda/potassa fluxed glazes, and (2) the effect of the addition of boric oxide (B_2O_3). Calcite/calcium carbonate (see pp. 115–16) is used to introduce CaO in Test 36A, and in Test 36B colemanite is used to introduce B_2O_3. Where necessary, calcium carbonate is abbreviated to Ca.carb.

Materials for Tests 36A to 36C

	Formula	*Molar weight*
Sodium carbonate	Na_2CO_3	106 g
Potassium carbonate	K_2CO_3	138 g
Colemanite	$2CaO \cdot 3B_2O_3 \cdot 5H_2O$	412 g
Calcite (calcium carbonate)	$CaCO_3$	100 g
Kaolin	$Al_2O_3 \cdot 2SiO_2 \cdot 2H_2O$	258 g
Quartz	SiO_2	60 g

(There are other similar materials. If you use one of these, obtain its formula and molar weight.)

Test 36A: Introducing Calcia

A little calcia is introduced in order to prevent devitrification; this gives us three fluxing oxides. Soda has been kept as the principal flux because it is an extremely powerful low-temperature flux, and part of the potassa has been replaced by calcia. Calcium carbonate is used to introduce the calcia (the carbonate fires away leaving only calcia). Thus our fluxes become

$0.5Na_2O$ (principal flux)
$0.3K_2O$
$0.2CaO$
1.0 total fluxes

By carrying out the adjustment in this way we still have a total of 1 mole of fluxes (i.e., unity in the fluxes) so that we may continue to relate this formula to the generalized formula for low-temperature glazes:

1 flux : 0.1 stabilizer : 1 glass-former.

Formula to be filled:

$0.5Na_2O$
$0.3K_2O$ $0.1Al_2O_3$ $1.0SiO_2$
$0.2CaO$

Calculation: Since this is a simple calculation, all the information will be entered together.

Materials	Oxides supplied				
		Na_2O	K_2O	CaO	Al_2O	SiO_2
all soda supplied by sod.carb.	0.5 sod.carb. →	0.5				
all potassa supplied by pot.carb.	0.3 pot.carb. →		0.3			
all calcia supplied by ca.carb.	0.2 ca.carb. →			0.2		
all the alumina and some of the silica supplied by kaolin	0.1 kaolin →				0.1	+ 0.2
remaining silica supplied by the single oxide quartz.	0.8 quartz →					0.8
total oxides found		0.5	0.3	0.2	0.1	1.0

Each material required is now multiplied by its molar weight, and the batch weight converted to a percentage recipe, as in previous tests.

Material		× Molar weight	= Batch weight
0.5 sod.carb.	×	106 g	= 53 g
0.3 pot.carb.	×	138 g	= 41 g
0.2 ca.carb.	×	100 g	= 20 g
0.1 kaolin	×	258 g	= 26 g
0.8 quartz	×	60 g	= 48 g
		total batch weight	= 188 g

Converting batch recipe to a percentage

$$\frac{53}{188} \times 100 = 28\% \qquad \frac{41}{188} \times 100 = 22\% \qquad \frac{20}{188} \times 100 = 11\%$$

$$\frac{26}{188} \times 100 = 14\% \qquad \frac{48}{188} \times 100 = 25\%$$

Percentage Recipe for Test 36A:

28% sodium carbonate
22% potassium carbonate
11% calcite
14% kaolin
25% quartz

Test 36B: Introducing B_2O_3 via colemanite ($2CaO \cdot 3B_2O_3 \cdot 5H_2O$)

To replace a little of the high-temperature glass-former SiO_2 by the low-temperature glass-former B_2O_3, using colemanite (borocalcite) to introduce the B_2O_3. To do this, the fluxes and alumina are kept the same and silica is reduced to 0.9 to let in the B_2O_3. Thus the formula used in Test 36A is adapted to

$$\begin{matrix} 0.5Na_2O & & \\ 0.3K_2O & 0.1Al_2O_3 & 0.9SiO_2 \\ 0.2CaO & & 0.1B_2O_3 \end{matrix}$$

Here one-tenth of the silica has been replaced by boric oxide ($0.1\ B_2O_3$).

Since this glaze is a little more complicated, the step-by-step method will be used, but first let us consider the colemanite. This material contributes $2CaO + 3B_2O_3$. Because we only want a very small amount of B_2O_3 we must concentrate on the B_2O_3 before considering the requirement for calcia. *Note.* If you tried to fill the calcia first, you would introduce too much B_2O_3. It is clear that we want a *very* small amount of colemanite to get 0.1 B_2O_3.

Calculation: The calculation to find the required soda and potassa is as before. To find how much colemanite is required, we divide the amount of B_2O_3 *wanted* in the formula by the amount of B_2O_3 we *have* in the colemanite. To quote Ivan Englund's splendid slogan "Divide what you want by what you have."

$$\frac{\text{we want } 0.1 \text{ B}_2\text{O}_3}{\text{we have } 3.0 \text{ B}_2\text{O}_3} = \frac{0.1}{3.0} = 0.03 \text{ colemanite}$$

Therefore, we must use 0.03 moles of colemanite to get 0.1 B_2O_3. We must now immediately check how much calcia is introduced by 0.03 moles of colemanite, and we find that this is 0.06. Proof:

$$1.0 \quad \text{colemanite contributes } 2\text{CaO} \cdot 3\text{B}_2\text{O}_3 \cdot 5\text{H}_2\text{O}\uparrow$$

$$0.03 \text{ colemanite contributes } (0.03 \times 2) \text{ CaO} = 0.06 \text{ CaO}$$
$$(0.03 \times 3) \text{ B}_2\text{O}_3 = 0.09 \text{ B}_2\text{O}_3$$

(0.09 B_2O_3 is as near as we can reasonably get to 0.1 B_2O_3.)

After carrying out these calculations, we may enter them in our checklist along with the other oxides required, as shown below. One pleasant thought about this test is that it contains all the necessary theory required to calculate any recipe from a formula and therefore represents the maximum difficulty encountered in glaze calculations.

Calculation:

	Materials	Oxides supplied					
		Na$_2$O	K$_2$O	CaO	Al$_2$O$_3$	SiO$_2$	B$_2$O$_3$
Step 1. The soda and potassa are found as in the previous Exercises.	0.5 sod.carb. 0.3 pot.carb.	0.5	0.3				
Step 2. Colemanite supplies all the B$_2$O$_3$ and some of the calcia.	0.03 colemanite			0.06			0.1
Step 3. Calcite can be used to supply the rest of the needed calcia. The formula requires 0.20 CaO. Colemanite has supplied 0.06 CaO. So we still require 0.14 CaO.	0.14 calcite			0.14			
Step 4. To complete the alumina required using kaolin: 0.1 kaolin gives 0.1Al$_2$O$_3$ and 0.2SiO$_2$.	0.1 kaolin				0.1	+ 0.2	
Step 5. Alumina is now filled, but we need more SiO$_2$.	0.7 quartz					0.7	
	total oxides	0.5	0.3	0.2	0.1	0.9	0.1

Step 6. Double check that all oxides have been found. We no longer need the checklist.

Step 7. The batch recipe is now converted to a percentage recipe.

Material		× Molar weight	= Batch weight	Percentage recipe
0.50 sod.carb.	×	106 g	= 53	27% sod.carb.
0.30 pot.carb.	×	138 g	= 41	20% pot.carb.
0.03 colemanite	×	412 g	= 12	6% colemanite
0.14 calcite	×	100 g	= 14	7% calcite
0.10 kaolin	×	258 g	= 26	13% kaolin
0.90 quartz	×	60 g	= 54	27% quartz
			200	

Test 36C: Increasing the Silica

We now have a good mixture of fluxes and some of the low-temperature glass-former, B_2O_3. A test has been included to see whether the amount of silica can be raised from the original 1 mole of SiO_2 to 1.5 moles. If so, we shall have a harder wearing glaze surface. Intermediate amounts of SiO_2 could be tried if you wish, but 1.5 SiO_2 will give a known satisfactory result. The same thing applies to B_2O_3. It should be noted that in altering the silica content, we are moving away from the generalized formula. If the new glaze is satisfactory, all is well; if not, the generalized formula still acts as a guide to balance the glaze again (more of this in Exercise 38 and Plate 16).

Formula to be filled:

$$\begin{matrix} 0.5Na_2O \\ 0.3K_2O \quad 0.1Al_2O_3 \quad \begin{matrix} 1.5SiO_2 \\ 0.1B_2O_3 \end{matrix} \\ 0.2CaO \end{matrix}$$

Calculation: In this test all amounts have been entered on the same checklist, using the same materials as in the previous test. You should follow the instructions given below together with the checklist.

Materials	Na₂O	K₂O	CaO	Al₂O₃	SiO₂	B₂O₃
			Oxides supplied			
0.50 sod.carb. →	0.5					
0.30 pot.carb. →		0.3				
0.03 colemanite →			0.06	————————→		0.1
0.14 calcite →			0.14			
0.10 kaolin →				0.1 + 0.2		
1.30 quartz →					1.3	
total oxides found	0.5	0.3	0.2	0.1	1.5	0.1

Step 1. Fill the Na_2O and K_2O required in the formula in the same way as before. You could check these off when the amounts given in the formula have been completely filled.

Step 2. Using colemanite to supply all the B_2O_3 and some of the CaO, we use Englund's formula to find the amount of colemanite required:

$$\frac{\text{Divide the amount of } B_2O_3 \text{ we want}}{\text{by the amount of } B_2O_3 \text{ in colemanite}} = \frac{\text{we want } 0.1\ B_2O_3}{\text{we have } 3.0\ B_2O_3} = 0.03 \text{ colemanite}$$

Thus we require 0.03 mole of colemanite to fill the B_2O_3. *Colemanite also gives some calcia.* Proof:

$$1 \text{ mole colemanite contributes } 2\,CaO \cdot 3B_2O_3 \cdot 5H_2O\!\uparrow$$

$$0.03 \text{ mole colemanite contributes } (0.03 \times 2)CaO \,=\, 0.06CaO$$
$$\text{and } (0.03 \times 3)B_2O_3 \,=\, 0.09B_2O_3 \text{ (rounded to 0.1)}$$

Step 3. To find the rest of the CaO required, calcite is the ideal material to use because it contributes only CaO to the melt. All we have to do is to subtract the amount supplied by colemanite from the amount required by the formula:

$$0.2 - 0.06 = 0.14\,CaO.$$

Step 4. If kaolin is to supply all the alumina required and some of the silica, we can use Englund's formula to find the amount of kaolin we require:

$$\frac{\text{Divide the amount of Al}_2O_3 \text{ we want}}{\text{by the amount of Al}_2O_3 \text{ in kaolin}} \,=\, \frac{\text{we want } 0.1\ Al_2O_3}{\text{we have } 1.0\ Al_2O_3} = 0.1 \text{ mole}$$

Thus 0.1 kaolin gives the Al_2O_3 we require and also some silica:

$$1.0 \text{ kaolin} = 1Al_2O_3 \cdot 2SiO_2 \cdot 2H_2O\!\uparrow$$
$$0.1 \text{ kaolin gives } 0.1Al_2O_3 \text{ and } 0.2SiO_2.$$

Step 5. We have 0.2 moles silica from the kaolin, therefore we still need 1.3 moles to give us the 1.5 moles SiO_2 required in the formula. This may be supplied by the single oxide quartz and entered in the checklist.

Step 6. The final steps are to convert the moles of materials required into a recipe by weight (batch recipe) and then to convert this to a percentage recipe as in the previous test.

Material		× *Molar weight*	= *Batch weight*	*Percentage recipe*
0.50 sod.carb.	×	106 g	= 53 g	24% sodium carbonate
0.30 pot.carb.	×	138 g	= 41 g	18% potassium carbonate
0.03 colemanite	×	412 g	= 12 g	5% colemanite
0.14 calcite	×	100 g	= 14 g	6% calcite
0.10 kaolin	×	258 g	= 26 g	12% kaolin
1.30 quartz	×	60 g	= 78 g	35% quartz
total batch weight			= 224 g	

Test 36D: Using a Frit

Many manufacturers of frits supply an alkali frit with precisely the same formula as that of Test 36C:

Stated as a percentage analysis:

$$50.8\% \ SiO_2, \quad 5.7\% \ Al_2O_3, \quad 17.5\% \ Na_2O$$
$$15.9\% \ K_2O, \quad 6.3\% \ CaO, \quad 3.8\% \ B_2O_3$$

Stated as a formula:

$$\begin{matrix} 0.5\ Na_2O \\ 0.3\ K_2O \\ 0.2\ CaO \end{matrix} \quad 0.1\ Al_2O_3 \quad \begin{matrix} 1.5\ SiO_2 \\ 0.1\ B_2O_3 \end{matrix}$$

It is therefore suggested that you apply a test of a commercial alkaline frit having this formula in the place provided on Tile B, i.e., Test 36D.

Assessment

After preparing and firing the tests to C.06 as suggested on p. 316, set them up together with their formulas in the correct order (see p. 317). The assessment must then take place in two stages:

1. Immediately after the tiles are drawn from the kiln, while still hot.
2. After a time lapse, preferably 24 hours or a week; *and* then again a month or a year later.

Comparing Tests from Exercises 35 and 36

Tests 35A–D

On drawing from the kiln, the tests should appear to be hard, shiny glazes. A few hours later, the soda-fluxed Test 35A will assume a slight irridescence, then become a sticky gel. You may test this with a stick. If you use your finger, *wash your hands immediately* as the mix has taken up water from the atmosphere forming a caustic sodium silicate. *Do not rub your eyes after touching the gel.* Small white crystals will begin to form: the glaze is coming out of the glassy, vitreous state. It is devitrifying. The potassa-fluxed test (35B) will also devitrify but may take several weeks. The same will eventually occur in the soda + potassa fluxed tests (35C and 35D).

Tests 36A–C

The tests with calcia should remain in the glassy state and should not devitrify even after a year has passed. If a few crystals, visible as tiny white flakes, begin to form, it is because the amount of CaO is only just within the amount needed to stabilize the glaze. With the introduction of the low-temperature glass-former B_2O_3 in 36B and even more so with the increase in silica in 36C, a more stable, harder glass is achieved by locking the constituents into a successful transparent glaze.

Test 36D

Given that this is a commercial frit it has been made to very exact standards and pre-fused. It will therefore soften to a fluid melt more quickly than the unfritted test of the same composition giving a hard, vitreous glaze. The only problem that you may encounter with the fritted version is that, if fired too high, it may become too fluid and soak into or flow off the tile. It should be noted, however, that frits are not used alone as glazes (see p. 122).

Conclusion

Soda and potassa will flux a glaze and produce a glass, but the glaze that forms on cooling will not be stable — it quickly devitrifies. However, with the addition of calcia, stability may be obtained, particularly when the composition has been fritted as in a commercial frit.

* * *

Recipe to Formula: Checking the Formula of a Given Glaze

There will be occasions when you want to check the oxide content of a given recipe, for instance when you need to adjust the recipe. To do this, correlate each step with the example given below.

1. Divide the amount of each material by its molar weight to find the number of moles of each material, e.g., 40 g potassium feldspar ÷ 556.5 = 0.072 moles of potassium feldspar.
2. Multiply the number of moles of each material in the recipe by the number of moles of each oxide in its formula. Taking potassium feldspar ($K_2O \cdot Al_2O_3 \cdot 6SiO_2$) for an example, we have $(1 \times 0.072)K_2O$, $(1 \times 0.072)Al_2O_3$, and $(6 g \times 0.072)SiO_2$.
3. Add up the total for each oxide; this gives the total amounts (i.e., proportions of each oxide in the recipe).
4. As it is the convention to state the formula with unity in the fluxes, add up the fluxes and divide through by this figure.

Example. Let us consider the recipe 40 g potassium feldspar, 20 g calcite, 10 g kaolin, and 30 g quartz (this glaze is discussed on pp. 285 and 287).

Molar		Oxide content		
Recipe ÷ weight = moles	K_2O	CaO	Al_2O_3	SiO_2
40 g pot.feld. ÷ 556.5 = 0.072	(1×0.072)	—	(1×0.072)	$(6 \times 0.072 = 0.432)$
20 g calcite ÷ 100.0 = 0.200		(1×0.200)		
10 g kaolin ÷ 258.0 = 0.039			(1×0.039)	$(2 \times 0.039 = 0.078)$
30 g quartz ÷ 60.0 = 0.500				$(1 \times 0.500 = 0.500)$
Divide each oxide by the total fluxes	0.072	0.200	0.111	1.010
$(0.072 + 0.200 = 0.272)$	0.265	0.735	0.408	3.713

Rounding off to one decimal place, we have a formula of:

$$0.3K_2O \quad 0.4Al_2O_3 \quad 3.7SiO_2$$
$$\underline{0.7CaO}$$
$$1.00$$

Note that the fluxes add up to 1.

High-Temperature Glazes

Herman Seger (1902), in his search for a means of measuring high temperature, carried out a series of trials to find the proportions for $K_2O : CaO$ and $Al_2O_3 : SiO_2$ that were the "most fusible" at the "melting heat of feldspar." Seger found the most fusible compositions to be

$$0.2K_2O \quad 0.5Al_2O_3 \quad 4SiO_2 \quad and \quad 0.3K_2O \quad 0.5Al_2O_3 \quad 4SiO_2$$
$$0.8CaO \qquad\qquad\qquad\qquad\qquad 0.7CaO$$

Of these the second one was chosen.

Extracts of these trials are given below in Groups 1 and 2. You may, if you wish, carry these out for yourself using potassium feldspar, calcite (Seger used pure white marble from Carrara, which is a form of calcite), kaolin, and quartz to fill the formulas. We have already seen in Test no. 14, "Blends of Four Materials," that a formula very near to Seger's gives a well-fused result, so we shall make a series of tests around this formula. This will then be followed by Exercises designed to give you experience in developing special glazes of your own.

EXERCISE 37: Testing Seger Formulas

Aim

To test the following Seger formulas at C.9 and select the most fusible from each group.

Group 1 (fluxes and silica held constant, alumina variable)

No. 1 $0.3K_2O \quad 0.40Al_2O_3 \quad 4SiO_2$
$0.7CaO$

No. 2 $0.3K_2O \quad 0.45Al_2O_3 \quad 4SiO_2$
$0.7CaO$

No. 3 $0.3K_2O \quad 0.50Al_2O_3 \quad 4SiO_2$
$0.7CaO$

No. 4 $0.3K_2O \quad 0.55Al_2O_3 \quad 4SiO_2$
$0.7CaO$

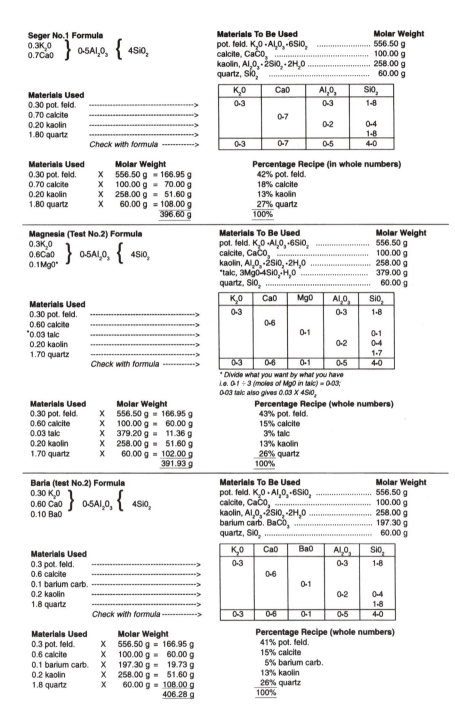

Seger No.1 Formula

$\left.\begin{array}{l} 0.3K_2O \\ 0.7CaO \end{array}\right\}$ $0.5Al_2O_3$ $\left\{\begin{array}{l} 4SiO_2 \end{array}\right.$

Materials To Be Used | **Molar Weight**
pot. feld. $K_2O \cdot Al_2O_3 \cdot 6SiO_2$ .... 556.50 g
calcite, $CaCO_3$ .... 100.00 g
kaolin, $Al_2O_3 \cdot 2SiO_2 \cdot 2H_2O$ .... 258.00 g
quartz, SiO_2 .... 60.00 g

Materials Used
0.30 pot. feld. -->
0.70 calcite -->
0.20 kaolin -->
1.80 quartz -->
Check with formula ------------->

K_2O	CaO	Al_2O_3	SiO_2
0.3		0.3	1.8
	0.7		
		0.2	0.4
			1.8
0.3	0.7	0.5	4.0

Materials Used | **Molar Weight**
0.30 pot. feld. X 556.50 g = 166.95 g
0.70 calcite X 100.00 g = 70.00 g
0.20 kaolin X 258.00 g = 51.60 g
1.80 quartz X 60.00 g = 108.00 g
396.60 g

Percentage Recipe (in whole numbers)
42% pot. feld.
18% calcite
13% kaolin
27% quartz
100%

Magnesia (Test No.2) Formula

$\left.\begin{array}{l} 0.3K_2O \\ 0.6CaO \\ 0.1MgO^* \end{array}\right\}$ $0.5Al_2O_3$ $\left\{\begin{array}{l} 4SiO_2 \end{array}\right.$

Materials To Be Used | **Molar Weight**
pot. feld. $K_2O \cdot Al_2O_3 \cdot 6SiO_2$ .... 556.50 g
calcite, $CaCO_3$ .... 100.00 g
kaolin, $Al_2O_3 \cdot 2SiO_2 \cdot 2H_2O$ .... 258.00 g
*talc, $3MgO \cdot 4SiO_2 \cdot H_2O$ .... 379.00 g
quartz, SiO_2 .... 60.00 g

Materials Used
0.30 pot. feld. -->
0.60 calcite -->
*0.03 talc -->
0.20 kaolin -->
1.70 quartz -->
Check with formula ------------->

K_2O	CaO	MgO	Al_2O_3	SiO_2
0.3			0.3	1.8
	0.6			
		0.1		0.1
			0.2	0.4
				1.7
0.3	0.6	0.1	0.5	4.0

* Divide what you want by what you have
i.e. $0.1 \div 3$ (moles of MgO in talc) = 0.03;
0.03 talc also gives 0.03 X $4SiO_2$

Materials Used | **Molar Weight**
0.30 pot. feld. X 556.50 g = 166.95 g
0.60 calcite X 100.00 g = 60.00 g
0.03 talc X 379.20 g = 11.36 g
0.20 kaolin X 258.00 g = 51.60 g
1.70 quartz X 60.00 g = 102.00 g
391.93 g

Percentage Recipe (whole numbers)
43% pot. feld.
15% calcite
3% talc
13% kaolin
26% quartz
100%

Baria (test No.2) Formula

$\left.\begin{array}{l} 0.30 K_2O \\ 0.60 CaO \\ 0.10 BaO \end{array}\right\}$ $0.5Al_2O_3$ $\left\{\begin{array}{l} 4SiO_2 \end{array}\right.$

Materials To Be Used | **Molar Weight**
pot. feld. $K_2O \cdot Al_2O_3 \cdot 6SiO_2$ .... 556.50 g
calcite, $CaCO_3$ .... 100.00 g
kaolin, $Al_2O_3 \cdot 2SiO_2 \cdot 2H_2O$ .... 258.00 g
barium carb. $BaCO_3$ .... 197.30 g
quartz, SiO_2 .... 60.00 g

Materials Used
0.3 pot. feld. -->
0.6 calcite -->
0.1 barium carb. -->
0.2 kaolin -->
1.8 quartz -->
Check with formula ------------->

K_2O	CaO	BaO	Al_2O_3	SiO_2
0.3			0.3	1.8
	0.6			
		0.1		
			0.2	0.4
				1.8
0.3	0.6	0.1	0.5	4.0

Materials Used | **Molar Weight**
0.3 pot. feld. X 556.50 g = 166.95 g
0.6 calcite X 100.00 g = 60.00 g
0.1 barium carb. X 197.30 g = 19.73 g
0.2 kaolin X 258.00 g = 51.60 g
1.8 quartz X 60.00 g = 108.00 g
406.28 g

Percentage Recipe (whole numbers)
41% pot. feld.
15% calcite
5% barium carb.
13% kaolin
26% quartz
100%

Figure 12.7. Formula to recipe calculations for tests in Exercise 38. Top, Seger no. 1 formula; middle, magnesia test no. 2; bottom, baria test no. 2.

After firing, choose the best proportion of alumina from your own tests, and use this in the next series of tests. For the purpose of this Exercise, Seger's result of 0.5 Al_2O_3 has been selected to use in the following tests.

Group 2 (fluxes and alumina held constant, silica variable)

No. 1	0.3K_2O 0.7CaO	0.5Al_2O_3	4.0SiO_2
No. 2	0.3K_2O 0.7CaO	0.5Al_2O_3	4.5SiO_2
No. 3	0.3K_2O 0.7CaO	0.5Al_2O_3	5.0SiO_2
No. 4	0.3K_2O 0.7CaO	0.5Al_2O_3	5.5SiO_2

Convert these formulas to recipes using potassium feldspar to fill the requirement for K_2O (the calculation for no. 1 is included in Figure 12.7, p. 332, where it also forms the first test for the next Exercise) and carry out the tests as in previous Exercises (see "Preparing and Applying the Tests," p. 314). (See Appendix 3, p. 397 to convert percentage analysis to unity formula, to calculate the molar weight, and to develop a percentage recipe.)

* * *

EXERCISE 38: Discovering the Effects of Additions of Magnesia and Baria

Aim

To run line addition tests to show that: (1) additions up to 0.2 mole MgO or BaO increase the fusibility of a glaze; (2) additions of either 0.3 MgO or 0.4 BaO, or more, give a matte glaze with stone-like quality as the excess is increased; (3) the results from a reduction firing are very different from an oxidation firing to the same top temperature. For the purposes of this Exercise, we shall start with the Seger formula

$$0.3K_2O \quad 0.5Al_2O_3 \quad 4SiO_2$$
$$0.7CaO$$

The Recipes

Refer to Plate 16, where the formulas for the magnesia series are given. The formulas for the baria tests are the same as the magnesia tests, replacing the MgO by BaO. Both series start with the Seger formula given above and for the calculation "formula to recipe" see Figure 12.7 (top). The center calculation shows the second test in the MgO series in which MgO is introduced, and at the bottom is the second test for the BaO series. The rest of the calculations for both series should be carried out using these as guides.

In the formulas for both test series, note that the MgO and BaO are increased up to 0.4 mole in no. 5. In no. 6, silica is reduced to 3 moles, with a further reduction of silica to 2.7 moles in no. 7.

Materials

The same four materials used in the previous Exercise plus magnesium carbonate and barium carbonate; two test tiles for an oxidation or reduction firing (four if firing in both). Each tile should be approximately 22×6 cm.

Method

A batch of 100 g (dry weight) of each glaze should be made. Tests should be weighed out, mixed, and applied as in previous tests and marked on the back with "Ba carb." or "Mg carb.," the firing temperature, "O" or "R," and an arrow pointing to the top of the tile. (The individual glazes can thus be identified after firing by reference to Plate 16.)

One baria and one magnesia test should be fired in "O," the other two in "R" to the top temperature of your choice (in the range C.8–10). On completing the tests, the glazes should be dried, labeled, and stored. When you use a different clay you should test these glazes with the new clay to make sure they still give satisfactory results. After firing, set up the tests with the formulas given in Plate 16 against each individual test (changing MgO for BaO for your baria series).

Assessment

Consult Figure 12.7 and Plate 16, while turning your tiles in the light, when making the assessment.

Note the addition required to give the maximum clear transparency in oxidation. Usually, this is 0.2 mole for MgO; in other words, the glaze becomes clearer with a small addition of MgO but then becomes increasingly opaque and finally matte. A similar change occurs with BaO, but the glazes do not clear to the same degree of transparency at 0.2 mole, and they are less shiny. In reduction both the MgO and BaO tests remain cloudy throughout and variations in the character of the surface may be seen.

Note the effect of reducing silica from 4 moles to 3 moles. In the results of the magnesia tests shown in Plate 16, the surface becomes matte and stone-like. With a further reduction of silica to 2.7 moles the surface becomes dry and in the BaO tests the surface is rough to the touch.

*　*　*

Further Investigation

The normal procedure would be to increase the proportion of glass-forming silica. However, in the tests illustrated, rather than retreat, it was decided to push beyond the limits (thereby departing from the standard formula), in the hope of finding a stony glaze with a smooth tactile surface that would be suitable for sculptural work. The low silica content was therefore kept, the MgO and BaO levels were lowered very slightly, and the potassa raised. From this experiment a very useful glaze with a pearly smooth tactile quality was found. The same experiment was applied to the last test in the baria series, and another useful glaze was obtained. The field of research of this kind can produce many useful and exciting glazes.

Before leaving this series of experiments, it is worth noting the extent to which iron is drawn into the glazes giving brown speckles. This has happened in nos. 6 and 8, but not in the underfired no. 7, which has not fused sufficiently to react with the body. Remember that different iron-bearing bodies give different fired results.

Middle-Temperature Glazes (C.4 to C.6)

In these tests we concentrate on transparent or white glazes: color will be dealt with in the next chapter.

The usefulness of the MT firing range has already been pointed out. Many of the qualities of high-fired stoneware bodies and stoneware glazes may be achieved at the upper end of the range. Indeed, many of the early Chinese stoneware glazes were fired at or just above C.5. Moreover, it is possible to obtain a reasonable degree of the subtle earth colors so popular in stoneware while enjoying a more economical firing with less wear and tear on the kiln fabric. At this temperature lead oxide cannot be used as the principal flux because even fritted lead glazes tend to volatilize over C.1. This does not mean that we have to rely solely on the alkalis soda and potassa for fluxing, as the alkaline earths calcia and magnesia may be usefully employed at this temperature in combination with other fluxes. We have also seen that zinc is of great value in the MT range and that zinc and baria (BaO) when used together or separately with boric oxide (B_2O_3) are useful (see Exercise 31). In addition, B_2O_3, acting as a glass-former, can offset the refractoriness of silica. Even wood ash glazes work marvellously well at middle temperature by replacing the fluxing mineral, feldspar, by a more fusible feldspathoid, such as nepheline syenite. Although the waxy sheen of lead glazes cannot be obtained at these temperatures, it is possible to produce excellent transparent and pure white opacified glazes. The lower end of this range is therefore an ideal one in which to experiment with the production of clear blue and aquamarine colors hitherto associated with LT alkali glazes. With so many fluxes available, a mixed fluxing effect may be used. Again, a multi-fluxed glaze gives a fluxing capability that works gradually as the temperature rises, rather than suddenly in a short range. The secret, then, of learning how to compose glazes for this range lies in having a thorough knowledge of the fluxing oxides and how and when to combine them. Exercise 39 is designed to this end.

EXERCISE 39: Fluxes for Middle-Temperature Glazes

Aim

To formulate glazes based on the generalized formula given in Figure 12.5 for the middle-temperature range:

$$1 \text{ mole fluxes} \quad 0.3 \text{ mole alumina} \quad : \quad 3 \text{ moles silica}$$
$$[1Al_2O_3 \quad : \quad 10SiO_2]$$

Since moderately shiny glazes are popular in studio pottery let us start by increasing the alumina to 0.4 mole in order to bring the alumina : silica ratio to the middle of the range for shiny glazes (see p. 280):

$$1 \text{ m fluxes} \quad 0.4 \text{ m alumina} \quad : \quad 3 \text{ m silica}$$
$$[1Al_2O_3 \quad : \quad 7.5SiO_2]$$

The alumina : silica ratio is very important when composing a glaze formula and should always be stated as above.

Materials

Sodium feldspar, potassium feldspar, calcite, magnesite, dolomite, zinc oxide (see p. 290 before using zinc oxide), kaolin, and quartz (see Appendix Figure A.4 for formulas and molar weights).

Method

In this Exercise you will be talked through each step in a series of changes. Such changes are never done haphazardly; there is always a good reason for making an alteration. The same applies to the choice of materials to fill the formula. There are many different choices that can be made, depending on the qualities you wish to achieve. These you will develop with experience. The following is an example of how and why such choices are made.

Formulation and Calculation

The fluxes. As we saw in the tests in Exercise 35, soda and potassa cannot be used alone as fluxes but need a little calcia to stabilize them, so let us start with the fluxes used in Exercise 36A:

Step 1.

$$0.5Na_2O$$
$$0.3K_2O$$
$$0.2CaO$$

This group of fluxes was satisfactory at low temperature when we had only 1 mole silica and 0.1 mole alumina. At middle temperatures there will be more heat-energy, and we can include fluxes that operate with maximum efficiency in this temperature range. For this, the Group 2 alkaline earth fluxing oxides may be used. This gives us the opportunity to use a mixed-flux effect for greater fusibility and to include a little magnesia (MgO) (which does not act as a flux at LT), thereby increasing the multiflux situation. It also opens the way to the use of dolemite, a calcium-magnesium carbonate. To let in the MgO and still keep the total amount of fluxes constant at 1 mole, we shall reduce the soda to 0.3 mole, leaving the potassa at 0.3. The reasoning here is that of these two, potassa is the more stable at the higher temperatures in the range.

Step 2.

$$0.3Na_2O$$
$$0.3K_2O$$
$$0.2CaO$$
$$0.2MgO$$

Since zinc (up to 0.2 mole) has proved itself as a powerful flux in the middle-temperature range (see p. 290), let us try 0.1 and 0.2 mole of ZnO and rearrange the above fluxes to accommodate this:

Step 3.

	(1)		(2)
	$0.3Na_2O$		$0.2Na_2O$
	$0.2K_2O$		$0.2K_2O$
	$0.2CaO$		$0.2CaO$
	$0.2MgO$		$0.2MgO$
	$0.1ZnO$		$0.2ZnO$

You may wonder why we have now reduced the potassa to let in the zinc oxide. Given that we are getting greater fluxing by using a multifluxing action, we can afford to reduce the oxides with high rates of expansion and contraction that cause crazing. We have, nevertheless, retained a little soda and potassa as starter fluxes (i.e., to get the fluxing action going as soon as possible). Calcia is also increased for a harder glaze. Our test results will show whether one of these will work.

Step 4.

(1)	(2)	(3)
$0.2Na_2O$	$0.1Na_2O$	$0.1Na_2O$
$0.2K_2O$	$0.2K_2O$	$0.1K_2O$
$0.3CaO$	$0.3CaO$	$0.4CaO$
$0.2MgO$	$0.3MgO$	$0.2MgO$
$0.1ZnO$	$0.1ZnO$	$0.2ZnO$

We now have some LT fluxes that are used here as starter fluxes, zinc as a powerful MT flux, and two excellent HT fluxes for that final spurt of energy.

Using the Fluxes with Alumina and Silica

The sets of fluxes in Steps 4.1 to 4.3 may be coupled with the proportions of alumina and silica chosen above to give 1 mole of fluxes : 0.4 Al_2O_3 : 3 SiO_2. This has an alumina : silica ratio of [1 : 7.5]. You should calculate recipes from these formulas using the composition of materials available to you (see p. 398). Do this very carefully: a good way is to convert the formula to a recipe then calculate this back again to see if you arrive at the same formula. To calculate recipe to formula, see p. 330.

In Steps 3 and 4 there are many fluxes; it should be said that it is not always necessary to have so many. This has been done here for practice, two or three fluxing oxides produce very good glazes.

Firing

These three glazes may now be test-fired to several points in the range of C.4 to C.6 — ideally, over a red body and a white slip. This will establish the limits of the firing range for these glazes and the qualities obtained at the various temperatures. If you can only fire at one temperature, then you will be checking the performance of the glazes at this temperature.

Assessment

If the glaze is underfired or overfired, adjustments can be made to the type or proportions of the fluxes used and/or the ratio of alumina to silica. In both cases very slight adjustments in the order of 0.01 to 0.02 mole for fluxes and 0.01 to 0.05 mole for alumina or silica are usually sufficient. For example, if your interest is with the upper end of the range (say, C.6) and the first tests are overfired, you may decide to lower the proportion of the more fusible fluxes or raise the alumina and/or silica:

Old glaze: 1 mole fluxes: $0.4Al_2O_3$: $3SiO_2$
$[1Al_2O_3$: $7.5SiO_2]$

New glaze: 1 mole fluxes: $0.45Al_2O_3$: $3.4SiO_2$
$[1Al_2O_3$: $7.5SiO_2]$

Here it may be seen that while the glaze has been made more refractory, the ratio of alumina to silica, and therefore the shiny character of the glaze, remains unaltered. Again, if your glaze is too shiny, the alumina : silica ratio can be adjusted by increasing the alumina, trying increments of, say, 0.025 (e.g., 0.425, 0.45, 0.475, 0.5, the last one giving an alumina : silica ratio of $[Al_2O_3$: $6SiO_2]$). If your glaze is too refractory, a little boric oxide may solve the problem (introducing the B_2O_3 in very small amounts, starting with, say 0.02 moles). From the above you can now see how the second, and sometimes the third, decimal place creeps into a formula. If the glaze is too shiny for your purposes, make adjustments in the fluxes. For example, baria can replace magnesia; zinc, which promotes shiny glazes (and sometimes causes spitting or pinholes in the glaze), can be omitted, and the fluxes balanced without it.

*   *   *

Chapter 13
Theory of Color and the Right Glaze for the Color

Introduction

Lying between Groups 2 and 3 of the periodic table are the transition metals that are chemically significant to potters for the several ways in which they combine with oxygen to provide coloring oxides. Titanium and zinc are also transition metals, and although they do not form specific coloring oxides, they have an important influence on color and are therefore included in this discussion. The source materials from which the coloring oxides are derived are often obtained as by-products when mining for other minerals or found as sedimentary deposits (particularly hematite, ochre, and iron-stained earths). Rutile and ilmenite (oxides of iron with titanium) are obtained from mineral sands (see p. 37). Another interesting source of color is ash, which is a mineral residue containing various amounts and combinations of the above elements left after burning carbonaceous matter (see p. 118).

Ways of Using Color in Ceramics

Color may be added to clay bodies, slips, and glazes. It may also be applied as surface decoration. As a general guide, 0.5–5 percent of coloring oxide may be added to a glaze, 5–15 percent to a clay slip, and 10–20 percent to a clay body. In the two latter cases, the resulting color will also depend on the color of the clay used for the slip. If a mixture of coloring oxides is used, the total amount should be kept within these reasonable limits. However, many studio potters work outside of these limits with magnificent results, using up to 25 percent color in clay bodies or adding a tiny amount to another coloring oxide to subtly change the color of a glaze. If you try amounts over 5 percent in a glaze it must be remembered that some coloring oxides have a fluxing effect and that those colorants with a low molar weight, such as FeO (72 g), CuO (80 g), and MnO_2 (86 g), have the greatest effect.

Remember that, if a color has been added to a body or slip, only partial vitrification takes place, so the color does not fully develop, If, however, a transparent (i.e., a fully fused) glaze is placed over it sufficient reaction occurs during firing to fuse the color and the full power of the color will then be seen.

Method of Stating Color Additions to a Recipe

If a color has been added to a percentage recipe, it may be stated as a percent addition (e.g., +5% add. means 5 g added to a total recipe weight of 100 g). This is done for the following reasons:

1. To enable comparisons of recipes and additions to bulk amounts to be made more easily.

Example: Adding color to a glaze

100% recipe (C.05–C.03)		3000 g batch weight (C.05–C.03)		
borax frit	90%	borax frit	90.0 × 30 =	2700 g
kaolin	10%	kaolin	10.0 × 30 =	300 g
total	100%	Total batch weight	=	3000 g
+2% add. copper carbonate		plus: copper carbonate	2.0 × 30 =	60 g
+0.5% add. cobalt carbonate		cobalt carbonate	0.5 × 30 =	15 g

2. To enable you to use the same recipe but change the color(s) without recalculating the recipe.

3. Since some coloring oxides combine with oxygen in several ratios (see Figure 1.4) they have different molar weights. If you are not precisely sure which oxide or mixture of oxides you have, you do not know what molar weight to assign to it, and cannot calculate an accurate recipe which includes the coloring oxide.

Natural Colors

Effect of Natural Color Present in Bodies

It is important to appreciate that any transition oxide naturally present in a clay deposit that gives or influences color may not be completely removed during the refining process. If this occurs, it can have a significant effect not only on the color of the fired body and on any glaze placed over it, but it may also affect the expected fired result of any other color added to the body, even when the color naturally present is not immediately visible. Iron oxide has the most important effect, followed by titanium dioxide and manganese dioxide. The oxidation state of an oxide also plays an important role, for example, whether the iron in the *fired* result is Fe_2O_3 or FeO.

EXERCISE 40: The Effect of Iron Naturally Present in Clay on the Fired Body and Glaze

This Exercise concentrates on high-temperature clays and glazes. It could also be used for middle- or low-temperature tests with the appropriate clays and glazes for the firing temperatures used.

Aim

To fire three or four stoneware bodies in oxidation and reduction, *partly* covered by clear and matte glazes (leaving part of the clay unglazed), and to study the fired bodies and glazes and their interaction, with particular reference to color. It is suggested that you include a red, buff, and white-firing body, or the complete range of HT stock clays in your studio.

Materials

A set of test tiles or objects (two sets if firing in "O" and "R") consisting of one of each of the clays to be tested. Also, 100 g dry weight of matte glaze and 100 g dry weight of a transparent glaze chosen from the previous chapter. For the preparation of the glazes, see Figure 5.12.

Method

Make the test pieces, and pour samples of the clear and the matte glaze over separate areas of each tile, leaving part of the body exposed without glaze.

Firing

See Chapter 5 for oxidation and reduction firing. If you are also testing porcelain, it could be fired with this group or in a special porcelain firing (see Exercise 41).

Assessment

Compare the difference in the color given by the different bodies and between the same clays fired in oxidation and reduction. Note whether the color is even or whether the iron has bled through to give speckles. The results of these tests prove that the same body must be used for repeatable results.

*   *   *

EXERCISE 41: Porcelain Body in Oxidation and Reduction

Although considered to be a white body, there is always sufficient iron in a porcelain body to give a warm, slightly creamy tint when fired in oxidation or a cooler, gray or bluish tint in reduction.

Aim

To fire in oxidation and reduction a porcelain body *partly* covered with a simple clear glaze (and partly with a matte one, if you wish) leaving some of the body exposed.

Materials

Two similar test objects made either in a commercially prepared porcelain body or one you have compounded; 100 g mix of Leach Glaze (No. 14 from Exercise 30) and a matte glaze from Exercise 38. If you plan to work with thin porcelain (for translucence), tests should be thinly and evenly plotted (see Plate 31 and Figure 9.2).

Method

Fire one test in oxidation, marked "O," and one in reduction marked "R." The test fired in "O" can follow the same firing cycle as that given for stoneware or your usual workshop firing cycle. For the other test you may like to try the following porcelain reduction firing:

Porcelain Reduction Firing Cycle

1. Fire up to C.03 (1100°C/2012°F) in "O"; then
2. Fire in "R" to the end of the firing. The choice of heavy, moderate, or light reduction should be dictated by results of past test firings.

This firing technique should prevent tiny blisters in porcelain that can result from the enormous amount of gases generated by repeatedly changing the kiln atmosphere, i.e., through constantly changing the oxidation state of iron in the body, even though the iron content is so small.

Both the oxidation and reduction tests should be fired to the same top temperature (one that you intend to continue using for porcelain) so that you can make a comparison of the results at the same temperature.

Thus your range could be, for example:

C.8–9   (1263–1280°C/2305–2336°F)
C.9–10   (1280–1305°C/2336–2381°F)
C.10–12 (1305–1326°C/2381–2419°F) or up to (1400°C/2552°F).

Assessment

Place the two objects closely side by side. Note the color difference between the tests fired in oxidation and reduction both in the unglazed body and the glazed area. The higher the firing temperature, the more marked the color difference: the body fired in oxidation has a warm, slightly cream color, the one fired in reduction throws a gray or bluish tint because of the small amount of iron in the body. This also affects the glazes. Some electric kilns fired in oxidation to 1305°C/2381°F or over may give a significantly reduced color. You can now appreciate how important it is to keep the ball clay content as low as possible, and also the value of "white-burning" ball clay where a white-fired body is required.

$$* \quad * \quad *$$

Added Color

Colors used in ceramics do not dissolve in water. However, placing them in a little water helps to break down the colorant into as fine a particle size as possible. Grinding the color also helps. The water then acts as a means of spreading the color evenly through the clay or glaze slip (or plastic clay).

Types of colorants used in ceramics:

1. Coloring oxides and carbonates
2. Colored stains
3. On-glaze enamels
4. Underglaze pencils and crayons

Coloring Oxides and Carbonates

These may be added as gram additions to the percentage recipes of clays, slips, and glazes. They may be used separately or in combination. Some combinations give splendid results, others are not so successful (e.g., manganese and chromium oxides give murky results). If a colorant is available in both oxide and carbonate form, the oxide will give a color that is at least one and a half times stronger (deeper in color) than the same amount of carbonate.

The constituents of the glazes are also important. For example, the oxide of chromium usually gives an opaque green, but if tin is present in a glaze, a chrome-tin pink is achieved. Also, because the oxide of chrome tends to volatilize (particularly over C.5), it will, if it settles on other glazes containing tin, produce pink flashings during firing that are usually unwanted. Copper in alkaline glazes (especially those containing soda) behaves similarly. This is important, particularly if you share a kiln. It will be remembered that the alkalis, especially soda, have a tendency to volatilize at temperatures over C.03 and more rapidly over C.5, and they may carry some of the copper with them to settle on other work during the firing.

Important: If oxides are used on unglazed biscuit ware or for underglaze decoration, make sure that the colorant does not leave a powdery surface, or the glaze will not adhere before or during firing. It is better to add a flux to the color and paint it onto greenware before biscuit firing, using a line addition test to assess the required amount of flux (see Appendix Figure A.7).

The visible color of most coloring oxides when bought is not the same as the fired color; these must be learned. A stain that has been pre-fused may give at least an indication of the fired color, but even here, as with oxides, the final color is affected by the other constituents present and the type of firing (see Figure 13.1 and Plate 4).

Colored Stains

These are prepared by melting together definite proportions of oxides, sulfides, and other natural mineral colorants. They give a more reliable and wider color range than oxides and may be used to color clay bodies, slips, and glazes as well as for underglaze decoration (but like oxides, must not be powdery after biscuit firing, see above). Stains may be prepared in the pottery as in Exercises 5 and 6, though more complicated equipment is required to produce bulk amounts and some stains require fritting temperatures beyond the reach of most studio pottery kilns. For economy, some potters buy basic stains and add fluxes or fillers, if necessary, for particular firing temperatures. Commercially prepared stains, though expensive, are particularly useful for colors that are even more expensive, or difficult to achieve, with coloring oxides, e.g., bright reds and vanadium yellows and blues fritted together with tin or zirconium silicate to produce stable colors. Another example is the fritting together of alumina with manganese to produce pink, which, if made from a mixture of oxides alone, would be too refractory at studio pottery firing temperatures.

A great range of colorants and raw materials that influence color are used in the preparation of stains, for instance, compounds of antimony, tin, titanium, molybdenum, praseodymium, iridium, zirconium, and yttrium. Various other materials are also incorporated. High-temperature stains contain appropriate amounts of quartz, feldspar, or alumina to render them more refractory, while low-temperature stains may have added fluxes (especially on-glaze colors, as discussed below). Such stains are compounded for and may only be used at low temperatures. Others have extended ranges throughout studio pottery firing temperatures. A group of modern stains based on zicon offer improved colors. For example, pink is made by heating a zircon-iron combination in such a way that the iron enters the zircon structure; the resultant stain can be used to give coral pink up to C.11 or C.12. Recently, from experiments using yttrium oxide, zirconium dioxide, and vanadium pentoxide, bright orange-yellows, deepening to reds with increasing yttrium, have been achieved for firing temperatures up to C.10. Other stains including yttrium can be fired to C.14 or even higher. These stains are free from the toxic soluble cadmium compounds that were previously used for this color range. Despite the usefulness of stains, some

	Lead oxide	Boric oxide potassia, soda	Calcia	Magnesia	Baria/Lithia	Alumina	Zinc oxide	Tin oxide	Other comments	Firing notes
Iron oxide	Richest amber yellow to deep brown.	Cooler tints.	Bleaches.	Inhibits color.	Bluish tint.	Favors color.	Dulls.	Makes the color milky.	Iron oxide with bone ash favors blue in celadon glazes.	'O' = amber/brown/rust 0.5 - 2% in 'R' = celadon gray green and blue.
Cobalt oxide	2% gives inky blue.	Brilliant purplish blue.	Pure blue. Addition of B_2O_3 helps.	Mauve. B_2O_3 helps. At 1280°C (2336°F) may give red or pink patches.	Greener blue.		Helps produce clear blue in calcium glazes.	Makes the color milky.	Impure cobalt gives purplish blue.	Blue in 'O' and 'R'.
Copper oxide	Bright green. DO NOT USE COPPER + LEAD ON FOOD/DRINK CONTAINERS.	Turquoise in low alumina earthenware glazes.	Grass green.		Favor blue in 'R'.	Affects turquoise in alkaline glazes. High Al_2O_3 = greener Low Al_2O_3 = bluer.	Small amounts heighten color in alkaline glazes.	3% tin oxide favors copper reds in 'R'.		Copper - red and metallic lustre in 'R'.
Manganese oxides	Brown.	Purple - brown, sometimes with red or blue tints.				High Al_2O_3 sometimes gives pink or pink flecks. Used together in pink stain.	Not recommended.	Milky coffee color.	MnO_2 converts to MnO at 1080°C/1976°F. Bubbles may remain in glaze.	Avoid firing manganese glazes in the range 1060 - 1100°C (1940 - 2012°F).
Chromia	2% at 900 - 950°C (1652 - 1742°F) gives red - orange. Temperature increases gives brown then green.	Opaque - green. High B_2O_3 destroys color.	Green, best with calcia and a little alkalis.			Low Al_2O_3 best for color development.	Mud brown.	Chrome - tin pink. The Al + Mn pink stain is better.	Chromia is valuable for toning down copper and cobalt.	Similar in 'O' and 'R'.

Figure 13.1. Effects of glaze constituents on color.

potters favor oxides for the incidental effects introduced by impurities in the raw material.

Testing Stains

Stains may be tested in exactly the same way as oxides. Specific stains are not cited in the Exercises as they vary according to the manufacturer, but they can be used by simply replacing a coloring oxide with a stain, heeding the manufacturer's advice on the firing temperature and optimum percentage additions, and testing around these figures. Remember that the glaze constituents affect the final surface colors. For this reason, you should obtain from the manufacturer a list of the constituents used to make the stain.

On-Glaze Enamels

These are pre-fused colored glasses or glazes that have been ground to very fine powders (usually 300s mesh). For use in the pottery, they are mixed to a smooth paste with a very light fine oil (e.g., oil of lavender, linseed oil, or turpentine) and applied with a brush to the surface of fired glazes (see Plate 25). Sometimes ceramists paint them directly onto fired unglazed bodies; this is best done on a fine-grained vitreous body. The ceramic is then re-fired at a low temperature to fuse the enamel and fix it to the body. The exact temperature is critical for each color and is supplied by the manufacturer; temperatures in the region of 730–800°C/1346–1472°F are usually required. If you are unable to obtain the firing temperatures from the suppliers, make a series of tests within this temperature range. If the correct temperatures are not used, the expected color may not be achieved; even a few degrees below and the color is not fully developed; a few degrees above and it is darkened or burned. Where several colors that require different temperatures are used, it is essential to apply the high-temperature ones first, fire the object, then apply the next, and so on, working down in temperature (in the ceramics industry, up to fourteen firings may be used to fix all the colors onto a ceramic). Fortunately, most color manufacturers have now developed palettes of colors that require the same firing temperature.

In the past, many enamels sat on top of the fired glaze and adhered to them simply by virtue of the enamel sticking to the glaze. Today, enamels and glazes are better tuned to one another so that the glaze softens a little, allowing the enamel to sink very slightly into the glaze, but not so much that the two merge completely. For this reason enamels are best used with low-temperature glazes because their firing range is sufficiently near to that of enamels. Even here you may need to try two or three different glaze compositions to find a match that will weld the two together without the enamels spreading into the glaze. This does not mean that enamels cannot be used with high-temperature glazes for decorative ware not subject to hard wear, but the above advice should still be considered.

Ceramics must be thoroughly dry before enameling. If necessary, they should be dried in a warm kiln or kept in a warming cabinet until ready to decorate. If moisture gets into the body, it will force its way out through the enamel during the enamel-firing, causing the enamel to spit and pin-hole. During the first 400 degrees, the kiln door should be kept open until the medium evaporates.

Water-Based Enamels

These modern colors may be used to decorate glazed or unglazed surfaces. The water-based enamels are perhaps easier to use, but the manufacturer's directions should be carefully followed.

Underglaze Pencils and Crayons

These may be used for fine-line drawings or for fillings in areas of color work. If you are unable to buy these, experimental ones may be made by adding color to a white clay slip, along with fluxes if necessary for the temperature you wish to use, and drying the slip back to the plastic state. The plastic clay may then be rolled into a long coil and cut into short lengths as "pencils," then soft biscuit-fired (try C.07–06). They should be fired hard enough for durability yet soft enough to leave a good deposit on the decorated surface. You should also consult Figure 13.1 before choosing your glaze constituents.

Where a porcelain slip has been used, a biscuit-firing temperature of C.02 could be used. The purpose of the biscuit firing is to harden the pencils sufficiently to prevent them from crumbling; do not make them too hard. You will need to experiment to find the optimum biscuit temperature.

Color Exercises: General Method

Color additions to clay slips were discussed in Chapter 10 simply because density and slip weight as well as Brongniart's formula were involved. In Exercise 23, a simple method of color additions was given (see "Mixing Test Quantities of Color"); here, more sophisticated methods are used. These apply equally to clay bodies and glazes in slip form.

Small Test Amounts Mixed in Slip Form

For small test amounts the color should be just covered with hot water for five minutes so that the particles separate. Do this in a small glazed test pot or crucible. A little of the clay or glaze slip should then be placed in a mortar and the color placed on top of it. If the color is put into the mortar first, it will stick to the bottom of the mortar; for this reason, a glass mortar is preferable. Thoroughly grind the mix to a smooth paste with a pestle, gradually adding the rest of the slip; a rubber kidney should be used to free any material that sticks to the mortar. The slip should finally be sieved through 120s or 200s mesh for an ultrafine blend.

Large Batch Amounts Mixed in Slip Form

The above method may be used, but if this is not practical, the color could be mixed to a paste with some of the slip until the color is evenly distributed and then mixed with the bulk slip. If possible, large batches should be mixed with a blunger, jar ball mill, or an electric mixer and left to stand for 24 hours, then blunged again before use (see Appendix Figure A.11).

Mixed in Dry Powder Form

If you are making a new batch from dry raw materials, the color may be added to the dry mix. Some potters like to add the color to the dry clay fraction, put the mix into a tightly secured plastic bag, roll it around until the color is well dispersed, and then add the mix to the rest of the powdered materials. (If you do this, wait until the dust subsides before opening the bag.)

Adding Color to Small Amounts of Plastic Clay

The usual technique is to render the clay down to a slip and proceed as above. However, for small amounts, if the body has good plasticity and workability some potters do not wish to disturb this. They prefer to soak the color just covered with hot water, then make several small hollows in the clay, pour the color into them and wedge the clay until the color is evenly dispersed. If you follow this method use only the minimum amount of water needed to cover the colored powder and wedge over a bowl so that you can catch any color that spills: wipe the bowl with the lump of clay to pick it up again.

Layouts of Test Tiles

For testing of color additions and blends, use the standard layouts shown in Appendix Figure A.7. For three colors, see Appendix Figure A.8.

Firing

For the tests in the following exercises use the procedures which by now you should have set up for yourself: that is, raw-glazing or biscuit firing and your own top temperatures for LT, MT, and HT. For clarification an average guide is given below:

LT (raku): C.09 to C.05
LT (earthenware): C.06 to C.2
MT: (middle temperature) C.4 to C.7
HT (stoneware): C.8 to C.9
HT (porcelain): C.9 to C.10+

EXERCISE 42: Adding Color to a White Body

Color may be added as oxides or as stains, as a single color or as a mix of colors. Remember that bodies require larger additions than slips or glazes. A complete range of color combinations is given in Appendix Figure A.10.

Aim

To add color to a white earthenware, white stoneware, or porcelain body. Tests for one color (or one color mix) are described. These may be repeated for other colors.

Materials

You will need 100 g dry weight of clay body rendered down to the plastic state (if the clay is already in the plastic state see the calculations on p. 160). You will also need your choice of single coloring oxide (or mix of coloring oxides). The color additions, given below, are for *oxides* (if using cobalt or copper carbonate record this in your notebook). If you use mixes of color, the total amount of color should equal the amounts given below.

A little transparent glaze will be required for the firing temperature to be used (see Exercise 30 for HT, Exercise 31 for MT, or Exercise 32 for LT glaze).

Method

1. Divide the clay into five equal parts (four for color tests, one test without color). Each portion will contain 20 g dry weight of clay.
2. Weigh out the four lots of color (see list below). Soak each color as instructed above, then wedge each lot of color into a lump of plastic clay, taking care not to lose any color. From each clay make a plastic button (make two if firing in "O" and "R"). Cover one side with a transparent glaze and inscribe the color addition on the other side.

Test 1: 20 g dry weight clay (no color)
Test 2: 20 g dry weight clay + 1 g color
Test 3: 20 g dry weight clay + 2 g color
Test 4: 20 g dry weight clay + 3 g color
Test 5: 20 g dry weight clay + 4 g color

This gives the percentage color additions of 0%, +5% add., +10% add., +15% add., and +20% add.

Firing

Fire the tests in the appropriate firing range for the clay body and glaze used and record the top temperature when you finish the firing.

Assessment

Study the quality and depth of the color and the texture of the body. Note whether the extra fluxing action of the color has had an effect. Assess this by comparing the colored results with the test without color. Choose the depth of color you would like to work with. If it has a high percentage of color, does it have a smooth surface, or is it blistered from overfiring? If overfired (and the correct firing temperature has been used) you should repeat the tests at a slightly lower temperature.

This method works well with single coloring oxides or stains. If you wish to make a black body, it is suggested that you use a stain for better dispersion of color. Three button tests should be tried containing +12% add., +15% add., and +18% add. of black body stain. Try to avoid a stain containing chromia, if possible, as it tends to flash and may settle on other ceramics during firing (see Plate 12).

* * *

EXERCISE 43: Colored Slips: Color Added to a White Slip; Making a Set of Color Samples

Aim

The addition of color to a white slip was dealt with in Chapter 10. Here, it is suggested that you make a set of single color samples, each with increasing increments of color, so that you can assess the colors and depth of color that you like. The samples will also act as a color reference for future work, and as a teaching aid. See also Plate 30.

Each tile should carry color additions of 5 g, 10 g, and 15 g. To do this a line addition test should be used (see Appendix Figure A.7.2 for layout). Colors suggested include cobalt carbonate (or oxide), copper carbonate (or oxide), iron oxide, manganese dioxide, and chromium dioxide (15 g of each color is required).

Materials

In addition to a white slip and the above colors, you will need a red-firing tile for each color tested and a little transparent glaze. A small glaze spoon (a spoon with one flat side) could be used to "waterfall" the slip and later the glaze onto the tile. If you put a hole at one end of each tile, the set could be tied together after firing.

Method

Check the density of your slip and adjust it if necessary (see Chapter 10 for method). Record this in your notebook. It is essential that you use the same density for repeat tests or work. If you wish to change the density of the slip see, Methods of Measuring Density, p. 215 and Exercise 22.

1. Weigh out three 5 g portions of color, (quick method: weigh out 15 g, and divide into three portions).

2. Place a sample of the slip without color in the first section. Then carry out the preparation of the colored slips, as described in the Introduction to Color Exercises, p. 348, adding the first amount of 5 g. Dribble a sample on the second section of the tile using the glazing spoon. Add the next portion of color to the slip (making a total of 10 g added color), mix well and sieve. Dribble this over the third section of the tile. Add the last 5 g color to the slip (making a total of 15 g additional color), mix and sieve again, and dribble a sample over the remaining area (leaving a small strip of the original body at the end).

3. After the slip has set (or after biscuit firing) apply a strip of transparent glaze across the length of the tile, partly covering the slips, leaving two-thirds of the tile with unglazed slip. The glaze could be applied by pouring with a glazing spoon carefully along the bottom of the tile. A very narrow strip of matte or opaque glaze can be applied to the other side in the same way (in order to see the masking effect such glazes have). *Leave a central panel unglazed.* This is the main part of this exercise, the added glazes are simply to demonstrate the effect they have on colored slips.

4. Clearly mark the back (e.g., Ex. 43/+cop.ox./C.06).

Firing

Fire to the appropriate temperature for the clay body and glazes used.

Assessment

Note how the transparent glaze develops the full color and that the matte glaze, if used, makes the color milky, much lighter, or totally hidden. If you have speckles in the cobalt test, they are due to insufficient grinding and mixing of the coloring oxide (the cobalt is still in tiny lumps). These tests give a quick guide to the effect of color in white slip and under glaze as well as the depth of color achieved from limit color additions. Later, you could experiment, by line adddition, with smaller increments of color in the area that interests you.

An important point to make here is that test tiles should *not* be cluttered with too much information, or they become difficult to "read" and assess. The tiles in this Exercise carry the limit of information.

* * *

EXERCISE 44: Color in Glazes: Adding Single Colors to HT and LT Transparent Glazes

Aim

To add increments of single colors to HT or LT transparent glaze(s) over a red- or buff-firing body.

Half the tile, lengthwise, should be covered with a white slip so that you can see the fired colored glaze over a white and colored surface. Two commonly used colors, cobalt and copper carbonates, are illustrated in Plate 13 (over a buff body). The layout and additions for other colors can be dealt with in the same way. This Exercise may also be used to test mixed color additions, and color additions to matte or opaque glazes.

Materials

Make test tiles about 6 cm wide by 18–20 cm long, one tile for each color to be tested. Select the type of firing(s) from the following suggestions: high temperature, oxidation and/or high temperature reduction; low temperature, oxidation, or low temperature, raku.

Mark out the tiles for a standard line addition test following the layout shown in Appendix Figure A.7.1 and enter the type of firing selected on the back of each tile. You will need 100 g transparent glaze for the firing range to be used (the glazes developed in Chapter 11 that suit your firing temperature are suggested) and 5 g total color for each color tested. For a raku firing make up a simple glaze of 90 percent alkaline frit and 10 percent kaolin.

Method

Mix and apply the tests as in previous Exercises. After each addition of color, remember to place a test on the tile before adding the next increment of color to the glaze.

The following increments give five color additions to the 100% recipe: 0.5%, 1%, 2%, 4%, and 5%.

1. adding 0.5 g gives +0.5% add.
2. adding 0.5 g gives +1.0% add.
3. adding 1.0 g gives +2.0% add.
4. adding 2.0 g gives +4.0% add.
5. adding 1.0 g gives +5.0% add.

Note that the increments double each time to 4% add., and the addition of one further gram gives +5% add.

Firing

By now you will have chosen your regular firing temperatures. These should be used. For the raku tests, quench in water for oxidation, or place in sawdust for reduction on drawing from the hot kiln. See Chapter 5 for the raku firing technique.

Assessment

Assess the depth of color produced by the gradual increase of color additions, and the depth of color achieved from additions of 5%, particularly with cobalt carbonate. From this it will be appreciated the additions of two or more colors could be dark, very dark with some colors, if the total color added exceeds five grams. Also note, if firing at HT and LT, the increasing depth of color at higher temperatures and the variation in the quality and hue of each color, at different temperatures, and between oxidation and reduction.

These color tests will serve as important permanent color samples. The set of tiles should be tied together or mounted on a card and correctly labeled. This test method may be adapted for testing colored stains in glazes, noting the supplier's recommendations for color limits.

*   *   *

The Right Glaze for the Color

The following should be read in conjunction with Figure 13.1 above. The chart should be studied before making further experiments and *before attempting to compound a glaze recipe*. All the oxides in a glaze have a role to play in the development of color. This is also true of clay slips and bodies, but is an extremely important consideration when compounding glazes. Consequently, before compounding a clay slip or glaze, the table should be consulted and a list drawn up of oxides that will promote the color you desire. Your glaze should then be compounded using a selection from this list.

Silica might seem to play the smallest role because it is not credited with favoring one particular tint of any color. Nevertheless, it is the vehicle for color development because the colorants dissolve or are dispersed as colloidal particles in silica glass to give colored glazes ("colloidal" is defined on p. 42). *Boric oxide*, while assisting silica as a glass-former, encourages the development of blue-green, turquoise in alkaline glazes.

Each different colored glass has a particular refractive index. This means that light passing through glass containing a particular coloring oxide is bent to a specific angle, creating a specific color.

Alumina must be considered carefully. If more or less alumina is required to adjust a color, careful balancing of the recipe is needed so that it is not too fluid or too viscous or too refractory as a result of the adjustment. Alumina is very refractory, thus if it is required to achieve a particular color, a commercially prepared fritted stain containing alumina and the colorant should be used, for instance the pink stain achieved by fritting alumina and manganese together (a further advantage, in this case, is that a clear pink is obtained). A bigger problem is that alumina may spoil a color if not reduced to a minimum, for instance the turquoise color achieved with copper in a LT alkaline glaze. Some alumina is necessary to prevent the glaze running (particularly on vertical surfaces), but at the same time only just enough must be used to stabilize the glaze. The all-important step at this point is to watch the firing very carefully and ensure that enough heat is used to fuse the glaze completely; at the same time, overfiring must be avoided.

The Group 1 and Group 2 oxides, once they have served their purpose as fluxes, still have further contributions to make. Group 1 alkali oxides and lead oxide promote brilliant colored, clear LT glazes. By referring to Figure 13.1, you will see that lead oxide promotes warm color, the alkalis cooler ones. With respect to the Group 2 oxides, we have already seen that the alkaline earth oxides, calcia, magnesia, and baria as well as acting as fluxes, help to form matte glazes. We now see a further contribution in their effect on color. Magnesia favors a purple tint with cobalt but tends to inhibit the development of iron colors. Calcia in oxidation tends to bleach the color obtained from iron and favors brilliant ambers and bright browns, while baria encourages a bluish tint in iron-browns and is useful for colder darker tones. A crossover line-blend test in which the calcite content of a glaze is gradually replaced by barium carbonate or magnesite could give a choice of brown tones. A simple test using a glaze containing, say 40 percent calcite, in which the calcite is gradually replaced by one of these in a cross-over line blend, would give several tones of brown. For example:

Test 1: glaze with 40% calcite
Test 2: glaze with 30% calcite + 10% magnesite
Test 3: glaze with 20% calcite + 20% magnesite
Test 4: glaze with 10% calcite + 30% magnesite
Test 5: glaze with 40% magnesite.

Of the remaining oxides, tin makes iron brown colors milky in oxidation, while small additions to a celadon glaze throw gray rather than green. Zinc oxide dulls an iron glaze while titanium oxide helps to develop the color. On the other hand, zinc oxide favors copper and cobalt blues.

Phosphorus and calcium phosphate. Calcium phosphate (bone ash) makes an important contribution to the development of blue celadons. It is believed that many of the beautiful blue celadons of the late Chinese Song period (1170–1260 A.D.) are due to traces of phosphorus in the ash in the glaze constituents or in the fly-ash in the kiln. In modern glazes the use of fruit wood ash containing phosphorus may achieve similar results.

Small additions of *ilmenite* give speckles, and in a high iron (11%) glaze plus ilmenite, an "aventurine" glaze results (a glaze with a glitter of tiny plate-like crystals). The ilmenite acts as seeds causing the iron to crystallize and glitter with gold, red, and brown.

EXERCISE 45: Effects of Specific Oxides on Color for HT Glazes in Oxidation and Reduction

Aim

To test increments of color in glazes composed of different oxides using an extension of the square blend method. Iron oxide and copper carbonate have been chosen for this exercise because they give the most spectacular results. One or both of these colors may be tested. Other colors may be similarly tested, using Figure 13.1 to choose oxides with particular color effects. Although the total number of tiles may be made at the same time (with a few extra in case of breakage), you are advised to undertake the glazing of one color at a time as this Exercise is complex and time-consuming. (See Plates 17 and 18.)

Method

Tiles

Make 24 tiles for the iron tests and 36 for the copper tests. Double this number if firing in oxidation and reduction and make them larger if you wish to set them up as a wall plaque. If the tiles are made from a red-firing body, they should be half-dipped diagonally in white slip. Rest the tiles on a pencil until the slip dries sufficiently for you to be able to mark the back of the tiles over the white slip with marking stain. You should start numbering the tiles from the bottom of each column, and work from the left-hand column to the right as follows:

Iron oxide tests:

```
4 8 12 16 20 24
3 7 11 15 19 23
2 6 10 14 18 22
1 5  9 13 17 21
```

Copper tests (numbered in the same order, but there are six columns and six lines giving 36 tiles):

```
6 12 18 24 30 36
5 11 17 23 29 35
4 10 16 22 28 34
3  9 15 21 27 33
2  8 14 20 26 32
1  7 13 19 25 31
```

Biscuit-fire, if this is your practice, and replace the tiles in correct order. Again, as you glaze each tile replace it in its correct position the right way up. The layout is important, and it should be noted that the arrangement for the copper tests is different from the iron tests.

Glazes

First make your own selection of the oxides you think are suitable for these glazes and try to write down suitable formulas. Those used in the illustrations are given with Plates 17 and 18.

You should calculate your glaze recipes from your own glaze formulas or those given with Plates 17 and 18 using the compositions of materials available in your area (see p. 398 for method) or use the theoretical formulas and molar weights given in Appendix Figures A.3 and A.4. Use the step-by-step method used for the calculations given in Figure 12.7 as a guide (you are advised to use a checklist as shown in Figure 12.7). Leave the color additions as additions to the percentage recipe. Do not put the color increments into the recipes (if you do you will have 36 calculations for the copper tests as opposed to six for each set of tests).

Do not forget to glaze two samples if you are firing in oxidation and reduction.

Iron tests. Glaze the first column as follows

1. Make 100 g of Glaze A; add 0.5 g color using the General Method, and apply a sample to tile 1 (the bottom tile of the first column).
2. Add a further 0.5 g of color, making a total of 1 g, and glaze tile 2.
3. Add a further 4.0 g of color, making a total of 5 g, and glaze tile 3.
4. Add a further 5.0 g of color, making a total of 10 g, and glaze tile 4.

This completes the first column. Continue working in this manner, making a new glaze for each column, and adding increments of color as above until all glazes have been completed.

Copper tests. Repeat the instructions given above, replacing iron oxide by copper carbonate, using the color increments given, and the glazes marked in Plate 18. Note: Color additions are 0.5 g; + 0.5 g = 1 g; thereafter + 1 g.

Firing

Fire the tests in each set close together in the kiln, to C.8–9. It is a good idea to arrange all the tiles in correct order on a suitable kiln shelf covered with bat wash (see Chapter 6); each set of tiles will then stay together and be in the correct order when they come out of the kiln. Note the exact top temperature used.

Assessment

Compare the color, texture, and other qualities produced by using different oxides with the same glaze formulas. If firing in oxidation and reduction, compare the different qualitites and colors obtained from the two different types of firing. These sets of tests form a catalog of surface treatments for many different purposes.

*   *   *

Low- and Middle-Temperature Tests

Single colors may be carried out and assessed in the same way as above. Possible color combinations are given in Appendix Figure A.10 and Figure 13.1 should be consulted to select oxides for their effect on color, for example, in a lead bisilicate glaze, an alkaline glaze, a glaze high in calcia, or one with zinc oxide for middle temperatures.

Blending Colors

Blending two colors is quite straightforward and may be accomplished by a square blend test using the layout given in Appendix Figure A.7, no. 6. Blending three and four colors can be accomplished by using the layouts in Exercises 29 and 30, respectively. Alternatively, you could use the traditional triangular layout for blends of three materials. If you decide to use this method it is suggested that, instead of using a single unwieldy slab of clay, you purchase a hexagonal tile cutter from a craft supplier (this is a special tile cutter that can be used to stamp out the tiles from leatherhard clay) or make a cardboard template (see Appendix Figure A.9) and make and assemble the tiles as shown in Appendix Figures A.8 and A.9 and surrounding text. This eliminates the difficulties of firing such a large slab; furthermore, by using single tiles for each colored glaze, you gain the important bonus of being able to pick up and isolate a particular color for assessment. The tiles should be arranged, as shown in Appendix Figure A.8, and clearly marked on the back, with a small number on the front, for assembly before glazing the tiles, as well as replacing the tiles after glazing.

Selecting Color Blends

This is not an easy decision to make as there are so many possible combinations to choose from. To facilitate your selection, a series of charts has been drawn up showing the possible combinations of oxides or carbonates of the most used colorants (see Appendix Figure A.10). This works well with oxides or carbonates. It is suggested that you choose a particular color area and follow this through from single colors to blends of two, and three colors (and possibly four colors, but not as a first experiment). You will, no doubt, find the color that satisfies you before you reach the end. During assessment you should carefully consider the effect, not only of the regular glaze constituents on colors but other materials such as zircon, titanium dioxide, and tin oxide. Remember to mark and catalog all tests so that you do not repeat them unwittingly at a later date.

The charts in Appendix Figure A.10 make it look relatively simple, but remember once you have made your selection each combination has to be tested in various proportions. It is suggested that you try limit proportions first to make sure you like the combination, e.g., for additions of mixes of two colors: 100 percent (dry weight) of glaze plus color mixes of A and B. Laid out in the following way, this represents a miniature cross-over line blend.

Test 1: 0.5% add. A + 3.0% add. B
Test 2: 2.0% add. A + 2.0% add. B
Test 3: 3.0% add. A + 0.5% add. B

These tests will give you an indication of the resulting color achieved from a small addition of one color to another and equal parts. For a more detailed test you can extend the above proportions as well as including in-between ones.

For additions of blends of three colors, use the instructions and chart in Appendix Figures A.8 and A.9 and the selective testing suggestions there for preliminary tests, again reduce the total amount of color added to 5 g by dividing each color by 10 (i.e., move the decimal point) and halve this.

For additions of blends of four materials, a similar program could be undertaken following the layout in Appendix Figure A.7, no. 6 but using your own increments.

A Discussion of Individual Colors

Iron Oxide

Iron oxide, found in hard rock and soft earth, is one of the best colorants in nature. It combines readily with oxygen to give iron oxides and with other elements to give the many iron-containing minerals, there is also iron sili-cate sand which in some parts of the world is used as a basis for "oil-spot" glazes. Again, ochre pigment is derived from an earth that consists of im-pure iron oxides, such as limonite, goethite, or weathered hematite, which give the earth a yellowish-tan color. Another iron earth composed of glauco-nite is an olive green to yellowish or gray color.

Iron carbonates, found as beds or nodules in sedimentary rocks, in-clude clay ironstone (a rock containing iron carbonate and clay minerals) and black-banded ironstone (a sedimentary rock composed of iron carbo-nate and coal). Basalt (see Chapter 2), a high-iron igneous rock, is very useful for making middle-temperature brown glazes.

Oxidation and Reduction of Iron Oxide

In the normal atmosphere in nature FeO oxidizes to Fe_2O_3 (we call this rust). The same thing happens during the firing of ceramics. If FeO is fired in a normal, fully oxidized atmosphere, that is, with sufficient oxygen enter-ing the kiln, the FeO oxidizes to Fe_2O_3. In a reduced atmosphere (when the kiln vents are closed or partially closed), the reverse occurs. The extent to which this takes place depends on the degree of oxidation or reduction to which the body and glaze are subjected. A further point of interest: at the end of a reduction firing, when the kiln is turned off and oxygen reenters the kiln, a little reoxidation may occur resulting in FeO with some Fe_2O_3 or perhaps the halfway stage, Fe_3O_4, where there is more oxygen than in FeO

but not quite as much as in Fe_2O_3. Some of the iron may even reach an in-between stage, $Fe_3O_4 \cdot Fe_2O_3$, where there is a mixture or intimate association of the two forms. The various stages of oxidation can be sketched as

$$Fe \rightarrow FeO \rightarrow Fe_3O_4 \rightarrow Fe_2O_3$$

Reduction is the reverse:

$$Fe_2O_3 \rightarrow Fe_3O_4 \rightarrow FeO \rightarrow Fe$$

Color Range of Iron in Clay Bodies

The following is only a general guide, the color being influenced, to a certain extent, by other oxides present and, most importantly, by the firing cycle and the type of iron present after firing. You should also refer to Chapter 7 and Figure 7.4.

Oxidation. Iron oxide in fired clay bodies gives warm tones: 2 percent to 7 percent gives terracotta, while over 7 percent gives brick red, the color darkening with an increase of iron. The color also darkens with an increase of firing temperature (see Exercise 8).

Reduction. Generally, clays fired in reduction give more earthy (less bright) tones than those fired in oxidation. The range passes through buff/gray and toasted-brown to a dark purplish-brown as the iron content increases. Take care when adding iron oxide to a body to be fired in reduction as FeO has a stronger fluxing action over 900°C than Fe_2O_3.

Clay bodies containing particles of iron minerals, which often originate from the fire clay used to compound the body or the presence of iron pyrite in a natural stoneware clay, give speckles or sometimes splodges that erupt into the glaze (see Plate 16). This is particularly noticeable in ceramics fired to C.10 and over in heavy wood-fired reduction.

Color Range of Iron Oxide in Glazes

The color range obtained from iron in fired ceramic glazes is wide and critically dependent on the following factors:

1. The percentage amount of iron oxide added to the glaze.
2. Iron present in the materials used in the glaze mix.
3. Oxides present in the glaze mix, which, though not contributing iron, influence the hue obtained from it.
4. The type of firing and top temperature.
5. The clay body on which the glaze is placed.
6. The fluidity of the glaze at top temperature. A fluid glaze permits the even dispersal of colloidal particles of iron oxide. If a thin section of the glaze is viewed through a microscope, a brilliant ruby-red glass may be seen.

7. The rate of cooling, which is important for the development of particular glaze effects, e.g., whether or not recrystallization takes place.

Colors obtainable in earthenware (oxidation) iron glazes:

1. In fully fused transparent glazes, 4 percent gives yellow to amber and over 4 percent rich brown. In matte glazes these colors will be creamy.
2. Lead glazes give brilliant warm colors with iron oxide while alkaline glazes give cooler tones.
3. In lime (calcium) matte glazes iron colors are more creamy: small amounts (2% Fe_2O_3) can give the quality of old parchment while 5% to 7% gives deepening tones of beige.
4. Zinc oxide dulls iron glazes, while titanium dioxide and tin oxide make them creamy.

In high-temperature iron glazes, colors in *oxidation*:

1. 1% to 4% add. gives yellow to pale brown. The colors are not as brilliant as those obtainable at earthenware temperatures.
2. 5% to 10% add. gives rust-red to very dark brown. If the iron content is high, the color is so dense that the glaze appears almost black. The thickness of the glaze brings variations: thin areas produce a rusty red color, thicker areas, brown-black. This characteristic is employed to produce tenmoku-type glazes where the dark color "breaks" to a lighter tone; this also occurs over relief decoration. If the glaze is made matte, especially one with 0.4 mole of baria or more, the colors will be creamy.

In *reduction*, glazes containing 0.5 percent to 2 percent iron oxide give gray-green, a pale jade green, or blue depending on the clay and glaze constituents used; this is traditionally called a celadon glaze. Quite often such a glaze may be obtained simply from the reaction of the glaze materials with iron oxide in the body, i.e., without added color.

Iron Oxide and the Formula

Before attempting to place iron oxide in a formula for a high-iron glaze, i.e., amounts over $+5\%$ add., you should run out a series of tests, with a range of additions to the percentage recipe between $+5\%$ add. to $+15\%$ add. and try different firing cycles to find the best result. If you then decide to include the iron oxide in the formula, remember the following: The formula represents the *fired* result (not the unfired oxides placed in the glaze mix). Thus, if you use red iron oxide in your glaze and fire in reduction, the final product will be black iron oxide or, more likely, a mixture of the two.

The question then arises which oxide of iron you will represent in the formula.

Copper Oxide

Copper is available in more than one form (see Figure 1.4), and changes occur during firing: cuprous oxide (Cu_2O) reduces to cupric oxide (CuO), and the carbonate breaks down leaving an oxide. The resulting color produced by the various forms of copper in a fired glaze are influenced both by the firing cycle used, and the presence of other oxides in the glaze (see Figure 13.1).

A repeat warning is given here. It is very easy to confuse CuO and CoO, and it is therefore suggested that you abbreviate copper oxide to cop.ox. and cobalt oxide to cob.ox. (replacing ox. by carb. for the carbonate) when inscribing or writing on the back of a small test tile.

Fusibility

Copper oxide has the greatest effect of all the coloring oxides on the fusibility of a glaze, having a fluxing ability equal to soda and potassa and almost as much as lead oxide. Parmelee (1973) suggests that in high-temperature glazes the fluxing ability of copper oxide is similar to calcia. Great care is therefore needed when testing a glaze to which copper in any of its forms has been added to make sure that the glaze does not run. This must be done before using it on a kiln load of ceramics. These tests should be stood in kiln test trays or placed on old pieces of kiln shelf well covered with bat wash and alumina powder.

A General Guide to the Colors Usually Associated with Copper

This is discussed separately under oxidation and reduction.

In *oxidation*, 1 to 5 percent produces green (blue-green with high soda and lithia); over 5 percent black (especially over a red-firing body), often with a burned look. However, with careful testing it is possible to achieve a metallic quality in a fluid copper glaze useful for sculptural work.

In a standard glaze (one conforming to the generalized formula), green color results from full oxidation of the copper; this applies to the oxide and the carbonate of copper. Because, as a student you may be careless or heavy-handed when weighing out colorants (the amounts look so small), it is a good idea to use the carbonate: it is cheaper and "weaker" than the oxide. The carbonate consists of three elements, copper, carbon, and oxygen, in contrast to copper and oxygen in the oxide. You are thus less likely to put too much copper into the mix and spoil the results. A further point is that the carbonate breaks down very quickly, dissolves, and disperses throughout a molten glaze, hence a small amount of color can give an exceptionally clear, transparent green glaze. When the copper oxides are used, very careful weighing techniques must be employed so that a burned look from excess copper is avoided. This particularly applies to a glaze applied too thinly over a clay body with a high iron content.

If you wish to achieve the brilliant low-temperature Persian turquoise, using copper, there are a number of problems to be overcome. A glaze high in the *alkalis*, K_2O and Na_2O, is needed, but if you look back at Exercise 35 you will see that glazes fluxed by these two oxides alone are unstable, and devitrify when exposed to moisture. It was also shown that a little calcia was necessary to stabilize such glazes, but calcia detracts from the turquoise color and favors a grass-green. The answer is to use in your recipe a high-alkaline frit that has been professionally compounded with just enough calcium to stabilize the glaze. A frit that also contains some *boric oxide*, B_2O_3, will assist the fusibility as well as the color, since boric oxide favors the development of turquoise. Of the other necessary glaze ingredients, silica does not have an unfavorable effect on the color but alumina throws the color toward green, and a glaze low in alumina will be too fluid. If you are making tiles that can be fired flat, the fluidity of a glaze low in alumina is not too much of a problem, unless there are other color glazes lying next to it. To prevent glazes from running into each other it is advisable to outline your design in some way which provides a physical barrier. You might use the fifteenth-century Spanish technique known as "cuerda seca" (dry cord), in which a line of unglazed pigment separates different colors, or apply coils of clay like the "cloisons" in enamel work. These then become a permanent part of the surface decoration. Extensive testing will be needed in order to arrive at a satisfactory balance of oxides in a glaze intended for use on a vertical surface. You may have to sacrifice some of the intensity of the color in order to achieve stability by the addition of more calcia and/or alumina. It may help to replace some of the soda or potassa by lithia, or to fire at a slightly higher temperature and include a little (about 0.1 mole) zinc, which aids viscosity. A modern approach would be to test the color response of strontia among the fluxes introduced in a frit (see Shaw, 1971).

Many ceramists who are able to fire only in oxidation sometimes feel that they cannot achieve the subtle variety of colors obtainable in reduction. They should be reassured that iron and copper separately and together can offer a great wealth of color in oxidation. The colors achieved are more brilliant, when desired, yet pastel when used in the right glaze with small amounts of colorant, probably softened with a little iron, vanadium, or cobalt (e.g., 0.2% of the modifying coloring oxide with 0.5% to 1.2% of copper carbonate).

In *reduction*, the colors usually associated with copper are blue and blue-gray, brought about by the additon of 1–5 percent copper, and "copper red," obtained from under 1 percent (with special treatment). The reduction blues and gray-blues, the subtle variations obtainable by blending copper with other oxides, and the raku copper reds are well within the capabilities of the beginner. The low-temperature copper lusters are a little more demanding, while high-temperature copper reds require considerable research. Much depends on working with a particular kiln (the firing cycle is crucial), and some kilns seem to like producing copper reds, while others do not. You therefore need a considerable interest in kiln firing to specialize in these glazes. For these reasons the HT copper reds have been placed in an advanced section (see Plate 18).

ADVANCED SECTION

Theory of the Reduction Process with Regard to Copper

The reduction fire draws oxygen from the glaze constituents so that the copper is reduced, often to the pure metallic state. This enables it to disperse evenly through the glaze melt as ultrafine colloidal particles. *It is the extremely fine size and almost "microcloud-like" distribution through the glaze that gives the red color. The finer the cloud of particles the more pure the red. This could be the reason why only a very small amount of copper oxide is needed for the best results.* Subsequently, nucleii form, and around these, tiny crystallites grow. This gives two phases: fresh (new) crystallites of copper and noncrystalline glass.

As Norton (1974) points out, "These crystallites are so small that they do not prevent complete transparency." Light is bent (refracted) when it passes through the crystallites, and the differential (the difference between the refractive index of the glass and the crystallites) produces the color. Although the general opinion has been that the pure copper crystals are responsible for the red color, Norton states, "There is still evidence that in some cases slightly reoxidized copper may also be responsible for the red color."

The size to which the crystallites grow, though still ultrafine, dictates the hue as well as its quality: the finer the size, the better the red. This, in turn, depends on the fluidity of the glaze at top temperature, which enables the copper to disperse through the glaze, and the temperature and time during the cooling stage when the crystals form (or "strike").

At the end of the firing, when the kiln is turned off, a little air flushes back into the kiln and there is a short burst of reoxidation. This affects the surface of the glaze with a lesser effect deeper down. If, however, too much oxygen enters and penetrates more deeply into the glaze, the red will be lost and an orange-red or a dirty bluish-red will be produced. Often a ceramic comes from the kiln with one side a dirty blue and the other red or pink; this is due to uneven reduction or because more air (oxygen) has entered on the "blue side."

Conditions that Favor the Production of Reduced Copper Reds

1. 0.5% to 2% copper oxide (the smaller the amount the better).
2. A fine-grained body, or one covered with fine white slip to give a smooth surface.

3. A fluid glaze to enable the copper oxide to disperse in the molten glaze as fine colloidal particles. An alkaline glaze helps to produce a fluid glaze; calcia may be included (up to 0.5 moles in a multifluxed glaze).
4. Baria but not magnesia.
5. Low alumina and no more than 0.2% zinc (if any).
6. Boric oxide to increase the fusibility of the glaze and improve the quality of the red color.
7. A little iron oxide and tin. These are sometimes added as they also reduce during firing, and with the slight reoxidation at the end of the firing, they take up oxygen more quickly than copper. This can prevent the copper from over-reoxidizing, but care must be taken because the iron can cause discoloration.
8. A reduction firing cycle, which is a very individual thing and unique to the particular kiln used.

The manner of reducing during firing has already been discussed. There is also a critical time at the top temperature after the reduction has been achieved. Some potters find that they need to open the ports for a few seconds just before they switch off to "clean" the kiln, i.e., allow a flush of oxygen to enter the kiln, and then close up all the ports tightly to prevent further reoxidation. This could be the case in an extremely well-built kiln that does not allow any air to creep back in when switched off and that drops the first hundred degrees to the point at which the glaze is too rigid to allow the first stage of reoxidation to take place. On the other hand, some potters find that it is necessary to "fire down," i.e., to lower the flame so that the temperature drops, but to keep enough combustion in the chamber to occupy oxygen that seeps into the kiln during the initial drop in temperature.

Materials That Influence the Red Color

Purple-reds may be achieved with additions of cobalt oxide or titanium dioxide. Hopper (1983) suggests up to 1 percent of the former and 5 percent of the latter. Yellow tints can sometimes be achieved by exceptionally fine particle size of the glaze (as well as the body or clay slip). For this, thorough ball milling helps, see Hetherington (1937). An orange-red is favored by calcia together with a little iron (under 0.5% add.) in the presence of tin oxide.

Suggested Techniques to Improve Color

If you do not achieve a reduction red from these tests (or from future work, since conditions may change without your realizing it), then you should consider your firing cycle. Do not start your first reduction before C.06, as you need to ensure that all carbon has been burned off. You could try postponing reduction to C.03 to C.02. Fire a little higher if your glazes look as though sufficient fluidity was not achieved to enable the copper to disperse in the glaze. If the glaze, although red, has a greenish cast or looks "dirty," perhaps you have allowed too much oxygen to flow back into the kiln at the end of the firing. This could reoxidize the top layer to green while the lower layers remain red, making the glaze look a dirty-red. If the construction of the kiln is such that reoxidation cannot be prevented during initial cooling, then you should "fire down" (see above).

After this, consider very carefully the constituents of the glaze and the smoothness of the body used. You may need to reduce the iron content of the glaze, or you may need to apply a fine-grained white slip to the body under the glaze. If these measures fail, you should try a different clay body. A porcelain body would be a good choice. The copper colorant may be added in the glaze, under the glaze as a wash, or in a white slip — the latter being useful if an isolated copper red decoration is desired.

Another technique is to cover the copper-containing glaze with a second glaze layer. The same glaze, but without the copper, could be used. This protects the underglaze from the influx of oxygen at the end of the firing. Do not put copper in this layer or you might end up with a blue layer over a red one. The thickness of the glaze is also important and several thicknesses should be tested. The thicker the glaze, the more concentrated the layer of copper. See Plate 33.

■　■　■

Titanium and Iron Series

Figure 13.2 shows the relationship between titanium dioxide (TiO_2) and hematite (Fe_2O_3) and the minerals that include both TiO_2 and Fe_2O_3. If you look first at titanium dioxide, you will see that it is free of iron. Next to it lies rutile, which is titanium dioxide containing iron as an impurity and sometimes traces of tin. Many chemists consider it to be one of the crystal forms of titanium dioxide and disregard the impurity, but to a potter the impurity is important as it brings with it a little iron oxide.

If you look at the next mineral in the chart, ilmenite, you will see that both titanium and iron appear in the formula. The iron present is no longer simply an impurity but a significant amount; this makes it necessary for the

THE TITANIUM -- IRON FAMILY			
TITANIUM DIOXIDE	**RUTILE**	**ILMENITE**	**HAEMATITE**
pure TiO_2	TiO_2	$FeTiO_3$	Fe_2O_3
	TiO_2 with an impurity of iron (and sometimes tin)	approx. 46% FeO 50% TiO_2	
	anatase and brookite have the same chemical formula.	+ impurities	

Figure 13.2. The titanium-iron family of oxides.

potter to distinguish between rutile and ilmenite. The last entry in the chart, hematite, has been discussed above under "Iron Oxide."

Titanium Dioxide and Titania

When titanium dioxide (TiO_2) enters a glaze melt, it loses some of its oxygen and becomes titanium oxide, or titania (TiO). Many authors (and this text) reserve the name *titania* for the oxide once it has entered the melt and keep the name *titanium dioxide* for the oxide used as a raw material. Note, particularly if you include this oxide in a formula, that titanium has several oxidation states and therefore different molar weights:

$$TiO \quad 48 + (16 \times 1) = 64 \text{ g}$$
$$TiO_2 \quad 48 + (16 \times 2) = 80 \text{ g}$$
$$TiO_3 \quad 48 + (16 \times 3) = 96 \text{ g}$$

Use in Ceramics

An important contribution of this oxide is that it makes the glaze harder. Up to 1 percent TiO_2 may enter the melt, 2 to 5 percent gives semiopacity, over 5 percent gives full opacity. The several forms of TiO_2, though white in themselves, have an effect on even the small amount of iron present in porcelain, giving a glaze the quality of vellum paper in oxidation and a slight bluish cast in reduction.

Titanium Dioxide and Crystal Growth

Microcrystalline opaque glazes. An excess of titania in a glaze (i.e., more than can be held in the melt on cooling, see supersaturated solutions, p. 42) enters the melt during firing. With slow cooling, some of it will recrystallize to form tiny fresh faced crystallites. The number of fresh crystals that form and their size depend on the rate of cooling and the viscosity of the glaze. They give a smooth matte glaze. The opacity is due to the difference between the refractive index of the noncrystalline glass matrix of the glaze and crystals. The refractive indices of commonly used opacifiers are

titania	2.5–2.9	recrystallize from the melt
zirconia	2.13–2.2	
tin oxide	1.99–2.09	inert opacifiers
zirconium silicate (zircon)	1.94	
bone ash	1.43	

The refractive index of most glazes is 1.5 to 1.6.

In LT opaque glazes, titania works well with zinc oxide, forming zinc silicate crystals during the slow cooling. Comparisons of the qualities obtained from mixes of these may be seen by making a square blend test of percent additions of these to a simple LT glaze. This may be accomplished by:

1. Selecting your best result from Exercise 34 or 35 (lead bisilicate or alkali/borax frit plus kaolin tests) and using this as your starting recipe.
2. Using the layout given in Appendix Figure A.7, no. 6, with

   A = titanium dioxide with increments of 2% add., 4% add., 6% add., 8% add., 10% add.
   B = zinc oxide with increments of 3% add., 6% add., 9% add., and 12% add.

Crystalline Glazes

Titanium dioxide is very important in crystalline glazes in which up to 25 percent may be used. (*Remember that some of this 25 percent enters the glassy phase, as stated earlier.*) The titanium oxide forms tiny nuclei, or seeds, around which the crystals grow. A further value of this oxide is its ability to draw color from the body which is then incorporated in the structure of visible crystals (see also Plates 27 and 28).

Rutile

Although given the formula TiO_2, rutile contains some iron; therefore, it cannot be used to replace titanium dioxide when the color effects of iron are not desired. In oxidation rutile gives a brown mottled appearance to glazes, particularly when used in a borax glaze, and rutile has been used on a great many commercial tiles (e.g., those to surround a fireplace) to give this effect. In reduction the presence of rutile can give a blue color, which is not always favored by potters. However, small amounts of rutile may be used to modify the color of other coloring oxides: cobalt and copper oxides and carbonate are very often treated in this way. Like titanium dioxide, rutile may be used as a crystallizer, the particles of rutile acting as seeds for crystal growth. In oxidation this will give amber to brown tints to the crystals, if no other color has been added, and bluish tints in reduction.

Ilmenite

Ilmenite, correctly speaking, is a "titanate of ferrous iron." Titanium is always present as well as iron. Ilmenite is supplied to potters ground to various grain-sized particles, usually described as ilmenite coarse and ilmenite fine, and may be used in clay bodies or glazes to give speckles. Daniel Rhodes (1989) describes this as a "peppery appearance." The particle size to obtain from your suppliers depends on the size of speckles you hope to achieve. Coarse-ground ilmenite is used to "seed" crystalline glazes.

In the glaze melt the surface of the grains dissolves, giving an amber halo. For this effect 1 percent to 3 percent is the usual addition. Both rutile and ilmenite are found as beach sands (also called black sands). To test the effects of rutile and ilmenite separately and together, a square blend test (see Appendix Figure A.7 for layout) may be used, with

A = rutile, with increments of 0.5% add., 1% add., 2% add., 3% add.
B = ilmenite, with increments of 1% add., 2% add., and 4% add.

Manganese Dioxide

The metal manganese (Mn) does not occur uncombined in nature. It is, however, widely distributed in several forms, often replacing calcium, barium, or magnesium in minerals. When refined, the pure metal (melting point 1260°C/2300°F) is a light pink-gray. Manganese carbonate powder has a similar color while manganese dioxide powder is black. Sometimes little fern-like patterns formed from manganese carbonate (rhodochrosite, $MnCO_3$) may be seen in sediments, for example, in clay pits where a cutting has been made, and also in moss agate. (It is interesting that a similar decoration may be achieved by dribbling a mix of manganese dioxide and tobacco juice into wet slip immediately after slip application.) It is also found as nodules or layered with iron sediments or sedimentary rocks, and as bog manganese where it has accumulated due to the action of tiny plants.

Uses of Manganese Dioxide and Manganese Carbonate in Ceramics

Manganese dioxide and carbonate are useful in both oxidation and reduction firings for producing brown to purplish colors. With iron oxide it gives rich dark browns and, if fritted with alumina, a pink stain. Manganese works well with cobalt, iron, rutile, and ilmenite. One color it does not blend with well is chromium dioxide. Manganese dioxide at 2 to 10 percent gives the following colors:

in lead glazes, brown
in alkali glazes, purplish brown
with a little cobalt oxide, purple at low temperature
coarse-ground manganese, speckles (useful in clays and glazes)
manganese + alumina, pink (the stain is advised, see p. 345).

Both forms of manganese may be tested in simple line addition tests, trying 2.5%, 5%, and 10% add.

Manganese dioxide, a black powder, and manganese carbonate, a pinkish buff color, are the types usually sold by craft suppliers.

Cobalt Oxide and Carbonate

Cobalt gives blue at all temperatures and in oxidation and reduction. The maximum limit for glazes is 0.2 to 5 percent add., less if combined with another color. Note that the oxide is about three times as strong as the carbonate.

Cobalt is usually obtained as a by-product when mining for nickel. The oxides and carbonates of cobalt are regularly used by potters, however, the cobalt stain is particularly valuable if a well-dispersed, even color is required.

It is an extremely strong colorant, less than 1 percent giving strong blue both in oxidation and reduction at all temperatures throughout the potter's firing range. Although the color blue persists with all glazes, the various oxide constituents of the glaze affect the hue (see Figure 13.1). An exception to this is the pink color induced by the presence of phosphate introduced via bone ash, but this is not a stable color (see Rado, 1988).

In the firing, the several forms of cobalt oxide (CoO_2, Co_2O_3, Co_3O_4), and $CoCO_3$ convert to (CoO). Later in the firing, this participates in the formation of silicates and borates, and the blue color is dispersed throughout the glass. There are several oxidation states of cobalt so it should not be included in the glaze formula but kept as an addition to the percentage recipe (e.g., +5% add.). Cobalt has a fluxing effect second only to copper among the transition metals and is very nearly as powerful as soda and potassa. However, only very small amounts of cobalt oxide are normally used in ceramics. The carbonate form is useful because it breaks down at 800°C/1472°F and disperses better in glazes and slips, but it must be given time to decompose and give up its carbon content in the early stages of firing. This is important in raku firing. If it is not given time to decompose, the cobalt carbonate ($CoCO_2$) may cause blisters; therefore, *cobalt oxide should be used for raku*. On the other hand, since the carbonate is a combination of cobalt, carbon, and oxygen, the cobalt is far more dilute than in the oxide form, and there is, therefore, less likelihood of using too much.

Depth of Color

Strong blues may be obtained with 0.5 to 2 percent add. of cobalt oxide. Transparent glazes will have great depth of color, but an excess of this oxide gives a patchy blue-black, metallic result. Be careful when combining cobalt with other coloring oxides, as it may overpower them; 0.1 to 0.2 percent is sufficient to affect other colorants. More can be added in slips and bodies — 1 to 5 percent for slips, 10 to 15 percent for bodies. Together with copper oxide and red iron oxide in equal parts, it gives a true black (e.g., 2% to 2.5% of each).

Chromium Sesquioxide (Cr_2O_3)

Chromium is usually found in nature only in combination and is reduced by the refining process to a brilliant white metal (as in chromium plating). It is used by potters in the oxide form, Cr_2O_3 (common name, chromia) which produces in standard glazes a dull green; it is popular for modifying other colors, in particular, cobalt and copper (e.g., 0.2 g chromia used to modify 0.5 g cobalt carbonate). Chromium is also found in the important iron mineral chromite ($FeO \cdot Cr_2O_3$), the fully oxidized form being iron chromate ($Fe_2O_3 \cdot Cr_2O_3$), which potters use to produce gray.

Chromia does not dissolve easily in ceramic firings. About 1 percent goes into solution; the rest usually disperses as tiny solid particles through the glaze, giving an opaque dull green. For sculptures, very small amounts in a lead glaze give a bright red at 900°C/1652°F or just below, but as alumina spoils the development of the red, it must be reduced to a minimum, thus making the glaze very runny. It should be noted that this is a *toxic glaze* and must *not* be used on anything that could, in any way, be used for food and drink, or a toy that could be sucked.

Vanadium Pentoxide

Vanadium metal does not occur in nature by itself, but extraction from the parent rock and refining gives a silvery white metal. This combines with oxygen readily, to give two oxides, vanadium trioxide, V_2O_3, which is not stable, and vanadium pentoxide, V_2O_5, which is extremely expensive.

The more popular form is the stain formed from it, which gives bright, clear yellow when prepared with tin oxide, and blue with zircon (zirconium silicate). It (and the oxide) must, however, only be fired in oxidation as even short exposure to reduction causes a bleaching of the color which cannot be restored. If a small amount of titanium dioxide is added to the frit batch (when making the stain) stronger, redder colors may be produced. In these forms the stain may be used at all temperatures up to and over C.10. As the prepared vanadium yellow stain it may be used in bodies, clay slips and glazes (see Plate 15).

Stains with vanadium include:

vanadium-tin: yellow
vanadium-tin-zirconium: redder yellow
vanadium-yttrium-zirconium: orange-yellow
vanadium-zirconium: turquoise
vanadium-silicate-zirconium: green

Nickel Oxide

Nickel oxygen compounds have a number of oxidation states, but the name *nickel oxide* is used for them all. The color given by nickel oxide alone is a somewhat uninteresting gray-brown. It is used in ceramics to modify other brighter colors, giving a quieter character to such colors as cobalt blue, and with copper a green-brown.

EXERCISE 46: Making a Malachite Glaze

Introduction

In this Exercise the methods of glaze development given in Chapter 11 and those of glaze formulation in Chapter 12 are brought together with methods of color experimentation to achieve a particular preconceived glaze quality and color so that you can see how the various technical methods may be used in conjunction with one another. This is the type of testing you would carry out for a specific piece of work. The glaze is suitable for placing on a porcelain or any other HT body of your own choosing. Several different thicknesses of glaze application should be tried initially. If too thin on a dark body, it will fire an unpleasant black.

Aim

To produce a matte glaze of the same color as the natural (unpolished) mineral malachite. This is a deep, slightly bluish green with lighter shades mixed with it (see Plate 14).

Formulating and Calculating the Recipe

This is considered in three steps:

1. Deciding the firing temperature and type of firing to be used and then building a formula and converting this to a percentage recipe.
2. Selecting the coloring oxides.
3. Consulting Figure 13.1 for the glaze constituents that promote the color required.

1. For the purpose of this Exercise, let us consider a C.8–9 glaze fired in oxidation. The generalized formula for C.8–9 is

$$1 \text{ flux} : 0.5 \text{ alumina} : 4 \text{ or } 5 \text{ silica,}$$

which gives an alumina : silica ratio of between [1 : 8] and [1 : 10]. Because we are trying to produce a rocklike but smooth surface, let us reduce the alumina : silica ratio to just above [1 : 5]. If you look at the results and formulas of Exercise 38 (also see Plate 16), you will see that nos. 6 and 8 give the quality we are seeking. No. 6 has an alumina : silica ratio of [1 : 6], no. 8 [1 : 5.4]; either could be tried. As this is a "beyond the limits" exercise, we are no longer considering a standard transparent glaze, and given the quality we are looking for, we could try [1 : 5.4].

Again, if we look at the results of Exercise 38 we shall see that both no. 6 and no. 8 have only 2.7 moles of silica, so we shall follow suit and reduce the silica, leaving the alumina at 0.5 moles. Our glaze is now:

$$1 \text{ fluxes} \qquad 0.5 \text{ aluminum} \qquad 2.7 \text{ silica} \\ [1 : 5.4].$$

The alumina : silica ratio in the above formula tells us that this glaze falls midway between 1 and 10 on the scale of dry to shiny glazes. It is a matte glaze.

If you are undertaking this Exercise you may wish, after studying the photograph of the fired result (see Plate 14), to raise the silica to 3 moles of SiO_2, giving an alumina : silica ratio of [1 : 6], or 3.5 moles of SiO_2, giving a ratio of [1 : 7]. These ratios would give more shiny glazes.

Note. HT glaze containing such a low proportion of glass-forming silica, while perfectly satisfactory for nonfunctional ware, would need to be tested for durability and permeability before use or sale as domestic ware. This can be done by testing in a laboratory or over a long period of heavy use in the home.

2. We must now consider the color additions. From the study of individual colors in this chapter, copper and chromium seem most useful. In this Exercise let us start with copper carbonate to give green in oxidation, and some chromia to see whether it will tone down the brilliant color from the copper to give a more earthy blue-green. We may find that adding some lithia will help to throw the green color toward a bluer tone but not the harsh tone which might result from cobalt additions. Without the chromia, copper produces turquoise in alkaline glazes, but with the softening effect of chromia and a little lithia, the right hue may be achieved. Here we see the value in keeping the color outside the recipe, as this expedites the testing of a number of different proportions of the colorants.

3. The glaze constituents are also important. If we consult Figure 13.1 we see that soda favors the blue-greens, so let us include some in our recipe. We should also have a little potassa and certainly some calcia, as it is the principal HT flux, but not too much, as it will favor the yellow greens. Baria is therefore included as a second HT flux (also, unlike calcia, it will not influence the color toward the yellow-green). So let us start with the following fluxes:

$$0.30 \ Na_2O$$
$$0.10 \ K_2O$$
$$0.05 \ CaO$$
$$0.50 \ BaO$$

This comes to a total of 0.95 moles. The baria is a little high, so let us compromise:

$$0.30 \ Na_2O$$
$$0.10 \ K_2O \qquad 0.5 \ Al_2O_3 \qquad 2.7 \ SiO_2$$
$$0.08 \ CaO \qquad\qquad\qquad\quad [1 : 5.4]$$
$$0.49 \ BaO$$

We now have a little more CaO, a little less BaO. This is still not quite unity, so let us make the soda 0.33. (We can use nepheline syenite to supply the soda.) We now have a glaze formula of:

$$0.33 \ Na_2O$$
$$0.10 \ K_2O \qquad 0.5 \ Al_2O_3 \qquad 2.7 \ SiO_2$$
$$0.08 \ CaO \qquad\qquad\qquad\quad [1 : 5.4]$$
$$0.49 \ BaO$$

This gives a recipe of:

> 60% nepheline syenite
> 2% calcite
> 29% barium carbonate
> 2% kaolin
> 7% quartz

Method

1. Make two tiles from the body of your choice about 15 cm long and 4 cm wide, divided into 5 sections. Make a note of the reference no. of the one you use. Prepare 100 g (dry weight) of the above glaze.

2. Choose a depth of color from your results of Exercise 44 or from Plate 13. (Run out a line addition test for additions of copper carbonate if you have not done this in Exercise 44). For the purpose of this Exercise let us select +2% add. copper carbonate. Soak the color just covered in hot water for a few minutes and add to the glaze.

3. Keeping the copper carbonate at +2% add. throughout, make the following increments of chromium oxide: +0.2% add., +0.4% add., +0.6% add., +0.8% add., and +1% add. taking out a test, and placing it on the tile, after each addition.

4. From the fired results of this test, shown in Plate 14 (see the top tile), it may be seen that the first three tests are still very blue. With the fourth test, carrying addition of +0.6% add. chromia, and the fifth test carrying +0.8% add. chromia, the color changes to a muted blue green.

5. The color addition of +2% add. copper carbonate and +0.8% add. chromia was then chosen for color and a further line addition test carrying increments of +2% add. to +8% additions of lithia was tested. (Lithia is tested for its *effect* on color: it is not a color.)

6. From the first two tests on the fired tile (see the bottom test tile in Plate 14) carrying 2% and 4% add. lithia respectively, with +4% add. chosen, the color required is maintained plus an improvement in the smoothness, but still matte quality of the glaze.

Thus, by the combination of +2% add. copper carbonate, and 0.8% add. chromia, with the further addition of +4% add. lithia, the color desired is achieved and compares well with the hand-specimen of malachite, also illustrated in Plate 14.

7. Finally test additions of coarse water ground zirconia were made in the hope of achieving a textural effect which would break up the color to simulate the textural quality found in a rough cut piece of malachite. Additions of +2% add., +4% add., and +8% add. zirconia were tried (see the last three tests on the second test tile in Plate 14). The results achieved were not a replica of the malachite sample, but simulated the idea of a broken texture. The first test (no. 3 on the tile illustrated) gave a coarse texture, with the second and third increasingly finer textural effects. The surface remained smooth in all tests.

Firing

If you carry out these tests, C.8–9 in oxidation is recommended, though testing in both oxidation and reduction will show that oxidation firing can be as exciting and certainly as full of color as reduction firings.

Assessment

In the tests shown in Plate 14, a smooth, stony-matte glaze is achieved by using the glaze recipe given above plus color additions of +2% add. copper carbonate and 0.6% to 0.8% percent chromia. Then, with the further addition of +4% add. lithium carbonate, a blue-green color was achieved.

This type of experimental glaze can act as a springboard for many other effects that could be extremely interesting. Further additions (e.g., 3 percent addition of tin oxide, or placing the glaze over a more fluid glaze for a "lizard skin" effect, or over black slip) can produce many interesting effects.

Once familiarity with clay body types, color, and glaze formulation is established and at your finger tips, you are free to let your imagination and creative ability run free knowing the directions you can take without expending your best energy searching for the means.

*   *   *

Glossary

Adsorbed—Added on. The prefix "ad" implies that the ions are "added" on to the crystal, not absorbed as an integral part of it.

Adsorbed ions—Ions that attach themselves to the broken edges of crystals.

Atom—A single unit of an element.

Batch recipe—These are larger, or smaller, "test" amounts than the percentage recipe. Large amounts may also be called bulk recipes. The use of the percentage recipe simplifies the calculation of a batch weight.

Bond—The term used for the linkage of one atom with another in a chemical compound.

Burette—A narrow graduated glass tube with a tap at the bottom for controlling the flow of liquids, thereby measuring very accurately small quantities of liquid released. A pipette serves a similar function, but, once filled by lowering the glass tube into the fluid to the required level the fluid is controlled by placing a finger over the top opening.

Chemical reaction—The interaction of two or more substances resulting in a chemical change in them.

Compound—A substance consisting of two or more elements chemically united in definite proportions by weight.

Crystal—A crystal has a definite and unique three-dimensional internal arrangement of its constituent elements. Where it is able to develop freely an external form grows, which expresses the internal structure. Solids that do not form crystals are said to be amorphous (noncrystalline).

Deflocculate—To cause large particles, or "aggregates" of solids suspended in a slip, to separate and disperse as very fine particles.

Dunt/dunting—Crack/cracking formed in ware by too rapid cooling. The edges of the crack(s) remain sharp as the glaze, now viscous, is no longer able to flow over the edges. Cracks formed during heating will not be sharp edged as the glaze on melting will cover and smooth them.

Element—A substance that cannot be resolved by chemical means into a simpler substance.

Eutectic composition—The proportions of two or more chemical substances that are able to melt (or crystallize) at the lowest possible temperature (the eutectic temperature) for a mixture of those substances, provided the mixture is held at that temperature long enough for the reaction to complete.

Fettle—To trim the seams of joins on the surface of cast objects that have been made from a two- (or more) piece mold.

Flocculate—To cause extremely fine particles of clay to aggregate forming particles (or flocs) of greater mass.

Formula—(1) The expression of a chemical substance using the chemical symbols for the constituent atoms of the elements involved; (2) the expression of a glaze in similar chemical terms.

Glass-former—A substance capable of forming a noncrystalline glass. Silica is the chief glass-former in ceramics; boric oxide is also used in small additions to silica.

Heat treatment/heat-work—The combined energy input during firing due to the combined effect of time and temperature.

Ion—An electrically charged atom or group of atoms.

Isotherms—Lines of heat drawn on a map or diagram, joining points of equal heat at a specific time.

Kaolin/China clay—A natural clay composed of the clay mineral kaolinite, quartz sand, and mica. A very small amount of iron is present, but it has a minimal effect on the fired clays and glazes. It is therefore described as a virtually iron-free white-burning clay. Once refined it corresponds closely to the composition of kaolinite and is accorded the same theoretical formula, $Al_2O_3 \cdot 2SiO_2 \cdot 2H_2O$.

Kaolinite—The pure clay mineral having the formula $Al_2O_3 \cdot 2SiO_2 \cdot 2H_2O$. It is the clay mineral found in the clay deposits called kaolin. It is also abundant in all other clay deposits, though in these it is not so obvious because of the presence of iron and other colored mineral constituents.

Magma—Molten rock.

Malachite—Hydrous carbonate of copper mineral. (Do not confuse this with *molochite,* defined below.)

Melting point/melting temperature—The temperature at which a material begins to melt.

Mineral—A homogeneous solid with a definite crystal structure and fixed chemical composition.

Mineralized sands—Sands that contain a sufficient proportion of a particular mineral, or group of minerals, considered to be of economic value.

Mole—The SI unit of quantity of a chemical substance (see Abbreviations for SI).

Molecule—The smallest portion of a substance capable of existing independently while retaining the properties of the original substance.

Molochite—The trade name for calcined kaolin manufactured by the English China Clay Company. It is fired to $1500°C/2732°F$ giving a composition of mullite and noncrystalline glass. It is therefore free of crystalline silica and free of shrinkage problems.

Monomer—A chemical *compound* consisting of single molecules, as opposed to a polymer, the molecules of which are built up by the repeated union of monomer molecules.

Orton cones—Orton pyrometric cones manufactured by the Edward Orton Jr Ceramic Foundation, and made from ceramic raw materials in specific mixtures to record the heat work in a kiln when fired at a specific rate of heating. Orton cones are the only ones used in this text where they are represented in the following manner: for example, C.8–9. The temperature equivalents to the numbers are given in Appendix Figure A.5. They are fully described in Chapter 5.

Oxide—A compound of another element with oxygen.

Percentage recipe (*% recipe*) —In this text recipes are quoted as percentage recipes, that is, so as to total 100 units. This means that they may be weighed out in any standard weight units; in this text grams are used.

Periodic table—An ordered arrangement of the chemical elements according to their atomic numbers such that elements having similar properties fall into the same group (see Appendix Figure A.2).

Pin-holes—Small bubbles, formed during the final stages of firing a glaze, which have burst but not been completely filled by the melted glaze due either to the glaze not being soaked (held) at top temperature long enough or because the glaze is too viscous.

Rate of firing—The number of degrees rise in temperature per hour. The "firing temperatures" or "top temperatures" stated in this text are based on a standard rate of firing of 150°C/270°F per hour.

Polymer— (see monomer).

Saggar—A container made from a refractory clay in which raw or biscuit-fired ware is placed for firing, usually to protect the object from direct flame. A coil of clay is usually placed between the container and a flat lid so that it may be cracked open easily after firing. The flat but not completely airtight lid allows the heating air to escape, but not unwanted fumes to enter, it also enables the saggars to be stacked for firing (such a stack is called a bung).

Seger cones—Pyrometric cones for gauging heat treatment (heat work) during the firing of ceramics. Temperature equivalents are given in Appendix Figure A.6.

Sinter—The softening and compacting of the points of contact of clay particles during the early stages of firing such that the particles adhere to one another.

Slip weight—Weight of a particular volume of slip, indicating its density. In this text the slip weight is stated as the number of grams per hundred milliliters (ml) of slip.

Système International d'Unites (SI units)—The modern system of measurement. For example, grams (weight); liters (volume); moles (number). (See SI, abbreviations.)

Viscosity—The resistance of a fluid to flow. High viscosity, less fluid; low viscosity, more fluid. In ceramics a glaze should have sufficient viscosity to stay on a vertical surface during firing, yet sufficient fluidity to flow out and cover a surface evenly. Rheology is the study of deformation and flow of matter.

Volatile—Passing readily into vapor; evaporating readily.

Yield point—The point at which clay moves under slowly increasing pressure exerted by the ceramist. If too much pressure is required the clay is not in a workable state.

Appendix 1
Basic Chemistry of Use to Ceramists

Atoms, Ions, and the Periodic Table

An *atom* is the smallest particle of an element that can exist without losing its identity. It can be described as a central *nucleus* with one or more electrons orbiting around it. The nucleus is in turn made up of *protons*, which carry a positive electric charge, and *neutrons*. The number of protons, known as the *atomic number*, determines the element. The number of neutrons affects the *atomic weight* of the element and may vary; atoms of the same element with different numbers of neutrons are called *isotopes* of the element. A change in the number of protons, as in an atomic bomb or other nuclear reaction, changes one element into another.

The *electrons* carry a negative electric charge. An atom is electrically neutral because there are the same number of protons as electrons. The electrons are situated in "shells" — concentric orbits — around the nucleus, at a relatively great distance from it. When an atom gains or loses one or more electrons, it becomes electrically charged and is called an *ion*. Much of the chemistry of interest to ceramists has to do with the electrical attraction and repulsion between ions.

Figure A.1 shows the electronic shell configuration for the first twenty elements in the *periodic table*, including some of great significance to ceramists.

The table given in Figure A.2 is part of a much larger table. It shows the area of interest to ceramists. The elements, arranged according to their nuclear charge, also called their atomic number, are placed in rows or *periods* across the page, each period containing eight elements, ending with a "noble gas." (Although ceramists are not concerned with these gases, they demonstrate that there is a rationale behind the arrangement of eight *Groups* across the page.)

Those elements of importance to ceramists are given with their symbols (e.g., Li for lithium) and atomic weights. These should be learned (the most important are those in Groups 1, 2, 3, 4, and oxygen in Group 6; the remaining few you can learn gradually). As you study Chapter 1 you will discover that the elements placed together in Groups 1 and 2 play very

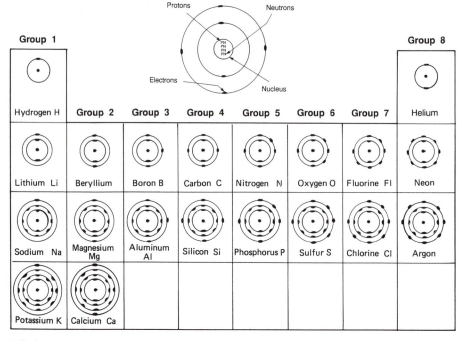

Figure A.1. Electronic shell configurations for the first twenty elements.

- • Nucleus
- ⚫ Electrons

special roles in ceramics. An other feature of interest is the zigzag line drawn across the table from boron to bismuth. This separates the metals (on the left) from the nonmetals (on the right). Many compounds are formed from the metals with the nonmetals, particularly the oxides formed from Group 1 and Group 2 metals with oxygen of Group 6. Lying in the center of the table are the transition metals. These supply the coloring oxides used in ceramics. Others (chiefly used to make commercial color stains) are named in Chapter 13. Titanium and zinc, while not colorants, play an important role by their influence on color.

Formulas and Molar Weights of Materials

The *molar weights* of all our materials can be quickly calculated by reference to the periodic table. For example,

$$CaO = 40 + 16 = 56 \text{ g}$$
$$MgO = 24 + 16 = 40 \text{ g}$$
$$SiO_2 = 28 + (16 \times 2) = 60 \text{ g}$$
$$CaCO_3 = 40 + 12 + (16 \times 3) = 100 \text{ g}$$

Note there are three elements in $CaCO_3$: Ca, C, and O.

Nonmetals

Metals

	GROUP 1 (Alkali metals)	GROUP 2 (Alkaline earth metals)	TRANSITION METALS — COLORING OXIDES										GROUP 3	GROUP 4	GROUP 5	GROUP 6	GROUP 7	GROUP 8
Atomic wt = 1 **H** HYDROGEN																		**HELIUM**
	7 **Li** LITHIUM	**Be** BERYLLIUM											11 **B** BORON	12 **C** CARBON	14 **N** NITROGEN	16 **O** OXYGEN	**F** FLUORINE	**NEON**
	23 **Na** SODIUM	24 **Mg** MAGNESIUM											27 **Al** ALUMINUM	28 **Si** SILICON	31 **P** PHOSPHORUS	32 **S** SULPHUR	**CHLORINE**	**ARGON**
	39 **K** POTASSIUM	40 **Ca** CALCIUM	**Sc** SCANDIUM	48 **Ti** TITANIUM	**VANADIUM**	**CHROMIUM**	**MANGANESE**	56 **Fe** IRON	**COBALT**	**NICKEL**	**COPPER**	65 **Zn** ZINC						
		88 **Sr** STRONTIUM	**Y** YTTRIUM	91 **Zr** ZIRCONIUM							**CADMIUM**			119 **Sn** TIN				
		137 **Ba** BARIUM												207 **Pb** LEAD	**BISMUTH**			

Figure A.2. A simplified version of part of the periodic table of the elements, showing the elements important in ceramics. When the elements are arranged in this way, those with the same number of electrons in the outer shell fall in the same column, or *group*.

The tables in Figures A.3 and A.4 give the molar weights for many compounds of use in ceramics.

With alkali, borax, and other purchased frits, the specific formulas or analyses and weights provided by the manufacturer must be used. Molar weights for other materials not listed here (e.g., regionally available materials) should be calculated using the instructions provided on pp. 397–98. (Note that the molecular weights of compounds are numerically the same as molar weights.)

	Formula	Molar weight in grams
Aluminum oxide, alumina	Al_2O_3	102
Barium oxide, baria	BaO	153
Boric oxide	B_2O_3	70
Calcium oxide, calcia	CaO	56
Carbon dioxide	CO_2	44
Ferrous oxide (black iron)	FeO	72
Ferric oxide (red iron)	Fe_2O_3	160
Lead monoxide, litharge	PbO	223
Lead oxide, red lead	Pb_3O_4	686
Lithium oxide, lithia	Li_2O	30
Magnesium oxide, magnesia	MgO	40
Manganese dioxide	MnO_2	87
Phosphorus pentoxide	P_2O_5	142
Potassium oxide, potassa	K_2O	94
Silicon dioxide, silica	SiO_2	60
Sodium oxide, soda	Na_2O	62
Strontium oxide, strontia	SrO	104
Tin (stannic) oxide	SnO_2	151
Titanium dioxide, titania	TiO_2	80
Vanadium pentoxide	V_2O_5	182
Zinc oxide	ZnO	81
Zirconium oxide, zirconia	ZrO_2	123

Figure A.3. Formulas and molar weights of oxides commonly used in ceramics, to the nearest whole number.

	Formula	Molar weight in grams
Alumina hydrate (aluminum hydroxide)	$Al_2(OH)_6$	156
Barium carbonate, witherite	$BaCO_3$	197.3
Bone ash (calcium phosphate)	$Ca_3(PO_4)_2$	310.2 (variable)
Calcite (calcium carbonate)	$CaCO_3$	100
Calcium borate	$Ca(BO_2)_2$	125.7
Calcite, calcium carbonate	$CaCO_3$	100
Calcium phosphate/bone ash	$Ca_3(PO_4)_2$	310.3
China clay (see kaolin)	$Al_2O_3 \cdot 2SiO_2 \cdot 2H_2O$	258.2
Colemanite	$2CaO \cdot 3B_2O_3 \cdot 5H_2O$	411 (variable)
Cornwall/Cornish stone	$0.3CaO \cdot 1.2Al_2O_3 \cdot 8SiO_2$ $0.34Na_2O$ $0.36K_2O$	674 (variable)
Dolomite	$CaCO_3 \cdot MgCO_3$	184.4
Feldspar, calcium (anorthite)	$CaO \cdot Al_2O_3 \cdot 2SiO_2$	278.3
Feldspar, potassium, orthoclase	$K_2O \cdot Al_2O_3 \cdot 6SiO_2$	556.8
Feldspar, sodium (albite)	$Na_2O \cdot Al_2O_3 \cdot 6SiO_2$	524.6
Hematite	Fe_2O_3	159.6
Kaolin (china clay)	$Al_2O_3 \cdot 2SiO_2 \cdot 2H_2O$	258.2 (variable)
Lead bisilicate frit	$PbO \cdot 2SiO_2$	343.4
Lead sesquisilicate frit	$PbO \cdot 1.5SiO_2$	313.4
Lead sulfide (galena)	PbS	240
Lepidolite	$Li_2F_2 \cdot Al_2O_3 \cdot 3SiO_2$	334 (variable)
Lithium carbonate	Li_2CO_3	74
Magnesite, magnesium carbonate	$MgCO_3$	84.3
Magnesium carbonate light	$3MgCO_3 \cdot Mg(OH)_2 \cdot 3H_2O$	365.2
Nepheline syenite	$0.75Na_2O \cdot Al_2O_3 \cdot 2SiO_2$ $0.25K_2O$	292
Petalite	$Li_2O \cdot Al_2O_3 \cdot 8SiO_2$	612.6
Potassium carbonate	K_2CO_3	138.2
Potassium feldspar (see feldspar)	$K_2O \cdot Al_2O_3 \cdot 6SiO_2$	556.8
Quartz (flint)	SiO_2	60.1
Sodium, feldspar (see feldspar)		
Spodumene	$Li_2O \cdot Al_2O_3 \cdot 4SiO_2$	372.2
Strontium carbonate	$SrCO_3$	147.6
Talc (steatite/soapstone)	$3MgO \cdot 4SiO_2 \cdot H_2O$	379.3
Whiting (see calcite)		
Witherite (see barium carbonate)		
Wollastonite	$CaSiO_3$	116.2
Zirconium silicate (zircon)	$ZrSiO_4$	183.3

When correcting to whole numbers, some authors correct potassium feldspar to 557 g, others use 556 g. Kaolin is marked as variable, but suppliers, in most cases, adjust each consignment so that the formula remains very close to the one stated above.

Figure A.4. Theoretical formulas and molar weights of minerals and other materials. Nepheline syenite and Cornwall stone, although rocks, are included and assigned generalized formulas, but it must be remembered that the compositions of these rocks are variable.

Standard Pyrometric Cones

Figures A.5 and A.6 provide temperature equivalents for Orton and Seger cones. To convert temperatures not listed, use the following formulas:

To convert degrees Celsius to Fahrenheit	To convert degrees Fahrenheit to Celsius
$°C \times \dfrac{9}{5} + 32 = °F$	$(°F - 32) \times \dfrac{5}{9} = °C$

	Low-temperature range			Middle-temperature range			High-temperature range	
Cone no.	Heating rate		Cone no.	Heating rate		Cone no.	Heating rate	
	150°C/hr	270°F/hr		150°C/hr	270°F/hr		150°C/hr	270°F/hr
C.010	894°C	1641°F	C.4	1186°C	2167°F	C.8	1263°C	2305°F
C.09	923°C	1693°F	C.5	1196°C	2185°F	C.9	1280°C	2336°F
C.08	955°C	1751°F	C.6	1222°C	2232°F	C.10	1305°C	2381°F
C.07	984°C	1803°F	C.7	1240°C	2264°F	C.11	1315°C	2399°F
C.06	999°C	1830°F				C.12	1326°C	2419°F
C.05	1046°C	1915°F				C.13	1346°C	2455°F
C.04	1060°C	1940°F				C.14	1366°C	2491°F
C.03	1101°C	2014°F				C.15	1431°C	2608°F
C.02	1120°C	2048°F						
C.01	1137°C	2079°F						
C.1	1154°C	2109°F						
C.2	1162°C	2124°F						
C.3	1168°C	2134°F						

1. The temperature equivalents in this table apply only to Orton pyrometric cones, heated at the rate indicated in air atmosphere.
2. The rates shown were maintained during the last several hundred degrees of temperature rise.
3. Temperature equivalents are not necessarily those at which cones will deform under firing conditions different from those of calibration determinations.
4. For reproducible results, care should be taken to ensure that the cones are set in a plaque with the bending face at the correct angle of 8° from the vertical with the cone tips at a consistent height above the plaque. Self-supporting cones are made with the correct mounting height and angle.
5. For other heating rates or if using small cones or self-supporting cones, specific tables of temperature equivalents should be obtained from your supplier.

Figure A.5. Temperature equivalents for Orton standard large cones. Source: American Ceramic Society.

Low-temperature range		Middle-temperature range		High-temperature range	
Cone no.		Cone no.		Cone no.	
022	595°C	2a	1150°C	7	1260°C
021	640°C	3a	1170°C	8	1280°C
020	660°C	4a	1195°C	9	1300°C
019	685°C	5a	1215°C	10	1320°C
018	705°C	6a	1240°C	11	1340°C
017	730°C				
016	755°C			12	1360°C
015a	780°C			13	1380°C
014a	805°C			14	1400°C
013a	835°C			15	1425°C
012a	860°C				
011a	900°C				
010a	920°C				
09a	935°C				
08a	955°C				
07a	970°C				
06a	990°C				
05a	1000°C				
04a	1025°C				
03a	1055°C				
02a	1085°C				
01a	1105°C				
1a	1125°C				

Figure A.6. Temperature equivalents for Seger standard cones. Source: Staatliche Porzellan-Manufaktur, Berlin.

Appendix 2
Test Tiles and Model Making

In all tests given in Figure A.7, mark the top of each tile with the proportions used over dry (or biscuit-fired) white slip. The letters A, B, etc., represent ceramic raw materials. On the back of each tile, mark the Exercise number, firing cone number (or firing temperature), type of firing cycle ("O" or "R"), and your initials if necessary. You should develop a standard abbreviated code that you place on the back of your test tiles and in your notebook, for example, EX.28/C.8/"R"(JL).

The traditional method of testing three materials, using a triangular clay slab, has not been used in this text. Instead, separate hexagonal tiles are used for each test; see Figure A.8. The advantages of this method over the traditional solid slab method include ease of construction and avoidance of warping or cracking. The tiles may be covered with glaze and picked up and examined separately. It also offers the possibility of selective testing and subsequently exploring further areas that gives interesting results from initial tests. Some craft suppliers offer special tile cutters that press out hexagonal shapes from leatherhard clay. They are a standard size and are quick to use. However, making your own template means that you can choose the size of tile convenient to you. This method and layout may also be used for additions (e.g., three colors) to a percentage recipe.

The template should be cut from strong cardboard. The size of your tile is determined by the length you make a–b (see Figure A.9). Lay the template on slab(s) of leatherhard clay and cut out your tiles, using a potter's knife. You are advised to number your tiles in the same order and in the same manner as the numbers on the chart. Mark them on the back over white slip as well as on the front (suggestion: dip one point of the tile in white slip and make this the top point of your tiles). Since it is essential to use the same clay for all tests, keep some of the clay, or note its catalogue number. Further tests must also be fired to the same temperature, using the same firing cycle and preferably the same kiln.

Figure A.9 also includes a template that can be used for making a model tetrahedron. This will help you visualize many of the physical relationships described in the text. Using stiff paper, draw the plan as illustrated

Line Addition Tests: addition of one material to 100% mix

1 Narrow range
100 g dry weight
clay or glaze

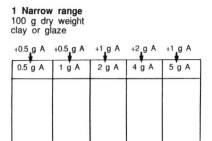

0.5 g A	1 g A	2 g A	4 g A	5 g A

An intermediate range could be achieved
with increments of 3 g giving 3, 6, 9, 12, 15 g

2 Wide range
100 g dry weight
clay or glaze

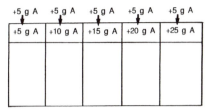

+5 g A	+10 g A	+15 g A	+20 g A	+25 g A

For a wider range, increments
of +10 g could be used

Crossover Tests of Two Materials

Additions of A + B such that the total remains the same

3 Narrow range
100 g dry weight
clay or glaze

+1 g A + 5 g B	+2 g A +4 g B	+3 g A +3 g B	+4 g A +2 g B	+5 g A +1 g B

4 Wide range
100 g dry weight
clay or glaze

+5 g A +25 g B	+10 g A +20 g B	+15 g A +15 g B	+20 g A +10 g B	+25 g A +5 g B

Note: Crossover tests may also be used to test percentage blends of two materials,
e.g., two types of clay bodies (see fig. 10.1 for layout).

Square Blend Tests
5 Blends of four materials

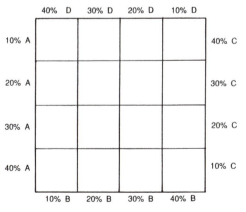

6 Additions of two materials to 100% glaze

(may also be used for test additions to clay)

	+5 g A	+10 g A	+15 g A	+20 g A	+25 g A
100% plain glaze					
+5 g B					
+10 g B					
+15 g B					
+20 g B					
+25 g B					

Figure A.7. Standard layouts for test tiles. Where test tiles are used for line addition
and crossover tests, each square in the layout represents one tile.

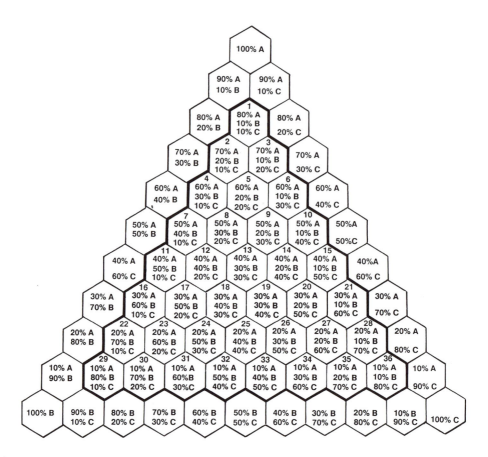

Figure A.8. Hexagonal tile layout for testing blends of three materials. The tiles inside the dark line show blends of all three materials. Those for blends of two materials are around the outside of the diagram, with a single material at each apex of the triangle.

in the figure and mark it as shown. To do this, draw the base line and along it mark 6 cm intervals (make sure this is accurate). Then cut out the whole as one piece and fold it so that x touches x and y touches y; the last triangle will fold inside the tetrahedron. Glue or tape together. To get a full idea of the structure of a single molecule of silica, thread a tiny bead on the end of a length of cotton threaded with a needle and push the needle up through an apex from the inside, draw the thread through until the bead sits exactly in the middle, glue three much larger beads to each of the four apexes, and hang up your model of a tetrahedron by the extra string (a small hole cut in one of the sides enables the bead to be seen). For teaching purposes it is a good idea to make the tetrahedron from four pieces of transparent fiber-glass and glue them together, with a small bead suspended at the center of the tetrahedron.

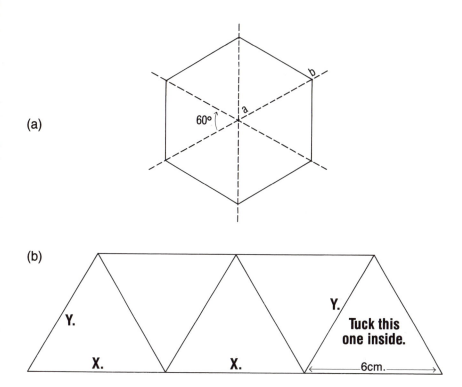

(a)

60°

a

b

(b)

Y.

X.

X.

Y.

Tuck this
one inside.

6cm.

Figure A.9. (a) Template for preparing hexagonal tiles; (b) diagram for constructing a tetrahedron.

Appendix 3
Equipment and Procedures

Color Combinations

The charts in Figure A.10 provide a way of "keeping score" for testing combinations of metal oxides and carbonates, commonly called coloring oxides/carbonates by ceramists, when added to glazes, slips, or clay bodies. The charts show all possible combinations irrespective of whether they give good or poor results, for example the dioxide of manganese (Mn) and the oxide of chromium (Cr) are included although they do not produce good colors. Nickel has not been included because it is usually used to tone down colors such as copper and cobalt. (See also Hamer and Hamer, 1991.)

Always note which oxide or carbonate of the colors you use (e.g., Fe_2O_3 or FeO). The strength of the color varies considerably with the oxide or carbonate used.

First, select the glaze, slip or clay body to use for all tests in a particular series of tests (record the clay body reference number, the recipe of slip, or glaze, in your notebook). Remember that different bodies have very different effects on color. Initially, color additions usually recommended are up to a total of 5% addition of color to 100% recipe of glaze, 5 to 10% add. for slips, and up to 20% add. for clay bodies. (Note that at this higher level the coloring oxides will have a significant fluxing effect. This should be all right in a refractory body, for example HT porcelain, but it can have a significant effect on, say, a white earthenware body.) As you are carrying out tests here it is reasonable to go a little beyond these figures, if you wish, so that you can see clearly the limits.

Second, select the group of colors you wish to test. For example, copper, chromium, and vanadium (using copper carbonate, chromium oxide, and vanadium pentoxide or vanadium stain).

Using the Charts

Two colors. Select all possible combinations of your choice of two colors from the first chart in Figure A.10 (it is suggested that you circle these lightly in pencil). Given the colors chosen above these would be 8, 12, and 15.

TWO COLOURS

	Co	Cu	Fe	Mn	Cr	V
Co	S	–	–	–	–	–
Cu	1. Cu Co	S	–	–	–	–
Fe	2. Fe Co	3. Fe Cu	S	–	–	–
Mn	4. Mn Co	5. Mn Cu	6. Mn Fe	S	–	–
Cr	7. Cr Co	8. Cr Cu	9. Cr Fe	10. Cr Mn	S	–
V	11. V Co	12. V Cu	13. V Fe	14. V Mn	15. V Cr	S

REPEATS ONLY

THREE COLOURS

#	Co	Cu	Fe	Mn	Cr	V
1.	Co +	Cu +	Fe			
2.	Co +	Cu		+ Mn		
3.	Co +	Cu			+ Cr	
4.	Co +	Cu				+ V
5.	Co		+ Fe	+ Mn		
6.	Co		+ Fe		+ Cr	
7.	Co		+ Fe			+ V
8.	Co			+ Mn	+ Cr	
9.	Co			+ Mn		+ V
10.	Co				+ Cr	+ V
11.		Cu +	Fe +	Mn		
12.		Cu +	Fe		+ Cr	
13.		Cu +	Fe			+ V
14.		Cu		+ Mn	+ Cr	
15.		Cu		+ Mn		+ V
16.		Cu			+ Cr	+ V
17.			Fe +	Mn +	Cr	
18.			Fe +	Mn		+ V
19.			Fe		+ Cr	+ V
20.				Mn +	Cr +	V

FOUR COLOURS

#	Co	Cu	Fe	Mn	Cr	V
1.	Co +	Cu +	Fe +	Mn		
2.	Co +	Cu +	Fe		+ Cr	
3.	Co +	Cu +	Fe			+ V
4.	Co +	Cu		+ Mn	+ Cr	
5.	Co +	Cu		+ Mn		+ V
6.	Co +	Cu			+ Cr	+ V
7.	Co		+ Fe	+ Mn	+ Cr	
8.	Co		+ Fe	+ Mn		+ V
9.	Co		+ Fe		+ Cr	+ V
10.	Co			+ Mn	+ Cr	+ V
11.		Cu +	Fe +	Mn +	Cr	
12.		Cu +	Fe +	Mn		+ V
13.		Cu +	Fe		+ Cr	+ V
14.		Cu		+ Mn	+ Cr	+ V
15.			Fe +	Mn +	Cr +	V

Figure A.10. Color combinations.

Three colors. Do the same on the chart for blends of three colors. We do not need the last chart for this series of tests.

Additions of Blends of Two Colors

Refer to the previous section to select a suitable layout. For example, the crossover test of two materials, no. A.7.1 narrow range, for additions of two-color blends to 100 percent recipe of a glaze. After assessing the fired results you may wish to make a more detailed test in a particular area and reduce the total amount of color added to say, 4% add. (i.e., 4 g total color added to every 100 g glaze) testing the range between:

$$0.5 \text{ g A} + 3.5 \text{ g B} \quad \text{and} \quad 3.5 \text{ g A} + 0.5 \text{ g B}.$$

For addition of blends of color to a clay body you can use the no. A.7.2 wide range crossover test of additions of blends of two colors. You should note that in this layout the total amount of color added is 30% add. This is often used for jewelry and highly decorative porcelain objects. You may wish to reduce this, testing blends between $5 \text{ g A} + 15 \text{ g B}$ and $15 \text{ g A} + 5 \text{ g B}$, or less.

A similar crossover test may be constructed for additions of two-color blends to slips, bearing in mind the limits suggested above.

Additions of Three-Blends

For these tests you should refer to Figure A.8 and the accompanying instructions.

Remember to use the correct firing temperature for the glaze you have chosen and be sure to fire to the exact top firing temperature for the glaze. Write the code number or top temperature on the back of your tiles, *after firing.*

Studio Equipment and Glassware

All the equipment illustrated in Figure A.11 is electrically driven except the rotary hand sieve and the glassware (bottom right). All equipment should be properly maintained and professionally checked.

Percentage Analyses of Wood Ashes

The purpose of the examples shown here in Figure A.12 is to illustrate the proportions of major constituents usually present in wood ashes, particularly the low level of alumina, the variable amount of silica, and the high proportion of calcia (particularly in fruit wood ashes). Remember that if you request an analysis of an ash you will be asked to state the oxides that the analyst should look for. The list of oxides given here should be a suitable list to submit.

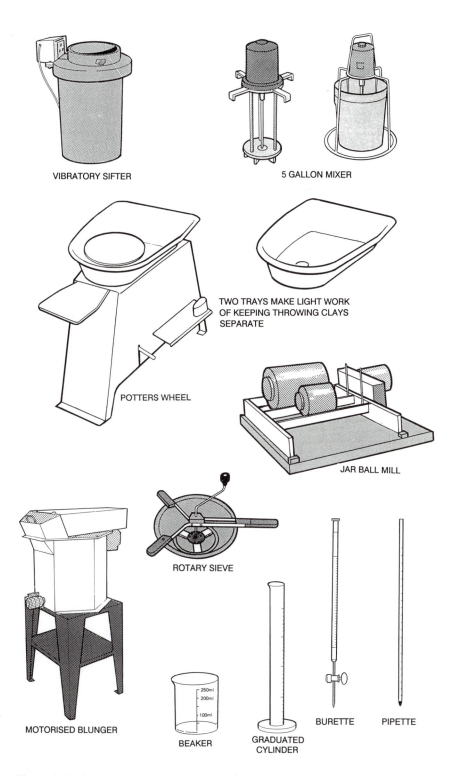

VIBRATORY SIFTER

5 GALLON MIXER

TWO TRAYS MAKE LIGHT WORK
OF KEEPING THROWING CLAYS
SEPARATE

POTTERS WHEEL

JAR BALL MILL

ROTARY SIEVE

MOTORISED BLUNGER

BEAKER

250ml
200ml
100ml

GRADUATED
CYLINDER

BURETTE

PIPETTE

Figure A.11. Studio equipment and glassware.

	Ash 1	Ash 2	Ash 3	Ash 4	Ash 5
SiO_2	42.20%	37.40%	35.00%	12.60%	8.60%
Al_2O_3	2.70%	1.20%	3.40%	0.90%	1.50%
Fe_2O_3	2.80%	3.40%	5.50%	1.00%	0.84%
MgO	3.00%	5.10%	3.90%	4.30%	3.70%
CaO	38.30%	38.80%	38.00%	62.00%	67.00%
Na_2O	0.62%	0.30%	0.60%	0.20%	0.30%
K_2O	5.20%	10.30%	8.50%	15.90%	13.00%
TiO_2	0.17%	0.10%	0.30%	0.10%	0.16%
P_2O_3	5.00%	3.20%	4.20%	2.80%	4.00%
MnO	0.1%	0.20%	1.00%	0.10%	0.70%
Total	100.00%	100.00%	100.00%	100.00%	99.80%

Figure A.12. Samples of percentage analyses of wood ashes.

Specific names have not been given in these sample analyses as there are so many variables, such as the soil type in which the original plant matter grew, the season during which the wood was felled, and perhaps slight variations in the species present. Hence the suggestion given in the text that wood ash should be collected in a useful (at least a year's) supply. It should be thoroughly burned, if necessary by placing it in a biscuit-fired container after the initial bonfire burning, and taking it to approximately 600°C/1112°F in an outdoor kiln, fired with a gas burner, before analysis.

Preparing Ceramic Raw Materials

The following preparation method may be used for crushed minerals, clay, or ash. Hard materials may need to be calcined before crushing (if you think your material is a mineral, show a hand specimen to a geologist for identification before crushing).

1. Clean the bulk amount as much as possible (e.g., burn off the carbon from wood ash) and ensure that it is well mixed so that the sample for analysis represents the bulk amount.

2. Take out a sample (about 50 ml by volume). Crush this to a fine powder and place in a glass test tube or small jar which should be labeled and lidded.

3. The sample should then be taken to the laboratory, placed in the laboratory drying cupboard unlidded, and held at 110°C/230°F for 24 hours (this could be done in a test kiln if necessary). Wood ash, clay, or other material containing water should be immediately placed in a dessicator for 24 hours. A dessicator contains silica gel in the bottom half of the container; this pulls away further free water from the material. Silica gel is blue when wet and red when dry. Re-lid the sample tightly.

The laboratory technician may prefer to complete the remaining steps or may expect you to carry them out, initially under supervision. Remember to have ready a list of oxides the analyst should look for. If the sample has been identified by a geologist give that list of oxides to the analyst. Otherwise see the list in Figure A.12 (to this add barium and lithium oxides). The analysis is carried out in a spectroscope and the analysis will be presented to you in the form of a percentage analysis by weight.

Converting a Percentage Analysis to a Unity Formula

The percentage analysis can then be converted to a unity formula by dividing each oxide by its molar weight and reducing this by dividing each amount by the weight of a chosen material. In the case of *clay* the standard practice is to divide through by the weight of *alumina*. For *glazes* the accepted convention is to bring the sum of the fluxes to unity (i.e., make the sum of the fluxes = 1, as explained below).

Several mineral materials, notably the feldspars and nepheline syenite, have variable formulas, hence you may need to convert a regionally available mineral or other material, expressed commercially as a percentage analysis, to a unity formula so that it is expressed in the same form as, for example, kaolin ($Al_2O_3 \cdot 2SiO_2 \cdot 2H_2O$), calcium carbonate ($CaCO_3$), and so on. You also need to calculate its molar weight. First the calculation is given, then the steps taken to calculate the unity formula and molar weight.

In this example a regionally found feldspar, which we shall call P.feld.X, is used.

% Analysis P.feld.X		Molar weight		Number of moles			Unity formula, P.feld.X
SiO_2	68.50%	÷	60	=	1.140		0.097 CaO
Al_2O_3	17.70%	÷	102	=	0.173		0.877 K_2O · 1.116Al_2O_3 · 7.35SiO_2
CaO	0.83%	÷	56	=	0.015	total number	0.026 MgO
K_2O	12.80%	÷	94	=	0.136	= of moles of	1.000 total
MgO	0.17%	÷	40	=	0.004	fluxes = 0.155	

Step 1. Divide each oxide by its molar weight to find the number of moles of each oxide.

Step 2. Add the fluxes 0.015 + 0.136 + 0.004 = 0.155.

Step 3. Divide the fluxes each by 0.155 and list them as shown under the unity formula. Add them up and you will find they total 1, so that we have unity in the fluxes.

Step 4. Divide the number of moles of the other oxides by 0.155 so that we retain the same proportions, and write the answers next to the fluxes as shown. This is now our unity formula.

Calculating the molar weight. This is done by multiplying the amounts of all the oxides in the unity formula by their molar weight and adding the results together. For this particular feldspar:

$$
\begin{array}{lll}
\text{CaO} & 0.097 \times 56\text{g} = & 5.432 \text{ g} \\
\text{K}_2\text{O} & 0.877 \times 94\text{g} = & 82.438 \text{ g} \\
\text{MgO} & 0.026 \times 40\text{g} = & 1.040 \text{ g} \\
\text{Al}_2\text{O}_3 & 1.116 \times 102\text{g} = & 113.832 \text{ g} \\
\text{SiO}_2 & 7.35 \ \times 60\text{g} = & 441.000 \text{ g} \\
& \text{Molar weight} = & 643.742 \text{ g}
\end{array}
$$

Converting a Unity Formula to a Percentage Recipe

For illustrative purposes in this calculation the formula and the molar weight (rounded to whole numbers) of P.feld.X are used as our regional material (see above).

The calculations are based on the assumption that the compositions for the kaolin, quartz, and dolomite are precise. Dolomite in fact varies in its natural composition, but it can be adjusted in the refining process, so manufacturers can keep to their advertised standard. If you are in doubt, the analysis/formula should be checked.

Formula to be filled	Materials used		Molar weight
0.3K$_2$O	P.feld.X:	0.877K$_2$O	643 g
0.6CaO 0.5Al$_2$O$_3$ 4SiO$_2$		0.097CaO · 1.116Al$_2$O$_3$ · 7.35SiO$_2$	
0.1MgO		0.026MgO	
	Dolomite:	CaCO$_3$ · MgCO$_3$	184 g
	Calcite:	CaCO$_3$	100 g
	Kaolin:	Al$_2$O$_3$ · 2SiO$_2$ · 2H$_2$O	258 g
	Quartz:	SiO$_2$	60 g

Remember (see Chapter 12)

1. The amount required of each material equals

$$
\frac{\text{what you want}}{\text{what you have}} = \frac{0.3\text{K}_2\text{O}}{0.877\text{K}_2\text{O}} = 0.342
$$

Therefore you need 0.342 potassium feldspar.

2. 0.342 P.feld.X also supplies 4 other oxides, so multiply 0.342 by the amount of each other oxide in P.feld.X.

Materials	K$_2$O	CaO	MgO	Al$_2$O$_3$	SiO$_2$
		Oxides supplied (check list only)			
0.342 P.feld.X	0.3	0.033	0.009	0.382	2.515
0.091 dolomite		0.091	0.091		
0.476 calcite		0.476			
0.118 kaolin				0.118	0.236
1.249 quartz					1.249
	0.3	0.6	0.100	0.500	4.000

Materials	× Molar weight	Batch	Percent recipe
0.342 P.feld.X ×	643	220.0	56.5% P.feld.X
0.091 dolomite ×	184	16.7	4.3% dolomite
0.476 calcite ×	100	47.6	12.2% calcite
0.118 kaolin ×	258	30.4	7.8% kaolin
1.249 quartz ×	60	74.9	19.2% quartz
		389.6	

Bibliography

BOOKS

Caiger-Smith, A. *Tin Glazed Pottery.* Faber and Faber, London, 1973.

Clarke, G., and M. Hughto. *A Century of Ceramics in the United States. 1878–1978.* E.P. Dutton, New York, 1979.

Cooper, E. *A History of Pottery.* Longman, London, 1972.

Cowley, D. *Moulded and Slip Cast Pottery and Ceramics.* B.T. Batsford, London, 1978.

Cox, K. G., N. B. Price, and B. Harte. *The Practical Study of Crystals, Minerals and Rocks.* Rev. edition. McGraw-Hill, New York, 1974.

Deer, W. A., R. A. Howie, and J. Zussman. *An Introduction to the Rock Forming Minerals.* Longman, London, 1986.

Fraser, H. *Glazes for the Craft Potter.* Pitman, London, 1973; Watson Guptill Publications, 1974.

———. *Ceramic Faults and Their Remedies.* A & C Black, London, 1986.

Frith, D. E. *Mold Making for Ceramics.* Chilton Book Co., Radnor, Penna., 1985.

Green, D. *A Handbook of Pottery Glazes.* Faber and Faber, London, 1978.

Griffiths, R. and C. Radford. *Calculations in Ceramics.* R. Griffith and C. Radford, Stoke-on-Trent, 1965; reprinted 1977.

Hamer, F. and J. Hamer. *The Potter's Dictionary of Materials and Techniques.* A & C Black, London, 1991; University of Pennsylvania Press, Philadelphia, 1991.

Hatch, F. H., A. K. Wells, and M. K. Wells. *Petrology of the Igneous Rocks.* Rev. edition. Allen and Unwin, London, 1972.

Health and Safety Booklets: You are advised to obtain the Regulations of the country in which you are working. If you are exporting you should discover the regulations of the country to which you are exporting. Three examples are given: Institute of Ceramics, *Health and Safety in Ceramics*, Pergamon Press, London, 1981. *Facts About Lead Glazes for Art Potters and Hobbyists*, Lead Industries Association, New York, 1972. *Lead in Glazes*, Department of Consumer and Corporate Affairs, Ottawa, Ontario, Canada, 1971. Your craft supplier, the above organizations, or your local health department should be able to assist you to find other recent releases as they are constantly updated.

Hetherington, A. L. *Chinese Ceramic Glazes.* Cambridge, London, 1937. Out-of-print but may be found in specialist libraries.

Holmes, A. *Principles of Physical Geology.* 3rd edition. Nelson, London, revised by Doris L. Holmes, 1978. Also published by Van Nostrand Reinhold, 3rd edition, 1978.

Hopper, R. *The Ceramic Spectrum.* Chilton Book Co., Radnor, Penna., 1983.

Keenan, C. W. and J. H. Wood. *General College Chemistry.* 6th edition. Harper and Row, New York, 1980.

Kenny, J. B. *Ceramic Sculpture, Methods and Processes.* Greenberg/Ambassador, New York and Toronto, 1953.

Kusnik, J. M. and K. W. Terry. "Physical Properties of Spodumene-Kaolin Mixtures in the Firing Range 1270°C/2318°F to 1300°C/2372°F." *Proceedings of the Australian Ceramic Conference and Exhibition*, Sydney, 1988.

Lane, P. *Studio Porcelain*, Pitman, London, 1980.

Lawrence, W. G. and R. R. West. *Ceramic Science for the Potter*. 2nd edition. Chilton Book Co., Radnor, Penna., 1982.

Leach, B. *A Potter's Book*. 2nd edition. Faber and Faber, London, 1945.

Levin, E. M., C. R. Robbins, and McMurdie. *Phase Diagrams for Ceramists. Journal of the American Ceramic Society.* Specific references given in text.

Lovatt, J. W. "Refractories for Fast Firing Kilns." *Ceram. Ind. J.* 93 (1045) (1984), 21.

Matthes, W. E. *Keramische Glasuren.* Verlagsgesellschaft Rudolf Muller GmbH, Koln, Germany, 1985.

McMeekin, I. *Notes for Potters in Australia: Raw Materials and Clay Bodies.* Rev. edition. New South Wales University Press, Sydney, 1978.

Nentwig, J., M. Kreuder, and K. Morgenstern. *General and Inorganic Chemistry Made Easy.* Verlagsgesellschaft, VCH, New York, 1992.

Norton, F. H. *Elements of Ceramics.* 2nd edition. Addison-Wesley, Reading, Mass., 1974.

Parmelee, C. W. *Ceramic Glazes.* 3rd edition. Cahners, Boston, 1973.

Pettijohn, F. J. *Sedimentary Rocks.* 3rd edition. Harper Collins, New York, 1974.

Pettijohn, F. J. and P. E. Potter. *Atlas and Glossary of Primary Sedimentary Structures: England, Spain, France, Germany.* Springer-Verlag, New York, 1964.

Preaud, T. and S. Gauthier. *La céramique du XXe siècle*, Office du Livre, Fribourg, Switzerland, 1982.

Rado, P. *An Introduction to the Technology of Pottery.* 2nd edition. Pergamon Press (Institute of Ceramics textbook series), Oxford, 1988.

Read, H. H. *Rutley's Elements of Mineralogy.* 26th edition. Allen and Unwin, London, 1970.

Rhodes, D. *Clay and Glazes for the Potter.* A & C Black, London, 1989.

Rogers, P. *Ash glazes.* A & C Black, London, 1991.

Ryan, W. *Properties of Ceramic Raw Materials.* 2nd edition. Pergamon Press, New York, 1978.

Rye, O. "Bone China." *Pottery in Australia* 22, 2 (1983).

——. *Pottery Technology.* Manuals on Archaeology 4, Taraxacum, Washington, D.C., 1981.

Sanders, H. H. *Glazes for Special Effects.* Watson-Guptill, New York, 1974.

Seger, H. *Collected Writings of Herman Seger*, I–II. Translated by members of the American Ceramic Society, 1902. Published jointly by the Society and the Chemical Publishing Co., available in specialist libraries.

Shaw, K. *Ceramic Glazes.* Applied Science Publishers Ltd., London, 1971.

Singer, F. and S. S. Singer. *Industrial Ceramics.* Chapman and Hall, London, 1963.

Singer, F. and W. L. German. *Ceramic Glazes.* Borax Consolidated, London, 1960.

Terry, K. W. "The Use of Spodumene in Ceramic Bodies and Glazes." *Journal of the Australian Ceramic Society* 25 (1989): 19–40.

Uvanov, E. B., D. R. Chapman, and A. Isaacs. *The Penguin Dictionary of Science.* 5th edition. Penguin, London, 1971.

Watts, A. S. *Journal of the American Ceramic Society* 38, 10:343–73; 46, 8:371–73.

Whitten, D. G. A. and J. R. V. Brooks. *The Penguin Dictionary of Geology.* London: Penguin, 1972.

Wood, N. *Oriental Glazes.* Pitman, London, 1978.

PERIODICALS

American Ceramics. Harry Dennis, 15 W. 44th St., New York, NY 10036.

American Craft. American Crafts Council, New York, NY.

Arts Atlantic. Confederation Centre Art Gallery and Museum, 145 Richmond St., Charlottetown, Prince Edward Island, C1A 1J1, Canada.

Arte Ceramico. c/o Fontanella, No. 18 - 2°. 2°. 08010-Barcelona, Spain.

Ceramics Art and Perception International. Art and Perception Pty. Ltd., 35 William St., Paddington, Sydney NSW 2021, Australia.

Ceramics Monthly. 1609 Northwest Boulevard, Columbus, OH 43212

Ceramic Review. 21 Carnaby St., London, W1V 1PH U, England.

Contact Quarterly. Alberta Potters' Assoc., PO Box 1050, Edmonton, Alberta, TJ5 2M1, Canada.

Craft Australia. Craft Council of Australia, 27 King St., Sydney 2000, Australia.

Fusion Magazine. Ontario Clay and Glass Association, 80 Spadina Ave., Suite 204, Toronto, Ontario, M5V 2J3, Canada.

Ontario Craft Magazine. Ontario Craft Council. 35 McCaul St., Toronto, Ontario, M5T 1V7, Canada.

Keramiek. Pueldijk 8, 3646 AW Waverween, Netherlands.

Keramik Magazin. Steinfelder Strasse 10, D-8770 Lohr am Main, Germany.

La Revue de la Céramique et du Verre. 61 Rue Marconi, 62880 Vendin-le-Vieil, France.

NCECA Directory. P.O. Box 1677, Bandon, OR 97411.

Neue Keramik. Unter den Eichen 90, D-1000 Berlin 45, Germany.

Pottery in Australia. 2/68 Alexander St., Crows Nest, NSW 2065, Australia.

Potter, New Zealand Potter. Box 147, Albany, New Zealand.

Sgraffito. Johannesburg, South Africa.

Studio Potter. P.O Box 70 Goffstown, NH 03045. Editor, Gerry Williams.

Index

Carolina stone. *See* Cornish stone

Cassiterite (tin stone), 12

Casting slip: and ion exchange, 229; density of, 230; and molds, 230–31; bone china, 232; standard recipes for, 233; accessory materials for, 234; water for, 234; deflocculant for, 234; important adjustments, 236; aging, 236; making, 237; preparation and mixing, 238–39; testing, 240; firing, 237; batch and storage, 241; Twaddell, 244

Ceramic change, 91

Chalk, 11

Chamotte. *See* Grog

Chemical: symbols, 5, 383; formulas, 384–85; reactions, 7

China clay. *See* Kaolin

China stone. *See* Cornish stone

Cornwall stone. *See* Cornish stone

Chromium, sesquioxide (chromia), 370

Chrome-tin pink, 344

Chuck, 105

Clay: evolution of, 43; primary and secondary types of, 45; ion exchange in, 47–48; changes in the character of, 52; use of word, 53; description of natural deposits of, 54; clay-water relationship, 56; crystal structure of, 54–60; classification of clay minerals, 60; accessory minerals, 60–62; fusible, vitrifiable, refractory, 62–63; classification and use of natural, 63–68; preparation of, 149; maturing (weathering, aging, souring), 79–80; grain sizes of, 80–81; care of and working with, 81–90; drying, 88; workability of, 80–82; yield point of, 81; cones reflect changes during firing of, 76–77; shrinkage, 89; buying, 80; recycling, 86–87

Clay slip: Albany, 61; use of, 204; composition of, 205; simple additions to, 205–6; application of, 206; increasing vitrification of, 207, 214; as a cover coat, 212–13; dry weight of raw materials in, 204; adjusting density of, 215–18; using slip weight of, 216, 218

Cobalt: occurrence of, 26; metal oxides and carbonate, 15–17; method of stating color addition to a glaze, 341; speckles in glazes, 352

Colemanite (boro-calcite or calcium borate), 50, 248, 288; in transparent glaze, 353–54

Colloids, 42

Color: in natural clays, 61, 63–64, 66–68, 155–56, 341–43; coloring oxides and carbonates, 344; colored stains, 345; method of stating additions of, 341; in glazes, 353; selecting glaze constituents for, 354–55; on-glaze enamels, 347; water-based enamels, 348; underglaze pencils/crayons, 348; zirconium/yttrium/vanadium based stains, 345, 358; effects of oxidation and reduction on, 343; reduced copper reds, 364–66; in-glaze decoration (maiolica) 301; on-glaze decoration, 302; preparation and testing, 348–49; discussion of individual colors, 359–71; maximum additions of, 354; effects of titanium-iron family on, 366; 54, 368; combinations of, 392–93; percent additions of, 341, 351

Cones. *See* Pyrometric cones

Copper: occurrence of, 26; oxide and carbonate, 15–17; flashing, 344; in transparent glaze, 353; luster, 363–64; reduced red glazes, 364–65

Cordierite, 187, 189, 196–97

Cornish stone, 32; use of, 115

Crackle (glaze), 255

Crawling, 290–91

Crazing, 95

Cristobalite, 27; conversion of quartz to, 92; inversion of, 93

Crystal structure, 17–18; crystalline glazes, 368

Damper (back-plate). *See* Kiln

Deflocculants, 228–29

Deflocculated slips, 227–29

Density: definition of, 215; specific gravity and, 215–16; requirement of a casting slip, 230–31; of water, 215–16; measuring, 216; standard, 216. *See also* Slip weight

Diatomaceous earth, diatomite rock, 50

Diopside, 27–30

Dolomite, 49; use of, 116

Dunt, 94

Earthenware. *See* Clay

Elements, 5, 381; metal and nonmetal, 382

Enamel. *See* Color

Enstatite, 180

Equipment, 74–79; studio equipment and glassware, 394–95; jar ball mill, 79; pyrometer, 76; oxygen probe, 76; pyrometric cones, 76; throwing wheels, 77. *See also* Kiln

Eutectic: point, 28; temperature, 28; composition, 30, 263, 265

Fast-firing, temperature equivalents for, 77

Feldspar, 7, 10, 20; decomposition of, 32, 45; chief types of, 34; use of, 115, 179

Feldspathoids, 12, 34, 179–80

Ferric, ferrous, ferroso-ferric. *See* Iron
Fieldwork, 64
Finger test for plasticity, 82
Fired bodies: standard assessment of, 152–58, 175; porosity of, 154; mechanical strength of, 169; resistance to thermal shock of, 169
Firing: changes during, 90; glaze fit and the firing cycle, 94; biscuit and glaze, 96; bisque and glost, 96; fast-firing, 77; flashing, 344; once-firing/twice-firing, 96; time and temperature profiles, 145; comparison of LT and HT, 170; development of mullite, 171; optimum range for LT and HT bodies, 170–71; average top temperatures for, 98; slip cast objects, 240. *See also* Atmosphere, oxidation and reduction
Flint, 11, 50
Flocculants, 228; flocculated slips, 227–28
Flux, 9, 17
Formulas: formula weights, 20; theoretical and molar weights, 384–85
Frits: study of, 12, 113; reasons for use of, 122; definition of, 122; preparation of, 122; making and testing, 130; and phase diagrams, 137; testing alkali and borax, 206; lead monoxide, 12; bisilicate, 12; sesquisilicate, 12; health reasons for making, 12

Galena, 38
Gibbsite (aluminum hydrate), 58
Glass, 19; definition of, 247; glass-formers, 9; silica and boric oxide, 248
Glaze, 13–14; definition of, 247–48; compositions of materials used in, 312; glaze-fit, 94–95; fluxes, stabilizer, and glass-formers, 248–53; types of, 253–57; "norm" as starting point for, 258; method for making, 258; adding dry materials to, 293; ratios of flux:glass-former in, 305; generalized ratios for formulating, 312; role of mullite in, 311; specific gravity/slip weight of, 260; surface tension in, 307. *See also* Calculations
Glaze types: clear transparent HT, 285–87; test, 260; LT tin opacified, 300; matte, 254; lime glaze, 146; magnesium, 333–35; barium, 333–35; iron, 359; copper, 362; maiolica decoration, 301; enameled decoration, 302; effect of iron in body, 335; value of MT, 335; lead-borosilicate, 95, 288; malachite, 371
Glazing: on raw and biscuit ware, 97; methods of application, 104; using a chuck in, 105; testing for thickness, 106

Glost firing. *See* Firing
Grain size, 80
Granite, 31; decomposition of, 32; classification of, 38
Grog (chamotte): types, 120–122, molochite, 121, 181
Growan. *See* Cornish stone

Health and safety, 72
Heat work (treatment), 145

Igneous rocks. *See* Rocks
Illite. *See* Clay, crystal structure of
Ilmenite, 368
Interface (body-glaze layer), 91
Ions: adsorbed, 18; ion-exchange, 18, 229, 381
Iron: oxide, 15–16; chromite, 37; hematite, 36; magnetite, 37; pyrite, 14, 38; in earth's crust, 61, 63–64; in common clay and natural stoneware, 63–64; in fire clay, 67; faults caused by, 157; speckles, 163; in ferro-magnesium minerals, 36; in yellow ochre (limonite) in buff MT body, 177–78; in dry surface treatment, 202; general discussion, 359–62

Kaolin: formation of 32; description and use of, 65–66
Kaolinite: crystal formation, 32; crystal structure, 59; classified, 60, 63
Kaolinization, 44–45
Kiln furniture, 75–76; back-plate (damper), 111; bung, 111; monitoring firings, 76–77
Kneading. *See* Wedging

Lead: element, 5, 6; oxide (litharge), 7, 12, 14; ore, 38; galena, 38; poisoning, 72; sesquisilicate frit, 12; bisilicate frit, 12; borosilicate (glaze), 288
Lepidolite. *See* Lithium
Leucite, 35; at HT, 273–74
Limestone (chalk, calcite), 11; formation of, 49–50; use of, 115–16
Lime-popping, 117
Limonite (yellow ochre), 178, 202
Line blends, 389
Lithium: element, 31; oxide (lithia), 8; carbonate, 10, 192; ionic bonding strength, 18; as constituent of tourmaline, 31; feldspathoids, 34–35; lepidolite (lithium mica), 36; petalite, 35, 192; in raku body, 194; other bodies, 196
Lizard skin, 375
Loess, 40

Magma, 23–27; magmatic minerals and rocks, 32–38

Magnesium: element, 5, 26; oxide (magnesia), 8–9; carbonate, 10; in magma, 26; in basalt, 26, 31; in tourmaline, 31; in mica, 36; glazes (*See* Glaze types)

Magnesite. *See* Magnesium carbonate

Maiolica, 257, 301

Malachite, 371

Malm. *See* Marl

Manganese: carbonate (rhodochrosite), 15–16; dioxide, 369

Marble, 331

Marking oxide, 124; white slip for, 124

Marl, 63

Maturing, plastic clay, 79

Melting point, 27

Mesh, sizes, 80

Mica, 36, 54, 58–61, 64–66; biotite (black mica), 36; muscovite (white mica), 36

Mineral sands, 40–42

Molar weights, 21

Molecular units, 6

Moles, 6

Molochite, 121, 181

Molybdenum oxide, 345

Montmorillonite: origin, 31; plasticity, 54; structure, 59–60; as constituent of bentonite and fuller's earth, 68

Mullite, formation of primary and secondary, 171–72

Muscovite. *See* Mica

Nepheline syenite, 35; use of, 115; comparison with Cornish stone, 115

Nickel oxide, 371

Ochre (limonite), 178, 202

Once-firing. *See* Firing

Opacifier, 254, 300–301

Orthoclase (potassium feldspar). *See* Feldspar, types of

Orton. *See* Pyrometric cones

Ovenware, 195

Oxides, 7–17; function of, 125; formula weights of, 28. *See also* specific compounds

Peeling, 95

Pegmatite, 30

Periodic table, 5, 381–84; and classification of oxides, 124

Perlite, 192

Petalite. *See* Lithium

Petuntse. *See* Cornish stone

Phase diagrams: diopside–calcium feldspar, 27–30; copper oxide–silica, 137–46;

calcium–alumina–silica, 142–45; alumina–silica, 267; potassa–alumina–silica, 271; potassa–alumina–leucite, 273; value of, 145–46; frits and, 145

Pin-hole, 290, 299, 348

Pitchers. *See* Grog

Plaster of paris, 230

Plasticity, 54–60. *See also* Accessory minerals

Poison, 5, toxic and other dangerous materials, 74. *See also* lead

Porcelain: resistance to thermal shock, 169; proportion of glass to solids in fired, 170; glaze recipes for, 190; as a body for ovenware, 195; color tests, 225; as casting slip, 237; firing slip-cast, 240; reduction firing problem, 241; as body for crystalline glazes, 257; adverse effects of baria in HT hard, 290; firing effects of iron in body, 342; effects on body fired in "O" and "R", 343–44; color added to body and glaze slips, 348–51; as a body for reduction red glazes, 366; effects of titanium dioxide in body, 367; as body for malachite glaze, 372

Potassium: carbonate, 11; feldspar (*see* Feldspar, types of)

Praseodymium oxide. *See* Color, stains, 345

Primary clay. *See* Clay, types of

Pugmill. *See* Equipment

Pyrite. *See* Iron, pyrite

Pyrometric cones, 76, 386–87

Quartz: crystal structure of, 11–12; crystallization of, 27; minerals, 35–36; phases of, 92–94; problems of too much cristobalite, 93–94; quartzite, 51; sediments and mineral sands, 40–41; quartz, quartz sand, flint, 116–18; moisture in powdered, 118; role in glaze, 248

Raku firing technique, 112

Raw glazing, 96

Recycling waste clay, 86

Refractive index, 254, 364, 367

Rhodochrosite. *See* manganese

Rocks: igneous, 30; sedimentary, 49–50; metamorphic minerals and, 51–52; classification, 38

Rutile, 368

Sand, types of, 40–41

Saturated solutions, 42; solubility of minerals and, 43

Screen. *See* Mesh

Secondary clay. *See* Clay, types of

Sediments: deposition, 40; resistant, 42; types of deposits, 45; changes in, 52

Seger cones. *See* Pyrometric cones

Seger, Hermann: measuring high temperature, 311; formulas, 331–32
Shivering, 95
Silica, as glass-former, 247–48
Sinter, 265
Slip casting. *See* Casting slip
Slip weight, 216–18
Solid state reactions, 139
Specific gravity, 216. *See also* Density
Spodumene, 35
Surface tension: in glazes, 307; viscosity and, 307; effect of oxides on, 308

Talc, 116. *See also* Enstatite
Temperatures: equivalents for pyrometric cones, 386–87; conversion of Celsius and Fahrenheit, 386. *See also* Fast-firing
Test tiles: making, 99–101; layouts for line additions, square blends, blends of three materials, 388–391
Thixotropy, 230
Time x temperature profiles, 145
Titanium: dioxide (anatase), 17; titanium-iron series, 366

Tourmaline, 31, 32
Transition metals, 15–16, 340, 382–83
Tuff, 30
Twaddell, °TW, 243–44
Twice-firing. *See* Firing

Vanadium pentoxide, 371
Viscosity / fluidity, definition, 306

Weathering: mechanical, 40; chemical, 40, 41, 79
Wedging and kneading, 83–85
Weights and numbers, 19–22
Wollastonite (calcium silicate), 51, 180
Wood ash, 118–120; percent analyses of, 394–96
Workability, 79–80, 82, 85. *See also* Yield point; Finger test

Yield point, 81, 85

Zinc oxide, 290–91